Teacher's Annotated Edition

German
today 1

THIRD EDITION

Jack Moeller
Helmut Liedloff
Clifford J. Kent

HOUGHTON MIFFLIN COMPANY   **Boston**

Atlanta   Dallas   Geneva, Illinois
Lawrenceville, New Jersey   Palo Alto   Toronto

Acknowledgments

The authors and the publisher wish to thank the following people who reviewed various stages and portions of manuscript: Tanja M. Moore (Aiken Senior High School, Aiken, South Carolina), Sonia Schweid Reizes (Bedford Public Schools, Bedford, Massachusetts), and Ellen Gottschalk Van Wart. We would like to thank Professor Dolores M. Burdick of Oakland University (Rochester, Michigan) for supplying the information on German cinema.

Printed in U.S.A.
Student's Edition ISBN: 0–395–38358–7
Teacher's Edition ISBN: 0–395–38359–5

Contents

Teacher's Guide

Annotated student text

Scope-and-sequence chart

1 Ich und du
Photo essay 1

		CULTURAL NOTES	WORTSCHATZ-ERWEITERUNG
KAPITEL 1	**Tag. Wie geht's?** 8 Wie heißt du? Wie geht's? Bist du zufrieden? Warum ist Volker so sauer?	BRD and DDR Handshakes Flavoring words Regional variations in greetings and farewells	Greetings and farewells Descriptive adjectives
KAPITEL 2	**Wie alt bist du?** 23 Jung oder alt? Wann hast du Geburtstag?	Republik Österreich Birthday customs	Zahlen: 1-19 Monate
KAPITEL 3	**Heute nachmittag** 36 Wo wohnst du? Marks Fotoalbum Was machst du?	Die Schweiz Hiking and walking	Musikinstrumente
KAPITEL 4	**Ich und meine Familie** 52 Der Brieffreund	German communities in the United States Family life	Berufe Zahlen: 20-1000 Zentimetermaß
	Noch einmal 71		

AUSSPRACHE	ÜBUNGEN
[i] [I]	Subject pronouns **ich, du, er,** and **sie** Present tense of **sein:** singular forms Negative word **nicht** *Grammatische Übersicht:* Notes about written German *Wiederholung*
[e] [ɛ]	Subject pronouns **wir, ihr,** and **sie** Present tense of **sein:** plural forms Pronouns **sie** (singular) and **sie** (plural) Present tense of **haben** Specific questions General questions *Grammatische Übersicht* *Wiederholung*
[y] [Y] Glottal stop	Present tense of regular verbs Present tense to express future time Using **gern** with verbs Using **gern** with **haben** The phrases **zu Hause** and **nach Hause** *Grammatische Übersicht:* Infinitive concept; present- tense meanings *Wiederholung*
[ø] [œ]	Verbs with stem ending in **-d** or **-t** Verbs with stem ending in a sibilant Position of the verb in statements Possession with proper names Possessive adjectives *Grammatische Übersicht:* Capitalization of **du** and **dein** / **ihr** and **euer** in letters *Wiederholung*

AUSSPRACHE	ÜBUNGEN	KULTURLESESTÜCK
[u] [U]	Verbs with stem-vowel change **a** > **ä** Singular definite articles **der, das, die** Noun plurals and plural definite article **die** Noun-pronoun relationship Nominative case of **ein** and **kein** *Grammatische Übersicht:* Nominative case; **kein** vs. **nicht** *Wiederholung*	Geld
[o] [ɔ]	Telling time Accusative case of **der, das, die; ein** and **kein** Accusative case of possessive adjectives Using **der, das, die** as pronouns *Grammatische Übersicht:* Official time *Wiederholung*	Zeugnis
[a] [A]	Subject pronouns **du, ihr, Sie** Possessive adjectives **dein, euer, Ihr** Verbs with stem-vowel change **e** > **i** Modal auxiliaries Omission of the dependent infinitive with modals *Grammatische Übersicht:* Mögen; negative of **müssen** *Wiederholung*	Wer geht ins Kino?
[ai] [ɔi] [ao]	Interrogatives **wo** and **wohin** Verbs with stem-vowel change **e** > **ie** Present tense of **wissen** The imperative forms: **du, ihr, Sie** Imperative forms of the verb **sein** Separable-prefix verbs *Grammatische Übersicht:* Verbs ending in **-eln** *Wiederholung*	Sammelfreuden
[ts] [z] [s]	Conversational past with auxiliary **haben** Past participles of weak verbs Past participles of strong verbs Past participles of separable-prefix verbs *Grammatische Übersicht* *Wiederholung*	Taschengeld und Jobs
[R]	The verbs **kennen** and **wissen** Verbs with stem-vowel change **au** > **äu** Accusative case of **wer** and personal pronouns Conversational past of inseparable-prefix verbs *Grammatische Übersicht* *Wiederholung*	König Fußball

3 Zum Städtele hinaus
Photo essay 225

AUSSPRACHE	ÜBUNGEN	KULTURLESESTÜCK
[ʌ]	Conversational past with auxiliary **sein** Narrative past of **sein** Special **der**-nouns in the accusative singular Prepositions with the accusative case Accusative prepositional contractions *Grammatische Übersicht* *Wiederholung*	Der Markt
[ə] [ən] [ər]	**Dieser**-words in the nominative and accusative Time expressions in the accusative case Present tense to express duration of time Coordinating conjunctions: **aber, denn, oder, sondern, und** *Grammatische Übersicht*: Independent clauses *Wiederholung*	Kaffeestunde
[χ] [k]	Comparison of adjectives and adverbs The verb **werden** Indirect statements Indirect questions *Grammatische Übersicht*: Verb in final position *Wiederholung*	Geographie
[ç] [ʃ] [χ]	Dative case of definite articles and nouns Dative case of **dieser**-words Dative case of indefinite articles and **ein**-words Dative case of special **der**-nouns Dative case of **wer** *Grammatische Übersicht* *Wiederholung*	Die Bahn
[l] [ŋ]	Prepositions with the dative case Dative prepositional contractions *Grammatische Übersicht* *Wiederholung*	Wien

Teacher's guide

Introduction

German Today speaks for itself. As soon as you open the texts you see how efficiently each chapter is organized, how naturally cultural material is integrated with language content, and how many ways students are engaged in active and personal participation. These features, in combination with vivid art and photography, create a dynamic two-year program that stresses language as a tool of people's lives and an instrument of their cultural expression. With such an emphasis, *German Today* provides students with a sound basis for learning German as it is spoken and written today.

Communication and culture

The program's most important purpose is to enable students to *use* German. This focus on communicative competence is woven into every aspect of *German Today,* so that students completing the course will be able to use each of the four language skills to do a number of things.

Speaking. From the start, *German Today* helps students develop practical speaking skills: asking for information; reporting what others say; stating individual opinions and concerns about home, school, shopping,' eating, travel, entertainment. Whatever the topic, students are encouraged to express their own moods and feelings; they learn to do more than give pat "yes or no" answers.

Listening. Listening skills have a practical emphasis, too. Students first understand the things they later learn to say. In addition, they learn to understand the gist of more complicated exchanges and other communications.

Reading. Students develop the skills to read everything they can say, without the help of a dictionary. With the aid of a dictionary, they will be able to read short newspaper and magazine articles, simple stories, and many other kinds of straightforward prose.

Writing. With guidance, students will be able to write complete sentences on many factual topics, express simple opinions, and write reports, descriptions, anecdotes, and personal letters.

A second aim of the program is to foster in students a sensitive appreciation of the German-speaking world. The kinds and quality of cultural information in *German Today* help students become aware of the diversity of the peoples and customs throughout the world.

Key strengths

Organization. There are several facets to the organization of *German Today:* the organizational clarity of the chapters, the manner in which topics were chosen and sequenced, and the program's unique superstructure. *German Today* is a two-level continuous course divided into six Stages. As students move from Stage to Stage, they progress from personal and local concerns to ever widening circles of cultural scope and focus. Stage 3 overlaps the two levels of the program to provide smooth articulation from one school year to the next. The Stages add a level of organization to the program that gives both teacher and student an opportunity to assess the work accomplished and consider the goals ahead.

Cultural integration. Cultural content is integrated with most elements of *German Today.* Each of the six Stages opens with an eight-page, full-color photo essay that illustrates some of the themes of the Stage in settings throughout the German-speaking countries. A section entitled "German Around You" opens the first-year book and shows students some of the many connections that exist between English and German.

Student involvement. The "German Around You" section is just one way that German is brought close to home for students. Throughout the program there is an emphasis on the student's personal and active participation in the learning process. The majority of the activities that follow core material are on a personal level; students may choose to respond in a variety of ways that parallel everyday conversation, as they express points of view, state their preferences or ideas, or ask questions. Even in the word study and grammar sections, open-ended activities provide an opportunity for students to use words and phrases imaginatively. This focus on self-expression builds students' confidence and skill in the use of the language.

Completeness of the program

German Today is a complete program. Although the Student Text can stand entirely on its own and constitutes a total course, you may wish to take advantage of the full complement of materials available with *German Today, One* to increase students' chances of reaching a high level of competency in German. The program consists of the following components:

Student Text. Much of what follows in this Teacher's Guide is a detailed description of the Student Text, after the brief summaries below of the ancillaries.

Teacher's Annotated Edition. Both a teaching aid and a resource, the Teacher's Annotated Edition includes this Teacher's Guide and an Annotated Student Text. The Teacher's Guide suggests procedures and activities for *German Today* and ways to adapt the program to different teaching styles and learners' needs. To provide the teacher with possible strategies for a typical lesson, sample lesson plans are given for Chapter 2 (Stage 1) and Chapter 9 (Stage 2). You will also find resource materials for teachers, including games and classroom expressions in German. Annotations overprinted on the relevant pages in the Student Text provide specific suggestions for introducing and practicing core material, varying exercises and activities, further personalizing activities, and expanding cultural information.

Workbook. The 112-page Workbook reinforces and strengthens a student's ability to write German correctly. Pages are perforated so that assignments can be handed in for correcting. Each chapter of the Student Text has a corresponding chapter in the Workbook. In addition, the Workbook has one page of culminating activities for students to do at the end of each Stage. Line art and realia illustrate the Workbook and heighten the exercise material's appeal to students.

Tests. A set of fifteen Tests is offered, one for each chapter in the Student Text. Each test is four pages long, and is supplemented by a pretest worksheet with questions intended to check test readiness, as well as an extra worksheet consisting of optional sections, which teachers may choose to treat as extra-credit work, include as part of the basic test, or simply omit.

Cassettes. Cassette recordings aid development in aural/oral skills. A set of 17 cassettes includes core material, pronunciation drills, grammar exercises, and readings from the Student Text. Special listening comprehension exercises, which do not appear in the Student Text, are also included for each chapter. The script for the listening comprehension exercises appears in a separate guide to the recordings. Listening comprehension sections of the Tests are also provided on tape.

Posters. The Posters are valuable visual aids. They are especially useful for introducing core material and vocabulary, drilling structures, and stimulating conversation. They can be adapted for individual or small group assignments as well as for use with the full class. The set contains 64 posters, 17 × 22 inches.

Flashcards. Handy in size, the Flashcards can be used for classroom activities such as vocabulary presentation and drill, and some grammar drills. The Flashcards can also be used in conjunction with the Posters to stimulate more complex and varied activities. The set includes 200 cards: 199 with a picture on one side and a word or phrase on the other, and an index card for quick reference.

Organization of the program

German Today, One contains fifteen chapters, and *German Today, Two* contains sixteen chapters (plus a number of special sections, which are discussed below). As mentioned earlier, the program also has an organizational superstructure that divides the thirty-one chapters of the two-year sequence into six Stages.

Each Stage has a theme designed to broaden the scope of the student's communicative abilities. The six Stages might be graphically depicted as a set of concentric circles, with Stage 1 at the center and Stage 6 outermost, representing the progression from the individual's immediate environment and everyday concerns to cultural issues of more lasting and widespread impact. Each Stage is introduced by an eight-page full-color photo essay. Culminating activities, called *Noch einmal,* are provided at the end of each Stage (and at the end of the first year) for a change of pace.

The organization of the program into Stages offers several benefits. First, considered from the standpoint of language acquisition, the Stage structure roughly reflects the sequence in which human beings expand their powers of communication and spheres of interest. The second benefit, though less linguistically based, is equally important. The Stages offer variety in both content and format, with the intent of maintaining a fresh level of interest for both students and teachers throughout the course of study. A third benefit is the ease of articulation between the first and second years that is made possible by having Stage 3 bridge the two levels.

The following is a brief summary of the Stages of *German Today.* See the Scope-and-sequence chart on pages TAE 4–9 for a detailed listing of the content of *German Today, One.*

Stage 1: Ich und du. Students learn basic forms of greeting, leave-taking, and thanking. They learn to identify and describe themselves, their families, and their friends with respect to age and certain traits of personality and appearance; and they learn to solicit such information from others. Students also learn to ask and answer questions about where they live, their health and personal moods, occupations, and activities. They also learn to express surprise, pleasure and displeasure, disbelief; to state some simple opinions; and to express and ask for agreement and disagreement. Stage 1 covers Chapters 1–4 of *German Today, One.*

Stage 2: So leben wir. The focus of this Stage is on the practicalities of everyday, teen-age life:

shopping with friends, going to school, buying tickets for concerts and movies, doing chores, and engaging in sports and hobbies. Students learn to extend and accept invitations or to decline them for appropriate reasons. They increase their range of communication skills to include expressing likes and dislikes, opinions and desires, indifference, and certainty. They learn to spice up their language through the use of flavoring words. Stage 2 covers Chapters 5–10 of *German Today, One.*

Stage 3: Zum Städtele hinaus. In this Stage, students learn to increase their linguistic ability to deal with adults and strangers in the world around them: shopping for food, ordering and eating in restaurants, making small talk about the weather, getting a driver's license, visiting and getting lost in new places, writing job letters, and participating in panel discussions. Students practice summarizing past events, asking and giving directions, making comparisons and simple evaluations, apologizing, expressing enthusiasm or indifference, and making polite requests. Stage 3 covers Chapters 11–15 of *German Today, One* and Chapters 1 and 2 of *German Today, Two.*

Stage 4: Wer die Wahl hat, hat die Qual. Within the context of a television program, letters to the editor, a house rental, and a photo-album, students learn to use language to express surprise, to protest, and to consider options. Students talk about teen magazines, television programs, mass transportation, the rooms of a house, and several possibilities for vacations. Stage 4 covers Chapters 3–6 of *German Today, Two.*

Stage 5: Hinaus in die Ferne. Students expand their ability to cope with social situations specific to German-speaking countries (such as taking flowers to a hostess) and to consider such issues as East/West and careers. They learn to evaluate intentions, to judge, to express personal preferences, and to give accounts in the past tense. Stage 5 covers Chapters 7–11 of *German Today, Two.*

Stage 6: Was die Welt zusammenhält. In this Stage, students deal more extensively with culture and the German heritage: science and technology, music, literature (in the form of a fairy tale and a short story), and German-American influence (exemplified by the history of comic strips). Students become acquainted with important names and facts in these fields of human endeavor and read their first pieces of German literary prose. Stage 6 covers Chapters 12–16 of *German Today, Two*.

Features of the Student Text

The following special sections supplement the fifteen chapters of *German Today, One*. Suggestions for their use are contained in the section of the Teacher's Guide entitled "Suggested procedures and activities," which begins on page TAE 14.

German Around You. This four-page section highlights some of the ways in which German speakers have influenced the English language and American culture. This light and appealing introduction to the course points out to students that they already know more German than they think they do by virtue of borrowed words, cognates, and the frequent use of English words by speakers of German.

Maps. Four maps are found on pages xii–xv: Europe, Federal Republic of Germany and German Democratic Republic, Austria, and Switzerland.

Photo essays. Each Stage is introduced by eight pages of full-color photographs, which have been selected for their relevance to the themes and topics of the Stage. The photo essays are designed to stimulate interest in the German-speaking world and may be used as the basis for numerous classroom activities.

Culminating Activities. At the end of Stages 1 and 2, and following Chapter 15 are Culminating Activities, entitled *Noch einmal*. These culminating activities offer a variety of enjoyable ways for students to combine and apply the skills they have learned in the preceding Stages.

Reference section. The following elements are found in the reference section at the end of *German Today, One*: (1) a selection of songs, poems, and non-standard expressions *(Jugendsprache)*; (2) a list of common German first names; (3) English equivalents for the dialogues of Chapters 1–15; (4)

grammar charts, which include pronouns, articles and adjectives, and verb forms; (5) supplementary word sets, categorized by topic and chapter; (6) groups of supplementary expressions arranged in idea groups; (7) German-English End Vocabulary; (8) English-German End Vocabulary; and (9) an index of the principal grammar and pronunciation topics and word sets introduced in the text.

Chapter format

A typical chapter of *German Today, One* contains the following elements:

Chapter opening text. In Stage 1, a brief passage in English opens each chapter. It gives some information about the geographical setting of the chapter and sets the scene for the core material.

Core material and activities. Dialogues, narratives, and simulated realia (schedules, notes, want-ads, etc.) introduce the cultural themes, new vocabulary, and grammatical structures. One to four core material selections are presented in each chapter. Most selections are followed by activities, called *Du hast das Wort*, that check and reinforce comprehension of the core material, present small amounts of new vocabulary, and provide opportunities for students to personalize the core material. Students also answer short comprehension questions on the core material in the *Fragen* and *Richtig oder falsch?* sections. Beginning in Stage 2, students practice new structures and vocabulary through directed statements and questions in the *Sag!* and *Frag!* sections.

Cultural notes. In each chapter there are several cultural notes in English. These notes, located in various places in the chapter, provide specific information on the customs, social conventions, or geography of a region; on special uses of language that occur in the core material; or on other matters of interest related to the theme or setting of the chapter.

Wortschatzerweiterung. The word study section presents word sets or groups of related words to help students expand their vocabulary. Each presentation is followed by related exercises and activities.

Aussprache. The pronunciation sections provide practice with specific sounds.

Übungen. The grammar sections consist of examples and brief explanations of the grammar points. Each presentation is followed by related exercises. Open-ended, personalized *Du hast das Wort* activities appear at appropriate intervals.

Grammatische Übersicht. The grammar summary is a reference section. It provides a concise overview of the grammar topics of the chapter. Where appropriate, material from previous chapters is summarized along with related new material.

Wiederholung. The review exercises focus on vocabulary and grammar of a given chapter and re-enter material from previous chapters.

Kulturlesestück. A reading selection that treats one of the cultural themes in the chapter and recombines familiar vocabulary and structures is found at the end of every chapter in Stages 2 and 3. New words that are not cognates are glossed in the margin as a reading aid. One or more activities follow the reading selection.

Vokabeln. The end-of-the-chapter vocabulary lists the active new vocabulary with English equivalents.

Suggested Procedures and Activities

Every group of students has different interests, needs, and abilities; every teacher has different ideas and techniques. No book or teacher's guide can replace the imagination, ingenuity, and sensitivity of the teacher. The guidelines in this section, therefore, are merely *suggestions* for effective use of the various elements of *German Today, One.* Each teacher should adapt and alter the procedures described to suit her or his style and situation.

Learning objectives

The formation of learning objectives is a good way to ensure that teachers and students alike are aware of the goals of the course. Such goals are necessarily an individual matter, and what is reasonable—or even possible—in one school or class may be out of the question elsewhere. There is no single correct set of objectives. A wide range of views exists, not only as to what level of expectation is proper, but also as to what form learning objectives should take and how detailed they should be. The following suggestions, therefore, are intended to help the teacher form learning objectives within the context of *German Today* that fit her or his own situation.

Several aspects of the instructional process need to be considered in forming learning objectives. First and foremost is the content: *what* is to be learned. Since few students will truly master all of what is taught, it is further necessary to determine what percentage of the content and what degree of accuracy constitute a minimally satisfactory level of attainment. Next to be considered is the amount of time within which students are to learn the material. Finally, one must decide how students are to demonstrate that they have learned the material. Again, there is no one answer to the question of what is adequate, reasonable, or fair. Teachers simply have to exercise their own judgment in light of what they know about their school, their students, and the amount of time available.

A useful tool for the process of forming learning objectives is the Scope-and-sequence chart on pages TAE 4 to TAE 9. This chart categorizes the course content according to the various kinds of information students should learn: cultural information, word sets (and vocabulary in general), pronunciation, grammar. The individual teacher can decide and then inform students exactly what will be expected, and to what level of proficiency or accuracy, within each of the categories. This procedure begins, but does not complete, the formation of meaningful learning objectives.

What will require a little more effort on the part of the teacher, but what is ultimately perhaps even more important, is a listing of the kinds of things students ought to be able to do with language by the time they finish a given chapter. This will involve analyzing the vocabulary, the topics and content of the various core material selections, and the kinds of expressions presented in the activities. The teacher should keep in mind what students are learning *to do* with language rather than just think about the grammatical structures or individual words students are supposed to learn. For each chapter, it should be possible to identify three to five "communication skills." Since these really form the heart of each chapter, around which the grammar, vocabulary, and the cultural information have been organized, it is important for students to know what the skills are and to be encouraged to master them.

A few examples will perhaps help. In Chapter 1, for instance, students learn (among other things) to exchange greetings and take leave of each other, to identify themselves, to describe themselves and others in terms of mood and personality, and to ask and answer some simple questions. At the end of the chapter, each student ought to be able to do each of those things, even if only on a fairly elementary basis. Similarly, in Chapter 3 they learn to express likes and dislikes, to discuss where they live, and to talk about their after-school activities. In later chapters the communication skills become more complex. In Chapter 6, students learn to express anxiety and reassurance; in Chapter 7, to extend, accept, and turn down invitations; in Chapter 15, to give directions.

Expressed in the form of communication skills, the goals of the course are more likely to make sense to students than goals that include only lists of vocabulary words or grammatical structures. Those are also important, of course, but their importance is frequently not as obvious or convincing to students as to teachers. By including among the objectives the kinds of communication skills the students should be trying to develop, teachers can help students see the point of what they are learning, and help them see language as a tool for a variety of tasks. Once again, since these *uses* of the language and the active participation that they require of the student are really the basis of the whole *German Today* program, their inclusion in the learning objectives of the course is extremely important.

Special sections of the program

German Around You. This section is an especially important feature because it comes at the very beginning of the first-year book. How students get started is likely to be a crucial factor in determining their attitude toward language study. Hence, the emphasis here is on the ways in which at least some bits and pieces of culture from the German-speaking countries—in the form of cognates and borrowed words, place names, and institutions—are not really so foreign after all. Many aspects of American culture have also found their way into German life and language. The point is to stress for students, at the outset, the familiar or common aspects of German rather than what is different or unusual about German. One of the aims of this section is to make students feel more comfortable with the experience of learning German by drawing attention to linguistic and cultural features they already know.

The degree to which the material presented in this section is, in fact, familiar will vary from class to class (even from student to student) and from one part of the country to another. But even if a student does claim total ignorance of everything on these pages, enthusiastic and vigorous presentation on the part of the teacher at this point can do much to overcome the beginner's feeling that everything having to do with German is "weird" or completely foreign.

A number of different kinds of activities can be devised to make these pages both an effective teaching device and a source of fun. One of the easiest ways to get students started is to look for things to add to each of the categories represented here. Newspapers and magazines, phone books, street maps and atlases, should all help produce additional examples of the influence of German. Students may want to learn the meanings, if they do not already know them, of the items that are presented on pages viii–xi of the Student Text. One word of caution should perhaps be expressed, however. Since the main purpose of this section is to get students interested and involved, it is important to treat these pages in a relaxed manner, to emphasize similarity and familiarity, and the usefulness of exposure to German as a way of enriching one's sense of English. Above all, it should be borne in mind that these pages are most likely to fulfill a useful purpose if they are treated as a lively means of introducing new material rather than as something to be presented and then tested. "German Around You" is important as much for its capacity to help set a positive tone as for its actual content.

Finally, one should keep in mind that this section is an introduction both to the language and to the culture. "German Around You" is just the first step in the *German Today* program, where language and culture are never really separated. In the material on these pages, partly because "grammar" is not at issue, teachers have an opportunity to help students see language as one part of a vast cultural complex. How students look at "German Around You" will have much to do with their success and their attitudes throughout their study of German.

You may wish to introduce (or try to elicit from students) some of the following words and phrases that are not included in the "German Around You" section.

Cognates: Parts of the body

der Arm	die Nase
das Haar	der Finger
die Lippen	

Cognates: Animals

die Katze	der Tiger
die Ratte	der Elefant

Cognates: Music

die Gitarre	die Musik
das Saxophon	die Flöte
die Klarinette	das Akkordeon
das Instrument	

Surnames

Mueller	Lehrer
Bauer	Baum
Schmidt	Weiss
Klein	Stein
Schiff	

Foods & Stores

Delikatessen	Zwieback
Knackwurst	Marzipan
Wiener Schnitzel	Sauerkraut
Apfelstrudel	Frankfurter
Sauerbraten	Hamburger

Borrowed words

Schnauzer	Zeppelin
Dachshund	Wanderlust
Weimaraner	Dirndl
Gestalt	Oktoberfest
Leitmotiv	Wunderkind

English words used in German

baby	jazz
babysitter	jeans
boss	job
camping	manager
clever	party
clown	pop-song
do-it-yourself	quiz
fair	shorts
gangster	show
golf	teen-ager
hit	test
hobby	toast
interview	western

For additional German place names in the United States, consult a map or atlas. You may wish to use an overhead projector and point out German names state by state, or you may wish to have students work in small groups (or pairs) to uncover German names in various regions or groups of states. In the latter instance you may need to assist students in their search. Where appropriate, supply English equivalents for students.

Photo essays. The full-color photographs at the beginning of each Stage are valuable for several reasons. The pure visual appeal of colorful pictures, which simply make the book more fun to use, is an obvious benefit. Likewise, the photographs are of self-evident value as a means of illustrating the places and topics described in the text and of giving the student a sense of reality and substance. The usefulness of the photo essays as the basis for activities, however, is more easily overlooked. A photograph can give rise to a practically unlimited number of comments and descriptions, especially with the help of a few timely suggestions from the teacher.

If a picture is worth a thousand words, in a foreign language course there is much to be said for eliciting as many of those words as possible from the students. Techniques for doing so range from asking students to make simple statements about a picture to asking them to "step into" a scene and create an appropriate narrative or conversation. Students can make up or answer factual questions about what is depicted; they can state their personal feelings about what they see; they can invent names for people, explanations for situations, or results of occurrences; they can say of what, where, or whom a picture reminds them.

You may wish to review the photographs from time to time as you prepare lesson plans, looking for ways to use them to elicit particular words and structures. Many pictures can serve repeatedly as cues for different kinds of utterances.

Most teachers prefer to keep to a minimum the amount of English spoken in the classroom. Certainly it is desirable to promote as much use of German as possible in talking about illustrations as in other activities. However, you may find that permitting occasional discussion of the photographs in English is worthwhile if it enables students to increase their awareness and understanding of the cultures that are represented.

Culminating Activities. Review and reinforcement are basic to a successful foreign language program. The ongoing re-entry that is included throughout the chapters of *German Today* is complemented by the Culminating Activities *(Noch einmal)* at the end of each Stage and at the end of the first-year book. This special section serves as the basis for a kind of "time-out," a break in the regular work pattern that acknowledges or reflects the natural plateaus students typically reach in the process of learning a language. Skills and topics from several chapters are used in these activities, helping tie together individual bits of information and concepts so that students can see the total picture and fully appreciate the communicative powers that they have acquired. Moreover, the section offers new and enjoyable ways for students to work with familiar material, as well as ways to expand their cultural awareness. While the section does provide review, the activities are meant to be fun rather than to be used as tests of any sort.

It is not expected that any one student will do all of the activities; rather, it is hoped that at least one or two activities will appeal to each student. The printed directions plus your imagination and help should suffice as guidelines. Some of the activities are intended for individual work (writing a letter), others for pairs or small groups (skits and displays), and still others for the entire class (games and large projects). The activities provide both oral and written practice; many involve use of visuals.

At least one Culminating Activity in each Stage is keyed to the color essay that introduces that Stage. Students are asked to develop a conversation, skit, or simple narrative based on one or more of the photos. One activity—writing an autobiographical description—is repeated at the end of each Stage, each time with a little more depth.

You may want to spend parts of several days working on this section, possibly alternating individual projects with group projects. (Some of these activities may be started before the end of the Stage.) Additional enjoyable activities such as slide shows, songs, and talks by visitors can be included during this period as part of the consolidation process that helps to give students the desired sense of accomplishment and understanding.

Chapter material

Chapter opening text. Students should begin the study of each chapter in Stage 1 by reading the brief introductory text in English. You may wish to expand on this material with information based on your own knowledge of the area. Be sure that students can locate the places discussed on a map. The maps in *German Today* will be useful, as well as a globe or various wall maps.

Besides providing a few details about the locale of the chapter and establishing a context for the core material, the opener may be used to stimulate discussion of current events and personal experiences and attitudes. Use newspaper articles, slides, or films of the area, if they are available. Ask students about their knowledge or impressions of the places mentioned in the text.

Core material and activities. Each chapter in *German Today* begins with one or more pieces of core material, which may be in the form of a short reading, a dialogue, a letter, or even a simple list of chores. Other pieces of core material include simulated realia: a photo album, a class schedule, catalog pages, etc. The considerable variety in the kinds of core material will quite likely affect the way you choose to present the new material to students, but several important functions of this section are shared in any case. First, the core material establishes a theme for the chapter, which is reflected in most of the other sections of the chapter as well. Second, core material introduces vocabulary and grammatical structures, many of which are treated in depth later in the *Wortschatzerweiterung* and *Übungen* sections. Third, cultural features are an integral part of the core material; many of these features are treated in cultural notes. Finally, one of the most important functions of the core material is to present examples of various categories of communication, which are then practiced and expanded upon in the *Du hast das Wort* sections that follow core material.

The suggested strategies for teaching core material and activities can be summarized briefly as follows: (1) present the material in several short sessions rather than fewer, longer ones; (2) return to material frequently for re-entry, variation, and reinforcement; (3) exploit to the greatest possible degree the interests, imagination, and creativity of both the students and the teacher.

The core material selections need not necessarily be memorized. A useful objective is for students to be able, at the end of a chapter, to understand and use the material in new contexts. This ability to comprehend and to produce language outside the familiar context in which it was presented is what marks true communicative competence.

With respect to comprehension, therefore, students should reach a point at the end of each chapter where they can answer questions based on the core material, paraphrase the material, and use the language correctly, within the parameters of familiar vocabulary and structures. They should be able to do so both orally and in writing, in response to either spoken or written cues.

There are many ways of presenting core material, but a few general guidelines are appropriate. How you present the dialogues will depend in part on the theme and the number of characters. Some dialogues lend themselves well to presentation by stick figures on the chalkboard or on overhead transparencies; others may be dramatized by the teacher with the assistance of one or two students. Some dialogues need props; others can be made more interesting by using recordings, posters, or cut-out illustrations from magazines. Paraphrasing in English is another technique used by many teachers to set the scene and ensure comprehension. As students progress, the teacher may wish to present new vocabulary by giving simple German definitions, antonyms, or synonyms, or by pointing out suffixes or word roots.

No matter what technique is used to introduce dialogues, it is recommended that students keep their books closed during the initial presentation. This helps focus their attention on what they are hearing, thus strengthening the often-neglected skill of listening comprehension. Cue cards on which the dialogue lines have been printed may be useful, but teachers will find that they can introduce dialogue lines more effectively if they, unlike the students, do memorize the material. Freed from the need to hold the book or a cue card, the teacher can use hand signals more easily, maintain eye contact with students, and observe more easily who is responding.

During the initial presentation, it is important that you model the lines at normal conversational speed, without distortion or undue exaggeration. It may be necessary, of course, to isolate a word, phrase, or phoneme for special work, but isolated practice should always be followed immediately by a repetition of the entire utterance at normal conversational speed. You may then wish to reread the entire dialogue with pauses to check on comprehension. Asking questions as you work through a section can help point out key elements and ensure that nobody gets lost along the way.

Once a dialogue is mastered students should be encouraged to adapt it in various ways. Adding a new beginning or ending, inserting adjectives and adverbs in appropriate places, changing characters' names, etc., can be fun. More to the point is that when students have an opportunity to "create" (within carefully controlled limits), they are apt to become less self-conscious and more fluent in their use of the language.

Make it clear to students that they are not expected to understand fully on the first exposure to the material, but encourage them to try to get a general idea of the meaning. There will be frequent opportunities to return to the selection and fill in the gaps in comprehension. Remind students frequently of basic techniques for understanding new material: logical guessing based on context; attention to morphological clues such as cognates and words related to other known words; attention to intonation, tone, and non-verbal clues such as gestures and facial expressions.

When narrative pieces first appear you will probably want to introduce them in much the same way as the dialogues: by stick figures, props, and so on. As students learn more German, you may be able to clarify the meaning of new words and expressions in German, by using them in sentences, or by referring to known words. After the first presentation, students may follow along in the text as they listen to you or to the recording. As with the dialogues, when meaning has been established, you may want to read the text or play the recording again, pausing after each sentence or two to ask questions. Before students take turns reading portions of the selection they should have acquired a considerable degree of understanding and fluency with the individual lines. It is a good idea, incidentally, to vary the purpose for which a selection is read. In some cases, students should be asked to read for the general gist of the story; in other cases, they should read for specific details; in still other cases, they should read with an eye to retelling the story later.

When you feel students are ready to begin reading the piece themselves, model the phrases and sentences for their repetition. Aim for correct pronunciation and intonation based on your model (or that in the tape) right from the beginning; it is at this point that the basis for proper pronunciation is laid. It is sometimes difficult to decide what degree of proficiency in pronunciation, intonation, rhythm, and speed should be attained by most students before you proceed to another activity. Students become discouraged and fatigued when impossibly high standards are set. At the same time, one must keep in mind that it is far easier to correct errors in pronunciation at the outset than it is to change poor pronunciation habits once they are firmly established. Corrections should be made in a natural tone of voice, devoid of criticism. It is often desirable to call on the entire class to repeat a corrected response before asking an individual to do so. In the end, most students should be able to pronounce utterances at normal conversational speed, without unnatural emphasis or exaggeration. Another technique is to have several individuals repeat a word or phrase, rather than just the students who made the error.

Many of these same techniques for presenting and checking comprehension of dialogues and narratives can be used for simulated realia, with one notable exception. Since items such as schedules or posters in real life are designed to be read, not heard, and since they are often illustrated, students should be able to see the text as they hear it. You may wish to display the material on an overhead projector or suggest that students follow in their books. Be sure students read the material with intonation that might be used in actually reading such an item; one reads abbreviated material differently from full prose. Make sure they understand what they are saying by occasionally asking them to paraphrase the information. When possible, students should try to paraphrase in German.

After the initial presentation, students can be encouraged to make slight variations. For example, in the concert poster on page 128, the name of the group and the ticket prices could be changed, within the limits of the students' vocabulary at that point.

It is very important not to spend too much time on a given section of core material without breaking to a different activity. In most circumstances, fifteen minutes is probably the maximum time that should be spent on any one activity. If one tries to analyze the material exhaustively during one session, students' concentration and level of interest are diminished. A more effective strategy is to limit the scope of each session, in terms of both the time spent and the material covered, and return to the selection the next day or even later in the same class period. Once the initial presentation of a section of core material has been completed, it is usually desirable to return to it two or three times during the study of that chapter. Most students will not master the material before several such presentations have taken place. The teacher's judgment will determine the time spent on new material. While students should not be allowed to become bored, they should not become frustrated by having to move ahead before they reach a reasonable level of understanding.

Most core material selections are followed by *Fragen* or *Richtig oder falsch?* activities. These checks are not only valuable in assessing student comprehension of core material; they also help students interpret the simulated realia.

Teachers may wish to adjust the level of difficulty of a question to the ability of each student. The question can be slightly modified but still reinforce the structure being practiced. Often the same question can be asked of two or three students in succession, so that the weaker student may have the opportunity to hear the correct answer before being asked to respond. Since in real conversations responses are often in the form of sentence fragments, you may wish to accept such responses from students. You can then provide practice in forming complete sentences in a different way.

As students progress in their mastery of the language, they should be given frequent opportunity to make up their own questions. Too often the teacher does all the asking and the students do all the responding. Students should be encouraged to work in pairs and in small groups as they ask and answer questions. Also, students should be given the opportunity to ask the teacher questions for practice with the formal form of address. The teacher's responses will provide extra listening comprehension practice.

The activities in the *Du hast das Wort* sections that follow most selections of core material are among the most important features of *German Today*. The way in which they are used can greatly affect the students' success in learning to communicate in German. All of the activities exist for the purpose of encouraging students to use German, often to talk about their own feelings and experiences. The teacher and students will frequently think of ways to expand or adapt the activities; such creativity is to be encouraged.

A limited amount of new vocabulary and structures is used in the activities. New material is indicated with a raised degree mark (°); English equivalents are provided in the end-of-chapter vocabularies. Much of this new material is analyzed later in the chapter. Many useful expressions may be treated as lexical items with little or no discussion of the grammar. In any case, it is usually best to do the activities first with minimal analysis, since the idea is to get the class started *using* the material as quickly as possible. After having worked on the appropriate parts of the *Wortschatzerweiterung* and *Übungen* sections, you may choose to go back to the activities to reinforce the students' understanding of how the words and concepts are practiced.

Many activities are in the form of a question (or statement) followed by a series of varied responses. Often these responses represent a variety of attitudes or moods, so that students can come close to presenting their own point of view in a given situation. Make clear to students that the printed variations do not represent all possible responses.

Rather, they are a selection of useful conversational tools covering a range of meanings. The activities will be most effective if students are allowed to choose the forms that actually express their own feelings—or their whims—and to invent or recall other expressions from previous chapters, and are not obliged to respond in set ways just so that everybody practices saying everything. Generally, in fact, all of the printed variations will eventually be used by somebody (if need be, the teacher can take a role and produce those that students do not use), and ideally the class will come up with a number of utterances to add to the ones provided. By returning to the activities several times during the course of a chapter they can be used effectively as warmups; the teacher can make sure that all of the material is learned and practiced in an enjoyable way.

Activities can be taught in much the same way as core material: presentation, practice, then reinforcement through variation. Initial presentation can be done with books open or closed, but subsequent practice should be done with books closed in order to maintain spontaneity. Ways to practice and use the responses in a realistic way are many and varied: 1. students practice in pairs, giving both cues and responses; 2. each student makes a statement or asks a question and the next one responds, going around the class in chain fashion; 3. as a game students must give a response not used by other students; 4. teacher makes a statement, asks a question, describes a situation, or shows a picture, and students give personal responses; 5. variations of the teacher-directed activities in number 4 are to have teacher tell students how to respond (directed dialog) or to give students a choice of two responses (both of these techniques are especially useful when the responses are first being learned). Whatever specific devices are used, the more often students are led to interact with one another as well as with the teacher, the more readily they will perceive German as a form of communication instead of an academic exercise.

Beginning in Chapter 8 of Stage 2, directed statements and questions in the *Sag!* and *Frag!* sections provide another means of practicing new structures and vocabulary. They also help accustom students to word order in dependent clauses long before that topic is taken up formally in the *Übungen* and *Grammatische Übersicht* sections. The teacher should give directed statements and questions in a natural tone of voice and personalize them whenever possible. Directed statements and questions can often be combined into simulated dialogues, which can then be role-played by students with little guidance from the teacher.

Cultural notes. Promoting awareness of diverse cultures is an integral part of *German Today.* The cultural notes are numerous and varied; their aim is to offer insights into the life of German-speaking people. It is not possible (or desirable) to include lengthy commentary and exhaustive details in the notes; they should serve instead as the basis for further discussion and in some cases, research. Annotations in the TAE provide additional information that you may wish to share with the students. Encourage students to be alert for news items and other references to the topics and locales of the book, and to bring them to the attention of the class. Many of the things they study in their other courses, especially social studies, literature, and art courses, are relevant to the subject matter of *German Today;* helping students to perceive such relationships among their different courses greatly benefits them and the entire school community.

All of the cultural notes of *German Today, One* are in English so that the information will be easily accessible and students will not consider them an added burden. As in the case of the other English sections of the text, you will want to use your own judgment as to how much time to allow for discussion in English. You may want to have students read the notes outside of class, then set aside a few minutes for class discussion afterwards. Perhaps you will wish to make up simple comprehension questions, to be asked and answered in German, based on the notes or the photos, drawings, or realia that complement them. Whatever method of handling them you prefer, it is hoped that the cultural notes and related activities or projects will prove enjoyable and informative.

Wortschatzerweiterung. The word study sections provide the basis for classroom activities designed to increase the students' basic vocabulary. New words are presented in related groups, since it is easier for many students to learn vocabulary in logical groups than as isolated words or expressions.

The majority of the groups are lexical word sets, such as sports terms, weather expressions, or food. Most word sets are presented through the use of illustrations to minimize interference from English and to place the vocabulary in context. Beginning in Stage 2 some sections are included that focus on linguistic features such as flavoring words, noun compounds, and suffixes -er and -er + -in. Such topics help students increase not only their vocabulary but also their word-building skills.

Several topics are presented in most *Wortschatzerweiterung* sections. Each topic generally relates to one of the core material selections; the topic can be presented after the core material selection has been introduced. Sometimes one or another of the topics lends itself to use as an introduction to the core material selection and could therefore be presented first. This technique will facilitate variation of the core material.

The exercises and activities that follow each presentation can be done with the entire class, small groups, or pairs of students. Exercises should be done orally first and can be followed by written work, if desired. Stress to students the need for mastering these words, which are intended to become part of their active vocabulary. It is suggested that you not spend too much time on a particular section during a single class period; once again, varying the kinds of things done in class will generally produce better results.

Aussprache. Each pronunciation section contains brief, simple explanations of one or two features of the German sound system, drills for practicing these features, and a few sentences to provide pronunciation and reading practice in context. The drills are based on minimal or near-minimal pairs. The illustrated proverb within each section offers students additional pronunciation practice, as well as a way to have fun learning set phrases that are an integral part of culture in the German-speaking countries. The proverbs are generally related to the sound being practiced.

Phonetic symbols are used in the pronunciation sections primarily for convenience of reference and to remind students that sounds and letters do not always correspond. Students are not expected to learn these symbols. Most of them correspond to symbols in the International Phonetic Alphabet; some have been modified to make them resemble alphabet letters more closely. Several key words are given for each sound so that students can learn to associate that sound with specific spellings. The key words are usually high-frequency words, and most of them are recently introduced vocabulary.

Students will attain widely varying degrees of proficiency in regard to pronunciation. One criterion for determining what constitutes acceptable pronunciation is whether or not a given utterance would be comprehensible to a native speaker not familiar with the text. Many factors, including innate aptitude, self-confidence, and motivation, will influence the extent to which an individual student's pronunciation may surpass the minimum acceptable level.

A student who clearly has difficulty distinguishing and reproducing the sounds of German should not be expected to achieve near-native pronunciation. On the other hand, a student who gives evidence of having a "good ear" and an ability to imitate sounds and speech patterns should be encouraged to improve her or his pronunciation as much as possible. Your perception of a student's relative potential, therefore, will determine to a considerable extent the kinds of corrections you make of that student's speech.

All of the pronunciation drills are included in the *German Today, One* recordings. Whether or not you use the recordings, you will probably want to model and then have students repeat the examples. Walk around the room as you model the words, so that students can see your mouth as you produce the sounds. Alternate choral repetition with individual practice, encouraging students to speak clearly and in full voice. It is important also to speak at a natural tempo, with normal stress patterns.

When presenting the proverbs, try first to elicit from students some possible interpretations or English equivalents, prompting as necessary. (English equivalents are provided in the annotations.) In many cases cognates, familiar words, and the illustration itself provide enough clues to point students in the right direction. Students should not be concerned about unfamiliar vocabulary and structures; the proverbs are not intended for active mastery, and linguistic analysis of them, especially early in the course, is unlikely to be profitable. As an optional activity, you might encourage students to come up with different artistic renderings of the proverbs and post the drawings on a bulletin board.

It is advisable to do portions of a pronunciation section over a period of several days, rather than attempt to cover it in one class period. Quick, lively drills on one or two sounds, repeated at appropriate points in later class periods, will produce better results than a concentrated one-time session.

Übungen. The grammar section of each chapter presents several grammar points, and each of these presentations is followed by one or more exercises for immediate practice and reinforcement of the topic. Each set of drills progresses in minimal steps, and often ends in a test drill. Two or three open-ended activities (*Du hast das Wort*) are interspersed throughout the grammar section.

Each presentation begins with an example of the grammar point at issue, either in chart form or as a German phrase or sentence. This example is followed by a succinct explanation in English. Grammar presentations may be done inductively or deductively, at your discretion. For example, you may wish to present some topics by having students do one of the exercises and then try to derive a grammar statement about the pattern practiced. In other instances, for a change of pace, you may wish to present examples and the explanation first, and then have students practice the concept in the related exercises. Alternating the use of inductive and deductive approaches, depending on the complexity of the particular grammar point, is one effective way of varying class procedures. In addition, this kind of variety can be a real help to the students; since not all students learn equally well with both approaches, the variety gives more of them a better chance of comprehending the material.

Most grammar exercises are given in context so that students can practice communicating with a purpose. Initially, drills should be done orally and with books closed, in order to focus students' attention on what they are saying. An extension of this oral practice is for the teacher to model the cues and responses for the students, who then write the responses after oral repetition. As a change of pace, students could cue the exercises instead of the teacher. As a general rule, intensive oral work should precede any written assignments. When dealing with a particularly difficult structure, many teachers find it helpful to repeat a drill, or a slightly modified version of it, two or three times within the same week. It may be helpful for some students to write out troublesome exercises after oral drill. Annotations often suggest variations for the drills. Students should be encouraged to offer their own variations; such variations are an important step toward competence in the language. *Du hast das Wort* activities are provided at strategic intervals to offer students greater freedom in the manipulation of new structures, in a new and personalized context. Students can do these activities in pairs or small groups. For a change of pace they can be done with the full class.

For the most part, *German Today* uses standard grammatical terminology, such as *noun, verb,* and *adjective.* However, certain terms that have proved confusing to students have been replaced by more descriptive terms. *Conversational past* is used instead of *present perfect,* and *der-, das-,* and *die-* nouns are used instead of *masculine, neuter,* and *feminine* nouns. The masculine and neuter forms of the definite and indefinite markers are presented first, followed by the feminine (and plural) form, although, as stated above, these terms are not actually used in the student text. This order simplifies the learner's task, since the masculine and neuter forms are identical in some cases, as are the feminine and plural forms.

The order of presentation of the cases is based on frequency of usage and relative ease of learning. The nominative forms are introduced first, then the accusative, and finally, the dative. The genitive case is postponed to the second level, since it occurs much less frequently than the other cases.

Grammatische Übersicht. This handy reference section summarizes the grammar points from the *Übungen* and sometimes presents additional information, which is intended for recognition only and is not practiced actively. The grammar summary brings together the topics presented step by step in the *Übungen* section. In some cases material from previous chapters is re-entered and summarized, along with related new material.

Grammar points are frequently presented in charts and tables for the purpose of quick review. Capital letters in parentheses following the grammar headings refer back to corresponding exercises in the *Übungen.* If students are having difficulty with any of the grammar topics, they should

be encouraged to repeat the appropriate drills in that section before taking the chapter test. Since this section is intended for reference, most teachers will not want to take class time to cover it.

Wiederholung. Systematic review and re-entry are key features of *German Today.* The review exercises in the *Wiederholung* focus on the vocabulary and grammar of the current chapter, and they re-enter such material from previous chapters. These exercises are intended for either oral or written work; some can be done both ways. In the earlier units especially, it is advisable for teachers to go over exercises orally before assigning them as written homework. You can assign selected exercises after completing the corresponding section of the grammar or wait until the chapter is finished. The *Wiederholung* is useful as a pre-test review.

Kulturlesestück. The cultural reading selections that are introduced in Stage 2 recombine familiar vocabulary and structures. Unfamiliar words that are not obvious cognates are glossed in the margin as a reading aid; they should be treated as passive vocabulary. The *Kulturlesestücke* are designed to give students an added cultural slant on one of the themes treated in the chapter. They offer students the opportunity to read extended blocks of material and provide training in understanding unfamiliar passages.

In most cases the reading selections can be presented in much the same way as the core material and activities are. (See pages TAE 17–21). As you work through the readings, encourage students to make intelligent guesses; they should try to use contextual clues to comprehend a word or phrase without referring to the chapter vocabulary.

The amount of time spent on a given reading selection will depend on the mood of the class as well as the nature of the reading selection. Activities after the *Kulturlesestück* have several aims: they help ensure that students understand the material; they may expand on the theme of the reading by personalizing the material and relating it to the students' own experience; and they may suggest research to further the students' cultural awareness. Many of the selections may be used as a point of departure for small-group activities or for individualized work. The teacher may wish to show slides, films, or filmstrips on related topics.

Vokabeln. The chapter vocabulary is a reference list of active new vocabulary with English equivalents. Students should master the words and expressions before going on to the next chapter. Vocabulary items are alphabetized within each of several categories as a learning aid: *Substantive, Verben, Andere Wörter, Besondere Ausdrücke,* and other categories as appropriate to the chapter. The *Besondere Ausdrücke* include idiomatic expressions as well as isolated words and set phrases introduced in core material or activities that students should learn as lexical items.

Reference section

Lieder und Gedichte. The reference section has been expanded to include materials requested by many teachers. Songs and canons have been selected for simplicity of language and melody and can be used successfully from early on. Poems by Heine, Mörike, and Goethe may be read for comprehension and cultural enrichment or they may be memorized.

Jugendsprache. This list of non-standard expressions popular with German teenagers will show students the creative way in which young Germans deal with their language in the 80's.

German first names. The most popular German boys' and girls' names are included in this up-to-date list. You may wish to assign names to students or let them choose their own.

English equivalents of dialogues. The English equivalents are intended mainly as a reference for home study, or for students who were absent when core material was introduced.

Grammatical Summaries. The third Appendix includes charts and tables of the inflected endings of nouns, determiners, and verbs. The paradigms include the nominative, accusative, and dative cases of *der-, das-,* and *die*-nouns, *ein*-words, *dieser*-words, and pronouns; prepositions that govern the accusative and the dative cases; numbers 1–1000; models of regular, irregular, and stem-changing

verbs in the present, imperative, and conversational past; and the modal auxiliaries *müssen, können, wollen, dürfen, sollen,* and *mögen.* This Appendix also includes a list of strong verbs with their past participles.

Supplementary word sets. The list of supplementary word sets is a useful tool in helping students increase the number of things they can say and write during the course of a chapter. In some of the activities such as conversations, letters, or skits, students may wish to use words not in their active vocabulary. Since it is unrealistic and pedagogically unsound to present long lists of words in a given group or set that all students must learn, these supplementary (and optional) word sets are made available to students with special interest in a topic. Some of the words presented are introduced as active vocabulary in later chapters.

Supplementary expressions. The list of supplementary expressions offers students another opportunity to express their feelings in various situations. From time to time you may wish to present some of these expressions with the English equivalents to students..

German-English Vocabulary. The end vocabulary gives the basic words and expressions introduced in the core material, activities, and *Wortschatzerweiterung* sections plus the chapter number where they are introduced. Teachers will find the chapter references useful in preparing additional exercises or quizzes. Words from headings, proverbs, photo captions, scene setters, and *Kulturlesestücke* are included also (except obvious cognates), but these are listed without chapter references.

English-German Vocabulary. This vocabulary includes the active words presented in *German Today, One.* Students will find the list helpful for some of the *Wiederholung* exercises as well as for skits and other open-ended activities.

Index. The Index at the end of the Student Text indicates the page(s) on which a grammar topic is introduced. The Index also contains page references to topics in the *Wortschatzerweiterung* and the *Aussprache* sections.

Sample Lesson Plans

Non-Linear teaching

Sample lesson plans for Chapter 2 (Stage 1) and Chapter 9 (Stage 2) are outlined below to demonstrate how a non-linear treatment of this text could be implemented. The exact amount of time needed to complete a chapter will depend on many factors, including the age and maturity of the students, the teacher's pacing, the length of the class period, and the amount of supplementary material used. The suggested plan for Chapter 2 spreads the teaching activities over 9 days, while the plan for Chapter 9 takes 10 days. Such an organization will make it possible to cover the 15 chapters of *German Today, One* in under 150 days, a pace that should still give teachers ample flexibility to adapt the plans to specific situations in their schools. Extra days can be used profitably doing the Culminating Activities for each Stage, showing slides or films, or special language attractions.

No one plan will work equally well for every class, but these suggestions may serve as models for teachers in preparing to teach the two chapters under discussion here as well as the remaining chapters. Perhaps the single most important general reminder is that variety and change of pace are crucial to a lively class. One way to achieve variety is to begin each chapter a little differently. A cultural note or a photo essay can serve as the basis for discussion that will help set the tone for a chapter, especially valuable when the chapter is set in a place that the students have not yet become familiar with. A topic from the *Wortschatzerweiterung* section may on occasion provide a good launching pad. The same is true of a topic in the *Übungen* section. And in some instances, one or more of the activities in a *Du hast das Wort* section may be a way of getting into a chapter, where you first help students master the variety of ways of responding to a comment or question before exposing them to the particular situation in the core material that calls such use into play.

Variety in technique is another way to build a successful language program. Probably nothing bores students faster than knowing that they can expect nothing other than teacher presentation followed by student response, in every class. Getting students to work in small groups or pairs occasionally, having students take over the role of

"teacher" at least to the extent of asking the questions, and working in chain drills rather than always having the teacher pose the next question or problem all help. One technique that can work well to give students a sense of being in some control of what goes on is to set aside three to five minutes at the beginning of the class during which students ask the teacher as many questions as they can think of.

Learning a foreign language within the rigid confines of a school class period does, of course, require practice and a certain amount of drill. But varying the sequence of activities and the instructional techniques and trying to keep things spontaneous will help make the language seem more like a real tool for communication rather than just a series of exercises. These sample lesson plans may help give you some ideas about how to proceed.

Planning a lesson

The detailed lesson plan for Chapter 2 and the somewhat abbreviated plan for Chapter 9 assume a forty-minute period. The numbers in parentheses represent a suggested number of minutes for each activity. If your class periods are shorter or longer than forty minutes, you can adjust the number of activities and the amount of time spent on them. Annotations frequently provide suggestions for games and supplementary activities. You may wish to use workbook exercises as extra practice in class or as homework assignments. Some teachers include a few minutes at the end of the period for students to begin their homework. Five or ten minutes is usually enough to make sure students understand what is required, and give a welcome change of pace.

Chapter 2 (Stage 1)

Day 1

(5) 1. Warm-up: Ask personalized questions based on structures and vocabulary of Chapter 1. For example: *Ingrid, bist du glücklich?*

(8) 2. Review Exercises D and E of *Wiederholung*, Chapter 1. After a student gives the correct German equivalent of one of the

English sentences, ask another student for the German equivalent of a slightly modified sentence. For example, in Exercise D:

1. Hi, how are you? — [Fine/not well].
2. What's the matter? Why are you [tired]?

(4) 3. Introduce Chapter 2. If you have prepared learning objectives, go over them with students. Mention theme of dialogues, word sets, communication skills, grammatical structures, cultural contents.

(5) 4. Read together the cultural note on Austria (p. 24). Initiate a discussion on some aspects of Austria by referring to the map on p. xv.

(15) 5. Introduce first dialogue, *Jung oder alt?* (p. 24), books closed. See suggested procedures, TAE p. 18. Watch pronunciation of *sechzehn*. After some control of dialogue lines, work with *Fragen*.

(3) 6. Introduce *Du hast das Wort* Exercise A (see TAE, p. 20).

Assignment: Study dialogue *Jung oder alt?* (p. 24). Write answers to *Fragen*. Practice *Du hast das Wort* Exercise A.

Day 2

(5) 1. Warm-up: Ask personal questions. *Wie heißt du? Heißt du [Inge]? Wie geht's? Bist du müde? Ist [Volker] krank?*

(10) 2. Review dialogue *Jung oder alt?* (p. 24). Ask *Fragen* with variations.

(13) 3. *Wortschatzerweiterung* (p. 26). Teach numbers 0–19. Watch pronunciation of *sechs* and *sechzehn*. Teach three numbers at a time: *eins, zwei, drei.*

(5) 4. Do Exercises A–C on numbers.

(5) 5. Introduce *Du hast das Wort* Exercise B. To get a variety of answers, assign an age to each student: *Inge, du bist neun.*

(2) 6. Do Exercise A on [e] and [ε] sounds in *Aussprache* (p. 28).

Assignment: Study numbers 0–19. Write out Exercise C (p. 26).

Day 3

(4) 1. Chain drill. Students take turns asking age, giving it, and then commenting: *Wie*

alt bist du? — Ich bin [sechzehn]. — Das ist sehr [jung].

(7) 2. Review numbers 0–19 and arithmetic problems. Vary the problems of Exercise C (p. 26).

(3) 3. Discuss cultural note on birthdays in German-speaking countries (p. 25). Practice birthday greetings.

(15) 4. Introduce second dialogue *Wann hast du Geburtstag?*, including *Richtig oder falsch?* (p. 25).

(7) 5. *Wortschatzerweiterung* (p. 27). Teach months. It is often helpful to teach in groups of three: *Januar, Februar, März.*

(4) 6. *Aussprache* (p. 28), Exercise B.

Assignment: Study dialogue *Wann hast du Geburtstag?* (p. 25). Learn months (p. 27).

Day 4

(5) 1. Warm-up: Have students give three sentences about themselves. *Ich heiße [Gerd Schulz]. Ich bin fünfzehn Jahre alt. Ich bin [faul].*

(10) 2. Review second dialogue *Wann hast du Geburtstag?* (p. 25). Vary *Richtig oder falsch?* Have students correct false statements.

(5) 3. Review months (p. 27). Practice Exercises D and E.

(10) 4. *Übungen.* Present plural subject pronouns and plural forms of *sein* (p. 29). Do Übungen A–C.

(3) 5. *Aussprache* (p. 28). Have students read aloud the three sentences containing words with [e] and [ε].

(7) 6. Game: *Tic-tac-toe* to practice numbers. See annotation (p. 26).

Assignment: Übungen A, B, C (p. 29).

Day 5

(5) 1. Warm-up: Review months with visuals. For variation see annotations (p. 27).

(5) 2. Review *Übungen* (p. 29). Personalize — have students ask each other the questions.

(10) 3. Introduce and practice *Übungen* D–F (p. 30).

(10) 4. Review dialogues by asking personalized questions about ages and birthdays: *[Frank], du hast im [Juli] Geburtstag,*

nicht? — Nein, im [April]. Du bist [siebzehn], nicht? — Nein, [fünfzehn].

(10)   5. Game: Bingo. See TAE p. 29. Let student draw and call out the numbers.

(5)   Optional: Do a Workbook exercise.

Assignment: Übungen D–F (p. 30). Prepare Wiederholung Exercises A and B (p. 34).

Day 6

(5)   1. Warm-up: Using visuals, have students make up two sentences about a boy or girl: *Sie heißt Ute. Sie ist sechzehn Jahre alt. Sie ist glücklich.*

(7)   2. Practice *Übungen* D–F (p. 30). Use visuals to cue *Übung* E. For other variations of *Übungen* D–F, see annotations (p. 30).

(5)   3. Practice *Wiederholung* Exercises A and B (p. 34). Have students read dialogue *mit verteilten Rollen.* Vary the questions.

(10)   4. Introduce and practice present tense of *haben* and questions (*Übungen* G–I, pp. 31–32).

(5)   5. Do one or two Listening Comprehension exercises.

(7)   6. Give written quiz on numbers 0–19. Correct in class.

(3)   Optional: Do a Workbook exercise.

Assignment: Practice Übungen G–I (pp. 31–32). Wiederholung: Write out Exercise D (p. 34).

Day 7

(5)   1. Warm-up: Do one or two Listening Comprehension exercises.

(10)   2. Practice *Übungen* G–I (pp. 31–32). Personalize and vary: see annotations (pp. 31–32).

(2)   3. Check *Wiederholung* Exercise D (p. 34).

(10)   4. Review core material by having students take turns asking each other questions on the dialogues: *Wann hat Petra Geburtstag? Hat Gerd auch im März Geburtstag?*

(5)   Optional: Do one or two Workbook exercises.

(3)   5. Quiz on months.

(10)   6. *Wiederholung:* Do Exercises E and F (pp. 34–35) together in class.

Assignment: Wiederholung Exercise C (p. 34). Prepare Wiederholung Exercise G (p. 35). Prepare pre-test for Chapter 2.

Day 8

(10)   1. Review vocabulary. Use visuals.

(10)   2. Correct *Wiederholung* Exercise C (p. 34). Have several volunteers present their answers to *Wiederholung* Exercise G (p. 35). Ask other students questions on what volunteers say.

(15)   3. Discuss answers to pre-test.

(15)   4. Do one or two Listening Comprehension exercises.

Assignment: Study for test on Chapter 2.

Day 9

(40)   Chapter test.

Chapter 9 (Stage 2)

Day 1

(5)   1. Warm-up: Have students take turns asking you questions to practice *Sie*-forms: *Haben Sie ein Hobby? Spielen Sie gern Tennis? Haben Sie einen Bruder?*

(5)   2. Introduce Chapter 9. If you have prepared learning objectives, go over them with students.

(15)   3. Introduce core material *Ich habe mein Zimmer aufgeräumt* (p. 180). Although this material is in conversational form, treat as a reading. Do *Fragen* and *Du hast das Wort.*

(5)   4. *Wortschatzerweiterung:* Practice *doch* as positive response (p. 183), Exercises A and B.

(10)   5. Conversational past, *Übung* A (p. 187).

Assignment: Study Ich habe mein Zimmer aufgeräumt (p. 180). Übung A (p. 187).

Day 2

(5)   1. Warm-up: Continue having students ask you personal questions to practice *Sie*-form.

(10)   2. Review *Ich habe mein Zimmer aufgeräumt,* including *Fragen* and *Du hast das Wort* (p. 180).

(15)   3. Introduce second selection *Ich habe eine Torte gebacken* (p. 181). Do *Fragen* and *Du hast das Wort.*

(10)   4. Review *Übung* A (conversational past, p. 187). Introduce past participles of weak verbs (*Übungen* B–D, pp. 187–188).
Assignment: Study *Ich habe eine Torte gebacken* (p. 181). Practice *Übungen* B–D, (p. 188).

Day 3

(5)   1. Warm-up: Have each student name one activity done over the weekend.
(10)   2. Review *Ich habe eine Torte gebacken,* including *Fragen* and *Du hast das Wort* (p. 181).
(7)   3. *Wortschatzerweiterung:* Introduce *Was hast du gestern gemacht?* (pp. 184–185). Do Exercise C and *Du hast das Wort.*
(10)   4. Practice *Übungen* B–D (p. 188).
(8)   5. Introduce past participles of strong verbs (p. 189). Do *Übung* E.
Assignment: Wortschatzerweiterung: Study *Was hast du gestern gemacht?* (p. 184). Practice *Übung* E (p. 189).

Day 4

(5)   1. Warm-up: Ask students if they have done certain chores. Use visuals.
(10)   2. Review Exercise C and *Du hast das Wort* on chores (p. 185). Do *Fragen* based on *Arbeitsplan* (p. 182).
(5)   3. Practice strong verbs with stem vowel *e* (*Übung* E, p. 189).
(10)   4. Introduce more strong verbs (*Übungen* F–I, pp. 189–191).
(10)   5. Pantomime game; see annotation, p. 185.
Assignment: Practice *Übungen* F–I, pp. 189–191. *Wiederholung* Exercises A and D (pp. 194–195).

Day 5

(5)   1. Warm-up: Students name one chore they have done.
(5)   2. Go over *Wiederholung* Exercises A and D (pp. 194–195).
(10)   3. Practice *Übungen* F–I (pp. 189–191).
(5)   4. *Aussprache:* [ts] (p. 186).
(10)   5. Introduce past participles of separable-prefix verbs (*Übungen* J–L, pp. 191–192).
(5)   6. Review both dialogues (pp. 180–181). (or Optional: Do a Workbook exercise.)
Assignment: Practice *Übungen* J–L (pp. 189–191). *Wiederholung* Exercise C (p. 195). Optional:

Read cultural note and accompanying recipe (p. 185).

Day 6

(5)   1. Warm-up: Have students ask you what chores you have done.
(5)   2. Go over *Wiederholung* Exercise C (p. 195).
(10)   3. Practice *Übungen* J–L (pp. 191–192).
(5)   4. Discuss cultural note and recipe (p. 185).
(10)   5. Do one or two Listening Comprehension exercises.
(5)   6. Personalized questions using conversational past. (Optional: Do a Workbook exercise.)
Assignment: Wiederholung Exercises B and E (pp.194–195). *Kulturlesestück* (p. 197), first paragraph.

Day 7

(5)   1. Warm-up: Questions about entertainment based on Chapter 7.
(5)   2. *Wiederholung* Exercises B and E (pp. 194–195).
(7)   3. *Kulturlesestück* (p. 197) first paragraph.
(8)   4. Sight-read *Kulturlesestück,* second paragraph.
(3)   5. Discuss cultural note on *Jobs for Youth* (p. 196).
(5)   6. *Aussprache:* [z], [s], and [ts], p. 186.
(7)   7. Do one or two Listening Comprehension exercises. (Optional: Do a Workbook exercise.)
Assignment: Kulturlesestück (p. 197), second paragraph. *Wiederholung* Exercises F and G (pp. 195–196).

Day 8

(5)   1. Warm-up: Vocabulary check, using visuals.
(7)   2. *Wiederholung* Exercises F and G (pp. 195–196).
(15)   3. *Kulturlesestück* (p. 197) entire piece.
(5)   4. *Aussprache:* Exercise C and proverb (p. 186).
(8)   5. Review conversational past and vocabulary. (Optional: Do a Workbook exercise.)
Assignment: Kulturlesestück, Activity A (p. 198). Pre-test, Chapter 9.

Day 9

(5)   1. Warm-up: Vocabulary drill, using visuals
(5)   2. *Kulturlesestück,* Activity A (p. 198).
(20) 3. Discuss answers to pre-test.
(10) 4. Game: Word Bingo.
Assignment: Study for test on Chapter 9.

Day 10

(40) Chapter test.

Resource Materials

Games for the classroom

Guten Tag. A volunteer stands with back to class, eyes closed. Someone says "Guten Tag, Ingrid." She must identify the voice and reply "Guten Tag, Frank." If she can't, another student replies.

Spelling bee. Two teams take turns giving words for their opponents to spell orally. Award a point for each correct spelling. Or, as you dictate a word, have a member of each team write it on the chalkboard.

Finish the story. Begin a story and have each student add one sentence to finish the tale. Record the story and play it back to students to hear the results.

Basket of objects. Use a wastebasket or other sizeable container. Hold up a variety of objects in succession for students to identify. As each item is identified, place it in the container. When twenty to thirty objects have been "filed," students (individually or as a group) compile a list of the contents of the container. Contents are then removed one by one as students check list.

I spy. "Ich sehe etwas und es beginnt mit. . . *S.*" The class guesses what it is. The guesser chooses the next object.

Description. A student briefly describes a person or object. The class must guess who or what it is, asking additional questions as necessary.

Dieter sagt. Tell class to do what you say, or point to the item you name only when you start with "Dieter sagt." Students who do what Dieter does not instruct are eliminated from the game.

Bingo. For practice of numbers, word sets, or verb forms. Prepare dittoed grids of 4 rows of 4 squares, or have students make their own. With the class, list on the board the items that will be used for calling, such as numbers from 1 to 31, foods, parts of the body, present or conversational past verb forms. Have a student write each word on a slip of paper to use for calling. Students fill in their grids, choosing words from the list on the board. Assign a caller who draws from the slips of paper. A win may be vertical, horizontal, four corners, diagonal, or four center squares.

Who is the fastest? Students are assigned numbers, the same ones to several students. The teacher asks a question and calls out a number. The students with that number race to the board to write the answer.

Aufpassen. Ask a volunteer to look around room and then leave. During the volunteer's absence rearrange several objects or people. Upon returning, the volunteer must name the changes.

Wortkette. Work with individuals or several teams. Team A says a German word. Team B must say a word that begins with the last letter of the preceding word. For example, Team A says *Buch,* Team B says *Haus,* and so on.

Was habe ich gemacht? Go through several actions and describe them as you perform them. Then have students tell what you did, using conversational past.

Anagrams. A useful game for the last minute or two of class. Write a jumbled word on the board and have students guess the word. For example: *chub = Buch.*

Silly sentences. Make up silly sentences or tongue-twisters which students take turns repeating as quickly as they can.

Mime. Form two teams. Prepare two lists of words, expressions, or sentences to be acted out without speech. Teams take turns; keep track of time needed to guess items (maximum three minutes per item). Team with lowest total time wins.

Portraits. Cut out ten pictures of people and display them. Describe one of the people and have students guess whom you have in mind.

Twenty questions. Choose an object from the *Tierreich*, *Pflanzenreich* or *Steinreich*. Students have twenty *ja/nein*-questions to guess the word. The student who guesses correctly chooses the next word.

Hangman. Think of a word and write on the board a blank space for each letter. Have class guess each letter in German. If the guess is correct, write the letter in the space it occupies. If the guess is incorrect, draw a part of the hanged man, until he is complete, or until students guess the word.

Einkaufen (Add-an-element game). Start by saying: *Ich gehe einkaufen und ich kaufe einen Hut.* The next person says: *Ich gehe einkaufen und ich kaufe einen Hut und eine Jacke.* To stay in the game, each successive student must repeat the list and add one purchase.

Synonym-antonym. One team gives a word. The opposing team must give either a synonym or antonym, as required, of the word given.

Das lange Wort. Write a long word on the board and ask students to write as many words as they can, using only the letters contained in the word.

What's my line? A student chooses a profession which is not revealed to the class. Other students try to guess the profession by asking questions.

Kreuzworträtsel. On a blank sheet of paper, have students create short, original crossword puzzles. Use a crossword from a newspaper as a guide. Have students prepare their puzzles in small groups. Groups may then exchange puzzles and fill them in.

Classroom expressions

Terms of praise and disapproval

Gut. Das ist (sehr) gut.
Schön. Das ist (sehr) schön.
Das hast du gut gemacht.
Ausgezeichnet.
Wunderbar.
Das ist schon besser.
Viel besser.
Nicht schlecht.
Richtig.
Natürlich.
Genau.

Bist du sicher?
Nein, das ist nicht (ganz) richtig.
Ein Wort ist nicht richtig.
Nein, das ist falsch.
Du hast mich nicht verstanden. Ich sage es noch einmal.
Du hast den Satz (das Wort) nicht verstanden.
Sag (Versuch) es noch einmal bitte!

General instructions

Ruhe bitte!
(Seid) nicht so laut bitte!
Seid bitte leise!
Ihr macht zuviel Lärm.
Paßt bitte jetzt auf!
Rede nicht mit deinem Nachbarn!

Schreibt jetzt bitte!
Lest jetzt bitte!
Ich fange (Wir fangen) jetzt an.
Fangt jetzt an!

Hört bitte auf zu schreiben (lesen)!
Gebt eure Aufsätze ab!
Gebt mir eure Aufsätze!
      Klassenarbeiten!
      Tests!
      Übungsarbeiten!
      Hausaufgaben!
Kann ich bitte eure Aufsätze haben?
[Jan], zeig mir bitte deinen Aufsatz!
Jeder verbessert seine eigene Arbeit.
Verbesser deine Arbeit bitte!
Verbessert eure Arbeiten!
Tausch mit deinem (Tauscht mit euren) Nachbarn!

Legt eure Sachen (Bücher) weg!
                           beiseite!
                           unter den Stuhl!

Macht die Bücher auf (zu)!
Schlagt Seite [11] in eurem Buch auf!
Schaut beim Sprechen nicht ins Buch!
Wiederholt den Satz (den Ausdruck)!
Noch einmal bitte!
(Etwas) Lauter!
              Deutlicher!
              Langsamer!
              Schneller!
Macht den Mund auf!
[Jan], du allein!
Alle zusammen!
Sprecht mir nach!

(Nicht) Nachsprechen bitte!
Hört nur zu! Nur zuhören bitte!
Hört gut zu!
Lies den Satz (den Absatz) vor!
Jeder liest einen Satz!
Fang mit Zeile [17] an!
Nicht auf Seite [19], auf Seite [20]!

Mach die Tafel sauber!
Geh an die Tafel!
[Jan], gehst du bitte an die Tafel?
Wer geht freiwillig an die Tafel?
Schreib den Satz (das Wort) an die Tafel!
Schreibt ab, was an der Tafel steht!
Schreibt alles ins Heft!

Wer weiß es (die Antwort)?
Wie sagt man das auf deutsch (auf englisch)?
Auf deutsch bitte!
Verstehst du die Frage (den Satz)?
Ist es (zu) schwer (leicht)?

Seid ihr fertig?
Wer fertig ist, kann Hausaufgaben machen.
                     lesen.
                     nach Hause gehen.
                     Vokabeln lernen.
                     Scrabble spielen.
Komm (morgen) nach der Stunde zu mir!

Transitions

Jetzt machen wir weiter.
Jetzt machen wir was anderes.

Jetzt lernen wir was Neues.
Das ist genug für heute.
Hat jemand Fragen? Habt ihr Fragen?

Student responses and questions

Das verstehe ich nicht. Das habe ich nicht verstanden.
Ah, ich verstehe.
Ich weiß es nicht.
Wie sagt man . . . auf deutsch (auf englisch)?
Können Sie den Satz noch einmal sagen bitte?
Kann er/sie den Satz wiederholen bitte?
Ich habe kein Papier (Buch).
Ich habe keinen Bleistift (Kuli).
Auf welcher Seite sind wir? Welche Zeile?
Wo steht das?
Ich habe eine Frage.
Was haben wir für morgen (Montag) auf?
Sollen wir das schriftlich oder mündlich machen?
Wann schreiben wir die nächste Arbeit?
                           den nächsten Test?
Für wann (sollen wir das machen)?
Ist das so richtig?
(Wann) Können Sie mir helfen?
(Wann) Kann ich mit Ihnen sprechen?

Computer terminology

der Anwender   *program user*
anzeigen   *to display*
mit dem Computer arbeiten   *to work on the computer*
auswählen   *to select a program*
der Bildschirm   *screen*
der Computer   *computer*
der Personalcomputer   *personal computer*
die Diskette   *diskette*
das Diskette-Laufwerk   *diskette drive*
der Drucker   *printer*
der Matrixdrucker   *matrix printer*
der Typendrucker   *letter quality printer*
laden   *to load*
ein Programm laufen lassen   *to run a program*
der Monitor   *monitor*
der Positionsanzeiger   *cursor*
programmieren   *to program*
die Programmiersprache   *computer language*
die Software   *software*   das Softwarepaket   *software packet*

speichern *to store*
auf Diskette speichern *to store on diskette*
ein 64 KB-Speicher *a 64 kilobyte memory*
die Tastatur *keyboard*
die Taste *key*   die Funktionstaste *function
key*
der Textverarbeiter, der Wortprozessor *word pro-
cessor*

Useful addresses

The following organizations may be of assistance in
obtaining cultural information and materials for
classroom use. Foreign language journals may
contain additional addresses as well as information
regarding study abroad and other exchange programs.

Austria

Austrian National Tourist Office
500 Fifth Avenue
New York, NY 10110

Austrian Institute
11 East 52nd Street
New York, NY 10022

Switzerland

Swiss National Tourist Office
608 Fifth Avenue
New York, NY 10020

German Democratic Republic

Embassy of the German Democratic Republic
1717 Massachusetts Avenue, N.W.
Washington, D.C. 20036

Gesellschaft Neue Heimat. This source will provide
materials about life in the DDR; Neue Heimat,
Mauerstraße 52, 1086 Berlin, GDR

Federal Republic of Germany

German Information Center
950 Third Avenue
New York, NY 10022

*Consulates of the Federal Republic of Germany in
the United States*. The offices listed below have

films and slides that may be borrowed by schools
and other institutions. The teacher may write to the
nearest Consulate for an up-to-date listing. In addition, taped recordings produced for *Inter Na-
tiones* are usually available through Consulate offices. Current catalogues are available upon
request.

Atlanta: 1000 Peachtree Center Cain Tower, 229
   Peachtree Street, N.E., Atlanta, GA 30043
Boston: 535 Boylston Street, Boston, MA 02116.
Chicago: Monroe Building, 10th Floor, 104 South
   Michigan Avenue, Chicago, IL 60603.
Detroit: Edison Plaza, Suite 2100, 600 Plaza Drive,
   Detroit, MI 48226.
Houston: 1900 Yorktown Street, Suite 405, Hous-
   ton, TX 77006.
Los Angeles: 6435 Wilshire Boulevard, Los Angeles,
   CA 90048
Miami: 100 North Biscayne Blvd., Miami, FL 33132.
New Orleans: 2834 International Trade Mart, 2 Canal
   Street, New Orleans, LA 70130.
New York: 460 Park Avenue, New York, NY 10022.
San Francisco: International Building, 601 California
   Street, San Francisco, CA 94108.
Seattle: 1617/IBM Building, 1200 Fifth Avenue,
   Seattle, WA 98101.
Washington, D.C.: 4645 Reservoir Road, N.W.,
   Washington, D.C. 20007.

German National Tourist Offices. These offices cir-
culate a modest number of films. In addition, tourist
brochures and some other printed material on the
Federal Republic are available upon request.

New York: 747 Third Avenue, 33rd Floor, New York,
   NY 10017.
Los Angeles: 444 South Flower Street, Suite 2230,
   Los Angeles, CA 90071.

Teacher Aid Depository. The office listed below
possesses a sizeable library of films, slides, and
tapes, as well as loan exhibits of German art. A
catalogue of materials is available upon request.

Teacher Aid Depository
AATG Administrative Office
523 Building, Suite 201
Route 38
Cherry Hill, NJ 08034

German

today **1**

German today 1

THIRD EDITION

Jack Moeller

Helmut Liedloff

Clifford J. Kent

HOUGHTON MIFFLIN COMPANY Boston

Atlanta Dallas Geneva, Illinois
Lawrenceville, New Jersey Palo Alto Toronto

About the Authors

Jack Moeller is the senior author of the series. Currently he is Chairperson of the Department of Modern Languages and Literatures at Oakland University in Rochester, Michigan. Professor Moeller has taught at both private and public high schools in the United States and Germany. He is a co-author of *Deutsch heute: Grundstufe, Blickpunkt Deutschland, Ohne Mühe!, Noch Dazu!* (Houghton Mifflin), and of several other texts.

Helmut Liedloff is Professor of German at Southern Illinois University in Carbondale, Illinois. Professor Liedloff is a native of Bremen, Germany, and has taught at the secondary school and university levels in Germany and at a number of colleges in the United States. He is a co-author of *Deutsch heute: Grundstufe* and *Ohne Mühe!* (Houghton Mifflin) and is a contributor to a number of professional journals.

Clifford J. Kent is Supervisor of Foreign Languages for the Beverly Public Schools in Beverly, Massachusetts, where he has helped develop an exchange program between Beverly High School and the Albert-Schweizer-Schule in Cologne, Germany. He has taught German at the junior high, high school, and college levels, as well as to adults, and he participated in an NDEA summer institute at Hofstra University.

LISTENING COMPREHENSION EXERCISES

Sonia Schweid Reizes is Assistant Program Administrator and teaches German, French, and Spanish in the Bedford Public Schools, Bedford, Massachusetts. She also teaches German at Middlesex Community College.

WORKBOOK

Sonia Schweid Reizes

CHAPTER TESTS

Constance E. Putnam taught German and Latin at John Marshall High School and at The Catlin Gabel School in Portland, Oregon. She also lived in Germany for several years and taught at the *Gymnasium* in Duderstadt and the *Pädagogische Hochschule* in Hildesheim.

Printed in U.S.A.
Student's Edition ISBN: 0–395–38358–7
Teacher's Edition ISBN: 0–395–38359–5

ABCDEFGHIJ-RM-93210/898765

Contents

2

So leben wir

Zum Städtele hinaus

German
around you

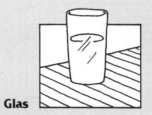

Glas

Hand

Blitz

As you begin to learn German, you will discover that you know more about the language than you think you do.

Maus

You can probably guess the meanings of the German words illustrated on this page, because they resemble English words. Words that are related in spelling and meaning and are derived from the same source language are called **cognates.** There are hundreds of German-English cognates.

Haus

Gras

Bär

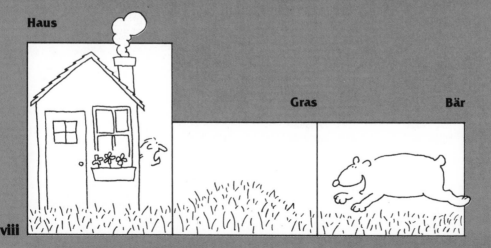

Kaufmann

The German language and culture have been present in the United States since the colonial days. German settlers fought in the Revolutionary War, and they continued to play an important role as their adopted country grew and prospered. The names of many towns and cities reflect the German origin of their founders. Towns like Berlin, Hamburg, Bremen, and Vienna all have counterparts in one of the German-speaking countries. You probably know many families with German names. As in English, the name often refers to the occupation of the person's ancestors.

Koch

Schuhmacher

ix

Kindergarten

Over the years, German immigrants have contributed to several areas of American life.

Rucksack

Oh Tannenbaum

Gesundheit!

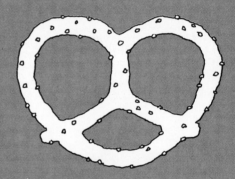

Brezel

Harmonika

X

Make-up   **Computer**   **Fan**

The exchange in culture and language has gone the other way, too. Speakers of German have borrowed many English words that are now part of the German language.

Look around you and you'll find that cognates, borrowed words, and German names have given you a head start in learning German.

City

Atlas
section

BUNDESREPUBLIK DEUTSCHLAND/DEUTSCHE DEMOKRATISCHE REPUBLIK

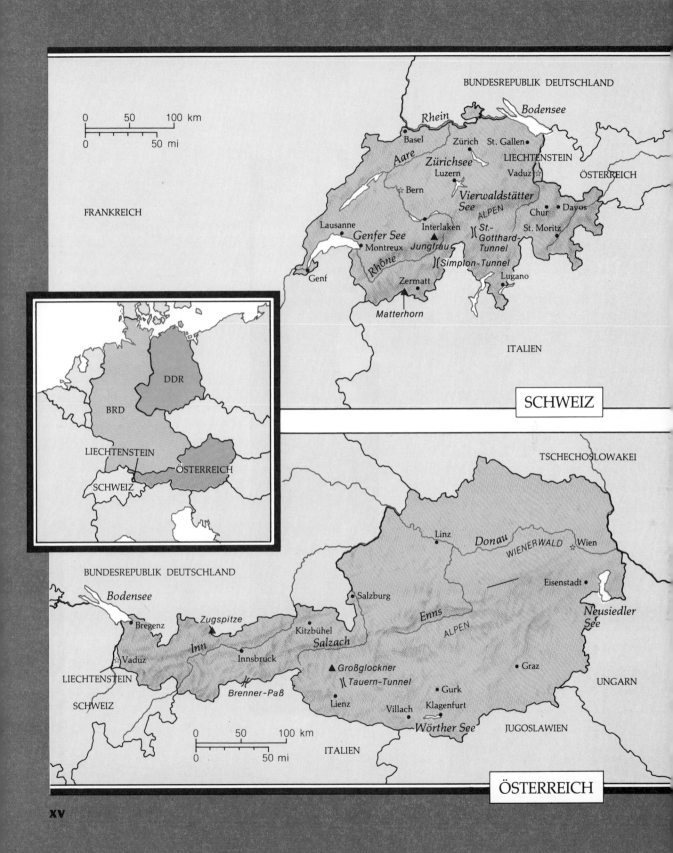

SCHWEIZ

ÖSTERREICH

XV

Ich und du

1

In der Schule. Classrooms everywhere look pretty much the same. From a crowded lecture hall at the university in Freiburg to individualized instruction in a school class in Munich, German students are expected to study hard. Education is considered very important, and even a bit of a privilege.

Was machst du? Walking home from school along the narrow streets in Dinkelsbühl is hardly typical of the many kinds of activities German young people enjoy — from a soccer game in Frankfurt to music making and life-sized board games in many towns.

Heute nachmittag. Quiet or even solitary pastimes are also popular: reading outdoors in Nuremberg or in a library, or just talking or going for long walks with a friend.

Kapitel 1

Tag. Wie geht's?

Nastätten 21 km
Dachsenhausen 8 km

Stadtmitte

Rüdesheim 53 km

Koblenz 11 km

The 100 million speakers of German live in a number of countries, located mostly in central Europe. The **BRD** (**Bundesrepublik Deutschland,** or Federal Republic of Germany) is the largest of the German-speaking countries. It is about the size of Oregon and has a population of 60 million. Its capital is Bonn. The **DDR** (**Deutsche Demokratische Republik,** German Democratic Republic) is a little larger than Ohio and has a population of 17 million. Its capital is East Berlin. Both the **BRD** and the **DDR** are modern, industrialized countries, with a high level of production in agriculture as well.

See *Introduction* for suggestions on how to present core material (dialogues and readings). Try to vary presentations by using stick figures on board, props, English equivalents, tapes, posters, etc. Employ choral as well as individual response.

Wie heißt du?

Ute Braun lives in Bonn. She meets a new girl at school and discovers they have something in common.

UTE BRAUN	Wie heißt du?
UTE SCHMIDT	Ute.
UTE BRAUN	Toll! Ich heiße auch Ute.

Du hast das Wort

See *Introduction* for suggestions on how to work with *Du hast das Wort.* New vocabulary in *DhdW* is indicated by a raised degree mark (°). After initial presentation, have students do both cues and responses, choosing those that reflect their mood or situation. Time spent on these exercises should be brief but frequent throughout the lesson.

A. Choose German names for yourselves from the list in the Appendix. Ask a classmate what her/his name is.

Wie heißt du?   [Barbara.]

B. Guess a classmate's name. If you're wrong, your classmate will correct you.

Heißt du [Mark]?   Ja°.
                         Nein°, ich heiße [Martin].

Wie geht's?

Ingrid runs into some friends and asks them how they are.

INGRID	Tag, Gisela. Wie geht's?
GISELA	Danke, gut.
INGRID	Tag, Dieter. Wie geht's?
DIETER	Schlecht.
INGRID	Was ist denn los?
DIETER	Ich bin müde.

Have students shake hands in the German fashion when they greet each other. See cultural note, p. 10.

Monitor *ü*-sound carefully. Have students say "me" with their lips rounded as for the *u*-sound in "moo."

 It is not uncommon for teen-agers in German-speaking countries to greet their friends with a handshake. The German handshake consists of a single movement downward rather than a series of up-and-down movements.

Ask various students how they are and let them select an appropriate response. Then chain drill.
S¹: *Wie geht's, [Ingrid]?*
S²: *Danke, gut. Wie geht's, [Dieter]?*
S³: *Sehr schlecht. Wie geht's, [Gisela]?*

Du hast das Wort

Students should master the material in this and subsequent exercises in this section and be encouraged to gradually carry on conversations with books closed.

Optional: Students may create own dialogues using phrases from both A and B. These could be performed for class, using German handshakes.

A. A classmate asks how you are. How would you respond?

Wie geht's?

Prima°!
Sehr° gut.
Nicht° schlecht.
Ganz° gut.
Danke, es geht°.

B. A classmate asks what's wrong. How would you respond?

Was ist los?

Ich bin müde.
Ich bin sehr müde.
Ich bin kaputt°.
Ich bin krank°.

An important characteristic of German is the use of "flavoring" words like **denn** to express the speaker's attitude about an utterance. These flavoring words relate the utterance to something the speaker or the listener has already said or thought. Depending on the choice of the word and sometimes on the tone of voice, the speaker may express interest, surprise, impatience, and so on.

Denn, for example, is often used in questions. It gives a little extra emphasis to the question and implies that one is interested in the answer.

Was ist los?	What's the matter?
Was ist **denn** los?	Well, what **is** the matter?

The meaning of flavoring words varies, depending on the context. Frequently there are no exact English equivalents. With experience, you will gain a feeling for the meaning and use of these words in German.

10   german today, one

Bist du zufrieden?

Monika and Volker are discussing the results of their last test.

VOLKER So, Monika, bist du zufrieden?
MONIKA Ja, sehr. Du auch?
VOLKER Nein, ich bin wirklich sauer.
MONIKA Das tut mir leid.

Du hast das Wort

Ask classmates whether they're satisfied with their work.

Bist du zufrieden?   Ja, sehr zufrieden.
                             Ja, ich bin glücklich°.
                             Nein, ich bin sauer.
                             Nein, gar° nicht.

After dialogues have been mastered, use questions and visuals to ask about Frank, Volker, and Monika. Then personalize:
  T: *Bist du unglücklich? Warum?*, etc.

Warum ist Volker so sauer?

Frank wants to know why Volker looks so gloomy.

FRANK   Wie geht's Volker?
MONIKA Schlecht.
FRANK   Ist er wieder krank?   Call students' attention to word order: predicate adjective at the end of sentence.
MONIKA Unsinn! Er ist nur faul.

Du hast das Wort

Other words students may enjoy learning are *fies* and *miserabel*.

How would you respond to a friend's question about a classmate?

Ist [Dieter] faul?   Ja, er ist sehr faul.
                             Nein, er ist krank.
                             Nein, er ist müde.

Ist [Gerda] zufrieden?   Ja, sie ist sehr zufrieden.
                             Ja, sie ist wirklich glücklich.
                             Nein, sie ist nicht zufrieden.

11

Greetings and farewells

Guten Morgen!
Guten Tag!
Guten Abend!

Auf Wiedersehen!
Tschüß!
Bis später.
Guten Abend!
Gute Nacht!

For regional variations, refer students to note on p. 14. Assign roles as Germans, Swiss, or Austrians. Have students greet each other appropriately.

Guten Morgen is used to say hello in the morning.
Guten Tag is used to say hello at any time during the day.
   Tag is an informal version of **Guten Tag.**
Guten Abend is used to say both hello and good-by during the evening.
Gute Nacht is used as a farewell late in the evening and at bedtime.
Auf Wiedersehen is used at any time of the day or night as an expression of farewell.
Tschüß is an informal farewell and is equivalent to *so long.*
Bis später is equivalent to *see you later.*

A   Respond appropriately to each of the following greetings and farewells.

Variation: Have students work in pairs; encourage them to use German first names.

■⊪   Tag, [Ingrid]!   *Tag, [Frank]!*

1. Guten Morgen!
2. Auf Wiedersehen!
3. Tschüß!

4. Bis später!
5. Guten Abend!
6. Gute Nacht!

B   How would you greet a person at the following times of the day or night?

1. 8:00 A.M.
2. 7:00 P.M.

3. 4:00 P.M.
4. 10:00 A.M.

5. 2:00 A.M.
6. 7:00 A.M.

Variation: Cue different times with poster or clock with moveable hands.

Descriptive adjectives

Gerda ist **gesund.**

Paul ist **krank.**

Heike ist **sauer.**

Jürgen ist **fleißig.**

Georg ist **faul.**

Martin ist **müde.**

Tanja ist **glücklich.**

Petra ist **unglücklich.**

Isabel ist **zufrieden.**

Optional: Teacher supplies adjectives; student performs with facial expression. Or teacher provides gestures and facial expressions and students guess adjective.

C   Ask a classmate whether he/she is tired, lazy, sad, etc.

    ■⦀   Bist du . . . ?

D   Ask a classmate how he/she is feeling. Then ask a second classmate to report what the first one said. Use the following conversation as a model.

YOU	Wie geht's?
CLASSMATE 1	[Schlecht]. Ich bin [krank].
YOU	[Stefan], wie geht's [Ingrid]?
CLASSMATE 2	[Sie] ist [krank].

Variation[1]: When *schlecht* is answered, vary with *Ich bin sauer / unglücklich.* When *gut* is answered, vary with *Ich bin glücklich / gesund / zufrieden.*

Variation[2]: Using visuals, ask why a student feels that way. Then have students ask each other.
T: *Warum ist Dieter unglücklich? (krank)*
S: *Er ist krank.*

Greetings and farewells may vary in the different German-speaking countries and even within one country. For instance, in southern Germany or in Austria one might hear **Grüß Gott** or **Grüß dich. Servus** is another common greeting in Austria. In Switzerland one often hears **Grüetzi** or **Salut.**

Auf Wiedersehen can be shortened to simply **Wiedersehen.** In some areas **Auf Wiederschauen** or **Adieu** are also used to say goodby.

14

See the *Introduction* for suggestions on how to use the *Aussprache* section. Contrastive drills and sentences are recorded in the tape program which accompanies the text.

_____ Aussprache _____

Students are not expected to learn the special symbols. They are provided to help make visually clear the relationship between sounds and letters.

In the pronunciation sections of this text, special symbols in brackets are used to represent various German sounds. Each symbol represents only one sound. In written German, different letters or letter combinations may represent the same sound. Vowels are classified as long or short.

long vowel [i]   pri**ma**, w**ie**
short vowel [I]   b**i**n, n**i**cht, Uns**i**nn

Check whether students can hear difference between long and short vowel sounds without seeing words.

A   Practice vertically in columns and horizontally in pairs.

[i]	[I]
L**ie**d	l**i**tt
b**ie**ten	b**i**tten
Ihnen	**i**nnen
B**ie**nen	b**i**nnen
K**ie**pe	K**i**ppe

Game: Prepare a list of German words with [i] and [I] sounds. Divide class into 2 teams. Say a word. If a student correctly identifies the vowel as long or short, her/his team wins a point.

Tell students to spread lips in wide smile when pronouncing long [i] as in *Lied*.

B   Practice the sounds [i] and [I]. Read the sentences aloud.

1. Ingrid ist wieder krank.
2. Unsinn. Sie ist nur müde.
3. Wie geht's Ilse?

The sentences provide students with an opportunity to practice sounds in a variety of positions. Check whether students can identify the words having long and short vowel sounds.

Have students repeat the proverb. Give the literal meaning ("Still waters *are* deep") and ask students for an equivalent saying in English ("Still waters *run* deep").

Stille Wasser sind tief.

See *Introduction* for suggested procedures to use in the *Übungen* section.

———————— Übungen ————————

The subject pronouns **ich, du, er,** and **sie**

Encourage students to study exercises so that they can be reviewed in class or lab without books. Let students play "Teacher" for practice in asking questions.

ich	I
du	you
er	he
sie	she

These exercises should be done at a lively pace and, whenever possible, with books closed. After sufficient practice, personalize where appropriate.

The subject pronouns **ich, du, er,** and **sie** are equivalent to the English pronouns *I, you, he,* and *she.*

A   Give the subject pronouns you would use in the following situations.

■ꕯ   You're talking about your mother.   *sie*

1. You're talking to a male friend.
2. You're talking about a female teacher.
3. You're talking about a male student.
4. You're talking about yourself.
5. You're talking to a female friend.

Present tense of **sein**: singular forms

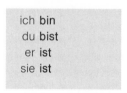

ich **bin**
du **bist**
er **ist**
sie **ist**

The forms of **sein** vary according to the subject used.

Hans! Bist **du** müde?   Hans, are *you* tired?
Ja, **ich** bin müde.   Yes, *I'm* tired.

B   Your friends are trying to find out what's wrong with you. Answer their questions in the affirmative.

■ꕯ   Bist du müde?   *Ja, ich bin sehr müde.*

1. Bist du sauer?   3. Bist du unglücklich?
2. Bist du faul?   4. Bist du kaputt?

C Your friends tell you how they're feeling. Ask them why they're feeling that way.

Game: Add-an-element. Each student must add an element (in this case, an adjective) to the preceding one. Students must repeat the adjectives in the order given.
S¹: *Ich bin müde.*
S²: *Ich bin müde und faul.*
S³: *Ich bin müde, faul und krank.*

■ꓕ Ich bin glücklich.   *Warum bist du denn glücklich?*

1. Ich bin kaputt.
2. Ich bin müde.
3. Ich bin sauer.
4. Ich bin unglücklich.
5. Ich bin zufrieden.

Sabine ist unglücklich. **Sie** ist krank.   *Sabine is unhappy. She's ill.*

Robert ist unglücklich. **Er** ist krank.   *Robert is unhappy. He's ill.*

D There's been a flu epidemic at school, but it's over now. When Christa asks about your friends, say they're well again.

■ꓕ Wie geht's Stefan?   *Er ist wieder gesund.*

■ꓕ Wie geht's Inge?   *Sie ist wieder gesund.*

1. Wie geht's Andrea?   4. Wie geht's Ilse?
2. Wie geht's Kurt?   5. Wie geht's Hans?
3. Wie geht's Nicole?   6. Wie geht's Georg?

E Form sentences, using the cued subject pronouns and adjectives.

■ꓕ er / fleißig   *Er ist fleißig.*

Variation: Students may make up their own combinations.

1. du / müde
2. ich / unglücklich
3. er / sauer
4. sie / krank
5. ich / faul
6. du / unglücklich
7. er / gesund
8. sie / glücklich
9. ich / zufrieden

The negative word **nicht**

At this stage it is probably best to avoid "rules" for position of *nicht*. It precedes an adjective, as in English.

Ich bin **nicht** müde.   I'm *not* tired.
Ilse ist **nicht** faul.   Ilse isn't lazy.

Nicht is equivalent to English *not*.

F   Tanja wants to know how your friends are feeling. Answer her questions in the negative.

■Ⅲ   Wie geht's Udo? Ist er
        wieder müde?   *Nein, er ist nicht müde.*

Personalize, using German names.

1. Wie geht's Frank? Ist er wieder krank?
2. Wie geht's Inge? Ist sie wieder glücklich?
3. Wie geht's Barbara? Ist sie wieder sauer?
4. Wie geht's Walter? Ist er wieder müde?
5. Wie geht's Jens? Ist er wieder glücklich?
6. Wie geht's Heidi? Ist sie wieder sauer?
7. Wie geht's Ingrid? Ist sie wieder zufrieden?

_____ Grammatische Übersicht _____

The *Grammatische Übersicht* is for reference and review. Occasionally some grammatical points are expanded.

The letters in parentheses following grammatical headings refer to the corresponding exercises in the **Übungen.**

The subject pronouns **ich, du, er,** and **sie**   (A)

ich	I
du	you
er	he
sie	she

The pronouns **ich, du, er,** and **sie** are equivalent to the English pronouns *I, you, he,* and *she.* They are used as the subject of a sentence.

Ist **Stefan** krank?   Nein, **er** ist nur faul.
Ist **Ingrid** unglücklich?   Nein, **sie** ist glücklich.

When talking about people, the pronoun **er** is used to refer to a male; the pronoun **sie** is used to refer to a female.

Present tense of **sein:** singular forms   (B-E)

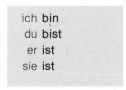
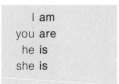

Subjects and their verb forms must agree. The German verb **sein,** like the English verb *to be,* has three different singular forms in the present tense.

The negative word **nicht**   (F)

Ich bin **nicht** krank.
Christa ist **nicht** faul.

Nicht is equivalent to English *not.* The position of **nicht** in a sentence can vary. One common position is just before the element that is being negated.

Notes about written German

1. All nouns are capitalized: **Morgen, Tag, Abend.**

2. The pronoun **ich** is not capitalized, unlike its English equivalent, *I.*

3. An apostrophe indicates the omission of the letter **e: Wie geht's?** = **Wie geht es?**

The letter ß (ess-tset) comes from an old German script form of the letters s (ess) and z (tset) written together.

4. The letter **ß** is called an **Ess-tset** and replaces **ss:**
    a. at the end of a word: **Tschüß**
    b. before a consonant: **du mußt** = you must
    c. after a long vowel: **fleißig**

5. In addition to **ß,** the German alphabet has three other letters that the English alphabet doesn't have: **ä, ö,** and **ü,** called **umlaut a, o,** and **u**. The symbol (¨) indicates that a vowel is umlauted.

Wiederholung

A   Give a greeting appropriate to the time of day shown in each picture.

◼ꕤ   *Guten Morgen!*

See Introduction for suggested use of *Wiederholung.* Many teachers prefer to do the exercises orally in class before assigning them as written homework. Additional exercises for written work may be found in the workbook that accompanies this text.

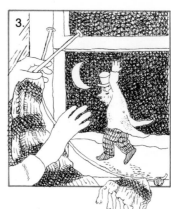

B   Complete each of the following sentences with the correct subject pronoun.

◼ꕤ   _____ bin müde.   *Ich*

1.   _____ bin glücklich.
2.   Bist _____ zufrieden?
3.   Wie geht's Peter? Ist _____ krank?
4.   Wie geht's Monika? Ist _____ wieder gesund?
5.   Warum bist _____ sauer?

C   Answer the questions after each dialogue.

INGRID	Wie geht's Frank?
DIETER	Er ist glücklich.
INGRID	Warum?
DIETER	Er ist wieder gesund.

1.   Wie geht's Frank?
2.   Warum ist er glücklich?

MONIKA	Wie geht's Gerda?
JÜRGEN	Ganz gut.
MONIKA	Ist sie nicht wieder krank?
JÜRGEN	Nein. Sie ist nur faul.

1. Wie geht's Gerda?
2. Ist sie krank?

D Express the following in German.

Variation: Have students make up a conversation with a classmate, using German equivalents of whichever sentences in Ex. D fit together sensibly.

1. Hi, how are you?
   I'm exhausted.
2. What's the matter?
   Why are you unhappy?
3. I'm sick again.
   You're not sick, you're just lazy.
4. So long!
   See you later!

Remind students about German word order here, predicate adjective last.

E Claudia meets Dieter at a party. Give the equivalent of their conversation in German.

Ex. E helps show students that "translating" is not just a substitution of one word for another, but that each language uses its own combinations of words to communicate a specific idea.

CLAUDIA	Good evening, Dieter. How are you?
DIETER	Bad.
CLAUDIA	Really? What's the matter? Are you sick again?
DIETER	No, just very tired.

It is expected that students will have mastered the vocabulary in the course of the lesson. This section is for reference and review.

——————— Vokabeln ———————

Be sure you can recognize and use actively the following words and expressions before going on to Chapter 2.

VERBEN (VERBS)

sein to be
  ich bin I am
  du bist you are
  er/sie ist he/she is

ANDERE WÖRTER (OTHER WORDS)

auch also, too
danke thanks, thank you
denn *flavoring word often used in questions*
du you
er he
faul lazy
fleißig industrious, diligent
ganz quite; complete(ly)
gesund healthy, well
glücklich happy
gut good
ich I
ja yes
kaputt exhausted
krank ill, sick
müde tired
nein no
nicht not
nur only, just
prima excellent, fine, great
sauer cross, annoyed; sour
schlecht bad
sehr very
sie she
so so
toll great, fantastic
und and
unglücklich unhappy
warum why
was what
wie how

ANDERE WÖRTER

wieder again
wirklich really
zufrieden content

BESONDERE AUSDRÜCKE
(SPECIAL EXPRESSIONS)

wie heißt du? what's your name?
ich heiße ... my name is ...
was ist (denn) los? (well,) what's the matter?
wie geht's? how are you (doing)?
es geht OK, can't complain
ganz gut OK, pretty well
das tut mir leid I'm sorry
Unsinn! nonsense!
gar nicht not at all
guten Abend! good evening!
guten Morgen! good morning!
gute Nacht! good night!
guten Tag! hello!; **Tag!** hi
auf Wiedersehen good-by
tschüß! so long!
bis später till later, see you later

Song:
O wie wohl ist mir am Abend
Wenn zur Ruh' die Glocken läuten
Bim, bam, bim.

Point out that nouns are capitalized: (*guten Abend*), but do not discuss gender or articles at this point.

Kapitel 2

Wie alt bist du?

A brief discussion of
Austria using a wall
map and the map on
page *xv* will orient the
students to the third
largest of the German-
speaking countries.
Name a few important
cities and point out the
Donau.

 Austria **(Republik Österreich),** with 7½ million people, is the third largest of the German-speaking countries. It is strong in both industry and agriculture. Austria's mountains, forests, and lakes attract visitors from all over the world and provide many opportunities for outdoor recreation.

Vienna, the capital, is world-famous for its music and theater and its excellent food.

Jung oder alt?

Warm-up: May begin
each class with a few
numbers (see p. 26).
They can add variety to
the exercises below.

Michael and his friends live in Vienna. Michael's birthday party prompts Heike and Dirk to compare ages.

HEIKE	Wie alt ist Michael?
DIRK	Sechzehn.
HEIKE	Und du?
DIRK	Auch sechzehn. Wir sind beide sechzehn.
HEIKE	Seid ihr *wirklich* sechzehn?
DIRK	Natürlich. Warum?
HEIKE	Ihr seid so jung.
DIRK	Wie alt bist *du* denn?
HEIKE	Schon siebzehn.
DIRK	Das ist aber sehr alt.

Point out that German has both a singular and a plural word for "you". May compare German *du* and *ihr* with Old English "thou" and "ye". Mention that other European languages also share this characteristic: French *tu* and *vous*; Spanish *tú* and *usted.*

Fragen

1. Wie alt ist Michael?
2. Wie alt ist Dirk?
3. Sind Michael und Dirk jung oder alt?
4. Wer° ist siebzehn?
5. Ist Heike alt oder jung?

Aber is a flavoring word that gives emphasis.

Personalize: *Wie alt bist du? Bist du schon 15?*, etc.

Du hast das Wort

Begin by asking stu-
dents the questions and
letting them select an
appropriate response.
Then have them take
over the complete con-
versation by asking
each other, books
closed.

A. A friend asks whether you're already fifteen. How would you answer her/his question?

Bist du schon fünfzehn?

Ja.
Ja, du auch, nicht°?
Nein.
Fünfzehn? Ich bin schon sechzehn.

Where a German uses *nicht?*, an English speaker would say "isn't that so?" or "right?"

When saying *ihr*, you may wish to point to two students, even though only one answers. Occasionally saying *ihr zwei* or *ihr beide* will reinforce the idea that *ihr* is plural.

B. Discuss the ages of various classmates with two friends.

Ihr seid beide sechzehn, nicht?

Ja.
Nein. Wir sind beide [fünfzehn].
Nein. [Petra] ist fünfzehn und ich bin sechzehn.
Ich bin sechzehn. [Petra] ist schon siebzehn.

Birthdays in German-speaking countries are usually celebrated either with family and relatives or with friends. There is apt to be a birthday cake with candles, often arranged in a circle around the edge, and some kind of display for birthday cards, flowers, and gifts. Frequently a group of friends will get together and sign a card to the **Geburtstagskind.** A common greeting on cards is **Herzlichen Glückwunsch zum Geburtstag.** Here are some other birthday greetings:

Alles Gute zum Geburtstag!	All the best on your birthday!
Alles Gute!	All the best!
Ich gratuliere dir auch.	I congratulate you, too.
Ich wünsche dir alles Gute.	I wish you all the best.

Have students learn *im* with months as vocabulary. Mention of dative is confusing and unnecessary at this point.

Wann hast du Geburtstag?

Petra finds she was mistaken about her friends' birthdays.

PETRA	Ich habe im März Geburtstag. Du auch, nicht?
DIRK	Nein.
PETRA	Wann hast du denn Geburtstag?
DIRK	Im April.
PETRA	Ach so. Hat Gerd nicht auch im April Geburtstag?
DIRK	Nein, erst im Mai.
PETRA	Ach ja, richtig.

May point out that the time element precedes *birthday.*

Richtig oder falsch?

Have students correct false statements.

1. Petra hat im März Geburtstag.
2. Dirk hat auch im März Geburtstag.
3. Petra und Gerd haben im April Geburtstag.

Contrast *erst* with *nur* from chapter 1. *Nur* sets a limit and implies "not more than this", as in *nur müde*; *erst* refers to a specific point in time, as in *erst im Mai.*

Wortschatzerweiterung

Teach numbers in groups of three, to aid learning.

Zahlen: 0–19

*Point out similarity to English: "*null* and void", or "to *null*ify" something.*

0	null	5	fünf	10	zehn	15	fünfzehn
1	eins	6	sechs	11	elf	16	sechzehn
2	zwei	7	sieben	12	zwölf	17	siebzehn
3	drei	8	acht	13	dreizehn	18	achtzehn
4	vier	9	neun	14	vierzehn	19	neunzehn

A   Ask a classmate how old he/she is.

B   Give your telephone number to a classmate.

Variation:
S[1]: Bist du schon 15?
S[2]: Nein, ich bin erst 14.

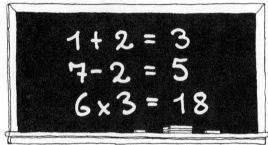

Wieviel ist eins und zwei?
Eins und zwei ist drei.

Wieviel ist sieben weniger zwei?
Sieben weniger zwei ist fünf.

Wieviel ist sechs mal drei?
Sechs mal drei ist achtzehn.

Point out German style of writing one *and* seven.

C   Do the following arithmetic problems with a classmate.

Game: Divide class into several teams. Think of a number. Students from each team take turns guessing the number. The team that succeeds wins a point.

■ıll $1 + 3 = ?$ *Wieviel ist eins und drei?*
Eins und drei ist vier.

1. $3 + 7 = ?$ 3. $4 + 13 = ?$
2. $2 + 9 = ?$ 4. $1 + 18 = ?$

Game: Play tic-tac-toe by filling squares with numbers chosen at random. Assign a math function to each team; members must create a problem whose answer corresponds to the square they want to get (e.g., 3 + 4 to get 7).

■ıll $10 - 7 = ?$ *Wieviel ist zehn weniger sieben?*
Zehn weniger sieben ist drei.

5. $18 - 12 = ?$ 7. $17 - 13 = ?$
6. $12 - 5 = ?$ 8. $18 - 1 = ?$

Variation: have students write out the problems.

■ıll $5 \times 3 = ?$ *Wieviel ist fünf mal drei?*
Fünf mal drei ist fünfzehn.

9. $4 \times 3 = ?$ 11. $6 \times 3 = ?$
10. $8 \times 2 = ?$ 12. $5 \times 2 = ?$

You may want to include the seasons for passive recognition: *Winter, Frühling, Sommer, Herbst.* Game: Name the seasons; students give the corresponding three months.

Wieviel ist es denn?

Game: Each student tells class when his/her birthday is. Afterwards students write down whose birthday is when. (*Ellen hat im Mai Geburtstag*, etc.) Student who correctly remembers the most birthdays wins.

Monate

Januar	April	Juli	Oktober
Februar	Mai	August	November
März	Juni	September	Dezember

D Ask a classmate when her/his birthday is.

■⊪ Wann hast du Geburtstag?   Im [*Mai*].

E Take a poll of your classmates to find out how many birthdays there are in each month. Write the total on the board.

■⊪ Wer hat im [Januar] Geburtstag?

Variation: S¹: *Hast du im Mai Geburtstag?*
S²: *Nein, ich habe im August Geburtstag.*

———————— Aussprache ————————

	long vowel [e]	Eva, S**ee**, g**eh**t	Students often respond well to pronunciation drills if they are presented in the form of games.
	short vowel [ɛ]	**e**s, d**e**nn, M**ä**nner	

A   Practice vertically in columns and horizontally in pairs.

Speakers of German vary in their use of long ä. Many pronounce long e and long ä alike. Other Germans pronounce the long ä much like the sound of English ai as in *fair*.

[e]	[ɛ]
B**ee**t	B**e**tt
d**e**n	d**e**nn
w**e**n	w**e**nn
st**eh**len	st**e**llen
f**eh**len	f**ä**llen

B   Practice the following words horizontally in pairs.

[i]	[ɪ]	[e]	[ɛ]
b**ie**ten	b**i**tten	b**e**ten	B**e**tten
st**ie**hlt	st**i**llt	st**e**hlt	st**e**llt
W**ie**sen	W**i**ssen	W**e**sen	w**e**ssen
v**ie**ler	F**i**lter	f**eh**le	F**e**lle
w**ie**gen	w**i**ckeln	W**e**ge	w**e**cken

C   Practice the sounds [e] and [ɛ]. Read the sentences aloud.

1. Was ist denn los, Eva?
2. Petra hat im Dezember Geburtstag.
3. Detlev Keller ist sechzehn.

Read sentences aloud while students have books closed. See if they can pick out the words with [e] or [ɛ] sounds. Have them find other examples of the sounds in the dialogues of chapters 1 and 2.

Have students pronounce the saying. Give English equivalent: "Speech is silver, silence is gold."

Reden ist Silber,
Schweigen ist Gold.

Übungen

The subject pronouns **wir, ihr,** and **sie**

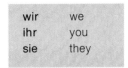

wir	we
ihr	you
sie	they

The subject pronouns **wir, ihr,** and **sie** are equivalent to the English pronouns *we, you* (plural), and *they*.

A   Give the subject pronouns you would use in the following situations.

1. You're talking to two friends.
2. You're talking about your teachers.
3. You're talking about yourself and a friend.
4. You're talking about Erik and Ingrid.
5. You're talking to your parents.

Present tense of **sein:** plural forms

wir **sind**
ihr **seid**
sie **sind**

Hans und Inge, seid **ihr** müde?   Hans and Inge, are *you* tired?
Ja, **wir** sind sehr müde.   Yes, *we're* very tired.

B   Beate expresses doubt about how you and your friend feel. Tell her it's true.

■⫶   Seid ihr wirklich glücklich?   *Ja, wir sind sehr glücklich.*

Some teachers prefer to do these and similar drills first with books open, then closed.

1. Seid ihr wirklich müde?   3. Seid ihr wirklich zufrieden?
2. Seid ihr wirklich kaputt?   4. Seid ihr wirklich sauer?

C   Ask whether Dieter and Gisela really mean what they say.

■⫶   Wir sind müde.   *Seid ihr wirklich müde?*

Use gestures to help convey meanings of *ihr* and *wir*. Personalize by treating the exercise as a dialogue.

1. Wir sind sauer.   3. Wir sind zufrieden.
2. Wir sind krank.   4. Wir sind kaputt.

Alex und Tanja sind sauer.   *Alex and Tanja* are in a bad mood.
Sie sind sehr müde.   *They're very tired.*

D   Jan always thinks people are a year older than they really are.
Correct him, as in the model.

This exercise may be
done first with books
open, then closed. Ask
individual students at
random.

■‖   Andrea und Erik sind sieb-   *Nein, sie sind erst sechzehn.*
zehn, nicht?

1. Hans und Ursel sind vierzehn, nicht?
2. Eva und Monika sind sechzehn, nicht?
3. Helmut und Uwe sind achtzehn, nicht?
4. Silke und Lutz sind fünfzehn, nicht?

Personalize: Have stu-
dent ask a neighbor the
question about two
others.

E   Form sentences, using the cued subjects and adjectives.

List pronouns and ad-
jectives; let students
make up their own sen-
tences.

Personalize by asking
about various students.

■‖   sie *(pl.)* / müde   *Sie sind müde.*

1. wir / faul
2. Thomas und Ilse / sauer
3. sie *(pl.)* / fleißig
4. ihr / glücklich

5. ich / krank
6. du / jung
7. Frank / alt
8. wir / gesund

The pronouns **sie** (singular) and **sie** (plural)

Ist **Birgit** müde?   Ja, **sie** ist sehr müde.
Sind **Eva und Jan** glücklich?   Ja, **sie** sind sehr glücklich.

F   You and Gabi are discussing mutual acquaintances. Confirm what Gabi
asks. Use either **sie** *(sg.)* or **sie** *(pl.)* as required by the question.

Make up simple sen-
tences with *sie ist* and
sie sind. See how fast
students can identify
singular and plural.

■‖   Brigitte ist krank, nicht?   *Ja, sie ist sehr krank.*

■‖   Trudi und Otto sind glück-   *Ja, sie sind sehr glücklich.*
lich, nicht?

1. Ursel ist sauer, nicht?
2. Marianne ist zufrieden, nicht?
3. Inge und Thomas sind unglücklich, nicht?
4. Michael und Wolf sind fleißig, nicht?
5. Heidi ist krank, nicht?

Ask students to reverse
the exercise, supplying
any name(s) that can
substitute for *sie ist* or
sie sind.
   T: *Sie ist sehr krank.*
   S: *Ingrid ist sehr
krank.*

You may wish to pre-
cede this drill with one
that separates singular
and plural forms.

Present tense of **haben**

At this point, don't expand practice of *haben* by using it with objects requiring the accusative.

ich **habe**	wir **haben**
du **hast**	ihr **habt**
er/sie **hat**	sie **haben**

G   Frank and his friends are comparing birthdays. Say that the people mentioned were born in the same month as their friends.

■ⅲ   Du hast im März Geburtstag. (Jens)   *Jens hat auch im März Geburtstag.*

1. Petra hat im Juni Geburtstag. (ich)
2. Wir haben im Februar Geburtstag. (Karin und Urs)
3. Jürgen hat im Mai Geburtstag. (ihr)
4. Ulrike und Thomas haben im September Geburtstag. (wir)
5. Anke hat im März Geburtstag. (du)
6. Ich habe im November Geburtstag. (Ellen)

Specific Questions

Check students' intonation. Tell them intonation is the same as in English: the voice normally falls at the end of a specific question.

Wie alt bist du?	Sechzehn.
Wann hast du Geburtstag?	Im Dezember.
Warum bist du so faul?	Ich bin müde.
Wer ist fleißig?	Christine.
Wieviel ist sechs und sieben?	Dreizehn.

Specific questions begin with interrogatives such as **wie, wann, warum, wer,** or **wieviel,** and require specific answers to supply the desired information.

H   At a crowded party, you can't hear everything Udo is saying. Ask questions to elicit the desired information.

You may mumble the word students must ask about. It lends reality to the situation:
T: *Jan ist . . .*
S: *Wie alt ist Jan?*
T: *Das ist . . .*
S: *Wer ist das?* .

■ⅲ   Jan ist *vierzehn.*   *Wie alt ist Jan?*

■ⅲ   Das ist *Ingrid Schmidt.*   *Wer ist das?*

1. Das ist *Jens Wagner.*
2. *Frank* hat im Mai Geburtstag.
3. Christa ist *siebzehn.*
4. Monika ist erst *zwölf.*
5. Es geht Inge *gut.*
6. Es geht Ralf *schlecht.*
7. Thomas hat *im Januar* Geburtstag.
8. Paula hat auch *im Januar* Geburtstag.

This drill may be done with books open, then closed. Personalize: *Wann hat Willi (hast du, habt ihr, etc.) Geburtstag?*

General questions

Tell students intonation is the same as in English: the voice normally rises at the end of a general question.

Bist du fünfzehn? **Ja.**
Ist Gerda auch fünfzehn? **Nein,** Gerda ist vierzehn.

General questions begin with a verb and require a **ja/nein-**answer.

I Ask whether the statements are really true.

As an introduction, give students a two-word statement (subject - verb) from which they must form a general question (verb - subject). They should raise their voices appropriately.
T: *du bist*
S: *bist du?*
T: *Frank hat*
S: *hat Frank?*

■III Frank ist vierzehn. *Ist Frank wirklich vierzehn?*

1. Ich bin fünfzehn.
2. Ursel ist elf.
3. Jens ist krank.
4. Gerda ist zufrieden.
5. Udo hat im Dezember Geburtstag.
6. Anke ist fleißig.

Draw arrows on board to indicate rising and falling intonation patterns. Many students are unaware of intonation patterns in their own language.

_____ Grammatische Übersicht _____

Subject pronouns (A)

The formal form *Sie* will be presented in chapter 7.

Review the function of the grammatical subject in a sentence. Have students find the subjects by writing familiar sentences on the board and replacing the subject with an X.
Wann hat X Geburtstag?
X sind wirklich krank.

SINGULAR	
ich	I
du	you
er	he
sie	she

PLURAL	
wir	we
ihr	you
sie	they

The plural subject pronouns **wir, ihr,** and **sie** function like the English pronouns *we, you,* and *they.*

The pronouns **sie** (singular) and **sie** (plural) (F)

Ist **sie** müde? Is *she* tired?
Sind **sie** müde? Are *they* tired?

Sie may mean *she* or *they.* A singular verb (for example, **ist**) indicates that **sie** means *she.* A plural verb (for example, **sind**) indicates that **sie** means *they.*

Present tense of **sein** (B-E)

SINGULAR	
ich **bin**	I am
du **bist**	you are
er/sie **ist**	he/she is

PLURAL	
wir **sind**	we are
ihr **seid**	you are
sie **sind**	they are

Like the English verb *to be*, the German verb **sein** has several forms in the present tense. The verb forms agree with their subject pronouns.

Present tense of **haben** (G)

ich **habe**	I have
du **hast**	you have
er/sie **hat**	he/she has

wir **haben**	we have
ihr **habt**	you have
sie **haben**	they have

Like the English verb *to have*, the German verb **haben** has several forms in the present tense. The forms must agree with their subject pronouns.

Specific questions and general questions (H-I)

Wie alt bist du?	How old are you?
Wann hast du Geburtstag?	When is your birthday?

A specific question asks for a particular bit of information and begins with an interrogative such as **wie, wieviel, wann, warum,** or **wer.** The voice normally falls at the end of a specific question.

Ist Gerda 15?	Is Gerda 15?
Hat sie im Mai Geburtstag?	Is her birthday in May?

A general question can be answered with **ja** or **nein** and begins with a verb. The voice normally rises at the end of a general question.

Wiederholung

A   Answer the questions after the dialogue.

INGRID	Tag, Peter! Wie geht's?
PETER	Sehr schlecht.
INGRID	Was ist denn los? Bist du krank?
PETER	Nein, nur kaputt.

1. Wie geht's Peter?
2. Ist Peter sehr müde?

B   Restate the sentences, inserting the flavoring word *denn* where indicated. Then give the English equivalents.

1. Wie alt bist du ____?
2. Wann hast du ____ Geburtstag?
3. Wie geht's ____?
4. Bist du ____ wieder krank?
5. Was ist ____ los?
6. Norbert ist sauer. Warum ____?

C   Form complete sentences from the cues below.

    ■‖   Peter / sein / wirklich /   *Peter ist wirklich sehr*
           sehr fleißig   *fleißig.*

    ■‖   wie / alt / sein / Dieter   *Wie alt sind Dieter und*
           und Meike /?   *Meike?*

1. wann / haben / du / Geburtstag /?
2. ich / haben / im Juli / Geburtstag
3. wie / alt / du / sein /?
4. sein / Ute / wirklich / unglücklich /?
5. ich / sein / sauer
6. wir / sein / beide / kaputt

D   Express in German:

1. See you later!   4. I am very lazy.
2. That's correct.   5. Anja is sick again.
3. I'm only fifteen.

E   Answer according to your mood and situation.

1. Wie geht's?   4. Wie alt bist du?
2. Wann hast du Geburtstag?   5. Bist du alt oder jung?
3. Bist du schon fünfzehn?   6. Bist du faul oder fleißig?

F Complete each sentence with an appropriate word from the list below.

aber   denn   los   nicht   nur   wie

1. Du bist auch sechzehn, ____?
2. Das ist ____ sehr alt.
3. Wie alt bist du ____?
4. ____ geht's?
5. Was ist denn ____?
6. Wir sind nicht sauer, ____ sehr müde.

G Choose a logical response or combination of responses from column B for each of the questions in column A.

▪▥   Du bist schon 17, nicht?   *Unsinn. Ich bin erst 15.*

A	B
Du bist erst dreizehn, nicht?	Unsinn. / Natürlich.
Du bist sehr jung, nicht?	Ja. / Nein.
Du hast im Juli Geburtstag, nicht?	Richtig. / Du auch, nicht?
Du bist zufrieden, nicht?	Ich bin schon [vierzehn].
Was ist los?	Ich bin erst [fünfzehn].
Bist du denn krank?	Ich bin nur müde.
	Ja, sehr.
	Ich bin krank. / Ich bin sauer.

Vokabeln

VERBEN

haben   to have
sein: wir sind   we are
ihr seid   you are *(pl.)*
sie sind   they are

ANDERE WÖRTER

aber   *flavoring word*
alt   old
beide   both
erst   only, first
falsch   wrong
ihr   you *(pl.)*
jung   young

ANDERE WÖRTER

mal   times
Monate   months *(p. 27)*
natürlich   naturally, of course
oder   or
richtig   correct, right
schon   already
sie *(pl.)*   they
wann   when
weniger   minus, less
wer   who
wieviel   how much
wir   we
Zahlen   numbers *(p. 26)*

BESONDERE AUSDRÜCKE

nicht?   isn't that so? *(at the end of a sentence)*
ach so   oh, I see!
wie alt bist du?   how old are you?
ich habe Geburtstag   it's my birthday
im [März]   in [March]

Kapitel 3

Heute nachmittag

Switzerland **(die Schweiz),** a country about half the size of Maine, is known for its scenery and industrial products. Much of the country is mountainous, and is ideal for skiing and hiking. The capital is Bern.

About 70% of Switzerland's 6½ million people speak a form of German called **Schwyzerdütsch.** The rest speak French, Italian, or Romansch, which is very close to Latin. The Latin name for Switzerland, **Helvetia,** is used on stamps and coins.

With the aid of a wall map or the map on p. xv, introduce Switzerland as the fourth largest German-speaking country. Name a few important cities and point out the language areas. Tell students that although the German Swiss speak *Schwyzerdütsch,* the written language is *Hochdeutsch* or *Schriftdeutsch.*

Help students vary dialogues by adding or subtracting lines or phrases, changing characters, using props and appropriate gestures. Personalize whenever possible.

Wo wohnst du?

Erik and Sabine live in Bern. School is out. Erik catches up with Sabine as she leaves for home.

ERIK	Gehst du jetzt nach Hause?
SABINE	Ja.
ERIK	Wo wohnst du denn?
SABINE	In der Gartenstraße.
ERIK	Ist das weit von hier?
SABINE	Nein, nur zehn Minuten.

Show how the word *Straße* is attached to the name of the street. For interest, show combinations with *Weg, Allee, Gasse: Blumenweg; Lindenallee; Schneidergasse.*

Use *Fragen* to discuss dialogues in the third person. Then distribute cards with street names; personalize questions: *Wo wohnst du? Ist das weit von hier?,* etc.

Fragen

1. Wer geht nach Hause?
2. Wohnt Sabine weit von hier?

Du hast das Wort

Show how *Bergdorf* is a compound meaning "mountain village." Have students try to think of similar place names in their area.

A. Ask a classmate on what street or in what town he/she lives.

Wo wohnst du?
In der [Garten]straße.
In [Bergdorf].

B. Ask how far that place is from where you are.

Ist das weit von hier?

Nein, nicht sehr weit.
Nein, nur fünf Minuten.
Ja, zehn Kilometer.°
Ja, ziemlich° weit.

Variation (hereafter V): Ask about a specific place.
S¹: *Ist [Bergdorf] weit von hier?*
S²: *Ja, sehr weit. /Ja, 19 Kilometer. /Nein, nur 5 Kilometer.* etc.
Remind students that 1 kilometer = 0.621 miles.

Marks Fotoalbum

Petra spielt gern Tennis.

Christa und Gerd spielen gern Basketball.

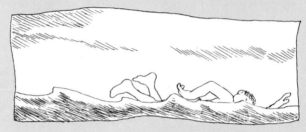

Herbert schwimmt gern.

Sie spielt auch gern Volleyball.

Ilse wandert viel.

Frank spielt sehr gut Fußball.

Ute und Frank gehen oft spazieren.

Other sports and activities: *Kegeln, Eishockey, Golf, Wettlaufen, Schilaufen, Tauchen, Schach, Dame, Scrabble.*
Do not introduce definite articles at this time. They are not needed for the exercises.

Fragen

1. Was macht Herbert gern?
2. Wer spielt Tennis? Basketball?
3. Was machen Ute und Frank?

Du hast das Wort

Ask a classmate whether he/she likes to engage in a particular sport or outdoor activity.

Encourage students to mix and match responses.

V: *Wann spielst du Tennis? (Jetzt, heute nachmittag, etc.)*

Spielst du gern [Tennis]?   Ja, ich spiele gern [Tennis].
    Ja, aber ich spiele nicht gut.
    Nein, ich spiele nicht gern [Tennis].

Gehst du gern spazieren?   Ja, sehr gern.
    Ja, natürlich.
    Nein, ich gehe nicht gern spazieren.

[Wanderst] du gern?   Ja, du nicht?
    Nein, ich [wandere] nicht gern.

Was machst du?

Fragen: Wann ist Gisela zu Hause? Was macht sie zu Hause?

Jan and Gisela are walking home from school together.

JAN	Bleibst du heute nachmittag zu Hause?
GISELA	Ja. Natürlich.
JAN	Was machst du denn?
GISELA	Hausaufgaben. Was sonst?

After students have learned *heute nachmittag*, let them guess the meaning of *heute abend* and *heute morgen.*

Du hast das Wort

A classmate asks you when you're going to do your homework. How would you respond?

While American students might have occasion to do homework in the morning (for example, in study hall), German students generally do not.

Machst du	heute nachmittag heute abend° heute morgen°	Hausaufgaben?	Ja, natürlich. Ja, du nicht? Nein, natürlich nicht. Nein, ich bin zu° müde.

Hiking and walking are favorite pastimes for Germans of all ages. There are well-maintained trails all over the country. Some are no more than paths through local scenic spots or city parks, while others are part of a vast complex of trails stretching from the Baltic Sea to Lake Constance. Some parks also feature **Trimm-dich-Pfade** (marked jogging paths with obstacles to climb over, and other suggested exercises).

Other instruments: *die Oboe, das Cello, die Harfe, die Tuba, die Trommel, das Saxophon, die Trompete (Trompete blasen, nicht spielen)*. Do not introduce definite articles at this time. They are not needed for the exercises.

Wortschatzerweiterung

Musikinstrumente

Klavier

Geige

Schlagzeug

Klarinette

Flöte

Gitarre

A   Ask a classmate whether he/she plays a particular instrument.

▪⫼   Spielst du [Klavier]?   Ja, natürlich.
                                       Nein, aber° [Geige].
                                       Nein, ich spiele nicht [Klavier].

B   Ask your classmate whether he/she plays well.

▪⫼   Spielst du gut?   Ja. Sehr gut.
                                 Ja, nicht schlecht.
                                 Ja, ganz gut.
                                 Nein, nicht sehr gut.

Pronunciation hint: For [y], tell students to keep tongue in the same position as for long [i], but round lips as for long [u]. Say *Kiel*, round lips and say *kühl*.

Aussprache

| long vowel [y] | müde, Schüler, Stühle |
| short vowel [Y] | fünf, Günter, Flüsse |

For [Y], keep tongue in same position as for short [I], but round lips as for short [U]: *Kissen > küssen.*

A Practice vertically in columns and horizontally in pairs.

Stand sideways and have students watch your lip movements as you model words. Remind students that they cannot smile and say *ü*. Lips must be pursed. (See hint for *müde* on p. 9).

[y]	[Y]
Füßen	Füssen
büßte	Büste
Düne	dünne
Mühle	Müll
fühlen	füllen

Activity: Write one of the two words on the board and pronounce either it or its pair. Class says *Ja* if you have pronounced the word you wrote, *Nein* if you pronounced the other.

B Practice the following words horizontally in pairs.

[i]	[y]	[I]	[Y]
Biene	Bühne	Binde	Bünde
diene	Düne	bitte	Bütte
Kiel	kühl	Kissen	küssen
liegen	lügen	Lifte	Lüfte

C Practice the sounds [y] and [Y]. Read the sentences aloud.

1. Günter, wieviel ist fünf und fünfzehn?
2. Warum seid ihr so müde?
3. Rüdiger ist unglücklich.

Eng., literal: *In brevity lies the spice.*
proverb: *Brevity is the soul of wit.*

In der Kürze liegt die Würze.

Glottal Stop

Say aloud *a nice man* and then say *an ice man.* The second phrase sounds different from the first because you break the stream of air between *an* and *ice.* This process of stopping and starting the air stream in the back of the throat is called a *glottal stop.* Both English and German use the glottal stop before vowels as a device to avoid running together words and parts of words. The glottal stop occurs more frequently in German than in English.

D Read the following sentences aloud. An asterisk (*) indicates a glottal stop.

1. Wo *ist *Erik heute *abend?
2. Wie geht *es *Eva?
3. Wie *alt *ist *Otto?

E Now try reading a few sentences without an asterisk.

1. Guten Abend!
2. Was ist das, Astrid?
3. Ist Udo wieder krank?

_____ Übungen _____

Present tense of regular verbs

Help students discover the relationship between verb endings and subject pronouns.

ich / du

ich geh**e**	du geh**st**
ich spiel**e**	du spiel**st**

The endings of regular verbs change according to a pattern. The **ich**-form ends in **-e,** the **du**-form ends in **-st.**

A Sabine is trying to find out more about you and your plans. Answer her questions affirmatively.

▪▥ Gehst du jetzt nach Hause? *Ja, ich gehe jetzt nach Hause.*

V: Have students ask each other the questions. Allow them to answer either affirmatively or negatively.

1. Wohnst du weit von hier?
2. Spielst du heute nachmittag Tennis?
3. Bleibst du heute abend zu Hause?
4. Machst du heute abend Hausaufgaben?

V: Have students answer question: *Ich spiele heute nachmittag Fußball.*

B

You didn't hear when Petra intends to do certain things. Ask her when it's going to be.

■‖   Ich spiele heute morgen   *Wann spielst du Fußball?*
           Fußball.

1. Ich gehe heute nachmittag schwimmen.
2. Ich spiele heute nachmittag Tennis.
3. Ich gehe heute abend spazieren.
4. Ich mache heute abend Hausaufgaben.

wir / ihr

wir geh**en**	ihr geh**t**
wir spiel**en**	ihr spiel**t**

The **wir-**form ends in **-en,** the **ihr-**form ends in **-t.**

V: Respond in the affirmative.

C

Bruno is curious and wants to know what your plans are. Keep him guessing by answering all of his questions in the negative.

■‖   Geht ihr nach Hause?   *Nein. Wir gehen nicht nach Hause.*

1. Bleibt ihr hier?
2. Geht ihr spazieren?
3. Spielt ihr Tennis?
4. Geht ihr schwimmen?
5. Spielt ihr Volleyball?

V¹: Have students substitute *wieder, jetzt.*
V²: Substitution drill for review purposes:
     T: *Wir spielen heute Tennis. (ich)*

D

Your friends tell you what they're doing today. Ask whether they do these things often.

■‖   Wir spielen heute Tennis.   *Spielt ihr oft Tennis?*

1. Wir spielen heute Fußball.
2. Wir spielen heute Basketball.
3. Wir gehen heute schwimmen.
4. Wir gehen heute spazieren.
5. Wir bleiben heute zu Hause.

er / sie (singular) / sie (plural)

er/sie geh**t**	sie geh**en**
er/sie spiel**t**	sie spiel**en**

The **er/sie-**form ends in **-t,** the **sie** (*plural*)-form ends in **-en.**

E   Marta asks how well several classmates play their instruments. Answer in each instance that they play either very well or very badly.

V¹: Personalize, using names of students.
V²: Hold up visuals to cue questions from students:
Spielt er gut Gitarre? Spielt sie gut Flöte?

▪⫶   Spielt Karin gut Klavier?   *Ja, sie spielt sehr gut.*
Nein, sie spielt sehr schlecht.

1. Spielt Bernhard gut Gitarre?
2. Spielt Astrid gut Klarinette?
3. Spielen Detlev und Erik gut Schlagzeug?
4. Spielt Detlev gut Flöte?
5. Spielen Rita und Christl gut Geige?

F   Say that the persons indicated play their instruments well.

Ex. F is a review of verb endings. If additional practice is needed, alternate subjects may be added: *ich (du, wir, etc.) / Klavier.*

▪⫶   Frank

Frank spielt gut Klavier.

1. du   2. ihr   3. wir   4. ich

Present tense to express future time

Ich mache heute abend Hausaufgaben.	*I'm going to do* homework tonight.
Spielst du heute nachmittag Tennis?	*Are you playing* tennis this afternoon?

German, like English, may use the present tense to express action intended or planned for the future. The time reference indicates whether a sentence refers to the present or the future.

G   The following people often engage in sports or outdoor activities. Ask whether they plan to do them this afternoon.

■||| Paul spielt oft Fußball.   *Spielt er heute nachmittag?*

1. Gerd und Rita spielen oft Tennis.
2. Gustav und Lutz spielen oft Basketball.
3. Gabi spielt oft Volleyball.
4. Tanja und Birgit spielen oft Volleyball.
5. Kai wandert oft.
6. Ute und Christl schwimmen viel.

Using **gern** with verbs

Ich **spiele gern** Basketball.   I *like to play* basketball.
Ich **spiele nicht gern** Tennis.   I *don't like to play* tennis.

The most common way of saying in German that you like or dislike doing something is to use **gern** or **nicht gern** with the appropriate verb.

H   Sometimes the things you enjoy most are those you don't do very often. Say that you enjoy the activities asked about below.

■||| Spielst du viel Tennis?   *Nein, aber ich spiele gern Tennis.*

V: Schwimmt ihr gut? Nein, aber wir schwimmen gern.

1. Schwimmst du viel?   4. Wanderst du viel?
2. Spielst du viel Klavier?   5. Gehst du viel spazieren?
3. Spielst du viel Gitarre?

I   When Lutz asks whether various classmates are involved in certain sports and activities, respond in the negative.

■||| Schwimmt Frank viel?   *Nein. Er schwimmt nicht gern.*

Personalize: Schwimmst du viel? gut? Spielst du oft Tennis?

1. Spielt Wolf oft Tennis?
2. Spielen Luise und Gerda oft Volleyball?
3. Wandert Michael viel?
4. Geht Klaus viel spazieren?
5. Spielt Cornelia oft Geige?

Using **gern** with **haben**

Jens **hat** Kirstin **gern.**   Jens *likes* Kirstin.
Kirstin **hat** Jens **nicht gern.**   Kirstin *doesn't like* Jens.

To express fondness for someone, German uses **gern** with a form of **haben. Nicht gern** is used to express a dislike.

J   Jochen and his friends are discussing which classmates they like. Form
sentences with *haben* and *gern*, using the cues provided.

V: Use the same cues
and *nicht gern*.

▪▥   wir / Martina   *Wir haben Martina gern.*

1. ich / Rolf
2. du / Ingrid / ?
3. Susanne / Rudi

4. ihr / Petra / ?
5. wir / Thomas

The phrases **zu Hause** and **nach Hause**

Gerd bleibt **zu Hause.**   Gerd is staying home.
Inge geht **nach Hause.**   Inge is going home.

When the verb expresses location, **zu Hause** is used.
When the verb expresses direction or movement, **nach Hause** is used.

K   Complete the sentences with *zu Hause* or *nach Hause*, as appropriate.

▪▥   Ich gehe heute nachmittag
_____.

*Ich gehe heute nachmittag
nach Hause.*

▪▥   Ich bleibe heute abend
_____.

*Ich bleibe heute abend zu
Hause.*

1. Wir bleiben heute morgen _____.
2. Petra und Erik gehen _____.
3. Dieter ist _____.
4. Gehst du _____?

5. Meike spielt _____.
6. Wann geht ihr _____?
7. Wann bist du _____?

L   Form sentences by supplying an appropriate verb.

bleiben   gehen   sein   spielen

Cue by *Wo bleibt
Dieter? Wo bleiben wir?*

▪▥   er / zu Hause   *Er ist zu Hause. / Er bleibt zu Hause.*

1. wir / zu Hause
2. wann / du / nach Hause / ?
3. Marta / zu Hause

4. ich / nach Hause
5. ihr / nach Hause / ?
6. wann / du / zu Hause / ?

Grammatische Übersicht

Present tense of regular verbs (A–F)

Have students think of other verbs they know (machen, wandern, wohnen). Write them on board and cross out the ending, leaving the stem.

Infinitive and infinitive stem

INFINITIVE	=	STEM	+	ENDING
bleiben		bleib		en
gehen		geh		en

The basic form of a German verb is the infinitive. Most German infinitives end in **-en;** a few end in **-n.** In vocabularies and dictionaries, verbs are listed under the infinitive form. The infinitive stem is the infinitive minus the **-(e)n** ending.

Point out that the present-tense wir and sie forms are identical with the infinitive.

Present-tense endings of regular verbs

INFINITIVE
spielen

SINGULAR		
ich	spiel	e
du	spiel	st
er/sie	spiel	t

PLURAL		
wir	spiel	en
ihr	spiel	t
sie	spiel	en

Contrast with English verb endings in the present tense: I/you/we/they come; he/she/it comes.

German verb endings change, depending on what the subject of the verb is. The verb endings are added to the infinitive stem. In the present tense most verbs have four different endings: **-e, -st, -t, -en.**

Present-tense meanings

Detlev **spielt** gut.

Detlev *plays* well.
Detlev *is playing* well.

Spielt er gut?

Is he *playing* well?
Does he *play* well?

Notice that German uses one present-tense form to express ideas that require several different present-tense forms in English.

Present tense to express future time (G)

Spielt Jutta heute nachmit- tag?	*Is* Jutta *going to play* this after- noon?
Wann **gehst** du nach Hause?	When *are* you *going to go* home?

In German, as in English, the present tense may be used to express action intended or planned for the future. The time reference indicates whether a sentence refers to the present or the future.

Using **gern** with verbs (H-I)

Ich schwimme **gern.**	I *like* to swim.
Ich spiele **nicht gern** Fußball.	I *don't like* to play soccer.

The most common way of saying in German that you like doing something is to use **gern** with a verb. To say that you dislike doing something, use **nicht gern** with a verb.

Using **gern** with **haben** (J)

Jens **hat** Kirstin **gern.**	Jens *likes* Kirstin.
Sie **hat** aber Jens **nicht gern.**	But she *doesn't like* Jens.

One way of expressing fondness for someone in German is to use **gern** with a form of **haben.** One way of saying that you *don't* like someone is to use **nicht gern** with a form of **haben.**

The phrases **zu Hause** and **nach Hause** (K-L)

Erika ist **zu Hause.**	Erika is at *home.*
Beate geht **nach Hause.**	Beate is going *home.*

The phrases **zu Hause** and **nach Hause** both mean *home,* but they are used in somewhat different ways. **Zu Hause** is used to talk about being at home. **Nach Hause** is used to talk about going home.

Wo wohnst du? Above, left: A quiet, residential street in Berlin. Right: A country village in Switzerland. Below: A suburban development near Hannover.

49

Wiederholung

A

Use first for sight-reading practice, then role-play with variations. Have students substitute their own names or those of friends and make other changes as they choose.

A   Answer the questions based on the following dialogue.

UTE	Tag, Karsten! Was ist denn los? Bist du sauer?
KARSTEN	Ja, sehr. Gisela ist nicht zu Hause.
UTE	Wo ist sie denn?
KARSTEN	Sie spielt wieder Basketball, und ich mache Hausaufgaben.

1. Was macht Gisela?
2. Warum ist Karsten sauer?

B   Ask a classmate the following arithmetic problems, beginning each question with *Wieviel ist . . . .*

1. $10 + 6 = ?$ 4. $15 - 2 = ?$
2. $19 - 1 = ?$ 5. $2 \times 7 = ?$
3. $3 \times 4 = ?$ 6. $8 + 9 = ?$

C   Begin each question with the appropriate interrogative.

1. _____ ist denn los?
2. _____ bist du so unglücklich?
3. _____ geht's?
4. _____ wohnst du?
5. _____ hast du Geburtstag?

Have students work in pairs and role-play.

D   You and a friend are discussing your plans for the afternoon. Express the following dialogue in German.

A	Hi, [. . .]! What are you doing this afternoon?
B	I'm going to play soccer. You, too?
A	No, I'm going home.
B	But why?
A	I'm going to do homework.

Personalize: Have students ask questions, using names of friends or classmates.

E   You are having a negative day. Answer everyone's questions in the negative, and then reinforce what you have to say by using an antonym in your second sentence.

  ■▷   Bist du krank?   *Nein, ich bin nicht krank. Ich bin gesund.*

1. Schwimmt Peter gut?
2. Ist Peter alt?
3. Ist Inge faul?
4. Bist du unglücklich?
5. Seid ihr glücklich?

After oral work, have students write as a paragraph.

F A new student is trying to find out more about you. How would you answer her/his questions?

1. Wo wohnst du?
2. Wie alt bist du?
3. Wann hast du Geburtstag?
4. Schwimmst du gern?
5. Spielst du gern Basketball? Spielst du oft?
6. Spielst du Gitarre? Spielst du gut?
7. Was machst du heute abend?

At this point, tell students there are three words for "the." For completeness, you may wish to have them learn the appropriate *der, das, die* with the vocabulary, but the articles won't be needed until chapter 5.

Vokabeln

SUBSTANTIVE (NOUNS)

Der, das, and **die** all mean *the.* The use of these articles will be practiced in Chapter 5.

der Basketball   basketball
die Flöte   flute
das Fotoalbum   photo album
der Fußball   soccer
die Geige   violin
die Gitarre   guitar
die Hausaufgaben *(pl.)* homework
der Kilometer   kilometer
die Klarinette   clarinet
das Klavier   piano
die Minute   minute
das Musikinstrument musical instrument
das Schlagzeug   drums
die Straße   street
das Tennis   tennis
der Volleyball   volleyball

VERBEN

bleiben   to remain, to stay
gehen   to go
machen   to do, to make
schwimmen   to swim
spazieren   to walk, to stroll, to go for a walk
spielen   to play
wandern   to hike, to go hiking
wohnen   to live

ANDERE WÖRTER

aber   however, but
gern   gladly, with pleasure
heute   today
hier   here
in   in(to)
jetzt   now
oft   often
viel   much, many, a lot
von   from
weit   far (away)
wo   where
ziemlich   quite
zu   to, too

BESONDERE AUSDRÜCKE

heute nachmittag   this afternoon
heute morgen   this morning
heute abend   tonight; this evening
was sonst?   what else?
nach Hause   home *(direction)*
zu Hause   (at) home
in der Gartenstraße   on Garden Street
gern haben   to like, to be fond of

Game: Students make bingo cards with 25 squares and fill in the numbers 1–19 at random, repeating whichever ones they choose. The teacher gives a series of math problems, the answers to which must be on the students' cards. Regular bingo rules apply.

Kapitel 4

Ich und meine Familie

In the United States, family names, names of towns, and certain customs recall the many Germans who have immigrated to this country. In cities like New York and Detroit there are still many families who speak German at home. They shop in German stores and keep up with news through German radio programs and newspapers. Many German-speaking communities have clubs that foster social and cultural activities, such as choral singing and dramatics.

Have students look at a map of their own or another state and guess which towns have German names. Other German influences are Christmas customs, Kindergarten, and the university system of teaching and research.

Der Brieffreund

Treat *den* as passive vocabulary in dates.

See *Introduction* for suggestions on how to present core material in narrative form. You may wish to introduce *Der Brieffreund* by using the tape recording. Ask students how much they can understand without help. Or ask them to listen for the answer to a specific question, first with books closed, then open.

Barbara lives in Wisconsin, a state with a large German-speaking population. She has just started corresponding with a pen pal in Germany.

Milwaukee, den 12. Dezember

Lieber Michael!

Mein Name ist Barbara Braun. Ich bin fünfzehn Jahre alt. Ich bin Schülerin und lerne schon zwei Jahre Deutsch. Mein Hobby ist Musik. Ich spiele gern Klavier, aber nur klassische Musik.

Mein Bruder heißt Bill. Er ist achtzehn Jahre alt. Er ist groß und schlank. Er spielt Gitarre und singt nicht schlecht. Er spielt oft Rock.

Meine Schwester heißt Susan. Sie ist erst elf Jahre alt. Sie ist klein und dünn. Sie spielt sehr gut Geige. Oft ist sie doof. Sie ist aber noch ein Kind.

Meine Mutter ist Apothekerin. Sie arbeitet von Montag bis Donnerstag. Am Freitag, Samstag und Sonntag ist sie zu Hause. Das ist natürlich schön. Sie ist sehr musikalisch. Sie spielt Klavier und Geige.

Mein Vater ist Elektriker. Er arbeitet viel und kommt oft spät nach Hause. Abends hört er gern Musik, und er kocht (er kocht gern und gut!). Er spielt Klarinette. Am Wochenende machen wir oft Musik, meine Mutter, mein Vater, meine Schwester, mein Bruder und ich. Das macht viel Spaß.

Was machst Du gern abends? Spielst Du Klavier oder Gitarre? Oder was? Hörst Du gern Musik? Wie findest Du klassische Musik? Treibst Du gern Sport? Tanzt Du gern? Hoffentlich schreibst Du bald.

Herzliche Grüße

Barbara

Ask detailed questions to check comprehension:
Wie heißt Michaels Brieffreundin?
Wie alt ist sie?
Wieviel Jahre lernt sie schon Deutsch?
Was ist ihr Hobby?
Was spielt sie gern?
Spielt sie Rockmusik?

Du hast das Wort

Optional: Assign as written review.

A. Describe Barbara's family.

Wie heißt Barbaras Bruder? Wie alt ist er? Ist er klein oder groß? Ist er musikalisch?

Wie heißt Barbaras Schwester? Wie alt ist sie? Ist sie klein oder groß? Was spielt sie? Warum ist sie oft doof?

Was ist Barbaras Mutter? Von wann bis wann arbeitet sie? Wann ist sie zu Hause? Was spielt sie?

Was ist Barbaras Vater? Was macht er abends? Was spielt er?

Optional: May use visual of family to present additional vocabulary (*Onkel, Kusine, Oma,* etc.).

B. Invent a family for Barbara's pen pal Michael. Describe the members as Michael would.

Meine Mutter heißt . . . Sie ist . . . Sie . . .
Mein Vater . . .
Mein Bruder [Thomas] . . .
Meine Schwester [Claudia] . . .

V: Ask a classmate
her/his name:
  S¹: *Wie heißt du?*
  S²: *Ich heiße* . . .

C. Ask a classmate for the names of family members (real or imaginary).

Wie heißt	dein Vater?	Er heißt . . .
	dein Bruder?	Er heißt . . .
	deine Mutter?	Sie heißt . . .
	deine Schwester?	Sie heißt . . .

D. A friend asks you what you're going to do this Saturday and Sunday. How would you respond?

Was machst du	am Samstag?	Ich mache meine Hausaufgaben.
	am Sonntag?	Ich spiele [Tennis].
	am Wochenende?	Ich spiele Karten°.
		Ich schwimme.
		Ich gehe tanzen.
		Ich arbeite.

Personalize: Have students answer the questions based on their own experience.

E. Have one of your classmates pretend to be Michael. Ask her/him the questions Barbara asked in her letter.

Was machst du abends?
Spielst du Klavier oder Gitarre?

At least half of the women (married and unmarried) in the Federal Republic work outside the home. In some households the man stays home to take care of the house and children. He cannot be known as the **Hausfrau,** so he is called the "**Hausmann.**"

Families often share leisure activities. When children are young, these activities include visits to friends and relatives, Sunday afternoon walks, outings to the country or to nearby cities and towns, and vacations. While teen-agers may choose not to go on the Sunday afternoon walks, they often participate in other kinds of family outings. They almost always join the family on vacation.

Berufe

Herr Schwarz ist **Geschäftsmann.**
Frau Schwarz ist **Geschäftsfrau.**

Herr Stein ist **Friseur.**
Fräulein Kneip ist **Friseuse.**

Herr Schmidt ist **Arbeiter.**
Frau Meier ist **Arbeiterin.**

Herr Weiß ist **Verkäufer.**
Fräulein Klein ist **Verkäuferin.**

Herr Wagner ist **Lehrer.**
Frau Wagner ist **Lehrerin.**

Herr Müller ist **Arzt.**
Frau Müller ist **Ärztin.**

Call students' attention to umlaut in *Ärztin*.

In German there are usually different forms of a noun to indicate a man and a woman in the same profession. Often, the feminine equivalent simply adds **-in** to the masculine form. Occasionally, an umlaut must also be added to the feminine form.

A Complete the sentences to say what the following people's parents do for a living.

Additional professions: *Mechaniker / Mechanikerin, Tankwart (m. and f.), Rechtsanwalt / Rechtsanwältin, Angestellter / Angestellte, Sekretär / Sekretärin, Krankenschwester / Krankenpfleger*

■⫙   Ritas Mutter ist Friseuse; Franks Vater ist ____.   *Friseur*

1. Utes Mutter ist Lehrerin; Jans Vater ist ____.
2. Peters Mutter ist Arbeiterin; Trudis Vater ist ____.
3. Ottos Vater ist Arzt; Elkes Mutter ist ____.
4. Georgs Mutter ist Geschäftsfrau; Ursels Vater ist ____.
5. Ritas Vater ist Apotheker; Gerds Mutter ist ____.
6. Sabines Mutter ist Verkäuferin; Werners Vater ist ____.
7. Franks Vater ist Friseur; Sylvias Mutter ist ____.

Zahlen: 20–1.000

20	zwanzig	50	fünfzig	80	achtzig	200	zweihundert
30	dreißig	60	sechzig	90	neunzig	500	fünfhundert
40	vierzig	70	siebzig	100	hundert	1.000	tausend

Review 1–19 quickly before introducing higher numbers.

Point out that German uses a period or space to set off thousands.

Dreißig ends in **-ßig** instead of **-zig.**
Sechzig loses the final **-s** of **sechs.**
Siebzig loses the final **-en** of **sieben.**
Hundert und **tausend** are generally used instead of **einhundert** und **eintausend.**

B You're at an auction. Each time a bid is made you raise it by 10.

Game: Point to students in various parts of the room and ask for numbers in sequence (20, 30, etc.). Whoever misses loses a point. Tell students to count by 2's, 5's, etc.: *in zweien, in fünfen, usw, zählen.*

■⫙   40 (vierzig)   (50) *fünfzig*

1. 90   3. 70   5. 60
2. 30   4. 20   6. 80

21	einundzwanzig		79	neunundsiebzig
22	zweiundzwanzig		101	hunderteins
34	vierunddreißig		121	hunderteinundzwanzig
57	siebenundfünfzig		265	zweihundertfünfundsechzig

Point out that compound numbers are not hyphenated in German.

The German numbers within the twenties, thirties, and so on, follow the number pattern used in the English nursery rhyme "four-and-twenty blackbirds."

In compound numbers with **eins**, the **-s** of **eins** is dropped:

eins > **einundzwanzig**

C   Your friends are trying to guess the numbers you're thinking of. Each time their guess is one short. Correct them.

▪▥   24 (vierundzwanzig)?   *Nein, fünfundzwanzig.*

1. 75?   4. 68?   7. 998?
2. 98?   5. 120?   8. 1.206?
3. 37?   6. 782?   9. 1.300?

Zentimetermaß

Games:
(1) A student thinks of a number; others in turn try to guess it. The first student to guess correctly chooses another number.
(2) *Aus.* Students count in sequence. Whenever 7, any number with a 7 in it, or a multiple of 7 comes up, students must say *aus* instead of the number.

1 Meter (1 m) = 39,37 in.
1 Zentimeter (1 cm) = 0,39 in.
2,54 Zentimeter (2,54 cm) = 1,0 in.

In German, a comma is used to write decimals.

Wie groß bist du?   1,62 m | Ein Meter zweiundsechzig.
                                          | Eins zweiundsechzig.

There are several ways to express height in German.

Remind students of equivalent ways to express height in the U.S.A.: *5 feet 4, five four.*

m/cm	ft/in.
1,95	6'5''
1,90	6'3''
1,85	6'1''
1,80	5'11''
1,75	5'9''
1,70	5'7''
1,65	5'5''
1,60	5'3''
1,55	5'1''
1,50	4'11''
1,45	4'9''
1,40	4'7''
1,35	4'5''
1,30	4'3''

Activity: Provide a metric measure to determine heights; use it to measure objects as well.

D   Ask a classmate how tall he/she is.

▪▥   Wie groß bist du?   [*Ein Meter fünfundvierzig.*]

E   Ask a classmate how tall various friends and relatives are.

If students don't know, let them make up probable answers.

▪▥   Wie groß ist dein Vater? dein Freund? deine Freundin? dein Bruder? deine Schwester?

Aussprache

> long vowel [ø]   schön, Flöte
> short vowel [œ]   zwölf, Wörter

A   Practice vertically in columns and horizontally in pairs.

Pronunciation hint: For [ø], tell students to place tongue against back of lower front teeth and say [e], as in *hehlen*. Keep tongue in same position, round lips, and glide to [ø].

[ø]	[œ]
Höhle	Hölle
Öfen	öffnen
fröhlich	Frösche
König	können
lösen	löschen

For [oe], the procedure is the same except have students start with [ε], as in *kennen*.

B   Practice the following words horizontally in pairs.

[e]	[ø]	[ε]	[œ]
lesen	lösen	kennte	könnte
hehlen	Höhlen	helle	Hölle
bete	böte	stecke	Stöcke
flehe	Flöhe	fällig	völlig

C   Practice the sounds [ø] and [œ]. Read the sentences aloud.

1. Jörg hört gern klassische Musik.
2. Petra spielt schön Flöte.
3. Sie wohnt in der Goethestraße.

Eng., literal: Many cooks spoil the porridge.
proverb: Too many cooks spoil the broth.

Viele Köche verderben den Brei.

Verbs with stem ending in **-d** or **-t**

finden	
ich finde	wir finden
du **findest**	ihr **findet**
er/sie **findet**	sie finden

arbeiten	
ich arbeite	wir arbeiten
du **arbeitest**	ihr **arbeitet**
er/sie **arbeitet**	sie arbeiten

Verbs with stem ending in **-d** or **-t** have an **-e** before the **-st** and **-t** endings in the present tense.

A Inform Gabi that all of the people she mentions work in the evenings.

◼▐ Was macht Inge abends?   *Sie arbeitet.*

1. Was macht Herr Klein abends?
2. Was machst du abends?
3. Was machen Hans und Volker abends?
4. Was macht Frau Kluge abends?
5. Was macht ihr abends?

B Hans-Jürgen asks what you and others think of rock music. Say that everyone finds it great.

◼▐ Wie findet Claudia Rockmusik?   *Sie findet Rockmusik schön.*

1. Und Dieter?
2. Frau Lenz?
3. Und du?
4. Margit?
5. Ihr?

Verbs with stem ending in a sibilant

heißen
ich heiße
du **heißt**
er/sie **heißt**

tanzen
ich tanze
du **tanzt**
er/sie **tanzt**

The **-st** of the **du**-form ending contracts to **-t** when the verb stem ends in any sibilant (**-s, -ss, -ß, -z,** or **-tz**).

C Ask whether each of the following persons likes to dance.

Use the same cues for an exercise with *heißen:*
Wie heißt Petras Bruder?
Wie heißt Inges Schwester?

■ıı   Petras Bruder   *Tanzt Petras Bruder gern?*

1. Inges Schwester
2. Dieters Bruder
3. du

4. ihr
5. Ritas Schwester

Position of the verb in statements

Be sure students understand that the element in first position can be a phrase or a single word.

1	2	3	4
Wir	arbeiten	abends	nicht.
Abends	arbeiten	wir	nicht.
Heute abend	arbeiten	wir	nicht.

In a German statement, the verb is always in second position, even when an element other than the subject is in the first position. When words other than the subject begin a sentence, the subject follows the verb.

D Günther asks you what your interests are. Say that of course you do each of the things he asks about.

V: Let students ask each other the questions.

■ıı   Spielst du Klavier?   *Natürlich spiele ich Klavier!*

1. Spielst du Tennis?
2. Hörst du gern Musik?
3. Arbeitest du viel?

4. Tanzt du gut?
5. Gehst du oft spazieren?
6. Kochst du gern?

E Say that you don't do any of the following things. Begin each sentence with *Nein* and the emphasized word or phrase.

Remind students that *heute abend, am Samstag,* and *klassische Musik* are each one element.

■ıı   Gehst du *abends* spazieren?   *Nein, abends gehe ich nicht*
                                        spazieren.

1. Arbeitest du *heute abend?*
2. Arbeitest du *am Samstag?*
3. Spielst du *Tennis?*

4. Singst du *gut?*
5. Bist du *musikalisch?*
6. Spielst du *klassische Musik?*

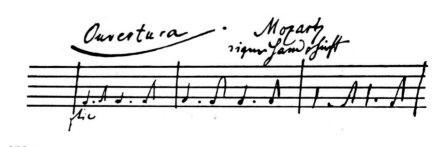

Original Mozart manuscript

Possession with proper names

Ist das **Inges** Gitarre?	Is that *Inge's* guitar?
Wie alt ist **Utes** Bruder?	How old is *Ute's* brother?

In German, an **-s** is usually added to a proper name to show possession or other close relationship.

The pronunciation of names like *Thomas'* in the genitive is *Thomases*.

Ist das **Thomas'** Mutter?	Is that *Thomas's* mother?

If the name already ends in an **s**-sound, no **-s** is added. In written German, an apostrophe is used after a name ending in an **s**-sound.

F The students mentioned below each have a brother who plays the same instrument. Point that out to a friend.

▪▥ Gerda spielt Klavier. *Gerdas Bruder spielt auch Klavier.*

1. Bernd spielt Geige.
2. Petra spielt Klarinette.
3. Hans spielt Gitarre.
4. Thomas spielt Schlagzeug.
5. Inge spielt Flöte.
6. Karin spielt Klavier.

Possessive adjectives

The concept of grammatical (as opposed to natural) gender will be presented in chapter 5, when noun gender is introduced.

mein/dein

Mein Vater arbeitet viel.	**Dein** Vater auch?
Meine Mutter arbeitet viel.	**Deine** Mutter auch?

The possessive adjectives **mein** and **dein** are equivalent to *my* and *your* (*sg.*). Possessive adjectives end in **-e** when they modify nouns referring to females.

G Gisela tells you about the activities in which various friends and relatives participate. Ask to make sure you heard the right person.

▪▥ Mein Freund schwimmt gern. *Wer? Dein Freund?*

Let students ask each other the questions, then personalize.

1. Meine Freundin schwimmt gut.
2. Mein Vater wandert gern.
3. Mein Bruder spielt Fußball.
4. Meine Schwester spielt Basketball.
5. Meine Mutter spielt Tennis.
6. Mein Freund spielt Volleyball.

H   Ute asks you questions about various people. Check to make sure you know which person she's asking about, and then confirm her judgment.

       ■╮   Ist deine Mutter jung?   *Meine Mutter? Ja, sehr.*

    1. Ist dein Vater jung?
    2. Ist dein Bruder faul?
    3. Ist deine Schwester fleißig?
    4. Ist dein Freund Hans-Dieter groß?
    5. Ist deine Freundin Inge glücklich?

sein / ihr

Give examples with *sein* and *ihre*:
Sein Vater ist Verkäufer.
Ihre Mutter ist Ärztin.

Seine Mutter ist Apothekerin.	*His* mother is a druggist.
Ihr Vater ist Geschäftsmann.	*Her* father is a businessman.

I   At a school event Ilse is trying to identify a number of spectators. Confirm Ilse's identifications.

       ■╮   Das ist Jochens Mutter, nicht?   *Ja, das ist seine Mutter.*

    1. Das ist Volkers Vater, nicht?
    2. Das ist Utes Schwester, nicht?
    3. Das ist Giselas Bruder, nicht?
    4. Das ist Walters Freund, nicht?
    5. Das ist Heidis Freundin, nicht?

J   Rolf asks about the occupation of a number of acquaintances. Say that his guesses are wrong.

       ■╮   Ist Martas Mutter Lehrerin?   *Ihre Mutter Lehrerin? Nein.*

       ■╮   Ist Martas Vater Lehrer?   *Ihr Vater Lehrer? Nein.*

    1. Ist Ritas Freund Verkäufer?
    2. Ist Ritas Freundin Geschäftsfrau?
    3. Ist Rudis Mutter Ärztin?
    4. Ist Rudis Vater Arzt?
    5. Ist Franks Bruder Apotheker?

unser / euer

In spoken German, *unsere* is often pronounced *unsre*.

Unser Arzt ist gut.	*Our* doctor is good.
Unsere Ärztin ist gut.	
Ist **euer** Arzt auch gut?	Is *your* doctor good, too?
Ist **eure** Ärztin auch gut?	

When **euer** has an ending, the **-e** before the **-r** is usually omitted.

K   You've just moved to a new town, and your relatives are curious about the professional people you've found there. Answer that they're good.

Indicate two students when saying *euer*, even though only one will answer.

◼❙❙   Wie ist eure Ärztin?   *Unsere Ärztin ist gut.*

1. Wie ist euer Apotheker?
2. Wie ist euer Lehrer?
3. Wie ist eure Friseuse?
4. Wie ist euer Elektriker?

L   You are talking to a pair of twins. Inquire why their friends and relatives feel or act as they do.

◼❙❙   Bruder / müde   *Warum ist euer Bruder so müde?*

1. Schwester / faul
2. Vater / sauer
3. Mutter / glücklich
4. Freund / doof
5. Freundin / unglücklich

ihr (singular) and ihr (plural)

Optional: Remind students that *ihr* is also the subject pronoun for *you* (plural).

Hier ist **Gerda.** Und das ist **ihre** Mutter.
Hier sind **Trudi and Jens.** Und das ist **ihre** Mutter.

Here's *Gerda.* And that's *her* mother.
Here are *Trudi and Jens.* And that's *their* mother.

Ihr can mean *their* as well as *her.* Context usually makes the meaning clear.

M   You and Heike are at a band concert. Heike asks about the identity of a number of people in the audience. Say that she has guessed correctly.

◼❙❙   Ist das Elkes Schwester?   *Ja, das ist ihre Schwester.*

1. Ist das Juttas Bruder?
2. Ist das Ottos und Pauls Lehrer?
3. Ist das Helgas und Eriks Lehrerin?
4. Ist das Evas Vater?
5. Ist das Günters und Tanjas Mutter?

N   Gerd asks you a number of questions about your friends and relatives. Answer him in the negative.

◼❙❙   Tanzt Gerdas Bruder gut?   *Ihr Bruder? Nein.*

1. Spielt Tanjas Schwester Tennis?
2. Kocht dein Bruder gut?
3. Spielt deine Schwester Geige?
4. Ist Stefans Vater Arzt?
5. Ist Volkers Mutter Geschäftsfrau?
6. Ist euer Arzt jung?
7. Ist eure Lehrerin alt?

Du hast das Wort

Describe some friends and members of your family by answering the following questions.

Ist deine Mutter jung oder alt?

Ist dein Vater jung oder alt?

Ist dein Bruder [Volker] prima oder doof?

Ist deine Schwester [Erika] faul oder fleißig?

Ist dein Freund [Hannes] groß oder klein? Und deine Freundin [Barbara]?

Ist deine Freundin [Cordula] glücklich oder unglücklich? Und dein Freund [Alex]?

Ist deine Freundin [Petra] oft sauer? Und dein Freund [Hans-Dieter]?

Ist dein Freund [Stefan] faul oder fleißig? Und deine Freundin [Angelika]?

Grammatische Übersicht

Verbs with stem ending in **-d** or **-t** (A-B)

finden		arbeiten	
ich finde	wir finden	ich arbeite	wir arbeiten
du **findest**	ihr **findet**	du **arbeitest**	ihr **arbeitet**
er/sie **findet**	sie finden	er/sie **arbeitet**	sie arbeiten

Verbs with stem ending in **-d** or **-t** require an **-e** before the present-tense endings **-st** or **-t.**

Verbs with stem ending in a sibilant (C)

heißen		tanzen	
ich heiße	wir heißen	ich tanze	wir tanzen
du **heißt**	ihr **heißt**	du **tanzt**	ihr tanzt
er/sie **heißt**	sie heißen	er/sie **tanzt**	sie tanzen

The sounds represented by the letters **s, ss, ß, z,** and **tz** are called sibilants. When a verb stem ends in a sibilant, the **-st** of the **du**-form ending contrasts to **-t,** making the **du-** and **er/sie**-forms identical.

Position of the verb in statements (D-E)

1	2	3	4
Brigitte	arbeitet	am Samstag	zu Hause.
Am Samstag	arbeitet	Brigitte	zu Hause.

In a German statement, the verb is always in second position, even when an element other than the subject (for example, an adverb or a prepositional phrase) is in first position. When a word or phrase other than the subject begins the sentence, the subject follows the verb.

Possession with proper names (F)

Das ist **Bettinas** Gitarre.   That's *Bettina's* guitar.
Wie alt ist **Peters** Schwester?   How old is *Peter's* sister?

In German, as in English, possession and other close relationships are expressed by adding **-s** to proper names. In written German, no apostrophe is used before the **-s.**

Ist das **Hans'** Vater?   Is that *Hans's* father?
Wie alt ist **Franz'** Bruder?   How old is *Franz's* brother?

Unlike English, German does not add an **-s** if a name already ends in an **s**-sound. In written German, an apostrophe is used after a name ending in an **s**-sound.

Possessive adjectives (G-N)

SUBJECT PRONOUN	POSSESSIVE ADJECTIVE	
ich	mein/meine	my
du	dein/deine	your
er	sein/seine	his
sie	ihr/ihre	her
wir	unser/unsere	our
ihr	euer/eure	your
sie	ihr/ihre	their

Mein Bruder arbeitet viel.
Meine Schwester arbeitet auch viel.

Possessive adjectives add no special ending when they modify nouns referring to males. They end in **-e** when they modify nouns referring to females.

Hier ist **Rita.** Und das ist
    ihr Vater.

Here's *Rita.* And that's *her* father.

Hier sind **Inge und Jens.**
    Und das ist **ihr** Vater.

Here are *Inge and Jens.* And
    that's *their* father.

Context usually makes clear whether **ihr(e)** means *her* or *their.*

Wie alt ist **euer** Vater?
Wie alt ist **eure** Mutter?

When **euer** has an ending, the **-e** before the **-r** is usually omitted:
euere>eure.

Capitalization of **du** and **dein** / **ihr** and **euer** in letters

Lieber Michael!

... Was machst **Du** am Samstag? Was macht **Dein** Bruder
Jens?
Geht **Ihr** tanzen? ... Hoffentlich schreibst **Du** bald ...

In letters or notes the German equivalents for *you* and *your* are capitalized: **Du, Dein(e), Ihr(e),** and **Euer(e).**

Wiederholung

A Identify the occupations shown in the drawings. Use the German name for each occupation in a brief sentence.

Meine Mutter ist Ärztin.
Ist deine Freundin Ärztin?

B You're showing some snapshots of people to Kurt, who tries to identify them. Confirm or deny his guesses, as in the model.

Das ist Gerdas Vater, nicht?   *Ja, das ist ihr Vater.*
Nein, das ist nicht ihr Vater.

1. Das ist Brunos Schwester, nicht?
2. Das ist Petras Bruder, nicht?
3. Das ist Andreas' Mutter, nicht?
4. Das ist Lottes Freund, nicht?
5. Das ist deine Freundin Katja, nicht?
6. Das ist dein Freund Stefan, nicht?
7. Das ist Kurts Vater, nicht?
8. Das ist euer Lehrer, nicht?
9. Das ist Jans and Ellens Mutter, nicht?

C Choose the phrase that best completes each statement based on the following paragraph.

May use for sight-reading.

Meine Schwester Inge hat am Samstag Geburtstag. Am Samstag abend kommen ihr Freund Hans und seine Schwester Gabi. Hans ist Verkäufer, und Gabi ist Friseuse. Sie sind beide sehr musikalisch. Gabi spielt gut Klavier. Hans spielt sehr gut Schlagzeug. Inge spielt nicht schlecht Gitarre. Ich spiele Klarinette — nicht gut, nur gern. Hoffentlich spielen wir am Samstag. Das macht wirklich Spaß.

1. Am Samstag . . .
   a. arbeitet Inge.
   b. kommen Inges Freund und seine Schwester.
   c. geht Inge nach Hause.
2. Gabi . . .
   a. spielt nicht gern Klavier.
   b. spielt Klavier, und Hans spielt Schlagzeug.
   c. ist die Freundin von Hans.
3. Inges Bruder . . .
   a. spielt auch Schlagzeug.
   b. spielt gern Klarinette.
   c. spielt gut Klarinette.

D Use a centimeter ruler to measure the following things. Give your measurements in German.

1. the length of your pencil (pen)
2. the width of this book
3. the length of your thumb
4. the length of a blackboard eraser
5. the width of your hand

Use a meterstick to measure larger items.

6. the circumference of your desk
7. the width of a blackboard
8. the length of the classroom
9. the length of a yardstick

Game: Write the subject pronouns and the infinitives of 5 or 6 verbs in two separate columns on the board. Divide class into two teams, and appoint a leader for each group. The leaders will take turns pointing to a subject pronoun and an infinitive. Students remaining at desks must match subject pronoun with correct verb form in present tense.

E Form questions, using the cues provided.

▪▥ warum / du / arbeiten / nicht / ?   *Warum arbeitest du nicht?*

1. dein Vater / arbeiten / abends / ?
2. du / tanzen / gern / ?
3. wie / deine Schwester / heißen / ?
4. wann / wir / gehen / nach Hause / ?
5. wann / Rita / arbeiten / ?

F Say in German that . . .

Remind students to use
mein in #1 and *ich* in
#2.

1. your friend likes to play tennis
2. in the evening, you play cards
3. that's fun
4. Peter's brother is home
5. he plays the piano well

Again, tell students that
there are three words
for "the" in German.
Have them learn the ap-
propriate definite article
as part of the vocabu-
lary (*das Jahr*, not
Jahr). However, post-
pone discussion of
"gender" until chapter 5.

Vokabeln

SUBSTANTIVE

der Apotheker/die Apothekerin pharmacist

der Arbeiter/die Arbeiterin worker

der Arzt/die Ärztin doctor, physician

der Brief letter

der Brieffreund/die Brieffreundin pen pal

der Bruder brother

das Deutsch German language

der Donnerstag Thursday

der Elektriker/die Elektrikerin electrician

die Familie family

(die) Frau Mrs.

(das) Fräulein Miss

der Freitag Friday

der Freund/die Freundin friend

der Friseur/die Friseuse hairdresser

der Geschäftsmann/die Geschäftsfrau
businessman/businesswoman

(der) Herr Mr.

das Hobby hobby

das Jahr year

SUBSTANTIVE

die Karten (*pl.*) (playing) cards

das Kind child

der Lehrer/die Lehrerin teacher

der Meter meter

der Montag Monday

die Musik music

die Mutter mother

der Name name

(der) Rock rock (music)

der Samstag Saturday

der Schüler/die Schülerin student

die Schwester sister

der Sonntag Sunday

der Vater father

der Verkäufer/die Verkäuferin salesperson

das Wochenende weekend

der Zentimeter centimeter

(Continued)

VERBEN

arbeiten   to work
finden   to find
hören   to hear
kochen   to cook
kommen   to come
lernen   to learn, to study
schreiben   to write
singen   to sing
tanzen   to dance

ANDERE WÖRTER

abends   evenings, in the evening
bald   soon
bis   till, until
dein   your *(sg.)*
doof   goofy, dumb, stupid
dünn   thin
euer   your *(pl.)*
groß   tall, big
hoffentlich   I hope, let's hope
ihr   her, their
klassisch   classical
klein   small, short, little
lieber/liebe   dear *(opening in letters)*
mein   my
musikalisch   musical
noch   still, yet
schlank   slender, slim
schön   nice
sein   his
spät   late; **zu spät**   too late, tardy
unser   our

BESONDERE AUSDRÜCKE

ich lerne schon zwei Jahre Deutsch   I've been studying German for two years
ich bin fünfzehn Jahre alt   I'm fifteen years old
sie ist aber noch ein Kind   she's still a child
wie groß bist du?   how tall are you?
treibst du Sport?   are you active in sports?
das macht Spaß!   that's fun!
herzliche Grüße   best wishes, kind regards, sincerely *(closing in letters)*
am Samstag   on Saturday

A **Wer bin ich?** Prepare a short autobiography. It may include information about your age, birthday, appearance, address, family members, parents' occupation, work habits, hobbies. The autobiographies are divided between two panels of five members each. First one team of panel members takes turns reading the information provided in the autobiographies, while the other team tries to identify the writer. The panels then switch roles. The team that guesses the most students wins. The quiz continues with new panels until all students have participated.

B **Deutsche Teenager.** Look at the pictures of the young people in the photographs on pages 1–7 and describe two or three of them in German as completely as you can (name, age, height, personality, hobbies, family); or, select several of the teen-agers you have met in the dialogues of chapters 1–4 and discuss them, based on the dialogue material. In either case, you may wish to invent some additional information.

C **Deutsche in der Welt.** Gather information on the German influence in the United States. Look through a telephone directory and list 25 names of people who might be of German origin. From a state map, see how many names of towns indicate they may have been settled by Germans. Collect magazine pictures that pertain to German-speaking people around the world. Report your findings.

D **Guten Tag!** With a partner, prepare a skit in which you introduce yourself to a teen-ager from a German-speaking country who is visiting your school and who speaks no English. You will probably want to say hello, introduce yourself, and tell about your interests and activities. Don't forget to ask your guest for information as well.

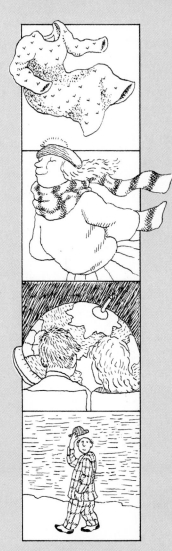

So leben wir

Arbeit . . . Traditional arts and crafts are still practiced in many parts of Germany — hand-woven baskets are for sale in Rothenburg, and violins are handmade in Mittenwald, for example — but modern, large-scale industry is also very much part of German life today. Hamburg's massive harbor helps tie Germany to the rest of the world.

. . . und Freizeit. Whether it's camping on Lake Constance, boating in a park in Cologne, playing chess in Bern, or going to an amusement park like this one in Munich, German-speaking people have a great variety of leisure-time activities.

Land und Stadt. Much European land has long been under cultivation, but in the cities, modern apartment complexes blend with older buildings while flowers add a touch of country color.

Kapitel 5

Brauchst du neue Sachen?

Das ist zu teuer

Astrid, Gisela, and Erik are window-shopping, looking at clothes.

ASTRID	Wie teuer ist das Kleid da?
GISELA	20 Mark, und das ist zu teuer.
ASTRID	Wie meinst du das?
GISELA	Ich finde, es ist häßlich.
ERIK	Die Jeans da sind wirklich klasse.
ASTRID	Meinst du? Wieviel kosten sie?
ERIK	50 Mark.
ASTRID	50 Mark! Das ist aber preiswert. Kaufst du sie?
ERIK	Ja.

May compare German *das Kleid da* ("the dress there") and *die Jeans da* ("the jeans there") to English equivalents "that dress" and "those jeans". Ask students to say "that" with articles of clothing on pp. 81–82.

Fragen

1. Ist das Kleid teuer?
2. Ist es schön?
3. Wie sind die Jeans?
4. Wieviel kosten sie? Ist das teuer?

Toll! Für Mädchen und Jungen!

1. das Hemd
   DM 19,–
2. die Jacke
   DM 68,–
3. die Hose
   DM 28,–
4. die Socken
   DM 5,–
5. die Bluse
   DM 25,–
6. der Gürtel
   DM 15,–
7. die Jeans
   DM 70,–

Schick! Für Damen und Herren!

1. der Pulli
   DM 47,—
2. der Rock
   DM 45,—
3. die Schuhe
   DM 65,—
4. der Anzug
   DM 150,—
5. die Krawatte
   DM 12,—
6. der Mantel
   DM 200,—
7. die Handschuhe
   DM 24,—

Fragen

1. Wieviel kostet das Hemd? die Jacke? der Rock?
2. Wieviel kosten die Jeans? die Schuhe? die Socken?

Du hast das Wort

Briefly discuss concept of grammatical gender so that students will better understand the following exercises.

A. What is your reaction to the price of each item of clothing mentioned below?

Das Hemd kostet DM 30,—.	Das ist furchtbar° teuer.
Die Krawatte kostet DM 7,—.	Das ist (sehr) teuer.
Der Mantel kostet DM 500,—.	Das ist preiswert.
Die Handschuhe kosten DM 4,—.	Das ist billig°.
Die Jacke kostet DM 99,—.	Das ist spottbillig°.
Die Bluse kostet DM 23,—.	
Das Kleid kostet DM 80,—.	
Der Gürtel kostet DM 15,—.	V: One student names an article of clothing and the price; another responds according to his or her concept of "expensiveness".
Die Hose kostet DM 30,—.	
Der Anzug kostet DM 350,—.	

B. A friend asks you to react to some of the clothes pictured on pages 81–82. How would you respond?

Wie ist	die Jacke?	Toll!
	der Rock?	Klasse!
	das Hemd?	(Sehr) schön.
		(Sehr) hübsch°.
		Nicht schlecht.
		Häßlich.
		Doof.

German fashion magazines are filled with terms that an American would recognize. Many German young people seem to be fascinated by things American or British, and as a result quite a bit of English has crept into the fashion language, especially in advertisements.

Sometimes English is used to describe various pieces of clothing, such as **T-Shirt, Blazer, Sweatshirt,** or **Jeans.** Jeans in particular seem to be under the influence of the American West, with labels such as **Pioneer, Bronco, Mustang,** or **Explorer.**

Styles or trends also often bear English names. A woman can buy **Make-up im College-Look** to go with her new **Overalls.** A man who doesn't go in for the leisurely **Sportswear-Look** can buy a **Cord-Anzug** or a **Tweed-Anzug.** A couple might want to buy coordinated outfits — they can be found in the catalogue under the heading **Er und sie im Partner-Look.** And to finish off their wardrobe, the fashion-conscious people can buy **Schuhe-Creationen mit viel Pep!**

Mal wie ein Pulli, mal wie ein Sweatshirt. So sind die neuen POLOS

Noch jemand ohne Overall?

Make-up macht einfach Spaß!

KONFEKTIONSGRÖSSEN: EUROPA/USA												
Kleidung für Damen							**Kleidung für Herren**					
Blusen, Röcke, Kleider, Mäntel, Hosen							*Anzüge, Jacken, Mäntel, Hosen*					
Europa	32	34	36	38	40	42	Europa	40	42	44	46	48	50
USA	4	6	8	10	12	14	USA	30	32	34	36	38	40
Pullis							*Hemden*					
Europa	38	40	42	44	46	48	Europa	35	36	37	38	39	40
USA	30	32	34	36	38	40	USA	13½	14	14½	15	15½	16
Schuhe							*Schuhe*					
Europa	36	37	38	39	40	41	Europa	38	39	40	41	42	43
USA	5	6	7	8	9	10	USA	5	6½	7½	8½	9	10

Fragen:
Wie ist der Mantel?
schön? warm? schön
warm?
Warum paßt er nicht?
Welche Größe trägt
Erik?

Welche Größe trägst du?

Astrid is helping Erik look for a new coat.

ASTRID — Hier ist ein Mantel in Braun. Schön, nicht?

ERIK — Ja, toll. Er ist auch schön warm.

ASTRID — Paßt er?

ERIK — Leider nicht. Er ist zu groß.

ASTRID — Welche Größe trägst du denn?

ERIK — Größe 40.

ASTRID — Hier ist deine Größe.

ERIK — Das ist aber kein Mantel. Das ist eine Jacke.

ASTRID — Ach ja. Schade.

Activity: Each student makes up a funny picture by cutting out from magazines various articles of clothing, which are put on a model the student makes. Display pictures in room.
(1) Use pictures to cue articles of clothing in drill.
(2) Have students tell what size their "figure" is wearing. It will be helpful if the teacher makes up a list of clothing items with current prices.

Du hast das Wort

A. Name an article of clothing you'd like to buy for a friend or relative. Give the size you need according to the chart.

Jacke — Er/sie trägt Größe . . .

B. Take the role of a salesperson trying to help a customer in a clothing store.

Paßt [der Mantel]? — Ja.
Ja, [er] paßt sehr gut.
Nein, [er] ist zu groß.
Nein, [er] ist zu klein°.
Nein, ich brauche Größe [40].

Remind students to change pronouns when necessary.

Wortschatzerweiterung

Die Farben

Other colors: *rosa, orange, lila, goldfarbig, beige.* May also introduce prefixes *hell-* and *dunkel-* for variations with "light" and "dark".

Point out that *Welche Farbe hat . . .* is a fixed expression for asking "What color is . . ." The verb *sein* is used in the response.

To reinforce colors, point to articles of clothing worn by students. Write them on the board: *Karins Jeans sind blau. Stefans Pullover ist braun.*, etc.

Can you guess these colors? The cognates in the following sentences should help you.

blau	Die See ist blau.
braun	Die Schokolade ist braun.
gelb	Die Banane ist gelb.
grau	Die Maus ist grau.
grün	Das Gras ist grün.
rot	Die Tomate ist rot.
schwarz	Die Kohle ist schwarz.
weiß	Das Papier ist weiß.

Game: *Ich sehe etwas.* Student thinks of an article of clothing worn by a classmate and says: *Ich sehe etwas. Es ist blau.* Others try to guess: *Ist es Gabis Pulli?* The student who guesses correctly chooses the next article of clothing and color.

A

May begin Ex. A by asking *Welche Farbe hat mein [Pulli]?* The student may respond with only the color. When questioning each other, students should expand to a complete sentence.

Explain that *Hose* is often used in the singular *(eine Hose = ein Paar Hosen).* Originally pants consisted of two leg parts held together around the waist, hence the plural.

Ask a classmate about the color of the clothes he/she is wearing.

■◁ Welche Farbe hat | dein Pulli?   *Mein Pulli ist [rot].*
                    | dein Hemd?
                    | dein Gürtel?
                    | dein Kleid?
                    | deine Jacke?
                    | deine Bluse?
                    | deine Hose?

Aussprache

long vowel [u]	gut, Bluse, Schuh
short vowel [U]	und, Pulli

A Practice vertically in columns and horizontally in pairs.

Pronunciation hint: For [u], tell students to say *oo* as in *moon*, but with exaggeratedly rounded lips and no glide.

[u]	[U]
Buße	Busse
Buch	Bucht
Huhne	Hunne
Buhle	Bulle
Mus	muß

After the two sounds have been practiced, say each word individually, letting students identify long and short vowels by saying *lang* or *kurz*. May play as two teams.

B Practice the following words horizontally in pairs.

[u]	[y]	[U]	[Y]
Fuße	Füße	mußte	müßte
Hute	Hüte	Busche	Büsche
Zuge	Züge	junger	jünger
Fuhre	führe	krummen	krümmen
gute	Güte	dunkel	Dünkel

C Practice the sounds [u] and [U]. Read the sentences aloud.

Ask students to identify the long and short *u*'s in each sentence.

Additional sentences:
In Ulm, um Ulm, um Ulm herum.
Morgenstund' hat Gold im Mund.

1. Wieviel kosten die Bluse und der Pulli?
2. Warum trägt Utes Bruder keine Schuhe?
3. Der Junge spielt gut Fußball.

Ende gut, alles gut.

Proverb: All's well that ends well.

Photo: Shoppers on the Kurfürstendamm in Berlin.

———————— Übungen ————————

Verbs with stem-vowel change a>ä

tragen
ich trage
du **trägst**
er/sie **trägt**

Drill: Students tell what shoe size the people wear.
Fritz / 40   (Fritz trägt Größe 40.)

Tragen has a stem-vowel change a>ä in the **du-** and **er/sie-**forms of the present tense.

A Find out what your friends are wearing to the party tonight.

■III Paula   *Was trägt Paula heute abend?*

1. Rita
2. Günter
3. Stefan
4. du
5. Birgit und Ute
6. ihr

The singular definite articles **der, das, die**

der Mann	**das** Mädchen	**die** Frau
der Gürtel	**das** Kleid	**die** Bluse

The definite articles **der, das,** and **die** are used with nouns, and are equivalent to the English definite article *the.*

B Inquire about the price of each article of clothing.

■||| der Pulli *Wieviel kostet der Pulli?*

1. die Jacke 3. die Bluse 5. die Krawatte
2. das Hemd 4. der Anzug 6. der Gürtel

C Give your opinion of each of the following articles of clothing.

■||| *Der Pulli ist klasse* [*häßlich, schön, etc.*]

Other adjectives: *toll, teuer, spott-billig, preiswert, hübsch, schick,* etc.

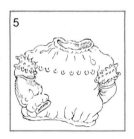

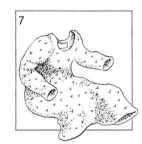

D You don't recognize a number of people at a school event. Ask a friend to identify them.

■||| die Frau da *Wie heißt die Frau da?*

1. die Lehrerin da
2. der Lehrer da
3. das Mädchen da
4. der Junge da
5. der Mann da
6. das Kind da

Noun plurals

Ein is used passively here. For now, use the number one as the English equivalent.

SINGULAR	PLURAL
ein Mantel	zwei **Mäntel**
ein Rock	zwei **Röcke**
ein Kleid	zwei **Kleider**
ein Hemd	zwei **Hemden**

Before introducing noun plurals in German, have students think of as many different types of plural endings as they can in English. Compare "book, books" [s]; "tree, trees" [z]; "box, boxes"; "man, men"; "mouse, mice"; sheep, sheep"; etc.

There is no simple way of predicting the plural form of a noun. German noun plurals are formed according to several basic patterns. The patterns are listed in the **Grammatische Übersicht** on pages 95–96.

E You and a friend are applying basic multiplication patterns to practical situations. Tell what the following purchases would cost.

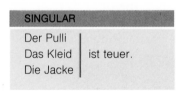 Ein Kleid kostet 200 Mark. *Zwei Kleider kosten 400* Was kosten zwei Kleider? *Mark.*

1. Ein Mantel kostet 300 Mark. Was kosten zwei Mäntel?
2. Ein Gürtel kostet 20 Mark. Was kosten vier Gürtel?
3. Ein Hemd kostet 30 Mark. Was kosten drei Hemden?
4. Eine Jacke kostet 100 Mark. Was kosten zwei Jacken?
5. Eine Krawatte kostet 15 Mark. Was kosten drei Krawatten?
6. Ein Anzug kostet 250 Mark. Was kosten zwei Anzüge?

The plural definite article **die**

SINGULAR		PLURAL	
Der Pulli		**Die** Pullis	
Das Kleid	ist teuer.	**Die** Kleider	sind teuer.
Die Jacke		**Die** Jacken	

The definite article **die** is used with plural nouns.

F You're shopping in a department store with Mark. Tell him what you think about the following items.

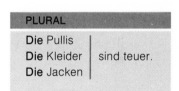 Schuhe / klasse *Die Schuhe sind klasse.*

1. Jeans / preiswert
2. Socken / schön warm
3. Hemden / häßlich
4. Pullis / toll
5. Gürtel / spottbillig

Refer to pages 81 and 82 for additional appropriate adjectives. See whether students can think of others from preceding chapters.

Noun-pronoun relationship

Additional practice: Give students a variety of nouns, referring to both people and things; use pictures if desired. See how fast students can supply the correct pronoun: *die Jacke — sie; die Frau — sie; das Hemd — es; etc.*

Singular

Der Junge ist toll. **Der Gürtel** ist toll.	**Er** ist toll.
Das Kind ist hübsch. **Das Kleid** ist hübsch.	**Es** ist hübsch.
Die Frau ist schick. **Die Jacke** ist schick.	**Sie** ist schick.

G Confirm Ute's guesses about the following articles of clothing.

V¹: Choice drill: *Ist der Pulli teuer oder billig? alt oder neu? groß oder klein? schön oder häßlich?*

■ıı   Ist der Pulli teuer?   *Ja, er ist sehr teuer.*

1. Ist der Anzug billig?
2. Ist der Rock hübsch?
3. Ist der Mantel schick?
4. Ist der Gürtel preiswert?

V²: Point to picture and ask question: *Wie ist der Pulli?* Student responds as he/she wishes: *Er ist schön, teuer*, etc.

H Say that the following people are good at certain sports.

V: Choice drill: *Spielt dein Bruder Fußball oder Tennis?*

■ıı   Spielt dein Bruder Fußball?   *Ja, und er spielt auch gut.*

1. Spielt dein Vater Tennis?
2. Spielt dein Freund Dieter Basketball?
3. Spielt dein Lehrer Volleyball?
4. Spielt Erik Fußball?

I Tell Frank that each item is the opposite of what he thinks.

V: Choice drill: *Ist die Bluse schick oder häßlich?*

■ıı   Ist das Hemd alt?   *Nein, es ist neu.*

1. Ist das Kleid billig?
2. Ist das Hemd schön?
3. Ist das Klavier gut?
4. Ist das Schlagzeug neu?

J Erna tells you which instruments various friends and relatives play. Ask whether they play well.

■ıı   Meine Lehrerin spielt Klavier.   *Spielt sie gut?*

1. Meine Mutter spielt Geige.
2. Meine Freundin Birgit spielt Flöte.
3. Meine Schwester spielt Klarinette.
4. Ilse spielt Gitarre.

V: Have students agree
with a friend that
various articles of
clothing are great.

K   Agree with Manfred about the following articles of clothing.

> ◼ⅲ   Die Bluse da ist schick, nicht?   *Ja, sie ist wirklich schick.*

1. Die Jacke da ist teuer, nicht?
2. Die Hose da ist spottbillig, nicht?
3. Die Krawatte da ist häßlich, nicht?
4. Die Hose da ist preiswert, nicht?

Plural

Die Jeans sind klasse.   **Sie** sind wirklich toll.
Die Hemden sind klasse.   Und **sie** sind billig.

L   You are at a flea market with Katrin. Say that you agree more or less with her opinions.

> ◼ⅲ   Die Schuhe da sind teuer, nicht?   *Ja, sie sind ziemlich teuer.*

1. Die Handschuhe da sind preiswert, nicht?
2. Die Jeans da sind billig, nicht?
3. Die Hemden da sind gut, nicht?
4. Die Jacken da sind alt, nicht?

M   Thomas is pointing out various items in a clothing catalogue. Ask him whether they're reasonably priced.

This is a test drill.

> ◼ⅲ   Der Mantel ist schön.   *Ist er preiswert?*
>
> ◼ⅲ   Die Socken sind warm.   *Sind sie preiswert?*

1. Der Rock ist schick.
2. Das Kleid ist klasse.
3. Die Bluse ist hübsch.
4. Das Hemd ist toll.
5. Der Gürtel ist schön.
6. Die Schuhe sind schick.
7. Die Jeans sind klasse.
8. Die Handschuhe sind warm.

Nominative case of **ein**

Help students discover that *ein* is used before *der-* and *das*-nouns in the nominative, *eine* before *die*-nouns in the nominative.

Der Anzug kostet 900 Mark.

Das Hemd kostet 100 Mark.

Die Jacke kostet 300 Mark.

Die Schuhe kosten 250 Mark.

Ein Anzug kostet wirklich 900 Mark?

Ein Hemd kostet wirklich 100 Mark?

Eine Jacke kostet wirklich 300 Mark?

Schuhe kosten wirklich 250 Mark?

The indefinite articles **ein** and **eine** are equivalent to English *a* or *an*. **Ein** and **eine** have no plural form.

N   You're trying to find out how much clothing costs in Germany. Ask your teacher about the price of the following things.

V: Have students answer the questions.

   ■‖   Anzug   *Wieviel kostet ein Anzug?*

1. Pulli	4. Hemd	7. Krawatte
2. Bluse	5. Jacke	8. Gürtel
3. Kleid	6. Rock	9. Hose

O   Some acquaintances brag about how much their clothes cost. You find the prices ridiculous. Say that the things *can't* be that expensive.

   ■‖   Meine Jacke kostet DM 200.   *Unsinn! Eine Jacke kostet nicht soviel!*

1. Meine Hose kostet DM 500.
2. Mein Hemd kostet DM 300.
3. Mein Mantel kostet DM 900.
4. Petras Bluse kostet DM 200.
5. Ellens Kleid kostet DM 800.
6. Hugos Jacke kostet DM 600.

Nominative case of **kein**

Comprehension check: Point to a student's article of clothing and ask whether it is something else.

The relationship between *ein* and *kein* can be made graphic by writing *ein* on the board, then adding a *k* at the beginning of *ein*.

Ist das **ein Pulli?** Nein, das ist **kein Pulli,** das ist ein Hemd.
Ist das **ein Hemd?** Nein, das ist **kein Hemd,** das ist ein Pulli.
Ist das **eine Bluse?** Nein, das ist **keine Bluse,** das ist eine Jacke.
Sind das **Blusen?** Nein, das sind **keine Blusen,** das sind Hemden.

Kein and **keine** are equivalent to English *not a, not an, not any,* or *no.* **Kein** is used before **der-** and **das-**nouns. **Keine** is used before **die-**nouns and plural nouns.

P Andreas is guessing the price of clothes in a catalogue. Disagree with his guesses.

Help students discover the similarity of *ein* and *eine* with the possessive adjectives. Have students make up prices and address classmates:
S¹: *Kostet dein Hemd 40 Dollar?*
S²: *Nein, es kostet nicht soviel.*

▪▮ Was kostet der Mantel? *Nein, kein Mantel kostet*
    2000 Mark? *2000 Mark.*

1. Was kostet der Pulli? 400 Mark?
2. Was kostet die Jacke? 500 Mark?
3. Was kostet das Hemd? 100 Mark?
4. Was kostet die Bluse? 150 Mark?
5. Was kostet die Krawatte? 50 Mark?
6. Was kosten die Handschuhe? 70 Mark?
7. Was kosten die Socken? 40 Mark?
8. Was kosten die Jeans? 120 Mark?

—————— Grammatische Übersicht ——————

Verbs with stem-vowel change **a** > **ä** (A)

tragen	
ich trage	wir tragen
du **trägst**	ihr tragt
er/es/sie **trägt**	sie tragen

A number of German verbs have a stem-vowel change (for example **a** > **ä**) in the **du-** and **er/sie-**forms of the present tense. In the vocabularies of this text, the stem-vowel change of the **du-** and **er/sie-**forms is shown in parentheses directly after the infinitive: **tragen (ä).**

Nominative case

Meine Schwester spielt Klavier.
Spielt **dein Freund** Klarinette?

German nouns show different cases depending on how they are used in a sentence. When a noun is used as the subject of a sentence, it is in the nominative case.

SUBJECT		PREDICATE NOMINATIVE
Das Mädchen	ist	meine Schwester.
Der Junge da	ist	der Bruder von Inge.

When a noun is used in the predicate after the verb **sein,** it is also in the nominative case.

The singular definite articles **der, das, die**   (B-D)

der Mann   **das** Mädchen   **die** Frau
der Gürtel   **das** Kleid   **die** Bluse

The singular definite articles **der, das,** and **die** function like the English definite article *the.* They are used with singular nouns in the nominative case.

There are three groups of nouns in German: **der**-nouns, **das**-nouns, and **die**-nouns. Most nouns referring to males are **der**-nouns; most nouns referring to females are **die**-nouns. (**Das Mädchen** is an exception.) Objects may belong to any group, for example **der Gürtel, das Kleid, die Bluse.** Since there is no simple way of predicting which group a noun belongs to, it is very important to learn the definite article when you learn the noun. Learn **der Gürtel,** not just **Gürtel.**

The plural definite article **die**   (F)

SINGULAR		PLURAL	
Der Rock		Die Röcke	
Das Hemd	ist klasse.	Die Hemden	sind klasse.
Die Bluse		Die Blusen	

The definite article used with plural nouns is **die.**

Noun plurals (E)

In German, noun plurals are formed according to five basic patterns. There is no simple way of predicting the plural form of a noun. You will, however, gradually discover that there is a kind of system to these patterns.

This "system" depends partly on whether the noun is a **der-, das-** or **die-**noun, and partly on how many syllables it has. From now on, learn the plural of the noun when you learn the singular form.

Pattern 1

no change in plural

das Mädchen	**die Mädchen**
der Gürtel	**die Gürtel**

plural adds umlaut

der Vater	**die Väter**
der Mantel	**die Mäntel**

Pattern 2

plural adds **-e**

der Freund	**die Freunde**
der Schuh	**die Schuhe**

plural adds **-e** *and umlaut*

der Anzug	**die Anzüge**
der Rock	**die Röcke**

Pattern 3

plural adds **-er**

das Kind	**die Kinder**
das Kleid	**die Kleider**

plural adds **-er** *and umlaut*

der Mann	**die Männer**
das Buch	**die Bücher**

Pattern 4

plural adds **-n**

der Junge	**die Jungen**
die Schwester	**die Schwestern**

plural adds **-en**

das Hemd	**die Hemden**

plural adds **-nen**

die Lehrerin	**die Lehrerinnen**
die Ärztin	**die Ärztinnen**

Pattern 5

plural adds **-s**

das Hobby	**die Hobbys**
der Pulli	**die Pullis**

In the vocabularies of this text, the plural of most nouns will be indicated directly after the singular. For example:

der Lehrer, -   indicates that there is no change in the plural form of the noun: **der Lehrer >die Lehrer.**

der Rock, ⸚e   indicates that an **-e** is added in the plural, and an umlaut is added to the appropriate vowel: **der Rock > die Röcke.**

Here are the plurals of some other familiar nouns.

der Apotheker,–	die Friseuse, –n
die Apothekerin, –nen	der Geschäftsmann, ⸚er
der Arbeiter, –	die Geschäftsfrau, –en
die Arbeiterin, –nen	das Jahr, –e
der Arzt, ⸚e	die Minute, –n
der Brief, –e	die Mutter, ⸚
der Bruder, ⸚	der Schüler, –
der Elektriker, –	die Schülerin, –nen
die Elektrikerin, –nen	die Straße, –n
die Familie, –n	der Tag, –e
die Freundin, –nen	der Verkäufer, –
der Friseur, –e	die Verkäuferin, –nen

Noun-pronoun relationship (G-M)

SINGULAR	
Der Mann ist alt. **Der Anzug** ist alt.	**Er** ist alt.
Das Kind ist schön. **Das Hemd** ist schön.	**Es** ist schön.
Die Frau ist hübsch. **Die Jacke** ist hübsch.	**Sie** ist hübsch.

PLURAL	
Die Männer sind schick. **Die Jeans** sind schick.	**Sie** sind schick.

The pronouns **er, es, sie** *(sg.)* and **sie** *(pl.)* may refer to either persons or things.

In the singular, **er** replaces **der-**nouns.

es replaces **das-**nouns.

sie replaces **die-**nouns.

In the plural, **sie** replaces all nouns.

Nominative case of **ein** and **kein** (N-P)

Das ist **ein** Hemd.   That's *a* shirt.
Das ist **kein** Pulli.   That's *not a* sweater.
Das ist **keine** Jacke.   That's *not a* jacket.

The indefinite articles **ein** and **eine** are equivalent to English *a* or *an*. The negative forms **kein** and **keine** are equivalent to English *not a (not an), not any,* or *no.*

SINGULAR	
der Pulli	Das ist **ein** Pulli. **kein**
das Hemd	Das ist **ein** Hemd. **kein**
die Bluse	Das ist **eine** Bluse. **keine**

Ein and **kein** are used before **der-** and **das-**nouns in the nominative case. **Eine** and **keine** are used before **die-**nouns in the nominative case.

PLURAL	
die Jeans	Das sind Jeans. Das sind **keine** Jeans.

Ein and **eine** have no plural form.
Keine is used before plural nouns in the nominative case.

Kein and **nicht**

Ist das **ein Hemd?**   Nein, das ist **kein Hemd.**
Trägst du **Jeans?**   Nein, ich trage **keine Jeans.**

Ist das **die Jacke?**   Nein, das ist **nicht die Jacke.**
Ist das **dein Hemd?**   Nein, das ist **nicht mein Hemd.**

Kein is used to negate a noun that would be preceded by **ein** or by no article at all in an affirmative sentence. **Nicht** is used in a negative sentence when the noun is preceded by a definite article or a possessive adjective.

Wiederholung

A Jan and Paul are talking about the forthcoming party on Saturday. Answer the questions, based on the dialogue.

> JAN   Trägst du am Samstag eine Jacke?
> PAUL Nein, ich trage keine Jacke. Ich trage nur ein Hemd.
> JAN   Warum?
> PAUL Ich trage nicht gern Jacken. Und eine Jacke ist auch zu warm.

1. Was trägt Paul am Samstag?
2. Warum trägt er keine Jacke?

B Form sentences, using the cues provided.

1. Petra / treiben / gern / Sport
2. tanzen / du / viel / ?
3. was / tragen / Paula / am Samstag / ?
4. ich / tragen / oft / Jeans
5. wie / heißen / der Junge da / ?

C You are in a negative mood, so you find fault with everything Susanne says. Use *er, es,* or *sie* in your answers, as appropriate.

> ▪▥   Das Hemd ist schick,   *Nein, ich finde, es ist häßlich.*
> nicht?   *Unsinn! Die Farbe ist furchtbar.*
>   *Ja, aber es ist furchtbar teuer.*

1. Die Bluse ist toll, nicht?
2. Claudias Kleid ist schön, nicht?
3. Ihr Rock ist hübsch, nicht?
4. Volkers Schuhe sind klasse, nicht?
5. Sein Pulli ist prima, nicht?

A sweater put on over the head can be called either a **Pullover** or a **Pulli**. Generally **der Pullover** is used for a heavier sweater with long sleeves. **Pulli** is the shortened form of **Pullover,** but is used mostly for lighter sweaters, often short-sleeved or even sleeveless.

D   Make up at least two sentences about the objects in each picture.

Hier sind zwei Hemden.
Sie sind preiswert.
Sie sind ziemlich neu.

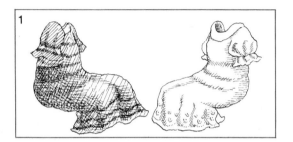

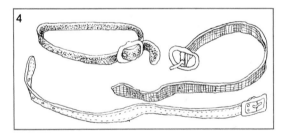

E   Complete each sentence with an appropriate antonym.

1. Die Jeans sind nicht zu teuer; sie sind _____ .
2. Der Rock ist nicht häßlich; er ist sehr _____.
3. Der Pulli ist nicht zu groß; er ist zu _____.
4. Die Jacken da sind nicht alt; sie sind _____.
5. Die Schuhe sind nicht gut; sie sind sehr _____.
6. Das Kleid ist nicht billig; es ist furchtbar _____.

F   Express the following in German.

1. Is Jörg going home?
2. He's going to play basketball this afternoon.
3. Does he play well?
4. Will you play tennis this afternoon?
5. When are we going to go swimming?
6. Why are they going?

G   Column A consists of questions or comments about clothing. Choose an appropriate response to each one from column B.

A	B
Ist der Rock teuer?	Schade.
Die Mäntel da sind wirklich klasse.	DM 12,45.
Wieviel kostet die Krawatte da?	Nein, er ist ziemlich billig.
Das Hemd hier kostet nur DM 5,–.	Meinst du?
Wie findest du die Jacke?	Das ist ja spottbillig!
Die Jeans passen leider nicht.	Wirklich klasse.

H   Express the following two-line conversational exchanges in German.

1. What's the name of that girl (over there)?
   Her name is [. . .].
2. What color is her dress?
   It's [. . .].
3. How expensive is the sweater?
   It's a very good buy.
4. How much do the shoes cost?
   They cost [. . .].
5. What size does your friend wear?
   Size [. . .].

German stores are permitted by law to have a clearance sale **(Ausverkauf)** twice a year: a winter sale **(Winterschlußverkauf)** at the end of January and a summer sale **(Sommerschlußverkauf)** at the end of July. In addition, there may be special offers **(Sonderangebote)** periodically.

Kulturlesestück

Geld°

money

Das ist eine Mark.
Eine Mark hat hundert Pfennig.

Das sind zehn Mark (DM 10,—).
Das ist ein Zehnmarkschein°.

10–Mark bill

Das sind auch zehn Mark (DM 10,—).
Das sind aber zwei Fünfmarkstücke°.

5–Mark pieces
(coins)

get

Was bekommt° man für zehn Mark?
Zum Beispiel°:

Zwei Tassen° Kaffee	DM 3,60
Zwei Stück Torte	DM 5,60
	DM 9,20

zum Beispiel: for
  example
cups

Kaffee ist teuer in Deutschland. Torte auch.

A   Say how long the following people have to work in order to earn enough money for the items they want.

1. Ingrid verdient *(earns)* zehn Mark die Stunde *(an hour).* Sie kauft neue Schuhe zu *(for)* DM 40,—. Wieviel Stunden arbeitet sie für die Schuhe?
2. Jan verdient sechs Mark die Stunde. Er kauft ein Polohemd zu DM 12,—. Wieviel Stunden arbeitet er für das Polohemd?
3. Peter verdient neun Mark die Stunde. Er kauft eine Gitarre zu DM 270,—. Wieviel Stunden arbeitet er für die Gitarre?

While German-speaking countries are similar in many ways, they do not share a common monetary system. The **BRD's** basic unit is the **Mark.** The **DDR** also uses a **Mark,** although its value is somewhat different from that of the Federal Republic's.

Switzerland's basic unit is the **Franken,** roughly equal in value to the **Mark** of the Federal Republic. There are 100 **Rappen** in a **Franken.**

Austria's basic unit is the **Schilling.** The **Schilling** is a much smaller unit than the **Mark:** a piece of cake would cost about twenty **Schilling.** There are 100 **Groschen** in a **Schilling.**

Vokabeln

SUBSTANTIVE

der Anzug, ̈e   man's suit
die Bluse, -n   blouse
die Dame, -n   lady, woman
die Farbe, -n   color
die Frau, -en   woman
die Größe, -n   size
der Gürtel, -   belt
der Handschuh, -e   glove
das Hemd, -en   shirt
der Herr, -en   gentleman
die Hose, -n   pants, slacks
die Jacke, -n   suit coat, jacket
die Jeans *(pl.)*   jeans
der Junge, -n   boy

SUBSTANTIVE

das Kleid, -er   dress
die Krawatte, -n   tie
das Mädchen, -   girl
der Mann, ̈er   man
der Mantel, ̈   coat
die Mark   German coin **(DM = Deutsche Mark = 100 Pfennig)**
der Pulli, -s   pullover
der Rock, ̈e   skirt
die Sache, -n   thing; **Sachen**   clothes
der Schuh, -e   shoe
die Socke, -n   sock

(Continued)

VERBEN

brauchen   to need
kaufen   to buy
kosten   to cost
meinen   to think; to mean
passen   to fit; to match
tragen (ä)   to wear

ANDERE WÖRTER

billig   inexpensive, cheap
blau   blue
braun   brown
da   here, there
das   that, the
für   for
furchtbar   terribly
gelb   yellow
grau   gray
grün   green
häßlich   ugly
hübsch   pretty, nice
kein   not a, not any

ANDERE WÖRTER

klasse   terrific
leider   unfortunately
neu   new
preiswert   worth the money, reasonably priced
rot   red
schick   chic, stylish
schön   beautiful
schwarz   black
spottbillig   dirt-cheap
teuer   expensive
warm   warm
weiß   white
welcher   which, what

BESONDERE AUSDRÜCKE

wieviel kostet der Pulli?   how much is the sweater?
welche Farbe hat dein Pulli?   what color is your sweater?
ein Mantel in Braun   a coat in brown
schade   too bad

Kapitel 6

Der Schultag

Ingrids Stundenplan

Ingrid Wagner					Klasse 10	
Zeit	Montag	Dienstag	Mittwoch	Donnerstag	Freitag	Samstag
8.00 – 8.45	Sport	Physik	—	Deutsch	—	—
8.50 – 9.35	Sport	Mathe	Chemie	Erdkunde	Geschichte	Physik
9.35 – 9.55	1. große Pause					
9.55 – 10.40	Englisch	Englisch	Latein	Chemie	Mathe	Deutsch
10.45 – 11.30	Geschichte	Latein	Deutsch	Geschichte	Mathe	—
11.30 – 11.50	2. große Pause					
11.50 – 12.35	Mathe	Erdkunde	Englisch	Kunst	Latein	—
12.45 – 13.30	Biologie	Musik	Biologie	Kunst	Deutsch	—

Use visuals or a clock face with movable hands to cue times. A comparison to monetary numbers from Chapter 5 (*acht Mark vierzig, neun Mark dreißig*) may be helpful.

Fragen

Point out the use of the 24-hour clock; see p. 118

1. Was hat Ingrid Montag um acht Uhr? Dienstag um 9.45 Uhr (neun Uhr fünfundvierzig)? Donnerstag um 11.50 Uhr (elf Uhr fünfzig)?
2. Was hat Ingrid am Samstag?

Du hast das Wort

Other school subjects (but not necessarily studied in a German school): *Sozialkunde*, "social studies"; *Zeichnen*, "drawing"; *Hauswirtschaft*, "home economics"; *Französisch*, "French".

A. A classmate asks you which subjects you have today. How would you respond?

Welche Fächer° hast du heute?

Heute habe ich [Bio, Chemie und Deutsch].

B. Ask a classmate which subjects he/she has this year.

Welche Fächer hast du dieses° Jahr?

[Deutsch, Mathe, Bio, Englisch und Geschichte.]

Activity: Have students make up their own schedules with German names of subjects.

Im Klassenzimmer

Personalize, varying at will, and perform skit.

Gisela and Dieter are waiting for class to begin.

GISELA   Was haben wir um neun? Chemie?
DIETER   Nein, heute haben wir keine Chemie. Wir haben Mathe.
GISELA   Oh, prima!
DIETER   Mathe und „prima"?
GISELA   Ja, ich finde Mathe interessant. Mathe ist mein Lieblingsfach.

Fragen

1. Was hat Gisela um neun Uhr?
2. Was ist Giselas Lieblingsfach?
3. Findet Dieter Mathe interessant?

Du hast das Wort

V: Students ask classmates what they think of their subjects:
S¹: *Wie findest du [Mathe]?*
S²: *interessant, langweilig, klasse, toll, schlecht,* etc.

A. Ask a classmate which subjects he/she likes and why.

Was ist dein Lieblingsfach?   [Englisch].

Warum?   Ich finde [Englisch] | toll.
                                      interessant.
                                      prima.
                                      leicht°.

B. Ask a classmate which subject he/she does not like and why.

Welches Fach hast du nicht gern?   [Bio].

Warum?   Es ist | langweilig°.
                 zu schwer°.

Most German students go to school from 8 A.M. to around 1 P.M. six days a week, although some now have school on Saturday only twice a month. Since classes do not meet every day, students often take ten or more subjects in one term. There are several recess periods during the day: one or two twenty-minute **große Pausen,** and often a ten-minute **kleine Pause** as well. These breaks usually occur after two class periods have been completed. During the breaks the students go outside (weather permitting) to relax and have a snack.

In the traditional German school system, the child, at age 10, enters an educational path which determines to a great extent the careers open to her/him. The *Gymnasium* (classes 5–13) leads to academic study at the *Universität.* The *Realschule* (classes 5–10) leads to *Fachschule* and then to *Fachhochschule.* The *Hauptschule* (classes 5–10) leads to *Berufsschule.* The recently formed *Gesamtschule* keeps children together longer, enabling them to switch tracks with greater ease. Many people disagree about this reform, however, and *Gesamtschulen* have yet to replace the traditional system.

In der Pause

Role-play dialogue.
Vary as students wish.

Karin and Norbert are in the school yard, discussing homework. Norbert is unhappy about the news he hears.

KARIN	Hast du deine Hausaufgaben schon fertig?
NORBERT	Welche? Die Matheaufgaben?
KARIN	Nein, die Chemieaufgaben.
NORBERT	Die mache ich heute abend. Was machst du heute nachmittag?
KARIN	Ich mache Bio.
NORBERT	Mensch! Bioaufgaben haben wir auch?
KARIN	Klar!

Fragen

1. Wann macht Norbert Chemie?
2. Was macht Karin am Nachmittag°?
3. Haben Norbert und Karin auch Bioaufgaben?

Du hast das Wort

Ask a classmate when he/she intends to do homework.

In most German schools, teachers rather than students move from one classroom to another. Students stay together as one class and remain in their homeroom for most subjects. Science and music are exceptions, however, and have special classrooms.

Wann machst du deine	Matheaufgaben?	Heute nachmittag.
	Bioaufgaben?	Heute abend.
	Deutschaufgaben?	Jetzt.
		Später.
		Morgen.

Wieviel Uhr ist es?

Dieter is always late for class. Sabine doesn't seem to find that a serious problem.

DIETER	Wie spät ist es?
SABINE	Es ist fünf nach zehn.
DIETER	Mensch! Ich komme wieder zu spät.
SABINE	Ist ja nicht so schlimm. Du bist ja gut in Chemie.

Introduce *ja* as a flavoring particle; see *Wortschatzerweiterung*.

Fragen

1. Ist es schon zehn Uhr?
2. Wie spät ist es?
3. Welches Fach hat Dieter jetzt?
4. Wer ist gut in Chemie?

The flavoring word **ja**

DIETER   Mensch! Ich komme   Oh no! I'm going to be late again!
              wieder zu spät!

SABINE   Ist **ja** nicht so schlimm.   That's not so bad.
              Du bist **ja** gut in Chemie.   You're good in chemistry (after all).

In Sabine's statements, the implication is that she and Dieter both know that Dieter is good in chemistry, so there's no need to worry. As a flavoring word, **ja** is often used to point out that both the speaker and the listener are aware of the circumstances to which the utterance refers. **Ja** also often has a reassuring tone.

A   Restate the sentences, inserting the flavoring word *ja* where indicated. Then give the English equivalents.

◼❙❙❙   Was? Der Mantel kostet nur   *Das ist ja spottbillig!*
          50 Mark?

1. Natürlich hat sie Mathe gern. Mathe ist ＿＿＿ ihr Lieblingsfach.
2. Jan geht jetzt schwimmen. Er hat seine Hausaufgaben ＿＿＿ fertig.
3. Diese Schuhe kaufe ich nicht. Sie sind ＿＿＿ viel zu klein!
4. Du gehst auch Tennis spielen? Das ist ＿＿＿ toll!
5. Meine Mutter spielt gut Tennis. Sie spielt ＿＿＿ auch viel.

Schulsachen

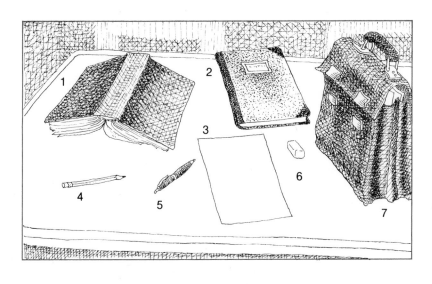

1. das Buch
2. das Heft
3. das Papier
4. der Bleistift
5. der Kugelschreiber
   (der Kuli)
6. der Radiergummi
7. die Mappe

Game: Add an object.
T: *Was packst du in deine Schulmappe?*
S¹: *Ich packe mein Buch in die Mappe.*
S²: *Ich packe mein Buch und mein Papier in die Mappe.*
etc.

Adjectives

Review adjectives from Chapter 1: *müde, glücklich, gesund, unglücklich, krank, fleißig, sauer, faul, zufrieden.*

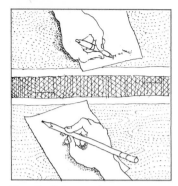

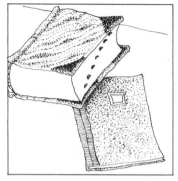

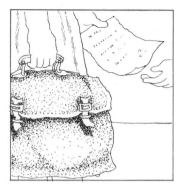

Der Kuli ist **kurz.**
Der Bleistift ist **lang.**

Das Buch ist **dick.**
Das Heft ist **dünn.**

Die Mappe ist **schwer.**
Das Papier ist **leicht.**

B Think of an object in the classroom. Have your classmates ask questions until they guess which object you've picked.

Remind students that schwer *and* leicht *also mean "hard" and "easy."*

Ist es lang?	Ja.	Ist es dünn?	Ja.
Ist es alt?	Nein.	Ist es blau?	Ja.
Ist es teuer?	Ja.	Ist es ein Kuli?	Ja.

Das Alphabet

The German alphabet has 26 regular letters and 4 special letters.

a	ah	f	eff	k	kah	p	peh	u	uh	z	tsett
b	beh	g	geh	l	ell	q	kuh	v	fau	ä	äh
c	tseh	h	hah	m	emm	r	err	w	weh	ö	öh
d	deh	i	ih	n	enn	s	ess	x	iks	ü	üh
e	eh	j	jot	o	oh	t	teh	y	üpsilon	ß	ess-tset

In speech, capital letters are indicated by using the word **groß: großes B, großes W.** Lower-case letters are referred to as **klein: kleines b, kleines w.**

C Pronounce the following abbreviations.

VW (Volkswagen) **BMW** (Bayerische Motorenwerke)
BRD (Bundesrepublik Deutschland) **DDR** (Deutsche Demokratische Republik) **USA** (U.S.A.)

D Spell the following words.

Physik preiswert billig Farbe Hose häßlich

Activity: Have students spell their names.

Aussprache

▌ long vowel [o]   s**o,** w**oh**nen, H**o**se, B**oo**t
▌ short vowel [ɔ]   k**o**mmen, S**o**cke

A Practice vertically in columns and horizontally in pairs.

[o]	[ɔ]
b**o**g	B**o**ck
Sch**o**te	Sch**o**tte
M**oo**s	M**o**st
T**o**ne	T**o**nne
Ofen	**o**ffen
S**oh**ne	S**o**nne

Pronunciation hint for [o]: Tell students to say *o* as in *so*, but with exaggeratedly rounded lips and no glide.

The following English-German contrastive drill may be useful. Have students indicate whether the German word is spoken first or second (mix the order): tone/*Ton*; boat/*Boot*; dome/*Dom*; hole/*hohl*.

B Practice the following words horizontally in pairs.

[o]	[ø]	[ɔ]	[œ]
gr**o**ße	Gr**ö**ße	K**o**pfe	K**ö**pfe
H**o**fe	H**ö**fe	k**o**nnte	k**ö**nnte
st**o**ße	St**ö**ße	St**o**cke	St**ö**cke
G**o**te	G**oe**the	H**o**cker	H**ö**cker
Ofen	**Ö**fen	T**o**pfe	T**ö**pfe

C Practice the sounds [o] and [ɔ]. Read the sentences aloud.

1. Kommt Otto am Sonntag oder am Montag?
2. Lotte und Monika hören gern Rockmusik.
3. Hoffentlich kostet die Hose nicht sehr viel.

This saying is common among school children in Germany. An English equivalent would be "There's no cure for stupidity."

Doof bleibt doof, da helfen keine Pillen!

Übungen

Telling time

Point out that *eins*
drops the *-s* in the ex-
pression *ein Uhr.*

Es ist zwei.
Es ist zwei Uhr.

Es ist eins.
Es ist ein Uhr.

A   Various friends want to know when you're coming to visit on Saturday.
Inform them that you'll come an hour later than they expected.

Let student assistant
cue time with cardboard
clock or by writing time
expressions on board.

V: *Wann kommst du?*
Wie spät ist es?
(Cue with clock.)

■▥   Kommst du um vier?   *Nein, um fünf.*

1.   Kommst du um drei?   4.   Kommst du um elf?
2.   Kommst du um sechs?   5.   Kommst du um neun?
3.   Kommst du um eins?

Es ist Viertel nach zwei.

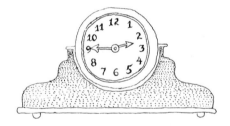

Es ist Viertel vor drei.

B   Tell Axel that you have classes a quarter hour later than he thinks.

■▥   Hast du um drei Bio?   *Nein, um Viertel nach drei.*

1.   Hast du um acht Deutsch?   4.   Hast du um eins Englisch?
2.   Hast du um neun Mathe?   5.   Hast du um zehn Chemie?
3.   Hast du um elf Geschichte?

C   Inform Inge that you have classes a quarter hour earlier than she thinks.

■▥   Hast du um acht   *Nein, um Viertel vor acht.*
     Musik?

1.   Hast du um zehn Kunst?   4.   Hast du um eins Erdkunde?
2.   Hast du um zwölf Sport?   5.   Hast du um elf Physik?
3.   Hast du um neun Latein?

Es ist zehn vor fünf.   Es ist zehn nach sechs.
Es ist zehn Minuten vor fünf.   Es ist zehn Minuten nach sechs.

D   Tell your friends that it's five minutes later than they thought.

V: *Es ist zwanzig Minuten nach acht.*

Avoid asking students to state time expressions that refer to 25 minutes before or 25 minutes after the hour, since the German (*fünf Minuten vor halb* and *fünf Minuten nach halb*) is difficult at this stage.

◼▥   Ist es Viertel nach acht?   *Nein, es ist schon zwanzig nach acht.*

1. Ist es fünf nach elf?   5. Ist es zwanzig vor eins?
2. Ist es sieben Uhr?   6. Ist es Viertel vor zwölf?
3. Ist es zehn nach sechs?   7. Ist es zehn vor acht?
4. Ist es fünf vor neun?

Es ist halb drei.
Es ist zwei Uhr dreißig.

E   Tell each friend who asks that you're going home a half hour later than the time mentioned.

V: *Nein, um vier Uhr dreißig.*

◼▥   Gehst du um vier nach Hause?   *Nein, um halb fünf.*

1. Gehst du um elf nach Hause?
2. Gehst du um sieben nach Hause?
3. Gehst du um eins nach Hause?
4. Gehst du um neun nach Hause?
5. Gehst du um sechs nach Hause?
6. Gehst du um drei nach Hause?

Du hast das Wort

Find out when a classmate has various classes.

Hast du um acht [Bio]?
Wann hast du [Chemie]?
Du hast um halb zehn [Englisch], nicht?
Um wieviel Uhr hast du [Mathe]?

Activity: Chain this set of questions throughout the class. The student giving the answer must ask the next question. Encourage class to vary questions.

Accusative case of **der, das, die**

NOMINATIVE
Der Mantel ist preiswert.
Das Hemd ist toll.
Die Hose ist klasse.
Die Schuhe sind spottbillig.

ACCUSATIVE
Meinst du **den** Mantel da?
Meinst du **das** Hemd da?
Meinst du **die** Hose da?
Meinst du **die** Schuhe da?

Call attention to plural form.

The direct object of a verb is in the accusative case. **Der** is the only definite article that has a different form before nouns in the accusative case: **der**>**den**.

F   You are shown some clothing. Say you find each article attractive.

■))   der Pulli   *Ich finde den Pulli hübsch.*

1. die Krawatte   3. das Kleid   5. der Mantel
2. der Gürtel   4. der Rock   6. die Bluse

G   Ute reacts favorably to a number of items in a clothing store. Ask her to specify which ones she means.

■))   Der Anzug ist preiswert.   *Meinst du den Anzug da?*

1. Der Gürtel ist klasse.   4. Das Hemd ist schön.
2. Die Bluse ist toll.   5. Der Mantel ist teuer.
3. Der Rock ist spottbillig.   6. Das Kleid ist hübsch.

V: Distribute objects or flash cards of objects to one half of the class. Ask the other students to tell who has each object:
T: *Wer hat den Bleistift?*
S: *[Uwe] hat den Bleistift.*

Accusative case of **ein** and **kein**

NOMINATIVE
Da ist **ein** Bleistift.
Da ist **kein** Bleistift.
Da ist **ein** Buch.
Da ist **kein** Buch.
Da ist **eine** Mappe.
Da ist **keine** Mappe.
Da sind Bleistifte.
Da sind **keine** Bleistifte.

ACCUSATIVE
Hast du **einen** Bleistift?
Hast du **keinen** Bleistift?
Hast du **ein** Buch?
Hast du **kein** Buch?
Hast du **eine** Mappe?
Hast du **keine** Mappe?
Hast du Bleistifte?
Hast du **keine** Bleistifte?

The indefinite article **ein** and its negative form **kein** become **einen** and **keinen** before **der**-nouns in the accusative singular. **Ein** has no plural forms.

H You've misplaced several of your school supplies. Try to borrow the following articles from various friends.

Game: Add an element.
T: *Was brauchst du?*
S¹: *Ich brauche einen Bleistift.*
S²: *Ich brauche einen Bleistift und eine Uhr,* etc.

■ıı ein Bleistift   *Hast du einen Bleistift?*

1. ein Kuli
2. ein Radiergummi
3. ein Heft
4. eine Mappe
5. ein Buch
6. ein Bleistift

I Christa asks what you and your friends are wearing to the party. Tell her you all don't plan to wear what she expects.

Personalize:
T: *Trägst du heute einen Rock?*
S: *Nein, ich trage ein Kleid.*

■ıı Trägst du heute abend eine   *Nein, ich trage keine Jacke.*
      Jacke?

1. Trägst du heute abend einen Pulli?
2. Trägt Erik einen Anzug?
3. Trägt Gisela ein Kleid?
4. Trägt sie einen Rock?
5. Trägt Günter Jeans?
6. Trägt er Schuhe?
7. Trägt er Socken?

Accusative case of possessive adjectives

Review genders of nouns by pointing to pictures and asking for *der, das, die.*

Ich habe **einen** Bleistift. Ich habe **ein** Heft. Ich habe **eine** Mappe.
Ich habe Bücher.

Ich habe **meinen** Bleistift. Ich habe **mein** Heft. Ich habe **meine** Mappe.
Ich habe **meine** Bücher.

J   You're always picking up after absent-minded Erik. When he asks where his school supplies are, say that you have them.

V: Ask who has various objects: *Wo ist mein Kuli? Wer hat meinen Kuli? Wo ist mein Radiergummi, mein Buch, mein Heft, meine Mappe? Wo sind meine Bücher, meine Bleistifte?*

■III   Wo ist mein Kuli?   *Ich habe deinen Kuli.*

1. Wo ist mein Radiergummi?
2. Wo ist mein Heft?
3. Wo ist meine Mappe?
4. Wo ist mein Bleistift?
5. Wo sind meine Bücher?
6. Wo ist mein Papier?

K   After an afternoon of swimming, everyone's clothes have become mixed up. Answer that you and Ulf have them.

Game: Teacher redistributes objects belonging to students. Student must guess who has her/his object.
T: *Wer hat deinen Bleistift?*
S: *Jochen hat meinen Bleistift.*

■III   Wer hat unsere Socken?   *Wir haben eure Socken.*

1. Wer hat unsere Schuhe?
2. Wer hat unsere Hemden?
3. Wer hat unsere Jacken?
4. Wer hat unsere Gürtel?

V: Student says that the things Erika has are her own:
T: *Hat Erika deinen Kuli?*
S: *Nein, sie hat ihren Kuli.*
T: *Hat Erika mein Buch, deine Mappe, unser Papier, meinen Bleistift, eure Hefte, deinen Radiergummi?*

Ilse points out that some of her friends are wearing new clothes. Ask what she thinks of them.

> ▪▥   Astrids Kleid ist neu.   *Wirklich? Wie findest du ihr Kleid?*

1. Christas Bluse ist neu.
2. Kirstins Rock ist neu.
3. Jochens Jacke ist neu.
4. Kurts Pulli ist neu.
5. Thomas' Hemd ist neu.
6. Gerdas Mantel ist neu.
7. Herberts Schuhe sind neu.

Du hast das Wort

Play a guessing game with your classmates. Think of a student in your class and name two or three articles of clothing that he/she is wearing. Your classmates will try to guess whom you have in mind.

Ich trage Hose und Hemd und einen Pulli.
Meine Hose ist braun.
Mein Pulli ist rot.
Wer bin ich?

Using **der, das, die** as pronouns

Demonstrative pronouns are commonly used and are introduced before accusative personal pronouns because they are easier.

Kaufst du **den Gürtel** da?
Nein, **der** ist zu teuer.

Are you going to buy that belt?
No, it is too expensive.

Wie findest du **den Mantel** da?
Den finde ich schön.

How do you like that coat?
I think that one is nice.

Der, das, die are often used as pronouns to replace nouns. The forms of these pronouns are the same as the forms of the definite articles.

M

You and Gabi are shopping. For some reason you don't seem to agree with any of her opinions.

> ▪▥   Ich finde den Pulli schön. Du auch?   *Nein, den finde ich nicht schön.*

1. Ich finde das Kleid hübsch. Du auch?
2. Ich finde die Bluse toll. Du auch?
3. Ich finde das Hemd teuer. Du auch?
4. Ich finde den Rock billig. Du auch?
5. Ich finde die Jacke hübsch. Du auch?
6. Ich finde den Mantel schön. Du auch?

Grammatische Übersicht

Telling time (A-E)

Time is expressed in the following ways:

1. on the hour: 1.00   Es ist eins.
                             Es ist ein Uhr.

On train schedules, the time is sometimes printed with *h*: 1ʰ25. *h* comes from Latin *hora*.

Notice that the **-s** of **eins** is dropped before the noun **Uhr.** Notice also that in written German a period is used after the numeral indicating the hour.

2. past the hour: 1.10   Es ist zehn (Minuten) nach eins.
                      1.15   Es ist Viertel nach eins.
                      1.30   Es ist ein Uhr dreißig.
                             Es ist halb zwei.

Notice that the expression with **halb** names the hour to come, not the preceding hour: **1.30 = halb zwei.**

3. before the hour: 1.40   Es ist zwanzig (Minuten) vor zwei.
                       1.45   Es ist Viertel vor zwei.

Official time

Ingrid hat **um 13 Uhr 30** Bio.   Ingrid has biology at 1:30 P.M.

Official time, used for concerts, train and plane schedules, and schools, is indicated on a twenty-four-hour basis: 8 Uhr = 8 A.M.
                                          20 Uhr = 8 P.M.

**Schnelle Züge
außerhalb des Taktfahrplans**

Wien–Salzburg–Wien

Wien Westbf	ab	0.10	7.10	8.20	9.45	14.00	18.10	20.10	21.45
Salzburg Hbf	an	4.05	11.05	11.49	13.19	17.20	21.30	23.35	1.48
Salzburg Hbf	ab	1.40	3.25	5.12	10.50	16.12	17.45	18.08	19.17
Wien Westbf	an	6.10	7.35¹	8.40	14.25	19.45	21.00	22.10	22.45

¹ An Samstagen, Sonn- und Feiertagen
Wien Westbf an 7.25 Uhr

Wien–Graz–Wien

Wien Südbf	ab	8.00	13.20	16.15	22.20
Graz Hbf	an	10.55	16.12	19.18	1.34
Graz Hbf	ab	4.10	7.15	11.10	
Wien Südbf	an	7.35	10.10	14.20	

Taktfahrplan
Wien-Salzburg-Wien
Wien-Graz-Wien

Accusative case

Kaufst du **den Mantel?**	Are you buying the coat?
Ich kaufe **eine Jacke.**	I'm buying a jacket.
Petra trägt heute **keinen Pulli.**	Petra isn't wearing a sweater today.

A German noun has different cases, depending on how it is used in a sentence. When a noun is used as the direct object of a verb, it is in the *accusative case.*

Accusative case of **der, das, die**   (F-G)

NOMINATIVE	ACCUSATIVE
Der Anzug ist billig.	Meinst du **den** Anzug da?
Das Kleid ist schick.	Meinst du **das** Kleid da?
Die Jacke ist klasse.	Meinst du **die** Jacke da?
Die Schuhe sind teuer.	Meinst du **die** Schuhe da?

Den is used instead of **der** in the accusative case. The other articles, **das** and **die,** have identical nominative and accusative forms.

Accusative case of **ein** and **kein**   (H-I)

NOMINATIVE	ACCUSATIVE
Da ist **ein** Bleistift.	Sie hat **einen** Bleistift.
Da ist **kein** Bleistift.	Er hat **keinen** Bleistift.
Da ist **ein** Heft.	Sie hat **ein** Heft.
Da ist **kein** Heft.	Er hat **kein** Heft.
Da ist **eine** Mappe.	Sie hat **eine** Mappe.
Da ist **keine** Mappe.	Er hat **keine** Mappe.
Da sind Bleistifte.	Sie hat Bleistifte.
Da sind **keine** Bleistifte.	Er hat **keine** Bleistifte.

Ein changes to **einen** before a **der-**noun in the accusative singular. **Ein** has no plural forms.
Kein follows the pattern of **ein,** except that **kein** has plural forms. In the plural, the nominative and accusative forms are identical. They are both **keine.**

Accusative case of possessive adjectives (J-L)

NOMINATIVE				ACCUSATIVE		
Wo ist	ein	Kuli?		Wer hat	einen	Kuli?
	mein				meinen	
Wo ist	ein	Heft?		Wer hat	ein	Heft?
	mein				mein	
Wo ist	eine	Mappe?		Wer hat	eine	Mappe?
	meine				meine	
Wo sind	meine	Bücher?		Wer hat	meine	Bücher?

The possessive adjectives **(mein, dein, sein, ihr, unser, euer)** have the same endings as the indefinite article **ein**.

Using **der, das, die** as pronouns (M)

Kaufst du **die Jacke** da?   Are you going to buy *that jacket?*
Nein, **die** ist zu teuer.   No, *it* is too expensive.

Der, das, die are often used as pronouns to replace nouns. They are then called demonstrative pronouns. Demonstrative pronouns usually occur at or near the beginning of a sentence. The English equivalent is usually a personal pronoun.

	SINGULAR			PLURAL
Nominative	der	das	die	die
Accusative	den	das	die	die

The forms of the demonstrative pronouns are the same as the forms of the definite articles.

Grades are based on class performance, written tests called **Klassenarbeiten,** and frequent quizzes called **Kurzarbeiten.** Pressure to achieve good grades is very strong because admission to a university (and to some jobs) depends primarily on the applicant's secondary school grades.

Extracurricular activities such as clubs, organizations, and sports are limited in German schools. Where such activities do exist, they are not really part of the school day.

Wiederholung

A \ Choose the phrase that best completes each statement, based on the dialogue.

PAUL	Tag, Ursel! Wie geht's?
URSEL	Es geht. Ich habe heute nachmittag viel Hausaufgaben.
PAUL	Das ist ja doof. Ich spiele jetzt Tennis.
URSEL	Du, Paul ... Wie spät ist es denn?
PAUL	Erst eins.
URSEL	Na gut. Ich spiele bis zwei.
PAUL	Das ist ja prima.

1. Es geht Ursel ...
   a. gut.
   b. prima.
   c. nicht so gut.
2. Paul ...
   a. geht jetzt nach Hause.
   b. macht Hausaufgaben.
   c. treibt heute nachmittag Sport.
3. Paul und Ursel ...
   a. haben jetzt Schule.
   b. gehen jetzt nach Hause.
   c. spielen jetzt Tennis.

B Explain to Gabi that things are not as she thinks, but rather exactly the opposite.

■▥   Ist dein Buch interessant? *Nein, es ist nicht interessant; es ist langweilig.*

1. Sind deine Matheaufgaben leicht?
2. Ist dein Kuli billig?
3. Ist deine Mappe neu?
4. Sind deine Englischaufgaben lang?
5. Ist dein Klassenzimmer groß?

C Take the role of the person in each picture. Tell what you are wearing.

■▥

*Ich trage keine
Jacke; ich trage
einen Pulli.*

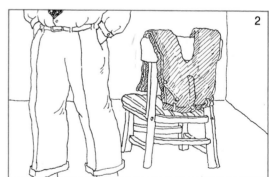

D   Supply additional information to each of the following sentences by beginning with one of the words or expressions below.

> **abends   heute nachmittag   hoffentlich**
>
> **jetzt   natürlich   morgens um halb neun**

∎ɪ   Mein Brieffreund wohnt in Bergdorf.   *Jetzt wohnt mein Brieffreund in Bergdorf.*

1. Er geht da in die Schule.
2. Er hat Chemie.
3. Er spielt Fußball.
4. Er macht seine Hausaufgaben.
5. Er schreibt bald.

E   A German student is visiting your school. You overhear various snatches of conversation during lunch. Tell your German friend what people are saying.

1. Ingrid: I have math this afternoon.
            Math is my favorite subject.
2. Mark: I'm going to do my chemistry homework this afternoon.
            I think chemistry is interesting.
3. Erik: It's already a quarter after twelve.
            I'm going to be late again.
4. Christl: Gerd likes Petra.
   Sabine: Yes, but Petra doesn't like Gerd.
5. Robert: Does your pen pal live in Kiel?
   Tanja: No. He lives in Stuttgart now.

Possible answers to Ex. F: *Ich arbeite, spiele Tennis, gehe spazieren, höre Musik, gehe tanzen, mache meine Hausaufgaben.*

F   Find out from a classmate what he/she does after school on certain days.

∎ɪ   Was machst du am [Montag]?   *Ich [spiele Fußball].*

G   Interview a classmate about school. You may want to ask some of the following questions. Summarize your findings.

Was ist dein Lieblingsfach?
Wann hast du [Deutsch]?
Wie findest du [Erdkunde]?
   Ist es leicht? schwer?
Hast du viel Hausaufgaben?
Machst du gern [Chemie]aufgaben?
   Wann machst du sie?
Welches Fach hast du nicht gern?

May be done orally, then in writing. Have students write as paragraph.

You may wish to begin: *Gerdas Lieblingsfach ist Bio. Sie . . .*

Kulturlesestück

1 = sehr gut

2 = gut

3 = befriedigend

4 = ausreichend

5 = mangelhaft

6 = ungenügend

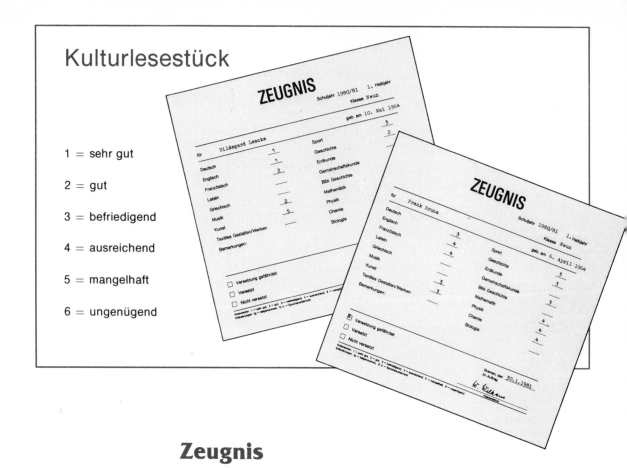

Zeugnis

Hilde geht in Bremen zur Schule. Sie ist in
Klasse Neun. Links° ist ihr Zeugnis. In
Deutsch und Englisch hat sie eine Eins. Das
sind ihre Lieblingsfächer. Da ist sie sehr gut.
In Mathe und Physik ist sie gut. Sie hat in bei-
5 den° eine Zwei. Nur in Kunst ist sie wirklich
schlecht. Da hat sie eine Fünf. Sie findet
Kunst langweilig.

Hildes Freund Frank ist nicht so gut. Er hat
viele Dreien und Vieren. Er arbeitet nicht
10 gern. Hoffentlich bekommt° er nächstes Mal°
nicht nur Vieren und Fünfen. Mit° drei
Fünfen zum Beispiel oder mit zwei Fünfen
und ohne° Dreien bleibt er sitzen°. Dann°
geht Hilde in Klasse Zehn, und er macht die
15 ganze Klasse Neun noch einmal°.

on the left

in beiden: in both

gets / nächstes Mal:
next time
with
without / bleibt . . .
sitzen: he repeats a
year / then
noch einmal: again

A   Answer the following questions, based on the reading.

Students may be interested in word for "flunk", *durchfallen: Axel fällt durch.* A student who receives a 6 in a major subject or three 5's *bleibt sitzen (sitzenbleiben);* that is, he/she must repeat the year and every subject (not only those he/she failed).

1. Wo hat Hilde eine Zwei?
   a. in Englisch
   b. in Deutsch
   c. in Mathe
   d. in Kunst
2. Wie findet Hilde Kunst?
   a. interessant
   b. leicht
   c. nicht interessant
   d. schwer
3. Warum ist Franks Zeugnis nicht gut?
   a. Er findet alle Fächer langweilig.
   b. Er ist faul.
   c. Die Fächer sind zu schwer.
   d. Er spielt zuviel Fußball.

Vokabeln

SUBSTANTIVE

die Aufgabe, –n   homework, lesson; **die Chemieaufgabe**   chemistry homework
die Biologie   biology; **die Bio**   bio
der Bleistift, –e   pencil
das Buch, ̈er   book
die Chemie   chemistry
der Dienstag   Tuesday
das Englisch   English
die Erdkunde   geography
das Fach, ̈er   (school) subject
die Geschichte   history
das Heft, –e   notebook
die Klasse, –n   grade, class
das Klassenzimmer, –   classroom
der Kugelschreiber, – (der Kuli, –s)   ballpoint pen
das Lieblingsfach, ̈er   favorite subject
die Mappe, –n   briefcase, book bag

SUBSTANTIVE

die Mathematik   mathematics; **die Mathe**   math
der Mittwoch   Wednesday
der Nachmittag, –e   afternoon; **am ~**   in the afternoon
das Papier   paper
die Pause, –n   break, intermission
die Physik   physics
der Plan, ̈e   plan; schedule
der Radiergummi, –s   eraser
die Schule, –n   school
der Sport   sport
die Stunde, –n   hour; class
der Stundenplan, ̈e   class schedule
die Uhr, –en   clock, watch
das Viertel, –   quarter

(Continued)

ANDERE WÖRTER

ach oh
dick fat, thick
dieser this
fertig ready, finished
halb half
interessant interesting
ja *flavoring word* (see p. 109)
kurz short
lang long
langweilig boring
leicht easy, light
schlimm bad
schwer difficult, heavy
um at, around
vor before

BESONDERE AUSDRÜCKE

Mensch! wow! brother! oh, boy!
klar! sure! of course!
wie spät ist es? what time is it?
wieviel Uhr ist es? what time is it?
es ist zehn Uhr it's ten o'clock
um wieviel Uhr? at what time?
um ein Uhr at one o'clock

Kapitel 7

Willst du ins Konzert?

The **Litfaßsäule** (a thick column on which advertising posters are displayed) was introduced to Germany in 1854 by Ernst Litfaß, a printer from Berlin. Litfaß had seen similar columns in other countries and recognized their value in advertising. The Berlin police gave Litfaß a monopoly on the poster columns; they saw them as a way of controlling the location of posters put up throughout the city. The **Litfaßsäulen** soon spread through the rest of Germany and are still in use today.

FRANKFURTER HOT DOGS
IM JUGENDZENTRUM

7.-9. Januar   20.00ʰ

Karten bei Buchhandlung Baumann
oder an der Kasse: geöffnet
täglich von 13ʰ bis 20ʰ

Eintritt: DM 5,— 8,— 12,— 16,—

Fragen

1. Wo gibt es ein Konzert°?
2. Wie heißt die Rock Band°?
3. Wieviel Tage spielen die *Frankfurter Hot Dogs?*
4. Wann beginnt° die Vorstellung°?
5. Wieviel kosten die Karten?

Du hast das Wort

A. Ask a classmate to name the rock group he/she likes best.

   Wie heißt deine Lieblingsgruppe?   [Die *Hot Dogs.*]

Encourage students to
use responses from
past chapters as well.

B. Ask a friend whether he/she would like to hear a concert by a certain rock group.

   Möchtest° du [die *Hot Dogs*]   Ja, [sie sind] toll.
     hören?   Ja, und wie!
                                         Klar!
                                         Ja, hast du Karten?
                                         Vielleicht°.
                                         Nein, ich habe keine Lust°.

Konzert im Jugendzentrum

Call students' attention to *du*. Preceding a proper name, it serves to get that person's attention.

Dieter and Ingrid are trying to find a time when they can both go to the Hot Dogs concert.

Point out *mal* as another flavoring word, short for *einmal*. See p. 133 for exercises.

INGRID	Du, Dieter, die *Hot Dogs* spielen heute abend.
DIETER	Das ist ja dumm. Ich kann leider heute abend nicht.
INGRID	Und morgen abend?
DIETER	Morgen abend geht's. Meinst du, wir bekommen noch Karten?
INGRID	Wir können's ja mal versuchen.

Dhdw teaching suggestion: Treat each question-answer pair as an individual exercise, keeping pace lively, with questions and responses varied. Build up to complete dialogue, eventually letting students take over all parts.

Fragen

1. Wer spielt heute abend?
2. Wann kann Dieter ins Konzert gehen?
3. Können die beiden noch Karten bekommen?
4. Hören sie die *Hot Dogs* gern?

Du hast das Wort

Create a dialogue between you and a friend. Try to make plans to go to a movie, play, or concert.

DU	
Was macht ihr	heute abend?
	am Samstag?

FREUND(IN)	
Wir wollen	ins Kino°.
	ins Theater°.
	ins Konzert.

Wann?	
Um wieviel Uhr?	

FREUND(IN)	
Um [8] Uhr.	Kommst du auch?
	Hast du Lust zu kommen?

DU	
Nein, ich habe	keine Zeit°.
	kein Geld°.
Nein, ich muß Hausaufgaben machen.	
Ich habe schon Lust, aber keine Zeit.	
Nein, ich darf° nicht.	

Schade.
Das tut mir leid.

Ja, gern. Gibt° es noch Karten?

Ich glaube° ja.
Vielleicht, vielleicht auch nicht.
Wir können ja mal fragen°.

The final product can be performed in class.

A musical member of the class may enjoy setting this song to music.

American music and rock groups are popular in German-speaking countries. German teen-agers listen to rock, disco, and country-western. American songs performed by European artists are usually sung in English. Even songs written by German artists often have English lyrics.

PRETTY BABY

Du bist so schön.
Ich muß dich seh'n,
Heute noch seh'n,
Oh, pretty baby!

Du hast mein Herz.
Das ist kein Scherz.
Oh, welcher Schmerz
Ohne dich, baby!

Glücklich zu sein,
Mit dir allein,
Immer zu zwei'n,
Oh, pretty baby!

Es kann nicht sein.
Ich bin allein,
Immer allein
Ohne dich, baby.

The *Frankfurter Hot Dogs* are a fictitious group. The song "Pretty Baby" was invented for them. Point out that an apostrophe (in *seh'n, zwei'n*) frequently indicates the omission of the letter *e*.

These dialogues lend
themselves to
classroom skits.

An der Kasse

The Hot Dogs *are a popular group. Ingrid and Dieter have a hard time
getting tickets.*

INGRID   Haben Sie noch Karten für morgen abend?

HERR   Es tut mir leid. Für morgen abend ist nichts mehr da. Ich habe noch ein
paar Karten für übermorgen.

INGRID   *(zu Dieter)* Was meinst du?

DIETER   Ich kann ja. Aber mußt du dann nicht arbeiten?

INGRID   Das schon. Aber ich bekomme sicher frei. Ich muß die *Hot Dogs* einfach hören.

DIETER   Also gut.

Dhdw: If attendant at
box office says "all sold
out", student must ask
for a different day so
that questions about
price can be asked.

Fragen

1. Gibt es noch Karten für morgen abend?
2. Für wann gibt es noch Karten?
3. Warum will Ingrid übermorgen nicht arbeiten?

Du hast das Wort

With a partner, make up a short dialogue about buying tickets to a performance. Use some of the questions and responses below.

DU
Haben Sie noch Karten für | heute abend?   morgen°?   übermorgen?

FRAU
Es tut mir leid.   Es ist alles ausverkauft°.   Für [heute abend] haben wir nichts mehr.   Für [heute abend] ist noch alles° da.   Für [übermorgen] haben wir noch Karten.

DU
Was kosten die Karten?

FRAU
Wir haben Karten zu [5, 8, 12 und 16] Mark.   Wir haben noch ein paar Karten zu [8] Mark.

DU
Ich nehme° [2] Karten zu [8] Mark.   Danke.   Oh, noch eine Frage°. Wann beginnt   die Vorstellung?

FRAU
Bitte. Das macht° [16] Mark.   Um [20] Uhr.

Wortschatzerweiterung

Noun compounds

German has many noun compounds. Their meaning can often be guessed from their component parts.

der Abend + die Vorstellung = die Abendvorstellung
das Theater + die Karten = die Theaterkarten

A noun compound takes the definite article of the last noun in the compound.

A   What do the italicized words mean?

1. Die *Abendvorstellung* beginnt um acht Uhr.
2. Gibt es für heute noch *Theaterkarten?*
3. Welche *Schuhgröße* hast du?
4. Hast du morgen *Klavierstunde?*
5. Wann machst du deine *Hausaufgaben?*
6. Am *Wochenende* mache ich meine *Matheaufgaben.*
7. Wie heißt dein *Deutschlehrer?*
8. Wo ist das *Deutschbuch?*
9. Was sind deine *Lieblingsfächer?*

Flavoring word **mal**

Wir können's ja **mal** versuchen.	Let's at least give it a try. (We can try it sometime.)
Du kannst ja **mal** ins Kino gehen.	You can go to the movies for a change.
Bernd will **mal** in Hamburg arbeiten.	Bernd wants to work in Hamburg someday.

The flavoring word **mal** is often used in commands, suggestions, or in statements of intent. The time for carrying out the intended action is not stated precisely. To express the same idea in English one often uses *sometime* or *someday*.

B   Choose a German response to complete each conversational exchange, based on the English guidelines.

> a.   Was können wir denn mal machen?
> b.   Möchtest du die *Hot Dogs* mal hören?
> c.   Das möchte ich auch mal machen.
> d.   Das muß ich auch mal lernen.
> e.   Ich muß bald mal neue Schuhe kaufen.
> f.   Ich muß Gerda auch mal schreiben.

1. *Jens says he also has to learn English someday.*
   Torsten: Dieses Jahr lerne ich Englisch.
   Jens: . . .
2. *Gerda would like to play more tennis.*
   Erika: Im Sommer spiele ich viel Tennis.
   Gerda: . . .
3. *Mark casually remarks that he needs new shoes soon.*
   Frank: Deine Schuhe sind kaputt.
   Mark: Ja. . . .
4. *Ursel asks what she and Barbara can do to relieve their boredom on a rainy afternoon.*
   Barbara: Es ist heute so langweilig.
   Ursel: . . .
5. *Gerd asks whether Uwe wants to play a different record for a change.*
   Uwe: Du, diese Gruppe ist furchtbar langweilig.
   Gerd: . . .
6. *Barbara has been corresponding regularly with Gerda. Renate remembers that she owes Gerda a letter, too.*
   Barbara: Morgen muß ich wieder an Gerda schreiben.
   Renate: . . .

Aussprache

| long vowel [a] | Vater, Staat, Frage |
| short vowel [A] | Kasse, alles, Mann |

A   Practice vertically in columns and horizontally in pairs.

Overhead transparencies of pronunciation drills are useful to show sound-symbol correspondences.

[a]	[A]
Bahn	Bann
kam	Kamm
Staat	Stadt
Schlaf	schlaff
lahm	Lamm

B   Practice the following words horizontally in pairs.

[a]	[ɔ]	[A]	[ɔ]
Bahn	Bonn	Bann	Bonn
kam	komm	Kamm	komm
stahlen	Stollen	Matte	Motte
Spaten	spotten	knalle	Knolle
fahl	voll	falle	volle

C   Practice the sounds [a] and [A]. Read the sentences aloud.

1. Hast du Astrids Mappe?
2. Ich habe noch eine Karte zu acht Mark.
3. Kannst du heute abend tanzen gehen?

Proverb: A bird in the hand is worth two in the bush.

Ein Spatz in der Hand ist besser als eine Taube auf dem Dach.

Most record stores in German-speaking countries have listening booths or stations where customers can listen to a recording before buying it.

Die Hot Dogs sind toll, nicht?

Übungen

The subject pronouns **du, ihr, Sie**

Additional exercise: Students ask the following people whether they're coming to the school play tonight.
Antje   (Kommst du heute abend, Antje?)
1. *Frau Karger*
2. *Inge und Volker*
3. *Herr und Frau Stassen*
4. *Jürgen*

The pronouns **du, ihr,** and **Sie** are all equivalent to English *you.*

> Tag, **Elke!** Was machst **du** denn?
> Tag, **Inge!** Tag, **Gerd!** Was macht **ihr** denn?

The familiar forms **du** and **ihr** are used in addressing relatives, close friends, and persons under about fifteen.

> Tag, **Herr Wagner!** Gehen **Sie** heute ins Konzert?
> Tag, **Frau Braun!** Tag, **Fräulein Schneider!** Gehen **Sie** auch ins Konzert?

Sie is a more formal form of address and is used in addressing strangers or adults whom the speaker doesn't know as close friends. **Sie** can refer to one or more persons.

A   Ask Mrs. Wagner the same questions you recently asked Günter.

> Gehst du heute abend ins Theater, Günter?
>
> *Gehen Sie heute abend ins Theater, Frau Wagner?*

1. Bekommst du noch Karten?
2. Was meinst du?
3. Hörst du gern Rockmusik?

4. Gehst du morgen ins Konzert?
5. Wie findest du die *Hot Dogs?*

The possessive adjectives **dein, euer, Ihr**

Hast du **deinen** Mantel, Inge?	Do you have *your* coat, Inge?
Habt ihr **eure** Mäntel, Kinder?	Do you have *your* coats, children?
Haben Sie **Ihren** Mantel, Herr Lenz?	Do you have *your* coat, Mr. Lenz?

German has three possessive adjectives meaning *your:*

> **dein** (familiar singular)
> **euer** (familiar plural)
> **Ihr** (formal, singular and plural)

B

Personalize: Teacher shows objects or clothing that belong to him/her and says:
T: *Ist das dein Bleistift?*
S: *Nein, das ist Ihr Bleistift.*

Mrs. Wagner is straightening up the classroom. She asks whether various objects belong to you. They don't. Express surprise that they're not hers.

◼ꜞꜞ Ist das dein Buch?   *Nein, ist das nicht Ihr Buch?*

1. Ist das dein Heft?
2. Ist das dein Radiergummi?
3. Ist das dein Kugelschreiber?
4. Ist das deine Mappe?
5. Sind das deine Bleistifte?

C Check to make sure all your friends and acquaintances have their tickets for the concert you're going to tonight.

◼ꜞꜞ Karin   *Hast du deine Karte?*
◼ꜞꜞ Inge und Klaus   *Habt ihr eure Karten?*
◼ꜞꜞ Frau Lenz   *Haben Sie Ihre Karte?*

1. Hans
2. Jens und Thomas
3. Gabi
4. Herr Hansen
5. Petra und Claudia
6. Frau Schneider

Verbs with stem-vowel change e>i

Personalize: Give a student a book and say:
T: *Ich gebe [Erik] ein Buch. Was gebe ich [Erik]?*
S: *Sie geben [Erik] ein Buch.*
T: *Nimmt [er] das Buch?*
S: *Ja, [er] nimmt das Buch.*

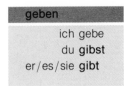

geben
ich gebe
du **gibst**
er/es/sie **gibt**

nehmen
ich nehme
du **nimmst**
er/es/sie **nimmt**

Geben and **nehmen** have a stem-vowel change **e>i** in the **du-** and **er/sie-**forms of the present tense.

D Stefan is selling off a block of tickets to a soccer game. Ask whether the following people are taking some tickets.

■⫶ Braucht ihr Karten? *Nehmt ihr Karten?*

1. Braucht Frau Lange Karten?
2. Braucht Fräulein Roth Karten?
3. Braucht Bernd Karten?
4. Brauchen wir Karten?
5. Braucht Herr Wagner Karten?
6. Brauchst du Karten?

E Marita wonders how Christa can afford to go to so many concerts. Tell her that various people give her tickets.

■⫶ Erik *Erik gibt Christa oft Karten.*

1. Inge
2. mein Bruder
3. ihre Schwester

4. du
5. ihre Freunde
6. ihr

Modal auxiliaries

Help students discover that the *ich-, er-, sie-,* and *es-*forms have no endings.

Personalize: *Kannst du gut Tennis spielen? gut schwimmen? gut tanzen?*

können can, to be able to

ich **kann**		wir **können**
du **kannst**	Sie **können**	ihr **könnt**
er/es/sie **kann**		sie **können**

Ich **kann** es mal **versuchen.** *I can try it.*

Modal auxiliaries are irregular in the present-tense singular. They are usually used with dependent infinitives. The infinitive is in last position.

F The library seems very noisy today. Say that the following people can't work.

> ▪▥ Ich arbeite nicht.   *Ich kann nicht arbeiten.*

1. Bernd arbeitet nicht.
2. Ingrid arbeitet nicht.
3. Wir arbeiten nicht.
4. Du arbeitest nicht.
5. Frau Lange arbeitet nicht.
6. Ihr arbeitet nicht.

G Say who can (or can't) do the following things.

> ▪▥ Wir können es machen. (Susanne)   *Susanne kann es machen.*

1. Die Jungen können es machen. (du)
2. Du kannst das Buch nehmen. (ihr)
3. Ihr könnt gut singen. (ich)
4. Ich kann die Vokabeln nicht lernen. (Erika)
5. Inge kann die Musik nicht hören. (wir)
6. Wir können heute nicht arbeiten. (Gisela)
7. Ich kann heute nicht ins Kino gehen. (Ute und Jens)

sollen   to be supposed to

ich **soll**		wir sollen
du **sollst**	Sie sollen	ihr sollt
er/es/sie **soll**		sie sollen

Du **sollst** jetzt **beginnen.**   You're supposed to begin now.

H   Decide which parts the members of your band should take.

Use pictures or posters as cues for Ex. H.

V: ich (Soll ich das Buch kaufen?) 1. wir 2. er 3. sie 4. ihr 5. Fräulein Lange.

■Ⅲ   Wer soll Klarinette spielen?   *Ja, Jürgen soll Klarinette*
Jürgen?   *spielen.*

1. Wer soll Gitarre spielen? Ich?
2. Wer soll Schlagzeug spielen? Jutta und Rainer?
3. Wer soll Klavier spielen? Kirstin?
4. Wer soll singen? Ich?
5. Wer soll Geige spielen? Stefan und Ute?

müssen   must, to have to

ich **muß**		wir müssen
du **mußt**	Sie müssen	ihr müßt
er/es/sie **muß**		sie müssen

Sie **muß** es bald **tun.**   She has to do it soon.

I   It's late. Say that the following people have to leave now.

■Ⅲ   Gabi   *Gabi muß jetzt gehen.*

1. Hans-Jürgen   4. ich
2. du   5. ihr
3. wir   6. Stefan und Barbara

J   Report to the class all the things you must do in the next few days.

■Ⅲ   schwer arbeiten   *Ich muß schwer arbeiten.*

Personalize: Mußt du heute viel arbeiten? Mathe machen? Vokabeln lernen? Schuhe kaufen?

1. Mathe und Englisch machen
2. Vokabeln lernen
3. Briefe schreiben
4. Schuhe kaufen

dürfen may, to be permitted to

ich **darf**		wir dürfen
du **darfst**	Sie dürfen	ihr dürft
er/es/sie **darf**		sie dürfen

Wir **dürfen** jetzt **gehen.**   We're allowed to go now.

K   Ask whether your friends really have permission to do what they plan.

■◗   Ich gehe heute ins Kino.   *Darfst du denn heute ins Kino gehen?*

V: *ich   (Ich darf nichts kaufen.)*
1. *du* 2. *er* 3. *wir*
4. *ihr* 5. *Paul* 6. *Petra*

1. Ich gehe morgen ins Konzert.
2. Ich gehe übermorgen ins Theater.
3. Inge spielt heute Volleyball.
4. Bruno spielt heute Fußball.
5. Stefan und Bettina gehen morgen abend tanzen.

L   It's against the rules! Respond to the following questions by saying the actions are not permitted.

V: Have students ask you in German for permission to go to the movies, to the disco, etc.

■◗   Warum spielst du nicht?   *Ich darf nicht spielen.*

1. Warum beginnst du nicht?
2. Warum schwimmst du nicht?
3. Warum kommt Ute nicht?

4. Warum bleibt Jens nicht?
5. Warum geht ihr nicht?

Have students give English equivalents of a few items. Be sure they do not equate *ich will* with "I will".

wollen to want, wish; to intend to

ich **will**		wir wollen
du **willst**	Sie wollen	ihr wollt
er/es/sie **will**		sie wollen

Ihr **wollt** hoffentlich **arbeiten.**   You want to work, I hope.

M   Say who is planning to do the following things.

■◗   Will Erik Musik hören? (du)   *Willst du Musik hören?*

V: *Erik   (Was will Erik am Wochenende machen?)*
1. *Petra* 2. *dein Bruder* 3. *wir* 4. *du*
5. *Ursel und Jörg*
6. *ihr*

1. Greta will heute nicht arbeiten. (wir)
2. Wir wollen Tennis spielen. (ich)
3. Ich will morgen schwimmen gehen. (Monika)
4. Will Ute Englisch lernen? (ihr)
5. Wollt ihr das Buch kaufen? (Hans-Jürgen)

Personalize: *Willst du heute Deutsch machen? heute abend tanzen gehen? Tennis spielen? ins Kino gehen?*

möchte would like to

ich **möchte**		wir **möchten**
du **möchtest**	Sie **möchten**	ihr **möchtet**
er/es/sie **möchte**		sie **möchten**

Sie **möchten** es **kaufen.**   They would like to buy it.

Ich möchte, du möchtest, etc., are special forms of the verb **mögen** (*to like*) and are equivalent to *I would like, you would like,* etc.

N   Tell your teacher that you would like to do the following things.

V: Repeat exercises with new subjects: *Ingrid, wir, er, du* (as question), *ihr* (as question).

Personalize: *Möchtest du heute abend ins Kino gehen?*, etc.

▪▥   jetzt Karten spielen   *Ich möchte jetzt Karten spielen.*

1. heute nachmittag Mathe machen
2. heute abend ins Kino gehen
3. morgen schwimmen gehen
4. am Wochenende wandern
5. die *Hot Dogs* hören

Du hast das Wort

Ask your teacher some questions about her/his leisure activities.

Können Sie [Klavier] spielen?
Möchten Sie am Wochenende [wandern]?
Wollen Sie heute abend [ins Kino] gehen?
Können Sie gut [schwimmen]?

Omission of the dependent infinitive with modals

Contrast with English: *I can't. I mustn't.*

Ich kann es nicht.   =   Ich kann es nicht tun.
Ich muß nach Hause.   =   Ich muß nach Hause gehen.

In sentences with a modal, the dependent infinitive is often omitted when its meaning is clear.

O   Give the English equivalents of the following conversational exchanges.

1. Es ist schon spät.
   Mußt du wirklich nach Hause?
2. Wir wollen ins Kino. Hast du Zeit?
   Nein, heute kann ich nicht. Ich muß arbeiten.
3. Ich kann die Aufgabe nicht machen. Ich habe keinen Bleistift.
   Möchtest du meinen Kuli?
4. Ist das nicht Christl Wagner da?
   Ja, was will sie denn hier?

142

Street musicians in German-speaking countries entertain their listeners with many different kinds of music. Town squares and pedestrian shopping streets make ideal gathering places for audiences. Facing page, top: A casual jam session in Vienna. Middle: One can hear classical music on the streets in Munich. Bottom: Students of medieval music perform on the steps of the town hall in Rothenburg. Right: Organ grinders can still be heard on the Kurfürstendamm in Berlin. Below: Passing the hat at a street concert in Nürnberg.

Grammatische Übersicht

The subject pronouns **du, ihr, Sie** (A)

> Tag, Frank! Was machst **du** heute?
> Tag, Inge! Tag, Claudia! Was macht **ihr** heute?
>
> Tag, Herr Wagner! Was machen **Sie** heute?
> Tag, Frau Lenz! Tag, Frau Becker! Was machen **Sie** heute?

There are three ways to express *you* in German: **du, ihr,** and **Sie.** The familiar forms **du** (singular) and **ihr** (plural) are used in addressing relatives, close friends, or persons under about fifteen. **Du** and **ihr** are also used frequently among members of a group such as students, athletes, laborers, or soldiers. **Du** is used to address a single individual. **Ihr** is used to address two or more individuals.

In the *Gymnasium*, teachers generally address students with *Sie* during the last three years (11th — 13th grades).

Sie is a more formal form of address. It is used in addressing strangers or adults whom the speaker doesn't consider close friends. **Sie** may be either singular or plural.

Often people agree to use **du** with each other once a relationship has become more familiar. Addressing someone with **du** is called **duzen.** Addressing someone with **Sie** is called **siezen.**

Historically speaking, **sie sind** *(they are)* and **Sie sind** *(you are)* are the same form. It was considered polite to address someone as **sie** *(they)* and to capitalize the pronoun in writing.

The development of formal pronouns to address a person was common to a number of European languages. English used to distinguish singular *thou/thee* from plural *ye/you; thou/thee* was restricted to informal usage, and *ye/you* was used both as informal plural and formal singular and plural. Today only *you* survives as our all-purpose pronoun.

The meanings and uses of **sie** and **Sie**

> Glaubt **sie** das?   Does *she* believe that?
> Glauben **sie** das?   Do *they* believe that?
> Glauben **Sie** das?   Do *you* believe that?

In spoken German, the meanings of **sie** *(she)*, **sie** *(they)*, and **Sie** *(you)* can be distinguished with the help of the corresponding verb form and the context.

> **sie** + singular verb form = *she*
> **sie** + plural verb form = *they*
> **Sie** + plural verb form = *you* (formal)

In written German, **Sie** *(you)* is always capitalized.

The possessive adjectives **dein, euer, Ihr** (B-C)

> Hast **du deinen** Mantel, Erik?
> Habt **ihr eure** Mäntel, Kinder?
> Haben **Sie Ihren** Mantel, Frau Lenz?

German has three possessive adjectives that correspond to the subject pronouns meaning *you*.

	SUBJECT PRONOUN	POSSESSIVE ADJECTIVE
familiar singular	du	dein/deine
familiar plural	ihr	euer/eure
formal, singular and plural	Sie	Ihr/Ihre

The meanings and uses of **ihr** and **Ihr**

> Hat sie **ihren** Mantel?   Does she have *her* coat?
> Haben sie **ihre** Mäntel?   Do they have *their* coats?
> Haben Sie **Ihren** Mantel?   Do you have *your* coat?

Context usually makes clear the meanings of **ihr** *(her)*, **ihr** *(their)*, and **Ihr** *(your)*. Note that **Ihr** *(your)* is always capitalized, like the corresponding subject pronoun **Sie.**

Verbs with stem-vowel change **e>i** (D-E)

geben		
ich gebe	Sie geben	wir geben
du **gibst**		ihr gebt
er/es/sie **gibt**		sie geben

nehmen		
ich nehme	Sie nehmen	wir nehmen
du **nimmst**		ihr nehmt
er/es/sie **nimmt**		sie nehmen

Point out that English has two verbs with stem-vowel change in the third person singular.
  I *say* vs. he *says* (sezz)
  I *do* vs. he *does* (duzz)

Geben and **nehmen** have a stem-vowel change **e>i** in the **du-** and **er/sie-**forms. Note that an additional spelling change occurs in **nehmen: er/sie nimmt, du nimmst.**

Modal auxiliaries (F-O)

Er **muß** jetzt arbeiten.	He *must* work now.
Sie **kann** es tun.	She *can* do it.

English has modal auxiliary verbs such as *must* and *can* that indicate an attitude about an action, rather than expressing the action itself.

German also uses modal auxiliary verbs. German modals are irregular in the present-tense singular. They lack endings in the **ich-** and **er/sie-** forms, and most modals show stem-vowel change.

	dürfen	können	müssen	sollen	wollen	möchte
ich	darf	kann	muß	soll	will	möchte
du	darfst	kannst	mußt	sollst	willst	möchtest
er/es/sie	darf	kann	muß	soll	will	möchte
wir	dürfen	können	müssen	sollen	wollen	möchten
ihr	dürft	könnt	müßt	sollt	wollt	möchtet
sie	dürfen	können	müssen	sollen	wollen	möchten
Sie	dürfen	können	müssen	sollen	wollen	möchten

Soll ich die Karten **kaufen?**
Frank **will** nicht **arbeiten.**

Modal auxiliaries in German are usually used with dependent infinitives. The infinitive is in last position.

Ich **muß** nach Hause.	=	Ich **muß** nach Hause gehen.
Ich **will** mein Geld.	=	Ich **will** mein Geld haben.

The dependent infinitive may be omitted when the meaning of the sentence is clear from the context.

Meanings of modals

INFINITIVE/MEANING		EXAMPLES	ENGLISH EQUIVALENTS
dürfen	permission	Ich **darf** arbeiten.	I'm *allowed to* work.
können	ability	Ich **kann** arbeiten.	I *can* work.
müssen	compulsion	Ich **muß** arbeiten.	I *must (have to)* work.
sollen	obligation	Ich **soll** arbeiten.	I'm *supposed to* work.
wollen	wishing, wanting, intention	Ich **will** arbeiten.	I *want (intend) to* work.
möchte	desire	Ich **möchte** arbeiten.	I *would like to* work.

Das Metropol Theater
ist in Ost-Berlin.

The modal **mögen**

Ich möchte, du möchtest, and so on, are special forms of the modal **mögen.** They are used frequently and are equivalent to English *would like.*

Mögen also has regular present-tense forms which are not used as often **(ich mag, du magst, er/sie mag, wir mögen, ihr mögt, sie mögen, Sie mögen).** The present-tense forms can be used to express a fondness or dislike for someone or something. **Mögen** rarely occurs in the affirmative. It is usually used in the interrogative or in the negative, without a dependent infinitive:

Mögen Sie Frau Lenz?	Do you like Mrs. Lenz?
Ich **mag** Rockmusik nicht.	I don't like rock music.

At this point, you will be expected only to recognize the present-tense forms of **mögen.**

Negative of **müssen**

Du **mußt nicht** arbeiten.	You *don't have to* work (if you don't want to).

The negative of **müssen** means *not to have to.* Note that **Du mußt nicht arbeiten** means *You don't have (you're not forced) to work,* whereas English *You mustn't work* means *You are forbidden to work.*

The German movie industry was extremely important during the era of silent films and early "talkies" (1919–1932). Directors like Fritz Lang, F. W. Murnau, and G. W. Pabst were considered among the finest in the world, and the German use of the "moving camera" was very influential.

During the 1930's and 1940's many great German filmmakers moved to other countries — mainly the United States — and there was a long period of mediocrity in German cinema due to this loss of talent. Since the early 1970's there has been a rebirth of German film, led by directors like Werner Herzog, Rainer Werner Fassbinder, and Wim Wenders, to name only the best-known of a large and growing group. Their films explore profound issues relating to politics, art, and human nature.

Wiederholung

A Christl and Peter are discussing the *Hot Dogs* concert. Answer the questions, based on the following dialogue.

CHRISTL Die *Hot Dogs* geben morgen abend ein Konzert hier!
PETER Das ist ja prima, aber ich kann sie nicht hören.
CHRISTL Warum denn nicht? Mußt du arbeiten?
PETER Nein. Ich habe kein Geld, und die Karten sind sehr teuer.
CHRISTL Kein Problem! Mein Bruder arbeitet an der Kasse. Ich habe zwei Karten für das Konzert. Ich bekomme eine, und du bekommst eine.
PETER Das ist ja klasse. Vielen Dank!

1. Wann geben die *Hot Dogs* ein Konzert?
2. Warum kann Peter nicht ins Konzert?
3. Wer arbeitet an der Kasse?
4. Wer gibt Peter eine Karte für das Konzert?

B Inform Ingrid that you're going to do the same things she is doing this week.

Do orally, then in writing. Vary the modal cues. Be sure students know meanings of sentences.

■■ Ich mache heute abend Hausaufgaben. (sollen)

Ich soll heute abend auch Hausaufgaben machen.

1. Ich spiele heute nachmittag Tennis. (können)
2. Ich gehe am Samstag ins Kino. (dürfen)
3. Ich kaufe morgen einen Pulli. (wollen)
4. Ich treibe am Sonntag Sport. (möchten)
5. Ich mache am Montag Chemie. (müssen)

C For each set of words below, pick out the three words that fit best into one category.

■■ Mark, tragen, kosten, wieviel

Mark, kosten, wieviel

1. Jugendzentrum, Konzert, Band, Lieblingsfach
2. wohnen, Karte, Kasse, ausverkauft
3. Stunde, Theater, Zeit, Uhr
4. Lust, Aufgabe, Geschichte, Englisch
5. Bleistift, Kuli, Geld, Radiergummi
6. Anzug, Schlagzeug, Größe, Farbe
7. Freund, Bruder, Schwester, Vater
8. Gitarre, Flöte, Geige, Fußball
9. Wochenende, Nachmittag, Café, Abend

D   It's Inge's birthday. Tell what she is getting from her family and friends.

> ▪▥   Erna/Bluse   *Erna gibt Inge eine Bluse.*

1. Carola/Kleid
2. Hans-Dieter/Pulli
3. ihr Vater/Schulmappe

4. ihre Mutter/Gitarre
5. Thomas/Kuli
6. Rüdiger/Buch

E   Udo isn't speaking loudly enough. Ask about the part of the sentence you didn't hear.

To be realistic, mumble the italicized parts of the sentences.

> ▪▥   Ich gehe *heute abend* ins Konzert.   *Wann gehst du ins Konzert?*

1. *Meine Freundin Ute* kommt auch.
2. *Die Hot Dogs* spielen.
3. Sie spielen *im Jugendzentrum*.
4. Die Vorstellung beginnt *um halb acht*.
5. Die Karten kosten *DM 12,50.*

F   Take the role of the ticket-seller in the illustration and answer the customers' questions.

Activity: Have students perform skits based on their answers and on the illustration.

1. Wer gibt das Rock-Konzert am Samstag abend?
2. Wieviel kosten die Karten?
3. Haben Sie noch Karten zu 8 Mark?
4. Wann beginnt die Vorstellung?
5. Wer spielt morgen abend hier?
6. Kann ich noch Karten für morgen abend bekommen?

Kulturlesestück

Wer geht ins Kino?

Deutsche Teenager gehen gern ins Kino. Einige° Filme sind sehr gut und laufen° zum Beispiel° auch in Amerika. Aber die Deutschen sehen° auch amerikanische Filme gern. Amerikanische Stars sprechen° in deutschen Kinos Deutsch. Die Deutschen mögen Untertitel° nicht.

some / run
for example
see, watch
speak

subtitles

Die Karten für gute Plätze° sind teuer — sie können sieben Mark oder mehr kosten. Natürlich kann man auch billige Karten bekommen. Die guten Plätze sind hinten°, die billigen Plätze vorne°.

seats

in the back
in the front

Meistens° gibt es eine Vorstellung am Nachmittag und zwei Vorstellungen am Abend, zum Beispiel um 19 und um 21 Uhr. Und man muß dann auch um 7 oder um 9 Uhr kommen.

usually

A Decide whether each statement is true *(richtig)* or false *(falsch)* based on the reading.

1. Deutsche Teenager dürfen nicht ins Kino gehen.
2. Deutsche sehen amerikanische Filme gern.
3. In deutschen Kinos haben amerikanische Filme Untertitel.
4. In deutschen Kinos kosten alle Karten sieben Mark.
5. Die Plätze vorne kosten mehr als *(more than)* die Plätze hinten.
6. Die Filme in deutschen Kinos laufen meistens nicht den ganzen Tag.

B Separate the following statements into two categories — those most typical of German movies and those most typical of American movies. If the statement is generally true of both German and American movies, put it in both categories: *deutsch und amerikanisch.*

1. Teenager gehen gern ins Kino.
2. Amerikanische Filme sind populär.
3. Die amerikanischen Stars sprechen Deutsch.
4. Die Stars sprechen Deutsch, aber der Film hat Untertitel.
5. Karten sind teuer.
6. Die Plätze vorne sind billig, denn *(because)* sie sind nicht so gut.
7. Die Vorstellung beginnt um sieben, aber man kann auch oft um acht hineingehen *(go in)*.
8. Es gibt eine Vorstellung am Nachmittag.

Vokabeln

SUBSTANTIVE

die Band, -s band
die Frage, -n question
das Geld money
die Gruppe, -n group
das Jugendzentrum youth center, club
die Karte, -n ticket
die Kasse box office
das Kino, -s movie theater
das Konzert, -e concert
die Lust pleasure, enjoyment
das Theater, - theater
die Vorstellung, -en performance
die Zeit time

VERBEN

beginnen to start, to begin
bekommen to get, to receive
dürfen (darf) may, to be permitted to
fragen to ask
geben (i) to give; **es gibt** (+ *acc.*) there is, there are
glauben to believe
können (kann) can, to be able to
möchte would like to
mögen (mag) to like
müssen (muß) must, to have to
nehmen (nimmt) to take
sollen (soll) should, to be supposed to
tun to do
versuchen to try
wollen (will) to want, to intend to, to wish

ANDERE WÖRTER

alles all, everything
an at
ausverkauft sold out
bei at
bitte please; you're welcome
bitte schön please; you're welcome
dann then
dumm dumb, stupid
ein paar a few, some
einfach simple, simply
frei free, not busy
mal *flavoring word* (see p. 133)
mehr more
morgen tomorrow; ~ **abend** tomorrow evening
nichts nothing
noch nicht not yet
sicher sure, certain(ly)
Sie you (*formal*)
übermorgen the day after tomorrow
vielleicht maybe

BESONDERE AUSDRÜCKE

hast du Lust? do you feel like . . . ?
ich habe keine Lust I don't feel like it
ja, und wie! sure, I do (I am)
es geht it's possible
ich bekomme frei I'll get (the day) off
das schon that's true
Karten zu drei Mark tickets for three marks
das macht sechzehn Mark that's sixteen marks
nichts mehr nothing left

Kapitel 8

Was hast du vor?

Ansichtskarten sind interessant

Thomas is curious about Petra's choice of a hobby. He thinks old post-cards are dull.

THOMAS	Sag mal, warum sammelst du gerade Ansichtskarten?
PETRA	Ich weiß nicht. Es macht Spaß.
THOMAS	Wirklich? Das verstehe ich nicht.
PETRA	Sehr einfach. Alte Ansichtskarten sind interessant und auch wertvoll.

Fragen

1. Was ist Petras Hobby?
2. Wie findet Thomas Petras Hobby?
3. Warum sammelt Petra alte Ansichtskarten?

The paradigm for verbs ending in -eln is given in the *Grammatische Übersicht.*

Du hast das Wort

Other collectable items and hobbies: *Münzen, alte Flaschen, Insekten, Puppen; Malen, Zeichnen, Basteln, Stricken.*

Ask a classmate whether he/she collects anything.

Sammelst du etwas°?   Nein, ich sammle nichts.
Ja. Ich sammle | Briefmarken°.
Schallplatten°.
Poster°.
Ansichtskarten.
Bierdeckel°.

The use of an article with a first name can express familiarity and fondness, but also a slight disparagement. Compare Eng.: *That Thomas!* (with emphasis).

Thomas braucht ein Hobby

Petra and Gerd think maybe Thomas needs a hobby, too.

GERD	Der Thomas ist wirklich eine lahme Ente.
PETRA	Ja, er ist immer müde. Und er findet immer alles langweilig.
GERD	Er hat aber auch zu nichts Lust.
PETRA	Was er braucht, ist ein Hobby.
GERD	Radioamateur vielleicht.
PETRA	Oder Keramik.

V: Chain drill:
S[1]: *Petra, hast du ein Hobby?*
S[2]: *Ja, mein Hobby ist Musik.*
Peter, hast du ein Hobby?
S[3]: *Ja, mein Hobby ist . . . etc.*

Richtig oder falsch?

1. Thomas ist immer müde.
2. Er findet alles interessant.
3. Er hat zu nichts Lust.
4. Er hat ein Hobby.
5. Er ist Radioamateur.

Sammelst du auch Briefmarken?

Du hast das Wort

A. A classmate asks you whether you have a hobby. How would you respond?

Hast du ein Hobby?   Ja, ich spiele [Tennis].
Ja, ich fotografiere° sehr gern.
Ja, ich sammle Briefmarken.
Ja, ich lese° viel.
Ja, ich gehe gern spazieren.
Ja, ich repariere° alte Autos°.
Nein, ich habe kein Hobby.

Have students use Ex. B as basis for a dialogue.

B. A friend suggests that you need a hobby. What are your excuses for not choosing the hobby he/she suggests?

Du brauchst ein Hobby.	Ja, ich habe oft nichts zu tun.
	Ja, ich habe oft Langeweile°.
	Meinst du?

Keramik	ist	vielleicht	Ach, [Keramik] ist zu schwer.
Radioamateur		interessant.	Ach, [Radios°] sind zu kompliziert°.
Ansichtskarten	sind		Ach, [Ansichtskarten] sind so langweilig.
Briefmarken			Ach, [Briefmarken] sind zu teuer.

Was habt ihr heute vor?

Astrid would like to know what Klaus and his friends have planned for the afternoon.

ASTRID   Du, Klaus, was habt ihr heute nachmittag vor?
KLAUS   Wir fahren nach Hamburg.
ASTRID   Kauft ihr ein?
KLAUS   Ja, wir kaufen Gerds Geburtstagsgeschenk.
ASTRID   Wo?
KLAUS   Ich weiß noch nicht. Bei Karstadt vielleicht.

Fragen

1. Wohin° fahren Klaus und seine Freunde?
2. Was wollen sie machen?
3. Wo kaufen sie ein?

Personalize:
Was hast du heute nachmittag vor? Kaufst du ein? Wo kaufst du ein? Was kaufst du? Ist es teuer? billig?

Du hast das Wort

A classmate inquires about your plans. How would you respond?

Was hast du	heute	vor?
	heute nachmittag	
	heute abend	
	am Wochenende	

Ich muß [arbeiten].
Ich muß [Deutsch] machen.
Ich gehe [ins Kino].
Ich spiele [Tennis].
Ich weiß noch nicht.
Nichts.
Ich habe zu nichts Lust.
Ich repariere mein Auto.

The government of the **BRD** regulates store hours to prevent competitors from taking advantage of each other and to maintain reasonable working hours. Monday through Friday stores are permitted to be open only between 7:00 A.M. and 6:30 P.M. On Saturdays stores must close by 2:00 P.M., with the exception of the first Saturday of the month **(langer Samstag),** when they may remain open until 6:00 P.M.

Stores in small towns and some city neighborhoods generally close for two or three hours during lunchtime on weekdays.

Treat prepositional contractions as part of fixed expression for now. Dative prepositional contractions are presented in *Chapter 15*.

Komm doch mit!

Photos, p. 159: Top left: Celle.
Top right and bottom: Nürnberg.

Astrid tries to persuade Erik to go shopping with her.

ASTRID	Kommst du heute nachmittag mit?
ERIK	Wohin?
ASTRID	In die Stadt. Zum Musikhaus Schumann.
ERIK	Heute, am Samstag?
ASTRID	Ja, heute ist doch langer Samstag.
ERIK	Ach ja, stimmt. Da machen die Geschäfte erst um fünf zu. Was willst du denn bei Schumann?
ASTRID	Die neue Platte von Katja Peters kaufen. Also, willst du nun mitkommen oder nicht?
ERIK	Ich habe eigentlich keine Zeit.
ASTRID	Ach, komm doch mit!
ERIK	Na gut.

Katja Peters is a fictitious singer.

Du hast das Wort

You have plans for this evening. Invite a friend to come along and inform her/him where you're going.

Suggested *Fragen: Wohin geht Astrid heute nachmittag? Kommt Erik mit? Welcher Samstag ist heute? Wann machen die Geschäfte heute zu? Was will Astrid bei Schumann?*

Kommst du heute abend mit?   Wohin?

In die Disco°.   Ja, gern.
In die Stadt.   Wann gehen wir?
Ins Café°.   Danke, ich kann nicht.
Ins Kino.
Ins Konzert.
Ins Jugendzentrum.   Cue with visuals.
Ins Theater.   Other places to go: *nach Bergdorf, ins Theater, in die Schule.*

Frag!

Ask a friend to obtain certain information from someone else. Note that when someone tells you to ask someone else a question, the verb comes at the end. In your question, however, regular word order is used.

Teaching suggestion: If students have difficulty understanding the questions at first, ask one the direct question (*Ute, was sammelst du gern?*), then ask a second student to ask the first (*Peter, frag Ute, was sie gern sammelt!*). Repeat this several times until they get the idea.

■▮   Frag [Ute], wie sie alte Ansichtskarten findet!   *Ute, wie findest du alte Ansichtskarten?*

1. Frag [Kai], was er sammelt!
2. Frag [Ute], was sie heute nachmittag macht!
3. Frag [Kai], was er bei Schumann kaufen will!
4. Frag [Ute], welche Platte sie kaufen möchte!
5. Frag [Kai], wann er ins Kino geht!
6. Frag [Ute],wieviel die Kinokarten kosten!

Frag! accustoms students to hearing the verb in final position. Students are not expected to generate transposed word order at this time.

Personalize by using students' names.
Have students answer the questions.

In recent years the downtown areas of many cities in German-speaking countries have been converted to traffic-free pedestrian zones **(Fußgängerzonen).** In addition to attractive shops and boutiques, the **Fußgängerzone** has many restaurants and outdoor cafés. The streets are frequently lined with flowers or trees, and they often lead into small squares with fountains or sculpture. Throughout the **Fußgängerzone** there are benches where people can rest their tired feet or simply sit and watch the others go by.

Musikhaus Schumann

1. der Cassetten-Recorder
2. das Radio
3. die Cassette
4. der Fernseher
5. die Schallplatte (die Platte)
6. die Stereoanlage
7. der Platten-spieler

Additional vocabulary:
das Tonband
das Tonbandgerät
Farbfernseher
Schwarzweißfernseher

A   Answer the following questions based on the illustration.

1. Wie teuer ist die Stereoanlage?
2. Was kostet mehr — das Radio oder der Cassetten-Recorder?
3. Ist der Fernseher preiswert?
4. Ist eine Schallplatte billig oder teuer?

Du hast das Wort   Compare your preferences with a classmate's.

Möchtest du einen Cassetten-Recorder kaufen oder hast du schon einen?
Kaufst du viele Platten? Cassetten?
Hörst du gern Radio?
Siehst du oft fern°?

Some useful commands

Have students tell what they are doing as they carry out commands: *Ich stehe auf,* (etc.). Have other students describe the action: *Er / Sie steht auf,* (etc.).

Mach die Tür bitte zu!	Please close the door.
Mach das Fenster bitte auf!	Please open the window.
Mach das Licht bitte an!	Please turn on the light.
Mach das Licht bitte aus!	Please turn out the light.
Steh bitte auf!	Please stand up.

B Carry out the commands as your teacher gives them.

C Tell a friend to carry out some of the commands above.

Flavoring word **mal** in commands

Sag **mal,** warum sammelst
   du gerade Ansichtskarten?
Schreib doch **mal!**

Say (Tell me), why do you collect
   post cards?
Why don't you write (sometime)?

Mal is frequently used to soften commands. The speaker leaves the time for carrying out the command vague and up to the receiver of the command.

Flavoring word **doch**

Komm **doch** mit!
Ja, heute ist **doch** langer
   Samstag.

Why don't you come along?
Today's the first Saturday of the
   month (remember?).

As a flavoring word **doch** has several meanings. In the first example the speaker uses **doch** to persuade the listener to do something. In the second example the speaker uses **doch** to imply that what is said is obvious and reminds the listener of something they both know.

D Give the English equivalents.

1. Sag mal! Gehen wir heute einkaufen oder nicht?
2. Hör mal! Das tut man doch nicht.
3. Wir gehen abends oft schwimmen. Komm doch mal mit!
4. Was machst du heute abend?
   Das weißt du doch.
5. Möchtest du mal die *Hot Dogs* hören?
6. Wir können es ja mal versuchen.
7. Schreib doch mal an Barbara.

For #5 and 6, you may need to review the use of *mal* in statements (Chapter 7).

Aussprache

Urge students to keep
diphthongs short.

[ai]	m**ei**n, M**ai**er
[ɔi]	h**eu**te, H**äu**ser
[ao]	br**au**n

A Practice the following words horizontally in pairs.

[ai]	[ɔi]	[ao]	[ɔi]
l**ei**te	L**eu**te	L**au**te	L**eu**te
h**ei**ser	H**äu**ser	bl**au**e	Bl**äu**e
S**ei**le	S**äu**le	s**au**re	S**äu**re
B**ei**le	B**eu**le	B**au**m	B**äu**me
H**ai**	H**eu**	H**au**fen	h**äu**fen

Do drills vertically, then
horizontally.

[i]	[ai]
L**ie**be	L**ei**be
W**ie**se	W**ei**se
s**ie**de	S**ei**de
B**ie**l	B**ei**l
W**ie**n	W**ei**n

B Practice the sounds [ai], [ɔi], and [ao]. Read the sentences aloud.

1. Meine Brüder spielen beide viel Fußball.
2. Das kleine Kind lernt fleißig Deutsch.
3. Warum gibt es so viele graue Häuser hier?

Additional proverbs:
Träume sind Schäume.
Ohne Fleiß kein Preis.

Proverb: Out of sight,
out of mind.

Aus den Augen, aus dem Sinn.

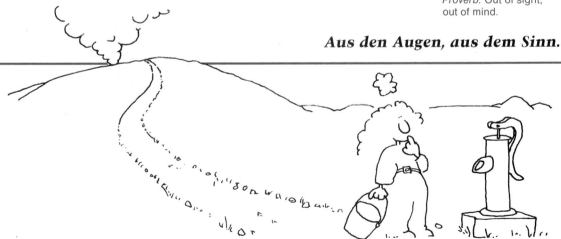

Übungen

Help students learn the *du-* and *er/sie*-forms of *fahren*. Compare to *tragen*, which they already know.

The interrogatives **wo** and **wohin**

Game: *Der Spion und der Schupo* (abbr. for *Schutzpolizist*): Use map for a police chase through Germany.

Wo ist Martina?   Where is Martina?
Wohin geht sie?   Where is she going?

Wo is used to ask about location. **Wohin** is used to ask about direction.

A You didn't hear the last part of the following statements. Ask to have the information repeated, using *wo* or *wohin*.

T: *Der Spion fährt nach Bonn. Wo ist er?*
S: *In Bonn.*
T: *Wohin fährt der Schupo?*
S: *Nach Bonn.*
T: *Der Spion bleibt also nicht in Bonn. Wohin fährt er?*
S: *Nach (Frankfurt).,* etc. at a rapid pace.

■ıı   Martina wohnt in München.   *Wo wohnt Martina?*

■ıı   Sie fährt morgen nach Bremen.   *Wohin fährt sie morgen?*

1. Utes Freund wohnt in Frankfurt.
2. Ilse geht jetzt nach Hause.
3. Tanja und Günter gehen ins Kino.
4. Herr Fleischer arbeitet zu Hause.
5. Frau Kaufmann fährt in die Stadt.

Have a second student briefly answer the question made up by the first student.
T: *Martina wohnt in München.*
S¹: *Wo wohnt Martina?*
S²: *In München.*

Verbs with stem-vowel change **e>ie**

Point out that the stem of *lesen* ends in a sibilant; remind students of the contraction in the *du*-form.

lesen
ich lese
du **liest**
er/es/sie **liest**

sehen
ich sehe
du **siehst**
er/es/sie **sieht**

Chain drill: Distribute flash cards to students.
S¹: *Ich sehe [die Tür]. Was siehst du?*
S²: *Ich sehe [den Fernseher]. Was siehst du?*

Lesen and **sehen** have a stem-vowel change **e>ie** in the **du-** and **er/sie-**forms of the present tense.

B Report on the leisure activities of the following people.

Point to various students in class.

■ıı   Dieter   *Dieter liest viel.*

1. Frau Weiß	3. Monika	5. wir
2. ich	4. du	6. ihr

C Say that the following people often watch television.

■ıı   Marita   *Marita sieht oft fern.*

1. Herr Hübner	3. Torsten	5. wir
2. ich	4. du	6. ihr

Present tense of **wissen**

ich **weiß**		wir wissen
du **weißt**	Sie wissen	ihr wißt
er/es/sie **weiß**		sie wissen

For practice with *wissen*, you may wish to refer students to the song on p. 291 of Chapter 13.

Wissen is irregular in the singular forms of the present tense.

D You and your friends are going to a disco. Confirm that everyone knows when you're going.

■‖ Jutta weiß, wann wir in die Disco gehen. Und Jürgen? *Er weiß das auch.*

1. Und Benno?   4. Und Ulf und Jochen?
2. Und Christl?   5. Und ihr?
3. Und du?

Use names of students in class.

Du hast das Wort

A. Answer according to your personal knowledge or experience. Use *Ja, das weiß ich* or *Nein, das weiß ich nicht.*

If students answer *yes*, have them supply the information concerned.

Weißt du, wie alt deine Mutter ist?
Weißt du, wann dein Vater Geburtstag hat?
Weißt du, wann deine Freunde Geburtstag haben?
Weißt du, wieviel Jeans kosten?
Weißt du, wieviel eine Mappe kostet?
Weißt du, wieviel Kinokarten kosten?

B. Ask your teacher some of the questions in Exercise A.

The imperative forms: **du, ihr, Sie**

Imperative forms are used to express commands. In both German and English, the verb is in first position.

du-imperative

Inge! **Frag(e)** bitte Frau Held!   Inge, ask Mrs. Held, please.
Dirk! **Arbeite** bitte jetzt!   Dirk, work now, please.

The **du**-imperative consists of the stem of a verb plus **-e**. The **-e** is often dropped in informal usage: **frage!**>**frag!** The **-e** may not be omitted if the stem ends in **-d** or **-t: arbeite!**

E   Frank is trying to put off repairing your car until tomorrow. Try to convince him to do it today.

   ◾⫴   Ich repariere es morgen.   *Ach, repariere es doch heute!*

1. Ich versuche es morgen.   3. Ich beginne morgen.
2. Ich mache es morgen.   4. Ich komme morgen.

Petra! **Nimm** bitte das Buch da!   Petra, please take that book.
Lies es heute abend!   Read it this evening.

If the stem vowel of a verb changes from **e** to **i** or **ie,** the imperative has the same vowel change and has no final **-e: nehmen**>**nimm!**

F   Monika is working with you in the library. Order her to do the things she asks about.

   ◾⫴   Soll ich das Buch da nehmen?   *Ja, nimm das Buch da!*

1. Soll ich das Buch lesen?   3. Soll ich Ute das Buch geben?
2. Soll ich das Heft nehmen?   4. Soll ich Jan das Heft geben?

*Interessante
Ansichtskarten*

ihr-imperative

Günter! Peter! **Fragt** bitte Frau Held!	Günter and Peter, please ask Mrs. Held.
Arbeitet bitte jetzt!	Please work now.

The **ihr**-imperative is identical with the **ihr**-form of the present tense, except that the pronoun **ihr** is omitted.

G

You and your friends are in a record store. Advise them to do the things they ask about:

▪▥ Sollen wir die Platte hier kaufen?	*Ja, kauft die Platte!*

1. Sollen wir auch die Cassette nehmen?
2. Sollen wir die Platte spielen?
3. Sollen wir jetzt beginnen?
4. Sollen wir es versuchen?

Sie-imperative

Herr Schmidt! **Fragen Sie** Frau Held!	Mr. Schmidt, ask Mrs. Held.
Arbeiten Sie bitte jetzt!	Please work now.

The **Sie**-imperative is identical with the **Sie**-form of the present tense. The pronoun **Sie** is always stated and follows the verb directly.

H

Frau Wagner is to pick up some theater tickets for you. Give her precise instructions as to what to do.

▪▥ Soll ich jetzt zur Theaterkasse gehen?	*Ja, gehen Sie bitte jetzt zur Theaterkasse!*

1. Soll ich drei Karten kaufen?
2. Soll ich die Karten zu 30 Mark nehmen?
3. Soll ich heute abend ins Theater gehen?
4. Soll ich um sieben kommen?
5. Soll ich mit Frau Lange fahren?

Du hast das Wort

Lead your class in a team game. Give various orders to individual members of each team. If they obey you, their teams gain a point. You may wish to use some of the commands from page 161.

Mach das Licht aus!	Steh auf!
Mach das Fenster auf!	Nimm [Utes] Buch!
Mach die Tür zu!	Gib [Erik] das Buch!

Sidebar notes (left margin):

A contrast between interrogative and imperative forms may be helpful. Write *Geht ihr jetzt?* on board; then cross out *ihr.* Change question mark to exclamation point.

V: Cue with imperative. Students change to questions.

Write on board: *Gehen Sie jetzt?* Change question mark to exclamation point.

Optional exercise: May precede H with contrast of question and command. *Gehen Sie jetzt zur Theaterkasse? Gehen Sie bitte jetzt zur Theaterkasse!*

Welche Platte soll ich denn kaufen?

Imperative forms of the verb **sein**

Inge!	**Sei** um sieben da!	
Günter! Peter!	**Seid** um sieben da!	Be here at seven.
Frau Lange!	**Seien Sie** um sieben da!	

I Urge the following people to change their attitudes.

Review meanings of adjectives before doing Ex. I. Use cut-out illustrations or posters of children, teen-agers, and adults to cue imperatives.

◼▮ Andrea, du bist aber faul.   *Sei nicht so faul!*

1. Astrid, du bist aber sauer.
2. Anton, du bist aber doof.
3. Bernd, du bist aber wirklich langweilig.

◼▮ Claudia! Gerd! Ihr seid ja so sauer.   *Seid nicht so sauer!*

4. Regina! Hugo! Ihr seid aber sehr faul.
5. Elke! Paul! Ihr seid so doof.
6. Inge! Franz! Ihr seid wirklich langweilig.

◼▮ Herr Kurz! Sind Sie sicher?   *Seien Sie nicht so sicher!*

7. Frau Lutz! Sie sind ja so fleißig.
8. Fräulein Weiß! Sie sind ja so fleißig.
9. Herr Lehner! Warum sind Sie so langweilig?

Separable-prefix verbs

The separable prefix

| mitkommen
zumachen | Ingrid **kommt** heute **mit**.
Wann **macht** das Geschäft **zu**? | Ingrid is coming along today.
When does the store close? |

Help students discover that in spoken German the stress falls on the separable prefix.

Many German verbs begin with prefixes such as **mit** and **zu.** Some prefixes are separable: in the present tense, they are separated from the base form of the verb and are in last position.

> Möchtest du heute **mitkommen?**   Would you like to come along today?
>
> Kannst du die Tür **zumachen?**   Can you shut the door?

In the infinitive form, the prefix is attached to the base form of the verb.

J   Ingrid asks what you and your friends have planned today. Verify her guesses.

Personalize.

■ⅲ   Kommst du heute nachmittag mit?   *Ja, ich komme heute nachmittag mit.*

1. Kommt Axel auch mit?
2. Hat Helga etwas vor?
3. Kaufst du bei Karstadt ein?
4. Macht Karstadt um fünf zu?

Nicht with separable-prefix verbs

| mitkommen
aufmachen | Ingrid kommt heute **nicht** mit.
Warum machst du das Fenster **nicht** auf? |

In a negative sentence, the adverb **nicht** usually comes directly before the separable prefix.

K   Werner wants to know what plans you and Trudi have. Keep him guessing by answering his questions in the negative.

V¹: Personalize.
V²: Make a statement, then ask a question based on it.
  T: *(Dieter) kommt heute mit. Wann kommt Dieter mit?*

■ⅲ   Kommt ihr heute nachmittag mit?   *Nein, wir kommen nicht mit.*

1. Kauft ihr heute nachmittag ein?
2. Kommt ihr heute abend mit?
3. Seht ihr heute abend fern?
4. Habt ihr vor, ins Kino zu gehen?

Have students describe
action of teacher.
T: *Was mache ich?*
S: *Sie machen die Tür
auf.*

Imperative forms of separable-prefix verbs

Gerd! **Mach** die Tür bitte **zu!**
Peter! Claudia! **Kommt** jetzt **mit!**
Frau Stein! **Machen Sie** bitte das Fenster **auf!**

In an imperative sentence, the separable prefix is in last position.

L You're getting the room ready for a party at the youth center. Tell each of your assistants what to do.

Additional practice:
Ute is in charge of
preparations for a
party. She gives orders;
student asks whether
he/she should do the
things now.
*Mach mal die Türen
auf!*
*Soll ich die Türen jetzt
aufmachen?*

■▥   Türen aufmachen   *Mach die Türen auf!*

1. Fenster aufmachen
2. Licht anmachen
3. bei Karstadt einkaufen

4. Fenster wieder zumachen
5. Türen wieder zumachen
6. Licht ausmachen

Grammatische Übersicht

Interrogatives **wo** and **wohin**   (A)

Wo ist Ingrid?   *Where* is Ingrid?
Wohin geht Dieter?   *Where* is Dieter going?

English uses the single word *where* for the two meanings *in what place* and *to what place*. German always distinguishes between these two meanings. **Wo** is used for *in what place* and **wohin** is used for *to what place*.

Verbs with stem-vowel change **e>ie**   (B-C)

lesen		
ich lese	Sie lesen	wir lesen
du **liest**		ihr lest
er/es/sie **liest**		sie lesen

sehen		
ich sehe	Sie sehen	wir sehen
du **siehst**		ihr seht
er/es/sie **sieht**		sie sehen

Lesen and **sehen** have a stem-vowel change **e>ie** in the **du-** and **er/sie-**forms of the present tense. Note that because the stem of **lesen** ends in a sibilant, the **-st** ending of the **du-**form contracts to **-t: du liest.**

Present tense of **wissen** (D)

ich **weiß**		wir wissen
du **weißt**	Sie wissen	ihr **wißt**
er/es/sie **weiß**		sie wissen

Wissen is irregular in the singular forms of the present tense.

The imperative forms: **du, ihr, Sie** (E-H)

Ernst!	**Schreib** bald!	
Peter! Inge!	**Schreibt** bald!	Write soon.
Herr Schmidt!	**Schreiben Sie** bald!	

The imperative forms are used to express commands. As in English, the verb is in first position. In written German an exclamation point is always used after a command.

du-imperative

INFINITIVE	IMPERATIVE	PRESENT
beginnen	**Beginn(e)** jetzt!	Beginnst du jetzt?
arbeiten	**Arbeite** jetzt!	Arbeitest du jetzt?
nehmen	**Nimm** das Papier!	Nimmst du das Papier?

The **du**-imperative consists of the stem of a verb plus **-e**, but the **-e** is often dropped in informal usage. If the stem of the verb ends in **-d** or **-t**, the **-e** may not be omitted in written German: **arbeite!**

If the stem vowel of a verb changes from **e** to **i** or **ie**, the **du**-imperative has the same vowel change and has no final **-e.** The pronoun **du** is not used in the imperative.

ihr-imperative

INFINITIVE	IMPERATIVE	PRESENT
beginnen	**Beginnt** jetzt!	Beginnt ihr jetzt?
nehmen	**Nehmt** das Papier!	Nehmt ihr das Papier?

The **ihr**-imperative is identical with the **ihr**-form of the present tense, except that the pronoun **ihr** is not used in the imperative.

Sie-imperative

INFINITIVE	IMPERATIVE	PRESENT
beginnen	**Beginnen Sie** jetzt!	Beginnen Sie jetzt?
nehmen	**Nehmen Sie** das Papier!	Nehmen Sie das Papier?

The **Sie**-imperative is identical with the **Sie**-form of the present tense. The pronoun **Sie** is always stated and follows the verb immediately.

In speech, one differentiates a command from a question by intonation. The voice falls at the end of a command and rises at the end of a general question.

Imperative forms of the verb **sein** (I)

Inge!	**Sei** um sieben Uhr da!	
Petra! Uwe!	**Seid** um sieben Uhr da!	Be here at seven
Herr Braun!	**Seien Sie** um sieben Uhr da!	o'clock.

Note that the **Sie**-imperative of **sein** is different from the **Sie**-form of the present tense.

Spinnen ist ein interessantes Hobby.

Separable-prefix verbs (J-L)

Have students think of other two-word verbs in English: *to pick up, to fill up, to dress up, to sit up*, etc.

to get up	I *get up* early.
to call up	Did you *call* your friend *up?*
to write down	Let me *write down* your address.

English has many two-word verbs, such as *to get up, to call up,* and *to write down.* These two-word verbs consist of a verb and a particle (for example, *up, down*). In sentences the particle is sometimes separated from the verb.

aufstehen	Warum **stehst** du nicht **auf?**
mitkommen	Erik **kommt** heute **mit.**
zumachen	**Mach** die Tür **zu!**

German has a large number of *separable-prefix verbs* that function like certain English two-word verbs. Examples are **aufstehen, mitkommen, zumachen.** In present-tense statements and questions and in imperative forms, the separable prefix (**auf, mit, zu,** and so on) is separated from the verb and is in last position.

> Ute kann nicht **mitkommen.**

In the infinitive form, the prefix is attached to the base form of the verb.

> Inge kommt heute **nicht** mit.

The adverb **nicht** usually comes directly before a separable prefix.

> Frank möchte **mit'kommen.**
> Petra kommt nicht **mit'.**

In spoken German, the stress falls on the prefix of separable-prefix verbs. In the vocabularies of this text, separable-prefix verbs are indicated by a raised dot between the prefix and the verb: **auf·stehen, ein·kaufen, mit·kommen, fern·sehen, vor·haben, zu·machen.**

Infinitives ending in **-eln**

sammeln		
ich **sammle**		wir sammeln
du sammelst	Sie sammeln	ihr sammelt
er/es/sie sammelt		sie sammeln

When the infinitive of a verb ends in **-eln,** the stem loses the **-e** in the **ich-**form.

Hamburg has long been one of the busiest seaports
in Europe. Above: Hamburg in 1730. Below: The city
today is a dynamic blend of the old and the new.

Wiederholung

Have students sight-read dialogue. Perform as skit.

A Erik is having a hard time getting Jürgen to do anything. Answer the questions based on the following dialogue.

ERIK Wir gehen heute abend zu Inge. Kommst du auch?

JÜRGEN Ach nein. Bei Inge ist es immer so langweilig. Da dürfen wir nicht richtig Musik machen.

ERIK Willst du vielleicht ins Kino?

JÜRGEN Ach nein. Filme finde ich doof.

ERIK Was möchtest du denn?

JÜRGEN Ich weiß es nicht. Ich habe zu nichts Lust.

ERIK Du bist aber eine lahme Ente!

1. Wohin möchte Erik heute abend?
2. Warum geht Jürgen nicht mit?
3. Will er ins Kino? Warum (nicht)?
4. Was will er denn?
5. Warum ist Jürgen eine lahme Ente?

B Make up two-line dialogues by choosing a line from column A and an appropriate response from column B.

Perform the made-up skit before the class.

A	B
Keramik ist interessant.	Ich kann's ja mal versuchen.
Du brauchst ein Hobby.	Ja, und wie!
Ich sammle alte Autos.	Meinst du?
Möchtest du fotografieren lernen?	Ich weiß es nicht.
	Vielleicht. Ich bin nicht sicher.
Benno ist Radioamateur, nicht?	Nein, eigentlich nicht.
[Wanderst] du gern?	Das kann sein.
	Ist das nicht furchtbar teuer?
	Nein, das ist zu langweilig.

C You and Jürgen have plans for tomorrow. Form sentences using the cues provided.

Tell students the words are in relative correct order, except for the dependent infinitive and the subject-verb in questions.

1. Jürgen / müssen / aufstehen / morgen / um sechs
2. er / wollen / fahren / nach Hamburg
3. ihr / dürfen / mitkommen / auch / ?
4. wir / können / einkaufen / da
5. Jürgen / möchten / kaufen / bei Schumann / eine Platte
6. die Platten / sollen / sein / da / sehr billig
7. du / wollen / kaufen / auch / eine Platte / ?

May do orally in class. Then assign as written homework.

D   Complete the second line of each two-line exchange by choosing an appropriate flavoring word. Give an English equivalent of each exchange.

1. Ich wohne nicht in der Gartenstraße.
   Wo wohnst du ____? (denn, doch)
2. Fährst du nach Bergdorf?
   Ja, komm ____ mit! (denn, doch)
3. Der Anzug da kostet nur 100 Mark.
   Das ist ____ billig. (mal, ja)
4. Petra sammelt alte Ansichtskarten.
   Das ist ____ interessant! (ja, denn)
5. Ist das Buch interessant?
   Ja. Lies es doch ____. (mal, ja)
6. Der Rock hier ist zu klein.
   Welche Größe trägst du ____? (mal, denn)

E   Thomas is in charge of a surprise party at his house this evening. Change the phrases in italics to the plural and restate his remarks.

1. Wo ist *das Geschenk?*
2. Hat Peter *den Bierdeckel?*
3. Ich brauche nun *die Schallplatte.*
4. Wer hat *die Cassette?*
5. Mach bitte *die Tür* auf.
6. Gib mir bitte *das Poster* da.
7. Hört ihr nicht *das Auto?*
8. Jetzt könnt ihr *die Tür* wieder zumachen.

F   The following sentences contain some unfamiliar words that are either cognates or compounds of familiar words. Give the meaning of each italicized word.

1. Hast du die *Kinokarten* gekauft?
2. Weißt du, wann die *Abendvorstellung* beginnt?
3. Karl spielt gern Fußball, Basketball und Hockey. Er ist wirklich ein *Sportfreund.*
4. Eishockey spielen wir im *Wintersportzentrum.*
5. Volker braucht ein deutsch-englisches *Wörterbuch.*
6. Zum Geburtstag bekommt ein *Baby* viele *Spielsachen.*

G   Answer the following questions. Then ask your teacher the same questions.

1. Hast du ein Hobby?
2. Sammelst du etwas?
3. Liest du gern?
4. Welches Buch liest du jetzt?
5. Gehst du gern spazieren?
6. Treibst du gern Sport?
7. Fotografierst du gern?

Kulturlesestück

Sammelfreuden

Germans love to go to the museum. In one year, the 2000 museums in the *BRD* have approximately 35 million visitors. In addition to seeing fine art, people like to learn about other aspects of their history. They therefore visit museums with special collections such as hats, typewriters, salt, tobacco, ivory, stoves, or shoes.

The Gutenberg-Museum in Mainz shows the beginnings of book printing. The Grimm Museum in Kassel is devoted to the Grimm brothers, famous for their fairy tales.

Viele Menschen° sammeln etwas: Briefmarken, Bierdeckel, Bücher, Ansichtskarten, Schallplatten, Poster. Auch als° Gemeinschaft° sammeln die Menschen: Museen° findet man° in vielen Städten.

5 Viele Deutsche gehen am Sonntag ins Museum, denn dann kostet es nichts. Sie sehen da Sammlungen° von Autos und Maschinen, von Bildern° und Postern, von Briefmarken, Büchern, Keramik und Möbeln°. Es gibt auch besondere° Museen, zum Beispiel das Gutenberg-Museum in Mainz, das Grimm-Museum in Kassel, ein Ledermuseum° in Offenbach, ein Uhrenmuseum in Furtwangen, ein Fahrradmuseum° in Neckarsulm und sogar ein Brotmuseum° in Ulm.

people

as
society / museums
one

collections
pictures
furniture
special

leather museum

bicycle museum
bread museum

A Choose the phrase that best completes each statement, based on the reading.

1. Die Gemeinschaft sammelt Sachen in . . .
   a. Möbeln
   b. Geschäften
   c. Bildern
   d. Museen
2. Man findet Museen in vielen . . .
   a. Städten
   b. Kassen
   c. Sammlungen
   d. Theatern
3. Am Sonntag sind viele Menschen im Museum, denn . . .
   a. die Karten sind am Sonntag sehr billig
   b. sie brauchen keine Karten zu kaufen
   c. am Samstag müssen sie arbeiten
   d. die Museen machen nur am Sonntag auf

B Below are lists of items, grouped so that two of them have something in common and might therefore be found in the same museum. Indicate which item does not belong in each group.

1. Briefmarken, Ansichtskarten, Autos
2. Möbel, Plattenspieler, Radios
3. Bilder, Brot, Poster
4. Autos, Schlagzeug, Fahrräder
5. Kleider, Anzüge, Bierdeckel
6. Uhren, Geigen, Gitarren

Vokabeln

SUBSTANTIVE

die Ansichtskarte, -n   picture postcard
das Auto, -s   car
der Bierdeckel, -   coaster *(used under a glass or mug)*
die Briefmarke, -n   postage stamp
das Café, -s   café
die Cassette, -n   cassette
der Cassetten-Recorder, -   cassette recorder
die Disco, -s   disco, discothèque
das Fenster, -   window
der Fernseher, -   television set
das Geschäft, -e   store
das (Geburtstags)geschenk, -e   (birthday) present
die Keramik   ceramics, pottery
die Langeweile   boredom
das Licht   light
die Platte, -n   record
der Plattenspieler, -   record player; turntable
das *(also* **der) Poster, -**   poster
das Radio, -s   radio
der Radioamateur, -e   "ham" radio operator
die Schallplatte, -n   record
die Stadt, ¨e   city
die Stereoanlage, -n   stereo system
die Tür, -en   door

VERBEN

an·machen   to switch on (the light)
auf·machen   to open
auf·stehen   to get up
aus·machen   to turn off (the light)
ein·kaufen   to shop; ~ **gehen** to go shopping
fahren (ä)   to drive

VERBEN

fern·sehen (ie)   to watch TV
fotografieren   to photograph
lesen (ie)   to read
mit·kommen   to come along
reparieren   to repair
sagen   to say, to tell
sammeln   to collect
sehen (ie)   to see, to watch, to look
vor·haben   to plan
verstehen   to understand
wissen (weiß)   to know
zu·machen   to shut

ANDERE WÖRTER

also   well
doch   *flavoring word (see p. 161)*
eigentlich   really, actually
etwas   something
gerade   exactly, precisely; just
immer   always
kompliziert   complicated
nun   now
wohin   where (to)
wertvoll   valuable

BESONDERE AUSDRÜCKE

eine lahme Ente   a dull, boring person
er hat zu nichts Lust   he doesn't feel like doing anything
ich habe Langeweile   I am bored
das stimmt   that's right

Ich habe zu Hause geholfen

179

Ich habe mein Zimmer aufgeräumt

Karin and Norbert found different ways to occupy their time over the weekend.

NORBERT   Was hast du am Wochenende gemacht?

KARIN   Ich habe geschlafen.

NORBERT   Mensch! Das ist doch nicht dein Ernst!

KARIN   Doch! Ehrenwort! Am Sonntag habe ich dann ein Flugzeugmodell gebastelt. Und was hast du gemacht?

NORBERT   Ich habe gearbeitet — wie immer.

KARIN   Was heißt das — du hast gearbeitet?

NORBERT   Ich muß zu Hause helfen. Ich habe mein Zimmer aufgeräumt und das Auto gewaschen.

KARIN   Das nennst du arbeiten?

NORBERT   Also, es ist wenigstens mehr als schlafen.

Fragen

Help students give answers in conversational past correctly.

1. Was hat Karin am Wochenende gemacht?
2. Was hat sie gebastelt?
3. Wer hat gearbeitet?
4. Welches Zimmer hat Norbert aufgeräumt?
5. Was hat Norbert sonst noch gemacht?

After students have done Ex. A, encourage them to give questions and answers with books closed.

Du hast das Wort

A. A classmate asks you what you've done recently. How would you respond?

Was hast du	am Wochenende gestern°	gemacht?

Ich habe	Hausaufgaben gemacht.
	[Tennis] gespielt.
	viel gearbeitet.
	[mein Zimmer] aufgeräumt.
	das Auto gewaschen.
	viel geschlafen.

B. You claim to have done certain things. When a friend expresses doubt or surprise, insist in your own words that what you say is true.

Vary with days of the week:
Was hast du am Samstag gemacht? am Montag? am Mittwoch?, etc.

Ich habe am Wochenende [zwölf] Stunden geschlafen.

Ich habe gestern [zwei] Bücher gelesen.

Ich habe letzte° Woche [zehn] Platten gekauft.

Mensch! Das ist doch nicht dein Ernst!

Wirklich?

Das ist schwer zu glauben.

Ich habe eine Torte gebacken

Paul feels he spent a constructive weekend, but Sabine seems to disagree.

SABINE Was hast du am Wochenende gemacht?
PAUL Nicht viel. Ich habe für meine Mutter eine Torte gebacken. Sie hat meine Großeltern zum Kaffee eingeladen.
SABINE Sehr interessant!
PAUL Sei nicht so sarkastisch! Du hast doch gefragt.
SABINE Hat die Torte wenigstens geschmeckt?
PAUL Ich weiß es nicht. Ich habe Gerda abgeholt, und wir haben einen Spaziergang gemacht. Wir haben dann bei Gerdas Eltern Kaffee getrunken.

Fragen

1. Was hat Paul gebacken?
2. Warum hat er die Torte gebacken?
3. Hat die Torte geschmeckt?
4. Was haben Gerda und Paul gemacht?
5. Wo haben sie Kaffee getrunken?

Du hast das Wort

Give a short account of what you did this weekend.

Am Freitag nachmittag habe ich [Tennis gespielt].
Am Abend habe ich [ferngesehen].
Am Samstag . . .

Arbeitsplan fürs Wochenende

Herr und Frau Gerdes haben vier Kinder. Alle müssen zu Hause helfen. Jedes Wochenende macht Frau Gerdes einen Arbeitsplan. Hier ist der Plan für letztes Wochenende.

	Freitag	Samstag	Sonntag
Werner	Badezimmer putzen	Geschirr spülen Garage aufräumen	Tisch decken
Gudrun	Tisch decken Mülleimer raustragen	abtrocknen Staub saugen	Geschirr spülen
Hilde	abtrocknen	Auto waschen Tisch decken	Frühstück machen
Erik	Geschirr spülen	einkaufen	abtrocknen

Fragen

Personalize in the present tense:
Mußt du zu Hause Geschirr spülen?
Habt ihr eine Spülmaschine?
Wer deckt den Tisch?
Mußt du dein Zimmer oft aufräumen?

1. Wer hat am Freitag Geschirr gespült?
2. Wer hat abgetrocknet?
3. Wer hat den Mülleimer rausgetragen?
4. Wann hat Werner das Badezimmer geputzt?
5. Wer hat fürs Wochenende eingekauft?
6. Wann hat Hilde den Tisch gedeckt?
7. Wann hat Gudrun abgetrocknet?
8. Wer hat am Sonntag Frühstück gemacht? den Tisch gedeckt?

Du hast das Wort

Optional: written review assignment. After doing this orally, students may write about their own chores last weekend.

Ask a classmate who must do various family chores next weekend and when.

Wer muß fürs Wochenende einkaufen?
Wer muß spülen?
Wer muß . . .

Doch as positive response

NORBERT	Das ist doch nicht dein Ernst!	You're not serious, are you?
KARIN	**Doch!**	Of course I am!
CAROLA	Gehst du denn nicht ins Kino?	Aren't you going to the movies?
OTTO	**Doch.**	Why, sure I am.

In Chapter 8 you learned that **doch** can function as a flavoring word. **Doch** may also be used as a one-word positive response to a negative statement or question. With **doch,** the speaker contradicts an assumption contained in a previous statement or question.

A Helga is making a number of wrong suppositions. Correct her, using *doch*.

    ■ıı   Gehst du nicht einkaufen?   *Doch. Ich gehe einkaufen.*

1. Gehst du nicht in die Stadt?
2. Kaufst du keine Platten?
3. Arbeitest du heute nicht?
4. Du gehst also heute nicht spazieren.
5. Du meinst das nicht.

B Say that you've done everything you're supposed to do.

    ■ıı   Hast du das Badezimmer geputzt?   *Ja, das habe ich geputzt.*

    ■ıı   Hast du den Tisch nicht gedeckt?   *Doch, den habe ich gedeckt.*

1. Hast du die Garage nicht aufgeräumt?
2. Hast du das Auto gewaschen?
3. Hast du die Torte gebacken?
4. Hast du deine Hausaufgaben nicht gemacht?

German cleaning products

Was hast du zu Hause gemacht?

Ich habe die Möbel abgestaubt.

Ich habe den Tisch abgeräumt.

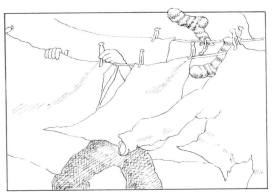

Ich habe Wäsche gewaschen.

Ich habe den Hund und die Katze gefüttert.

Ich habe Gartenarbeit gemacht.

Ich habe Kaffee gekocht.

C   Confirm the fact that you've already done your chores for the day.

■⊪   Hast du schon die Möbel   *Ja, die habe ich schon ab-*
        abgestaubt?   *gestaubt.*

1. Hast du schon die Torte gebacken?
2. Hast du schon den Müll rausgetragen?
3. Hast du schon den Hund gefüttert?
4. Hast du schon die Gartenarbeit gemacht?

Du hast das Wort   State three chores that you or various members of your family did this past weekend.

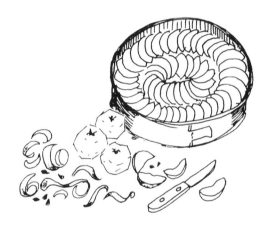

A German **Torte** has several layers, often with a cream filling. Another favorite pastry in German-speaking countries is the **Kuchen,** which consists of a single layer and sometimes has a fruit topping. The recipe below is for an **Apfelkuchen.**

Zutaten

150 Gramm Butter
125 Gramm Zucker
1 Ei
Eine abgeriebene Zitronenschale
150 Gramm Mehl
1 Teelöffel Backpulver
2-3 große Äpfel, geschält und in Streifen geschnitten

Butter und Zucker schaumig rühren, dann das Ei und die Zitronenschale dazu rühren. Mehl und Backpulver langsam hinzufügen. Eine Form mit Butter einfetten und mit Mehl bestreuen, dann den Teig in die Form füllen. (Wenn nötig, die Hände mit Mehl bestreuen, damit der Teig nicht an den Händen kleben bleibt.) Die Apfelstreifen vorsichtig in den Teig stecken und etwas Zitronensaft darüber träufeln. Backzeit: Ungefähr 45 Minuten bei mittlerer Hitze (bis der Teig schön hellbraun ist).

Ingredients

1⅓ sticks butter
½ cup sugar
1 egg
grated peel of 1 lemon
¾ cup flour
1 teaspoon baking powder
2-3 large apples, peeled and sliced in thin wedges

Combine butter and sugar and beat until creamy, then stir in egg and grated lemon peel. Sift together flour and baking powder and add gradually to mixture. Grease and flour a spring-form pan and press dough into the pan. (Add flour as necessary to keep dough from sticking to hands.) Arrange apple slices in concentric circles on the crust and sprinkle with a few drops of lemon juice. Bake at 350°F for about 45 minutes or until crust is golden brown.

Aussprache

If initial [ts] proves difficult, practice *nuts, zehn.*

[ts]	gan**z**, Pla**tz**, geh**t's**, **z**ehn, **z**u
[z]	**s**ein, **s**ehr, Blu**s**e, ge**s**und
[s]	e**s**, e**ss**en, wei**ß**

The letter **z** is pronounced [ts]. Before a vowel the letter **s** represents the sound [z]. In most other positions **s** represents the sound [s]. The letters **ss** and **ß** are both pronounced [s].

A Practice the sound [ts] in final position and initial position.

Tan**z**, schwar**z**, Schwei**z**   **z**ehn, **Z**immer, **z**u

B Practice the following words horizontally.

[z]	[s]	[ts]
rei**s**en	rei**ß**en	rei**z**en
Kur**s**e	Kur**s**	kur**z**
hei**s**er	hei**ß**er	Hei**z**er
Fel**s**en	Fel**s**	Fil**z**

C Practice the sounds [ts], [z], and [s]. Read the sentences aloud.

1. Sie kommen um zwölf in die Klasse.
2. Gisela kauft eine Bluse und eine Hose.
3. Franz und Inge gehen zweimal die Woche tanzen.

Proverb: When the cat's away, the mice will play.

Wenn die Katze aus dem Haus ist, tanzen die Mäuse.

Conversational past with auxiliary **haben**

German has several past tenses. One of them is the *conversational past,* which is commonly used in conversation to refer to past actions or states.

ich **habe** es gehört		wir **haben** es gehört
du **hast** es gehört	Sie **haben** es gehört	ihr **habt** es gehört
er/sie **hat** es gehört		sie **haben** es gehört

Have students say *ich hab'* to practice colloquial usage.

The conversational past is made up of an auxiliary verb and a past participle. Most verbs use **haben** as the auxiliary. The participle is in last position.

A   Konrad is eager to pass on a bit of gossip to you and to various friends. Explain to him that you have already heard it.

■|| Und du?   *Ich habe es schon gehört.*

1. Und Frau Weiß?
2. Und Herr Lange?
3. Und Jens und Inge?
4. Und Erika?
5. Und dein Bruder?
6. Und unsere Freunde?
7. Und ihr?
8. Und du?

Past participles of weak verbs

INFINITIVE	PAST PARTICIPLE	CONVERSATIONAL PAST
machen arbeiten	ge+mach+t ge+arbeit+et	Ingrid hat ihre Aufgaben nicht **gemacht**. Sie hat schwer **gearbeitet**.

Have students give examples of "weak" verbs in English.

Other verb ending in -t is *kosten.*

German verbs may be classified as weak or strong according to the way in which they form their past tenses.

The past participle of a weak verb is formed by adding **-t** to the unchanged stem. The **-t** expands to **-et** in verbs like **arbeiten.** In the past participle, most weak verbs also have the prefix **ge-.**

Erik hat die
Wäsche gewaschen.
Hilde hängt sie auf.

Personalize: Let stu-
dents select own an-
swers:
T: *Was hast du gestern
    gemacht?*
S¹: *Ich habe gearbeitet.*
S²: *Ich habe Fenster
     geputzt.* etc.

B Ilse asks whether you did certain things yesterday. Tell her you did.

▣ Habt ihr gestern Musik gehört? *Ja, wir haben Musik
                                      gehört.*

1. Habt ihr Platten gespielt? 4. Habt ihr gearbeitet?
2. Habt ihr auch getanzt? 5. Habt ihr Geschirr gespült?
3. Habt ihr Vokabeln gelernt? 6. Habt ihr Staub gesaugt?

If this exercise proves
difficult at first, review
the past tense forms:
*Hast du das Badezim-
mer geputzt?*
*Hast du Geschirr
gespült?*, etc.

C You've been very industrious. Say you've already done your chores.

▣ Machst du jetzt die Garten- *Nein, die Gartenarbeit habe
    arbeit?*   *ich schon gemacht.*

1. Putzt du jetzt das Badezimmer? 4. Machst du jetzt Frühstück?
2. Spülst du jetzt Geschirr? 5. Fütterst du jetzt den Hund?
3. Deckst du jetzt den Tisch?

D The following people are as busy today as they were yesterday. Tell what
they did.

Test drill.

Optional: Ex. D may
also be assigned as a
written review.

▣ Ich putze Fenster. *Ich habe gestern Fenster geputzt.*

1. Ich spüle Geschirr.
2. Frank bastelt Flugzeugmodelle.
3. Thomas kocht Kaffee.
4. Ingrid und Sabine machen Mathe.
5. Gisela und Jan lernen Vokabeln.
6. Du arbeitest wirklich viel.
7. Du spielst Tennis.
8. Erik saugt Staub.

Past participles of strong verbs

Students should be able to do Ex. E and F easily because there is no vowel change in the participle.

INFINITIVE	PAST PARTICIPLE	CONVERSATIONAL PAST
geben	ge+geb+en	Ich habe Erika ein Radio **gegeben**.
lesen	ge+les+en	Ich habe gestern ein Buch **gelesen**.
sehen	ge+seh+en	Ich habe Ilse nicht **gesehen**.

The past participle of a strong verb is formed by adding **-en** to the stem. The past participles of most strong verbs have the prefix **ge-**.

E   Hans-Dieter asks about your visit with some old friends. Satisfy his curiosity.

V¹: Free response:
Was habt ihr Gisela gegeben?
Was habt ihr gelesen?
Habt ihr Sonntag die Hot Dogs gesehen?
V²: Cue with different person:
Hast du Frank eine Platte gegeben? (er, sie pl., etc.)

■III   Was habt ihr Gisela gegeben? Das Poster?   *Ja, wir haben Gisela das Poster gegeben.*

1. Was habt ihr Frank gegeben? Eine Platte?
2. Was habt ihr gelesen? Thomas' Buch?
3. Wann habt ihr sein Buch gelesen? Letzte Woche?
4. Wo habt ihr Erik gesehen? Im Jugendzentrum?
5. Wo habt ihr die *Hot Dogs* gesehen? In München?

INFINITIVE	PAST PARTICIPLE	CONVERSATIONAL PAST
backen	ge+back+en	Ich habe eine Torte **gebacken**.
schlafen	ge+schlaf+en	Ich habe gut **geschlafen**.
tragen	ge+trag+en	Ich habe eine Jacke **getragen**.
waschen	ge+wasch+en	Ich habe mein Auto **gewaschen**.

F   Restate in the conversational past.

Point out that new verbs *backen, schlafen* have stem-vowel change *a>ä* in the present tense.

■III   Wäscht Frank das Auto?   *Hat Frank das Auto gewaschen?*

■III   Nein, Martina wäscht es.   *Nein, Martina hat es gewaschen.*

1. Bäckt Ingrid die Torte?
   Nein, Thomas bäckt sie.
2. Schläfst du gut?
   Ja, ich schlafe gut.
3. Trägst du Jeans ins Konzert?
   Ja, und Udo trägt auch Jeans.
4. Wann wäschst du die Wäsche?
   Ich wasche sie am Samstag.

INFINITIVE	PAST PARTICIPLE	CONVERSATIONAL PAST
helfen	ge+**holf**+en	Ich habe zu Hause **geholfen.**
nehmen	ge+**nomm**+en	Ich habe das Heft **genommen.**
schreiben	ge+**schrieb**+en	Ich habe Erika **geschrieben.**
trinken	ge+**trunk**+en	Ich habe Kaffee **getrunken.**

Many strong verbs change their stem vowel (and occasionally consonants) in the formation of the past participle.

G

Ask students to point out the changes in participle of these verbs. Have students give examples of "strong" verbs in English.

Repeat each item several times with additional names.

Sabine wants to know who did the following things. Confirm her guesses.

▪▥   Wer hat Rudi geschrieben? Eva?   *Ja, Eva hat Rudi*
                                          geschrieben.

1. Wer hat Heike geschrieben? Udo?
2. Wer hat zu Hause geholfen? Stefan?
3. Wer hat Dieter geholfen? Ingrid?
4. Wer hat den Pulli genommen? Gerda?
5. Wer hat die Mappe genommen? Ulf?
6. Wer hat schon Kaffee getrunken? Mutter?
7. Wer hat noch nichts getrunken? Vater?

H

Review irregular present-tense forms.

Point out that *helfen* has stem-vowel change *e>i* in the present tense.

You still haven't received answers to your questions. Ask them again in the present tense.

▪▥   Warum hast du Beate die   *Warum gibst du Beate die*
     Briefmarken gegeben?   *Briefmarken?*

1. Warum hat Jan Gisela seinen Cassetten-Recorder gegeben?
2. Was habt ihr in Englisch gelesen?
3. Wo hast du Tanja gesehen?
4. Warum hat Stefan soviel geschlafen?
5. Wer hat die Wäsche gewaschen?
6. Warum hast du keine Torte gebacken?
7. Warum hast du meinen Bleistift genommen?
8. Wer hat Meike geholfen?
9. Welche Jacke hast du getragen?

Du hast das Wort

Ask various classmates what they did over the weekend.

Was hast du am Wochenende gemacht?
Hast du dein Zimmer aufgeräumt?
Hast du geschlafen?
Hast du etwas gebastelt?
Hast du gearbeitet? Wo?
Hast du das Auto gewaschen?

I Restate in the conversational past.

Repeat each item several times with different subjects:
Hilfst du zu Hause?
(sie, ihr, etc.)

- ▪ Wir sehen unsere Großeltern am Samstag.

  Wir haben unsere Großel-
  tern am Samstag gesehen.

- ▪ Wir trinken um vier Kaffee.

  Wir haben um vier Kaffee
  getrunken.

1. Hilft Gerd zu Hause?
   Ja, er wäscht die Wäsche.
2. Bäckt Frank die Torte?
   Nein, er schläft am Samstag bis elf.
3. Gibst du Gerda das Buch?
   Ja, sie liest es am Wochenende.

Past participles of separable-prefix verbs

INFINITIVE	PAST PARTICIPLE	CONVERSATIONAL PAST
abstauben	ab+ge+staubt	Kirstin hat die Möbel **abgestaubt**.
einladen	ein+ge+laden	Ihre Mutter hat Schmidts **eingeladen**.
fernsehen	fern+ge+sehen	Abends haben sie **ferngesehen**.

The prefix **ge-** of the past participle comes between the separable prefix and the stem of the participle.

J Ute is a hard worker. Identify her as the one who did all the chores.

Repeat each item, asking for answers with various subjects:
Wer hat abgetrocknet?
(wir, sie, etc.)

- ▪ Wer hat das Zimmer
  aufgeräumt?

  Ute hat das Zimmer
  aufgeräumt.

1. Wer hat abgetrocknet?
2. Wer hat die Fenster aufgemacht?
3. Wer hat die Möbel abgestaubt?
4. Wer hat den Tisch abgeräumt?
5. Wer hat eingekauft?

K Your mother is checking whether you've done your chores yet. Inform her that you'll do them later.

- ▪ Hast du das Zimmer
  aufgeräumt?

  Nein, das räume ich später
  auf.

1. Hast du die Garage aufgeräumt?
2. Hast du die Möbel abgestaubt?
3. Hast du die Fenster aufgemacht?
4. Hast du den Tisch abgeräumt?
5. Hast du das Geschirr abgetrocknet?
6. Hast du den Mülleimer rausgetragen?

Restate the following exchanges in the conversational past.

- ▪▪▪   Kaufst du heute ein?   *Hast du heute eingekauft?*

- ▪▪▪   Ja, ich kaufe bei Karstadt ein.   *Ja, ich habe bei Karstadt eingekauft.*

1. Kaufst du nur bei Karstadt ein?
   Nein, ich kaufe auch bei Hertie ein.
2. Wann macht Karstadt auf?
   Heute machen sie schon um neun auf.
3. Macht Karstadt um fünf zu?
   Nein, sie machen erst um halb sieben zu.
4. Siehst du Samstag nachmittag fern?
   Ja, und ich sehe auch am Abend fern.
5. Wann räumst du die Garage auf?
   Ich räume sie gar nicht auf.

Grammatische Übersicht

Conversational past   (A-L)

Hast du schon Mathe **gemacht**?   *Have you done* your math?
Nein, **ich habe** Tennis **gespielt**.   No, *I played* tennis.

There are several past tenses in German. The conversational past, as the name implies, is common in conversation. It is used in many situations that require the simple past tense in English.

Auxiliary **haben**

ich **habe** Detlev **gefragt**		wir **haben** Stefan **gefragt**
du **hast** Petra **gefragt**	Sie **haben** Ingrid **gefragt**	ihr **habt** Silke **gefragt**
er **hat** Marta **gefragt**		sie **haben** Benno **gefragt**

The conversational past is made up of an auxiliary verb and a past participle. **Haben** is used as the auxiliary of most verbs. The past participle is in last position.

Ich habe gestern **nicht** gearbeitet.

Nicht often comes directly before the past participle.

Past participles of weak verbs

INFINITIVE	PAST PARTICIPLE	CONVERSATIONAL PAST
kaufen	ge+kauf+t	Erik **hat** eine Platte **gekauft.**
kosten	ge+kost+et	Wieviel **hat** sie **gekostet?**

German verbs may be classified as weak or strong according to the way they form their past tenses. A weak verb is a verb with a stem that remains unchanged in the past-tense forms. The past participle of a weak verb is formed by adding the ending **-t** or **-et** to the infinitive stem. Most past participles have the prefix **ge-**.

Past participles of strong verbs

INFINITIVE	PAST PARTICIPLE	CONVERSATIONAL PAST
schreiben	ge+schrieb+en	Ich **habe** eine Karte **geschrieben.**
nehmen	ge+nomm+en	**Hast** du die Karte **genommen?**
sehen	ge+seh+en	Nein, ich **habe** sie nicht **gesehen.**

A strong verb is a verb that changes its stem vowel (and occasionally consonants) in at least one of the past tenses. The past participle of a strong verb is formed by adding **-en** to the stem. Most strong verbs also add the prefix **ge-** in the past participle. Since there is no way to guess how or even if the stem vowel changes from infinitive to past participle, you should memorize the past participles of strong verbs.

For a list of the strong verbs used in this book, with their past participles, see the Appendix. Past participles of strong verbs are noted in the vocabularies as follows: **schreiben (geschrieben).**

Past participles of separable-prefix verbs

INFINITIVE	PAST PARTICIPLE	CONVERSATIONAL PAST
aufräumen	auf+ge+räumt	**Hast** du das Zimmer **aufgeräumt?**
einladen	ein+ge+laden	Wir **haben** Schmidts **eingeladen.**

The prefix **ge-** of the past participle comes between the separable prefix and the stem of the participle.

A   Create captions that describe the activity in each picture.

B   Restate the following exchanges in the conversational past.

1. Hilft Bruno zu Hause?
   Ja. Er räumt die Garage auf.
2. Wann holt ihr Schmidts ab?
   Um vier. Wir trinken um halb fünf Kaffee.
3. Was machst du Samstag nachmittag?
   Ich spiele Tennis.
4. Petra bäckt eine Torte.
   Hoffentlich schmeckt sie.
5. Dieter räumt hoffentlich sein Zimmer auf.
   Leider nein. Er liest ein Buch.

C   The following people recently went shopping. Say what they think of their purchases. Use a possessive adjective in each sentence.

    ◼▮▮   Peter / Pulli / schick   *Peter findet seinen Pulli schick.*

1. Frank / Mantel / klasse
2. Hannelore / Kleid / hübsch
3. wir / Jeans / prima
4. du / Gürtel / preiswert
5. ihr / Jacken / toll
6. ich / Hemd / schick

D   The following statements are all answers to questions beginning with *Wo?* or *Wohin?* Ask the questions.

1. Karsten wohnt in Hamburg.
2. Er fährt am Samstag in die Stadt.
3. Bei Karstadt kauft er einen Anzug.
4. Dann fährt er wieder nach Hause.
5. Er möchte heute abend ins Theater.

E   Give orders to the people indicated.

    ◼▮▮   Peter: Badezimmer putzen   *Putz bitte das Badezimmer!*

1. Karin: Geschirr spülen
2. Norbert: abtrocknen
3. Werner und Dietmar: Garage aufräumen
4. Herr Schwarz: die Wäsche waschen
5. Frau Schwarz: Tisch decken
6. Sabine: Kaffee kochen
7. Inge: Katze füttern

F   Several kinds of words can come at the end of a German sentence. Complete each of the following sentences with an appropriate word, according to the sense.

ab   auf   fahren   gefragt   gekauft
gefüttert   mit   spülen

1. Hat Gabi schon den Hund _____?
2. Muß sie noch das Geschirr _____?
3. Möchte sie morgen nach Frankfurt _____?
4. Ja. Sie steht früh _____.
5. Kommt ihr Freund Peter _____?
6. Hat er ein Auto _____?
7. Wann holt er Gabi _____?
8. Ich habe sie nicht _____.

G Complete the response in each conversational exchange with *Ja, Nein,* or *Doch,* as appropriate.

1. Hast du ein Hobby?
   ____, ich sammle Bierdeckel.
2. Kauft ihr heute ein?
   ____, wir bleiben zu Hause.
3. Fährt Detlev heute nicht mit?
   ____, er kommt mit.
4. Können Sie mein Auto reparieren?
   ____, ich habe leider keine Zeit.
5. Herr Siemens wohnt nicht in der Gartenstraße.
   ____, er wohnt da.
6. Spielst du oft Fußball?
   ____, es macht viel Spaß!

H Your German guest wants to know what your American friends are saying. Interpret the following conversational exchanges for your guest.

1. What did you do yesterday?
   Gerda and I took a walk.
2. Didn't you work?
   Not much. I washed our car.
3. When did you pick Gerda up?
   I picked Gerda up at four.
4. Did you invite Gerda for coffee?
   No, we had coffee with Gerda's parents.

Child-labor laws (covering anyone under the age of 14) prohibit young Germans from working at many of the part-time jobs that might be common for their American counterparts. Students between the ages of 15 and 18 who are enrolled in apprenticeship programs earn a small amount of money as they learn a trade. Students in college preparatory schools must depend on a regular allowance **(Taschengeld)** from their parents and on occasional jobs which are fairly difficult to obtain. Summer jobs require a minimum of four weeks' commitment and tend to be low-paid. They are not very popular because the summer vacation is only six weeks long and not enough time is left for the family vacation after four or five weeks of work.

Taschengeld und Jobs

Taschengeld° ist oft ein Problem für deutsche Schüler. Viele bekommen Taschengeld von den Eltern. Und in vielen Familien bekommen sie auch Geld für gute Zeugnisse°. Und
5 zum Geburtstag und zu Weihnachten°. Aber das ist natürlich oft nicht genug° für Kino und Konzert, für Cassetten und Schallplatten, für Klassenfahrten° und Sport.

Viele Schüler wollen also etwas Geld ver-
10 dienen°. In Deutschland ist das aber nicht so leicht. Babysitterjobs gibt es schon, aber nicht sehr oft. Ein paar Schüler können Nachhilfestunden° geben. In den Supermärkten gibt es Jobs, aber diese Jobs sind nicht leicht zu be-
15 kommen. Zeitungsjobs° gibt es auch, aber nicht für Schüler. In Deutschland kommen die Zeitungen am Morgen. Am Morgen haben die Schüler natürlich keine Zeit. So bleibt für sie die Reklame°: Sie können Reklame austra-
20 gen°.

pocket money

grades
Christmas
enough

class trips

earn

tutoring sessions

newspaper jobs

advertisements
distribute

A Below is a list of statements about teen-agers, jobs, and spending money. Indicate which statements seem more characteristic of German-speaking countries, which of the United States, which of both.

1. Taschengeld ist oft ein Problem für Teenager.
2. Barbara hat jede Woche einen Babysitterjob.
3. Viele Schüler arbeiten in den Supermärkten.
4. Paula kann keinen Babysitterjob finden. Ihre Freundinnen auch nicht.
5. Thomas arbeitet abends und am Wochenende im Supermarkt.
6. Paul macht jede Woche Gartenarbeit. So bekommt er Geld von seinen Eltern. Wenn er extra Geld braucht, räumt er die Garage auf, oder er putzt die Fenster.
7. Claudia kauft zwei neue Schallplatten. Sie bekommt das Geld von ihren Eltern, denn sie hat ein sehr gutes Zeugnis.
8. Jens kann keine Zeitungen austragen. Er muß am Morgen in die Schule.
9. Zum Geburtstag hat Inge Geld bekommen. Jetzt kann sie das kaufen, was sie haben will.
10. Erik trägt am Dienstag und am Freitag Reklame aus.

Vokabeln

SUBSTANTIVE

die Arbeit, -en   work
das Badezimmer, -   bathroom
der Eimer,-   pail
die Eltern *(pl.)*   parents
das Flugzeugmodell, -e   model airplane
das Frühstück   breakfast
die Garage, -n   garage
die Gartenarbeit   gardening, yard work
das Geschirr   dishes
die Großeltern *(pl.)*   grandparents
das Haus, ¨er   house
der Hund, -e   dog
der Kaffee   coffee
die Katze, -n   cat
die Möbel *(pl.)*   furniture
der Müll   garbage
der Spaziergang, ¨e   walk, stroll; **einen ~ machen**   to go for a walk
der Staub   dust
der Tisch, -e   table
die Torte, -n   fancy layer cake
die Wäsche   laundry
das Zimmer, -   room

VERBEN

ab·holen   to call for, to pick up
ab·räumen   to clear, to remove
ab·stauben   to dust
ab·trocknen   to dry up, to wipe dry
auf·räumen   to put in order
backen (ä; gebacken)   to bake
basteln   to tinker (with), to work at a hobby
decken   to set (the table)
ein·laden (ä; eingeladen)   to invite
füttern   to feed
helfen (i; geholfen)   to help

VERBEN

nennen (genannt)   to name, to call
putzen   to clean
raus·tragen (ä; rausgetragen)   to carry out
schlafen (ä; geschlafen)   to sleep
schmecken   to taste (good)
spülen   to wash dishes
Staub saugen   to vacuum
trinken (getrunken)   to drink
waschen (ä; gewaschen)   to wash

ANDERE WÖRTER

alle   all, everyone
als   than
fürs = für das   for the
gestern   yesterday
jeder   each, everyone
letzt   last
sarkastisch   sarcastic
wenigstens   at least
wie (immer)   as (always)

BESONDERE AUSDRÜCKE

was heißt das?   what do you mean?
das ist doch nicht dein Ernst!   you can't be serious!
doch!   yes (*in answer to a question containing a negative word*)
Ehrenwort!   honest! on my honor!
Kaffee trinken   to drink coffee (*with breakfast or with afternoon pastries*)
zum Kaffee einladen   to invite for coffee and cake
fürs Wochenende   for the weekend

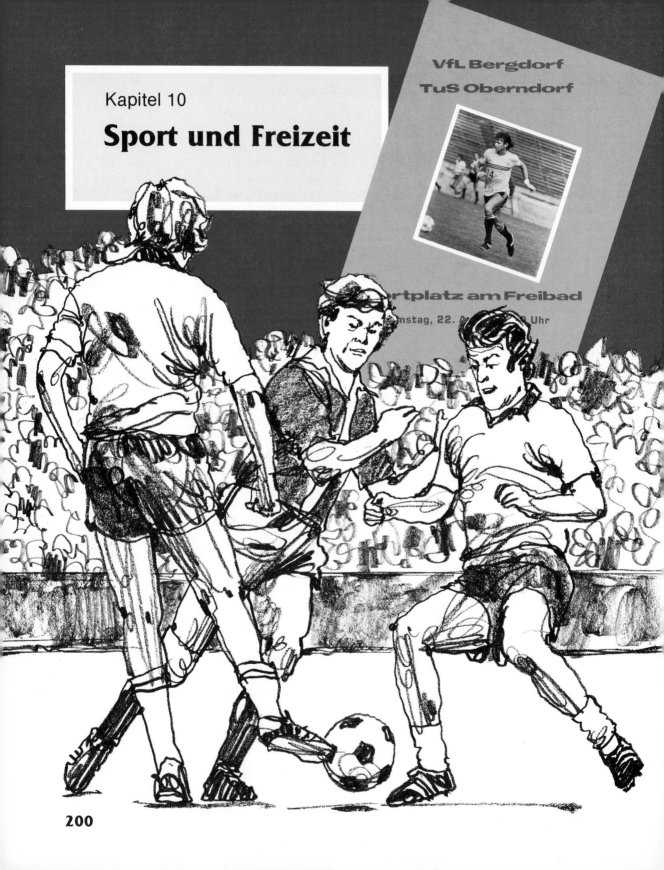

Kapitel 10

Sport und Freizeit

VfL Bergdorf

TuS Oberndorf

...rtplatz am Freibad

...mstag, 22. A... ... Uhr

Most young people in German-speaking countries are interested in a sport of some kind. Physical education is compulsory in all schools, both elementary and secondary. In spite of this, however, there is no stress on school teams.

A person who wishes to participate in competitive sports can join a sports club (**Sportverein**). In the **BRD** there are 40,000 such clubs, and more than 1 out of every 4 Germans is a member. Many teen-agers enjoy playing in youth soccer leagues sponsored by their local **Sportverein.** Soccer is by far the most popular sport; next in order are gymnastics, tennis, marksmanship, track-and-field, handball, swimming, table tennis, horseback riding, and skiing.

Berliner Turnerschaft
Korporation
1863
Turn- und Sport-Verein

Turngruppe 4		
• Männer:	Freitag	20 - 22 Uhr
• Jugend:	Freitag	20 - 22 Uhr
• Knaben:	Freitag	18 - 20 Uhr
• Gymnastik Frauen:	Mittwoch	19³⁰- 21³⁰ Uhr
• Frauen:	Dienstag	20 - 22 Uhr
• Jugend weibl.:	Dienstag	20 - 22 Uhr
• Mädchen:	Dienstag	18 - 20 Uhr
• Kleinkinder:	Mittwoch	17³⁰- 19³⁰ Uhr

Chain drill:
S¹: *Ich habe gestern Tennis gespielt. Hast du Tennis gespielt?*
S²: *Nein, ich habe Fußball gespielt. Hast du . . .*

Wer hat gewonnen?

Jan is on the Bergdorf soccer team. He tells Gisela the outcome of yesterday's game against Oberndorf.

Help students understand the difference between *Mal* (one of several points in time) and *Zeit* (a certain period of time).
for the last time (*Mal*)
do you have time (*Zeit*)
I have no time (*Zeit*)
one time only (*Mal*)

GISELA	Was hast du gestern gemacht?
JAN	Wir haben Fußball gespielt.
GISELA	Gegen wen?
JAN	Gegen Oberndorf.
GISELA	Habt ihr gewonnen?
JAN	Nein, wir haben zwei zu drei verloren.
GISELA	Ach, Mensch. Das tut mir leid. Aber zwei zu drei gegen Oberndorf ist ja nicht so schlecht.
JAN	Das stimmt. Oberndorf ist gut.
GISELA	Na, vielleicht spielen wir nächstes Mal wenigstens unentschieden.

Fragen

1. Gegen wen hat Bergdorf gespielt?
2. Wer hat gewonnen? Wie hoch° haben sie gewonnen?
3. Wie spielt Bergdorf vielleicht nächstes Mal?

Du hast das Wort

Expand: Students may create original dialogues based on similar questions and answers.

Ask which team won a particular game and ask about the score.

Wer hat das [Fußball]spiel gewonnen?
Wie hoch haben sie/wir gewonnen?
Wie hoch haben sie/wir verloren?

Ich lade dich ein

Ingrid is reluctant to go to a party to which she wasn't invited.

INGRID   Was hast du heute abend vor?

DIETER   Ich gehe auf eine Party. Was machst du denn?

INGRID   Eigentlich nichts.

DIETER   Nichts? Das ist ja prima. Dann komm doch mit!

INGRID   Wohin? Auf die Party?

DIETER   Natürlich.

INGRID   Du gibst doch nicht die Party!

DIETER   Nein. Gerd. Aber ich kann dich einladen.

INGRID   Ach Quatsch! Das geht doch nicht.

DIETER   Doch. Natürlich geht das. Du kennst ihn doch gut, nicht?

INGRID   Ja ... Also schön. Wann geht's denn los?

DIETER   Ich glaube, um acht. Ich rufe dich noch an.

INGRID   O.K. Tschüß. Bis später.

Have students suggest possible substitutions for elements in dialogue and then role-play with variations. For example, *morgen abend* or *Samstag abend* for *heute abend*, etc.

Fragen

1. Was hat Dieter heute abend vor?
2. Was hat Ingrid vor?
3. Wer gibt die Party? Dieter?
4. Warum darf Ingrid mitkommen?
5. Wann geht die Party eigentlich los?
6. Wen ruft Dieter an? Wann?

Du hast das Wort

Suggestion: Do an exercise a day as a warm-up, or at various times during class. Have students try to eventually ask and respond without their books.

V: Student asks teacher: *Was haben Sie heute vor?*

A. A friend asks what you have planned for this evening. How would you respond?

Was hast du heute abend vor?

Ich gehe | auf eine Party.
          | in die Disco.
          | ins Kino.
          | ins Jugendzentrum.

Ich sehe fern.
Ich höre Musik.
Ich will [Briefe schreiben].

B. React to a classmate's announcement that he/she is giving a party.

Ich gebe am [Samstag abend] eine Party.

Prima!
Schön!
Toll!
Wann geht's los?
Wirklich?
Schade, ich habe schon Pläne für [Samstag].

C. Suppose you find out that a friend of yours hasn't been invited to a party. How would you react?

Jan gibt eine Party. Er hat aber [Dieter] nicht eingeladen.

Mensch! Das geht doch nicht.
Was!? Warum denn nicht?
Was ist denn los?
Wirklich?
Na und°?
Natürlich nicht.
Das ist ja prima.

Sag!

Your teacher will ask you to repeat a bit of information to another class-mate. Note that in requests of this kind, the verb comes at the end of the sentence.

See Chapter 8, p. 158, for suggestions in doing this type of exercise.

■ Sag [Kai], daß du auf eine Party gehst!   *Ich gehe auf eine Party.*

1. Sag [Ute], daß Gerd die Party gibt!
2. Sag [Kai], daß du Gerd gut kennst!
3. Sag [Ute], daß sie mitkommen kann!
4. Sag [Kai], daß die Party um acht Uhr losgeht!

German teen-agers like to spend their free time in various kinds of places. In a **Café** they can engage in quiet conversation while enjoying a soda or a cup of coffee, and sometimes a pastry. Another popular spot with a very different type of atmosphere is a **Pinte** or **Kneipe.** Beer and other alcoholic drinks are available, and usually some snacks, like sausages. There might be a pinball machine **(Spielautomat)** or a juke box **(Musikbox)** to provide entertainment. Students also like to get together in a **Diskothek.** But conversation is usually out because the music is too loud. Sometimes a disc jockey keeps people entertained with records and general chatter.

Wortschatzerweiterung

Freizeit

Im Winter gehen Ute und Bernd Schi laufen.

Bernd kann auch gut Schlittschuh laufen.

Im Frühling zelten Paul und Norbert oft.
Camping macht Spaß.

Gisela und Jan machen gern Picknicks. Dann
gibt's viel zu essen.

Im Sommer gehen Gisela und Jan windsurfen.
Jan fällt oft ins Wasser.

Ralf und seine Freunde gehen oft segeln. Ilse
segelt nicht gern.

Im Herbst gehen Karin und Uwe oft bergsteigen.

Ilse reitet gern, Ralf aber nicht.

Help students discover that *Camping* is a noun. "To camp" (in tents) is *zelten*. Some Germans use *Camping machen* as well as *zelten*.

Activity: Take a class poll of favorite sports.

Game: *Was mache ich?* Students take turns acting out activities. Other students guess in German what the activity is: *Tennis spielen, reiten, segeln, bergsteigen, Schlittschuh laufen, Fußball spielen, tanzen, essen, trinken, die Tür aufmachen*, etc.

A   Answer the following questions based on the illustrations.

1.   Was machen Karin und Uwe im Herbst oft?
2.   Was macht Ute im Winter?
3.   Wer kann gut Schlittschuh laufen?
4.   Wer zeltet gern?
5.   Warum machen Gisela und Jan gern Picknicks?
6.   Wer geht oft windsurfen?
7.   Wer kann nicht gut windsurfen?
8.   Wer geht mit Ralf segeln?
9.   Wer geht nicht mit Ralf segeln?
10.   Was macht Ilse gern, Ralf aber nicht?

Du hast das Wort

Tell the class some of the outdoor activities you like to engage in.

Give three groups of months and have students name the season. Use visuals if possible.

Welchen Sport treibst du im Winter? im Sommer? im Frühling?
Spielst du im Winter Tennis?
Reitest du?
Gehst du Schi laufen? Schlittschuh laufen?
Gehst du windsurfen?

Suffixes -er and -er + -in

Compare with English -ess: stewardess, actress, waitress.

| fahren   to drive | fahr + er | = | der Fahrer | driver *(m.)* |
| | fahr + er + in | = | die Fahrerin | driver *(f.)* |

The suffix **-er** is often added to a verb stem to form a noun that indicates the male doer of an activity. The additional suffix **-in** indicates the female doer of an activity.

| segeln | segl + er | = | der Segler |
| | segl + er + in | = | die Seglerin |

To form a noun from a verb ending in **-eln,** the **-e** before the **l** is dropped.

| Schi laufen | der Schiläufer |
| | die Schiläuferin |

Some nouns formed from verbs show umlaut.

B   Name the male and female doers of the activities related to the following verbs and verb phrases.

> ▰ⅲ   Tennis spielen   *der Tennisspieler, die Tennisspielerin*

1. schwimmen
2. arbeiten
3. Briefmarken sammeln
4. basteln
5. bergsteigen
6. reiten
7. backen (ä)
8. tanzen (ä)
9. verkaufen (ä)

> Rainer ist Verkäufer.   Rainer is *a* salesman.
> Sabine ist Verkäuferin.   Sabine is *a* saleswoman.

German does not use **ein** or **eine** with a noun used to identify a member of a profession or someone temporarily engaged in an activity.

C   Complete each sentence with a noun derived from the verb.

1. Lutz and Anja arbeiten bei Volkswagen.
   Er ist ____. Sie ist ____.
2. Frau Krupp und Herr Anders backen viel.
   Sie ist ____, und er ist ____.
3. Herr und Frau Braun sammeln Briefmarken.
   Er ist schon vier Jahre Briefmarken ____; sie ist erst zwei Jahre Briefmarken ____.
4. Im Sommer spielen Tanja und Erik den ganzen Tag Tennis.
   Im Sommer ist Tanja nur Tennis ____, und Erik ist nur Tennis ____.

Aussprache

▌ [R]   **R**ock, P**r**eis, wa**r**um

The German **r** can be pronounced in two different ways. Some German speakers use a tongue-trilled [r] in which the tip of the tongue vibrates against the gum ridge behind the upper front teeth, like the **rrr** that small children often make in imitation of a car or truck starting up. Most German speakers, however, use a uvular [R] in which the back of the tongue is raised toward the uvula (the little flap of skin hanging down in the back of the mouth). It may help you to pronounce the uvular [R] if you make a gargling sound before the sound [a]: **ra.** Keep the tip of your tongue down and out of the way. It plays no role in the pronunciation of the uvular German [R].

Practice [R] in non-sense syllables:
aga, aga, aga / aka, aka, aka / ara, ara, ara; prah, prah, prah / brah, brah, brah / troh, troh, troh / druh, druh, druh / krih, krih, krih / greh, greh, greh.

A   Practice vertically in columns and then horizontally.

[R]	[R]	[R]
f**r**agt	wa**r**um	**r**agt
K**r**okodil	ba**r**ock	**R**ock
t**r**ugen	füh**r**en	**r**ufen
P**r**eis	Nie**r**en	**R**eis
b**r**ing	da**r**in	**R**ing
g**r**ünen	schü**r**en	**r**ühmen

Rhyme using [R]:
Ri-ra-rutsch,
Wir fahren mit der Kutsch,
Wir fahren mit der Eisenbahn,
Ri-ra-rutsch.

B   Practice the sound [R]. Read the sentences aloud.

1. Frau Braun trägt heute einen Rock.
2. Können Sie mein Radio reparieren, Herr Grün?
3. Frag mal Rita, warum sie nicht schreibt!

Zungenbrecher: Ein krummer Krebs kriecht über eine krumme Kruste.

Proverb: The biter will be bitten.

Wer anderen eine Grube gräbt, fällt selbst hinein.

The verbs **kennen** and **wissen**

Review conjugation of wissen.

Tell students that dependent clauses are set off by commas.

Ich **kenne** Frau Hofer.
Ich **kenne** Rainers Haus.

Ich **weiß**, wer Frau Hofer ist.
Ich **weiß**, wo Rainer wohnt.

Kennen means to know (to be acquainted with) a person, place, or thing. **Wissen** means to know something as a fact.

A Answer Torsten's questions in the negative.

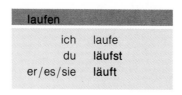

    ■Ⅲ Weißt du, wo Jörg
        Schneider wohnt?

Nein, das weiß ich nicht.

    ■Ⅲ Kennst du seine Schwester?

Nein, seine Schwester kenne ich nicht.

1. Weißt du, wie alt Jörg ist?
2. Weißt du, wie Jörgs Schwester heißt?
3. Kennst du Jörgs Freundin?
4. Kennst du denn Jörg Schneider?

Du hast das Wort

Personalize: Kennst du Chicago? New York? Paris? Kennst du die Bücher von Hemingway? Steinbeck? Kennst du Musik von Mozart? Beethoven? Kennst du Frau . . .? Herrn . . .?

Ask a classmate whether he/she is acquainted with certain people, places, or things, or knows certain facts.

Kennst du [Ingrid/Thomas]?
Weißt du, wo [sie/er] wohnt?
Weißt du, wie alt [sie/er] ist?
Kennst du [meine Schwester/meinen Bruder]?
Kennst du [meine Freundin Erika/meinen Freund Thomas]?
Kennst du [Berlin]?
Kennst du die Musik von [Beethoven]?

Verbs with stem-vowel change **au**>**äu**

Use directed dialogue:
T: Ilse, frag Heike, ob sie gern Schlittschuh läuft.
S¹: Heike, läufst du gern Schlittschuh?
S²: Ja, ich laufe gern Schlittschuh.

laufen	
ich	laufe
du	läufst
er/es/sie	läuft

Laufen has a stem-vowel change **au**>**äu** in the **du**- and **er/sie**-forms of the present tense.

B   Margit is trying to recruit members for a ski club. Tell her that the following people ski well.

     ▪⫿   Peter   *Peter läuft gut Schi.*

1. Uschi
2. Gerd und Paul
3. du

4. deine Freunde
5. Silke
6. ihr

Accusative case of **wer**

NOMINATIVE	ACCUSATIVE
Wer kommt heute abend?	**Wen** laden wir ein?

The accusative of **wer** is **wen.**

C   Helga is chatting about various people, but you don't hear her clearly. Ask whom she is referring to.

Activity: Write short
sentences on board,
using transitive verbs
like *hören, sehen, anrufen,* + first names.
Cover one of the names
and have students ask
questions with *wer* or *wen.*
Frank kennt Erik.
. . . kennt Erik?
. . . kennt Frank?

     ▪⫿   Ich habe Erik im Jugend-   *Wen hast du gesehen?*
               zentrum gesehen.

1. Ich habe Christl im Kino gesehen.
2. Ich habe Dieter für heute abend eingeladen.
3. Ich habe Ingrid angerufen.
4. Ich habe die *Hot Dogs* gehört.

V¹: (with conversational past):
Hast du mich verstanden?
Hast du mich gemeint?
Hast du mich gehört?
Hast du mich gefragt?

V²: *Wen hast du verstanden?*
     Mich? Ja, ich habe dich verstanden. (gefragt, gemeint, gehört)

Accusative case of personal pronouns

mich / dich

NOMINATIVE	ACCUSATIVE
Ich verstehe Christl.	Christl versteht **mich.**
Du verstehst Christl.	Christl versteht **dich.**

D   Express surprise at your classmate's statements.

     ▪⫿   Ich kenne dich gut.   *Wirklich? Du kennst mich gut?*

1. Ich verstehe dich.
2. Ich meine dich.

3. Ich höre dich.
4. Ich frage dich.

E   Karl is feeling rejected today. Reassure him that what he says isn't true.

▪▥   Du lädst mich nicht ein.   *Doch, ich lade dich ein.*

1. Du rufst mich nicht an.
2. Du hast mich nicht gern.
3. Du kennst mich nicht gut.
4. Du fährst mich nicht nach Hause.

uns/euch

NOMINATIVE	ACCUSATIVE
Wir verstehen Frank. **Ihr** versteht Frank.	Frank versteht **uns.** Frank versteht **euch.**

F   Answer the following questions in the affirmative.

V: *Habt ihr uns gehört? Natürlich haben wir euch gehört. (gemeint, gefragt, verstanden)*

▪▥   Kennt ihr uns?   *Ja, natürlich kennen wir euch.*

1. Hört ihr uns?
2. Meint ihr uns?
3. Fragt ihr uns?
4. Versteht ihr uns?
5. Braucht ihr uns?

G   Petra and Erik are feeling gloomy today. Try to cheer them up.

Show consonant/vowel relationships by writing articles and pronouns on board thus:
den (Bruder)
ih<u>n</u>
da<u>s</u> (Kind)
e<u>s</u>
die (Schwester)
si<u>e</u>

▪▥   Ihr nehmt uns nicht mit ins Konzert.   *Doch, wir nehmen euch mit.*

1. Ihr ladet uns nicht ein.
2. Ihr habt uns nicht gern.
3. Ihr ruft uns nicht an.
4. Ihr braucht uns nicht.

ihn/es/sie

NOUN	PRONOUN
Kennst du **meinen Bruder?** Kaufst du **den Fernseher?**	Ja, ich kenne **ihn.** Ja, ich kaufe **ihn.**
Kennst du **das Kind?** Kaufst du **das Radio?**	Ja, ich kenne **es.** Ja, ich kaufe **es.**
Kennst du **meine Schwester?** Kaufst du **die Uhr?**	Ja, ich kenne **sie.** Ja, ich kaufe **sie.**
Kennst du **meine Freunde?** Kaufst du **die Platten?**	Ja, ich kenne **sie.** Ja, ich kaufe **sie.**

H   Gisela is in charge of invitations to Gerd's party. Say that she intends to call the following guests later.

■III   Wann ruft Gisela meinen Bruder an?   *Später. Sie ruft ihn später an.*

1. Wann ruft sie Erik an?
2. Wann ruft sie meine Schwester an?
3. Wann ruft sie ihren Freund Peter an?
4. Wann ruft sie meine Freunde an?
5. Wann ruft sie Petra und Jens an?

V: Answer each question in the conversational past: *Sie hat ihn schon angerufen,* etc.

I   After an hour in the music store, Jan impatiently urges you to make up your mind. Decide that you don't want the things after all.

V¹: Let individual students make choice: *Ja, ich will ihn. Nein, ich will ihn nicht.*
V²: Cue first by using pictures, then expand by pointing to classroom objects.
V³: Have students do same with clothing, using cut-out pictures: *Willst du die Jeans oder nicht?*

■III   Willst du nun den Cassetten-Recorder oder nicht?   *Nein, ich will ihn nicht.*

1. Willst du nun den Plattenspieler oder nicht?
2. Willst du die Stereoanlage oder nicht?
3. Willst du das Radio oder nicht?
4. Willst du die Platte oder nicht?
5. Willst du die Cassetten oder nicht?

Teen-agers in German-speaking countries like to talk on the phone almost as much as their American counterparts. Germans usually identify themselves at once when they answer the phone. Callers also give their names before asking for the person they're trying to reach. When people end a telephone conversation, they often say **Auf Wiederhören** (literally, until we hear each other again). For example:

— Hier Ingrid Reimann!
— Tag, Ingrid! Hier Gerda. Ist Thomas zu Hause?
— Nein, er spielt heute Fußball.
— Ach ja, richtig. Ich rufe später wieder an. Auf Wiederhören, Ingrid!
— Auf Wiederhören, Gerda!

Lesen macht Spaß.

Sie

NOMINATIVE	ACCUSATIVE
Verstehen Sie **mich?**	Ja, ich verstehe **Sie.**

J

V: Students ask teacher the questions: *Haben Sie mich gehört?*

Answer your teacher's questions in the affirmative.

◼ıı   Hast du mich gehört?   *Ja, ich habe Sie gehört.*

1. Hast du mich gemeint?
2. Hast du mich gefragt?
3. Hast du mich angerufen?
4. Hast du mich zum Kaffee eingeladen?

K

Test drill. May wish to review previous drills on individual pronouns first.

Angela is having difficulty with a math problem. Suggest that she ask various friends and classmates for the answer.

◼ıı   Frank weiß es.   *Warum fragt sie ihn denn nicht?*

1. Wir wissen es.
2. Ingrid weiß es.
3. Du weißt es.
4. Heike weiß es.
5. Ihr wißt es.
6. Mein Bruder weiß es.
7. Meine Freunde wissen es.

Conversational past of inseparable-prefix verbs

INFINITIVE	PAST PARTICIPLE	CONVERSATIONAL PAST
beginnen	begonnen	Wann **hat** das Spiel **begonnen?**
bekommen	bekommen	**Hast** du noch Karten **bekommen?**
gewinnen	gewonnen	Oberndorf **hat** das Spiel **gewonnen.**
verlieren	verloren	Wir **haben** das Spiel **verloren.**
verstehen	verstanden	**Habt** ihr das **verstanden?**
versuchen	versucht	Wir **haben** alles **versucht.**

The remaining prefixes are listed in the *Grammatische Übersicht*.

Some prefixes (including **be-, ge-, ver-**) are never separated from the verb stem.

Inseparable-prefix verbs do not add **ge-** in the past participle. Both weak and strong verbs may have inseparable prefixes.

L   Werner has a few questions about yesterday's soccer game. Answer in the affirmative.

Write following words on board and have students pronounce them with proper stress: *auf-machen, beginnen, bekommen, einkaufen, fernsehen, gewinnen, mitkommen, verlieren, verstehen, versuchen, wiedersehen, zumachen.*

■III   Hast du wirklich eine Karte bekommen?   *Ja, ich habe wirklich eine Karte bekommen.*

1. Hat Marta auch eine Karte bekommen?
2. Hat das Spiel erst um vier begonnen?
3. Hat München wirklich gewonnen?
4. Und Hamburg hat verloren?
5. Hast du das Spiel verstanden?

M   Astrid and Klaus had some problems getting to the soccer game on time yesterday. Tell what happened by restating in the conversational past.

Optional: May be assigned as written review.

■III   Astrid bekommt kein Geld von zu Hause.   *Astrid hat kein Geld von zu Hause bekommen.*

1. Astrid versucht alles.
2. Klaus bekommt Geld von zu Hause.
3. Aber sie bekommen keine guten Karten.
4. Sie versuchen alles.
5. Das Spiel beginnt um sieben.
6. Hoffentlich gewinnt Berlin.

Du hast das Wort

Discuss a recent school game with your classmates.

Hast du Karten bekommen?
Wann hat das Spiel begonnen?
Wer hat gewonnen? Wer hat verloren?
Wie hoch hat sie / haben sie gewonnen / verloren?

The verbs **kennen** and **wissen**   (A)

Ich **kenne** Frau Braun gut.	I know Mrs. Braun well.
Ich **weiß**, wer Herr Braun ist.	I know who Mr. Braun is.

The English equivalent of both **kennen** and **wissen** is *to know*. **Kennen** means to be acquainted with a person, place, or thing. **Wissen** means to know something as a fact.

Verbs with stem-vowel change **au>äu**   (B)

laufen		
ich laufe	Sie laufen	wir laufen
du **läufst**		ihr lauft
er/es/sie **läuft**		sie laufen

Laufen has a stem-vowel change **au>äu** in the **du-** and **er/sie-**forms of the present tense.

Accusative case of **wer**   (C)

Nominative	**Wer** hat Detlev gefragt?	*Who* asked Detlev?
Accusative	**Wen** hat Detlev gefragt?	*Whom* did Detlev ask?

The accusative of **wer** is **wen.**

Accusative case of personal pronouns (D-K)

| Ralf kennt **mich** gut. | Ralf knows *me* well. |
| Er kennt **dich** auch, nicht? | He also knows *you*, doesn't he? |

Pronouns used as direct objects are in the accusative case. Nominative and accusative forms of personal pronouns correspond as follows:

Nominative	ich	du	er	es	sie	wir	ihr	sie	Sie
Accusative	mich	dich	ihn	es	sie	uns	euch	sie	Sie

Note that **es, sie,** and **Sie** are the same in nominative and accusative.

ACCUSATIVE NOUN	ACCUSATIVE PRONOUN
Kennst du **den Mann?**	Ja, ich kenne **ihn.**
Kaufst du **den Plattenspieler?**	Ja, ich kaufe **ihn.**
Kennst du **das Kind?**	Ja, ich kenne **es.**
Kaufst du **das Radio?**	Ja, ich kaufe **es.**
Kennst du **die Frau?**	Ja, ich kenne **sie.**
Kaufst du **die Platte?**	Ja, ich kaufe **sie.**
Kennst du **die Kinder?**	Ja, ich kenne **sie.**
Kaufst du **die Platten?**	Ja, ich kaufe **sie.**

The accusative pronouns **ihn, es,** and **sie** can refer to either persons or things.

Conversational past of inseparable-prefix verbs (L-M)

INFINITIVE	PRESENT TENSE	CONVERSATIONAL PAST
beginnen	Wann **beginnt** das Spiel?	Wann **hat** das Spiel **begonnen?**
verlieren	Wir **verlieren** oft.	Wir **haben** oft **verloren.**
versuchen	Ute **versucht** alles.	Ute **hat** alles **versucht.**

The prefixes **be-, emp-, ent-, er-, ge-, ver-,** and **zer-** are never separated from the verb stem. These inseparable prefixes may occur with both weak and strong verbs. Inseparable-prefix verbs do not add the prefix **ge-** in the past participle.

In spoken German, inseparable prefixes are unstressed: **begin'nen, versu'chen.**

Chess, gymnastics, basketball, and skiing are popular activities in the German-speaking countries.

Wiederholung

A Read the excerpts from Dieter's diary and answer the questions that follow.

MONTAG

Ein prima Tag! In Englisch habe ich eine Zwei bekommen und in Deutsch eine Eins. In Mathe habe ich leider eine Vier. Aber Mathe ist schwer. Und für mich ist eine Vier eigentlich nicht schlecht.

DIENSTAG

Die *Hot Dogs* geben am Samstag abend ein Konzert. Karten habe ich aber nicht bekommen. Nichts mehr da. Alles ausverkauft. Ich bin wirklich sauer.

DONNERSTAG

Ich habe Jörg im Jugendzentrum gesehen. Er hat zwei Karten für die *Hot Dogs*. Erika kann nicht mitkommen, und er braucht jetzt nur noch eine Karte. Ich habe Erikas Karte gekauft. Ute gibt am Freitag eine Party. Sie hat mich eingeladen.

SAMSTAG

Eine tolle Party. Ich habe viel mit Ute getanzt. Sie tanzt wirklich gut. Und heute abend gehen wir ins Konzert. Ute hat auch eine Karte. Jörg und ich holen sie um sieben ab.

1. Was hat Dieter in Mathe bekommen?
2. Warum kann Dieter am Dienstag keine Karten bekommen?
3. Wen hat er im Jugendzentrum gesehen?
4. Warum braucht Jörg nur eine Karte?
5. Wer hat Dieter eingeladen?
6. Wer geht mit Dieter ins Konzert?
7. Wann holen Jörg und Dieter Ute ab?

B You and Sabine are chatting about Jörg and his forthcoming party. Answer Sabine's questions in the affirmative.

Have students make up original sentences with nouns, then substitute pronouns.

■III   Kennst du Jörgs Freundin Uschi?   *Natürlich kenne ich sie.*

1. Hast du Jörg gesehen?
2. Hat er dich eingeladen?
3. Darf meine Schwester auch mitkommen?
4. Kannst du uns abholen?
5. Hast du dein Auto gewaschen?

C   Express the following conversational exchanges in German.

1. Christl bought a dress.
   What did it cost?
2. Last night Peter called Meike.
   What did she say?
3. You didn't see Erika this morning?
   No, I had no time.
4. Did you invite Jörg?
   Yes, but he can't come.
5. What did you do yesterday afternoon?
   We watched television.
6. We played against Oberndorf yesterday.
   Who won?

Suggested activity: After teacher has corrected sentences in Ex. D, have them copied correctly. Distribute them to other students, who then read them aloud. Students guess who wrote the description.

D   Prepare five or six sentences about activities you like to do. You may wish to include answers to the following questions.

Treibst du gern Sport? Hast du ein Hobby? Sammelst du etwas? Läufst du gern Schi? Liest du gern? Schläfst du viel?

Remind students to use only vocabulary and structures they know.

E   Ask your teacher five questions about what he/she likes to do in various seasons. For example:

Was machen Sie gern im Winter? Treiben Sie gern Sport?

F   Describe the activities in the illustration. What are the people doing? What time of year is it?

Kulturlesestück

König Fußball

Im deutschen Sport ist der Fußball König°. Man° kann sagen, daß Fußball
der deutsche Nationalsport ist. Und das ist er nicht nur in Deutschland.
Man kann sicher sagen, daß Fußball der beliebteste° Sport der Welt° ist.
    Überall° in Deutschland kann man sehen, daß Fußball sehr beliebt ist.
5 Was spielen die Kinder auf der Straße? Fußball. Was spielen sie im Park?
Fußball. Wohin gehen viele Männer, Frauen und Kinder am Samstag-
oder Sonntagnachmittag? Zum Fußballplatz° oder ins Fußballstadion°.
Oder sie sehen Fußball im Fernsehen. Auch kleine Dörfer° haben einen
Fußballplatz, und die großen Städte haben große Stadien°.
10   In den Schulen und Universitäten gibt es auch Fußballmannschaften°,
aber da spielen sie fast keine Rolle°. Die großen Fußballmannschaften
und Fußballspieler kommen aus den Sportvereinen°. Und jedes Kind
kennt die Namen der großen Fußballspieler. Die besten Spieler spielen in
der Nationalmannschaft. Weltmeisterschaften° gibt es alle° vier Jahre.

king / one

favorite
der Welt: in the world
everywhere

soccer field
soccer stadium
villages
stadiums
soccer teams
spielen . . . Rolle: are not
important / sports clubs
world championships /
every

Choose the word or phrase that best completes each statement, based on the reading.

1. Der beliebteste Sport der Welt ist . . .
   a. Basketball   b. Fußball   c. Segeln   d. Schilaufen
2. Im Park spielen deutsche Kinder . . .
   a. Golf   b. Baseball   c. Basketball   d. Fußball
3. Viele Deutsche sehen am . . . ein Fußballspiel.
   a. Sonntagnachmittag   b. Sonntagabend   c. Samstagmorgen
   d. Samstagabend
4. Auch kleine Dörfer haben . . .
   a. große Stadien   b. eine Universitätsfußballmannschaft
   c. einen Fußballplatz   d. viele Sportvereine
5. Die großen Fußballmannschaften kommen aus den . . .
   a. Schulen   b. Sportvereinen   c. Universitäten
   d. Dörfern
6. Die besten Spieler können alle . . . Jahre in den Weltmeisterschaften spielen.
   a. zwei   b. drei   c. vier   d. fünf

Sonntag abend is written as two words when referring to a specific Sunday evening, as one word when not.

German soccer cheers:

Zicke-Zacke, Zicke-Zacke
Hoi, Hoi, Hoi!

Tempo, Tempo, Tempo!

Ha, Ho, He
Hertha BSC! (BSC-Berliner Sport-Club)

Vokabeln

SUBSTANTIVE

das Camping   camping
die Freizeit   leisure time
der Frühling   spring
das Fußballspiel, –e   soccer game
der Herbst   autumn, fall
das Mal   time, occasion;
  nächstes Mal   next time
die Party, –s   party
das Picknick, –s   picnic
der Schi, –er (*also* **Ski**)   ski
der Schlittschuh, –e   ice skate
der Sommer   summer
das Spiel, –e   game
das Wasser   water
der Winter   winter

VERBEN

an·rufen (angerufen)   to call, to telephone
essen (i; gegessen)   to eat
fallen (ä)   to fall
gewinnen (gewonnen)   to win
kennen (gekannt)   to know, to be acquainted
  with
laufen (äu)   to run, to walk
los·gehen   to go, to take off
reiten   to ride (horseback)

Past participles of verbs conjugated with *sein* are
given in Chapter 11.

VERBEN

Schlittschuh laufen (äu)   to ice-skate
Schi laufen (äu)   to ski
segeln   to sail
verlieren (verloren)   to lose
windsurfen   to go wind surfing
zelten   to camp

ANDERE WÖRTER

gegen (*+acc.*)   against
hoch   high
na   well
nächst   next
unentschieden   undetermined; tied (*in scor-
  ing*)
wen (*acc. of* **wer**)   whom

BESONDERE AUSDRÜCKE

wie hoch hat Oberndorf gewonnen?
  by how much did Oberndorf win?
auf eine Party gehen   to go to a party
wann geht's los?   when does it start?
das geht nicht   that doesn't work; that won't
  do
Quatsch!   nonsense! rubbish!
na und?   so what?
bergsteigen gehen   to go mountain-climbing

noch einmal

Eine deutsche Zeitung. Publish a newspaper **(die Zeitung)** in German with features, interviews, and ads. The following list may give you some ideas on what kinds of articles to include:

— Calendar of school events for a month
— Interview of student or teacher about a hobby
— Interview of a foreign student, giving her/his impressions of American schools
— Sports report
— Poll of students listing chores they do at home, favorite school subjects, favorite music or band
— Ad from bookstore for books and supplies, listing prices in **Mark, Schilling,** or **Franken**

Junge Deutsche. The class is divided into several groups. Using pictures from German magazines, each group prepares a display. Topics can be clothing, sports, entertainment, and teen-agers at parties, school, or home. Each group may include illustrations on all of these subjects, or single topics can be assigned: one group takes clothing, another sports, and so on.

Ein(e) Brieffreund(in). At the end of Stage 1, one of the suggested activities was to write a short autobiography to be submitted to a panel. Use some of that information — age, appearance, family — to begin a letter to a German friend. Continue to tell about your school subjects, hobbies, interests, and activities. Describe a typical school day; tell what you and your friends like to do after school or on weekends.

If you would like to have a real German pen pal, ask your teacher for the names of some organizations that can arrange such contacts. It might be possible for your class as a whole to correspond with an English class in a high school in Austria, Germany, or Switzerland.

Nach der Schule. Prepare a skit with three to four classmates. You are in a school hangout. A waiter or waitress has already taken your order, and you are involved in conversation with your friends about music, clothing, hobbies, chores, and sports.

E **Musik.** Learn the words and music to one or more German songs; records may be available from your city library, or you may ask your teacher for other sources. Have a volunteer compose music to "Pretty Baby" (page 130), and then organize a group to perform it.

F **Hier und dort.** Study the pictures on pages 73–79. Discuss the features in the photographs that seem to you more characteristic of German-speaking countries than of life in America.

G **Schicke Sachen.** With several classmates, prepare a skit in which you go shopping for clothes. You will need a salesperson, and you may want to have a friend accompany you. Dialogues may include a discussion of sizes, colors, prices, and style; possible settings may concern a somewhat pushy salesperson, an indecisive customer, or an urgent phone call home to request additional spending money.

H **Tagebuch.** In German, keep a diary (**das Tagebuch**) — one which you can read aloud or discuss in class, if requested. Include topics such as (1) school — classes you most enjoyed or disliked, amount of homework, any tests or special programs; (2) home — chores, family activities; (3) free time — shopping trips, hobbies you worked on or records you enjoyed listening to, friends you saw, and movies, concerts, or sports events you attended.

I **Wo hört man Deutsch?** The class is divided into four groups, each of which is responsible for creating a pictorial essay on one of the four German-speaking countries. Each group chooses one member to give a short talk to the class about the essay. Afterwards, take a class poll to find out in which of these countries the most students would like to live. Discuss some reasons for these choices.

You may wish to present these talks to other language classes and invite them to tell you about the countries they are studying.

3

Zum Städtele hinaus

226

Ein Stadtbesuch. Rothenburg is almost everyone's favorite medieval town, though Heidelberg, on the Neckar, is also popular. If you prefer the country, Wengen is just one of many villages in the Swiss Alps.

Sehenswürdigkeiten. Everyone likes castles. Some, like Neuschwanstein, have dramatic settings; others, like Linderhof, have lovely formal gardens. Costumed attendants or museum displays can make castle interiors fascinating, too. At the Hofburg in Vienna the annual Kaiserball includes an elegant meal.

229

Guten Appetit! Cafés are wonderful places to meet friends; if the setting allows a panoramic view of Salzburg, so much the better. Fruits and vegetables can be bought in open-air markets, often, as in Bonn, set up in a large square.

Kapitel 11

Bäcker,
Metzger,
Supermarkt

Einkaufen in Deutschland

Teaching suggestion: Assign this section to be read independently, with discussion during the next class session.

Barbara Braun besucht ihren Brieffreund in Nürnberg. Sie schreibt einen Brief an ihre Deutschklasse.

Nürnberg, den 3. März

Liebe Klasse!

Ich habe hier schon viel gesehen und gelernt. Meine Gastfamilie°, Herr und Frau Kraft, Ingrid und Michael, ist sehr nett. Letzte Woche bin ich dreimal° mit Frau Kraft einkaufen gegangen. Die Supermärkte sind hier fast so wie zu Hause. Nur darf man das Obst und Gemüse hier nicht anfassen°. Das habe ich natürlich falsch gemacht. Ich habe die Tomaten angefaßt. Da hat die Verkäuferin gesagt: „Einen Moment, bitte! *Ich* gebe Ihnen° die Tomaten. Die Tomaten kann doch schließlich° nicht jeder anfassen." — „Entschuldigung! Das habe ich nicht gewußt."

    Wir haben alle Sachen in einen Einkaufswagen° gepackt und bezahlt, wie in Amerika. Aber dann hat Frau Kraft alle Lebensmittel selbst eingepackt. Fast alle Kunden haben nämlich große Einkaufstaschen. Große Papiertüten gibt es nicht. Und für Plastiktüten° muß man bezahlen.

    Das Fleisch, das Brot und den Kuchen fürs Wochenende hat Frau Kraft aber nicht im Supermarkt gekauft. Fleisch, Wurst und Schinken haben wir beim Metzger gekauft und den Kuchen und das Brot beim Bäcker. Frau Kraft hat da „ihren" Metzger und „ihren" Bäcker. Beim Bäcker und beim Metzger sagen alle Kunden immer schön „Grüß Gott" und „Auf Wiederschauen". Und die Verkäufer antworten jedes Mal. Wie oft sagen sie wohl jeden Tag „Auf Wiederschauen"?

    Am Samstag sind wir dann noch zum Markt gegangen und haben dort eingekauft. Wir waren schon früh dort, denn dann ist noch alles frisch. Und es ist noch viel da. Aber auch hier darf man Obst und Gemüse nicht anfassen.

    Das ist alles für heute. Bald mehr!

Herzliche Grüße

Barbara

Glosses (right margin):

- host family
- three times
- handle, touch
- to you / after all
- shopping cart
- plastic bags

Point out the various English equivalents for *man* and the past participle of the irregular weak verb *wissen: gewußt.*

Fragen

1. Wie oft ist Barbara letzte Woche einkaufen gegangen?
2. Ist sie allein° gegangen?
3. Was hat Barbara falsch gemacht?
4. Wer hat die Lebensmittel eingepackt?
5. Warum hat Frau Kraft keine Plastiktüte genommen?
6. Was hat Frau Kraft beim Metzger gekauft? Und beim Bäcker?
7. Was sagen die Verkäufer jeden Tag sehr oft?
8. Warum ist Frau Kraft am Samstag schon früh zum Markt gegangen?

Personalize: *Wann geht deine Mutter einkaufen? Gehst du auch einkaufen? Hast du eine Einkaufstasche?*, etc.

Du hast das Wort

Optional: Have students discuss how grocery shopping in Germany differs from that in America, and how it is the same.

Barbara apologized for touching the vegetables in the supermarket. How would you apologize if a classmate told you you had broken something?

Du hast [meine Platte] kaputtgemacht.

Entschuldigung.
Habe ich das gemacht?
  Ach, Entschuldigung.
Entschuldigung. Das
  habe ich nicht gewußt.
Das tut mir leid.

Sag!

Dependent word order after *daß* is still for recognition only. If there is comprehension difficulty, give students the correct answer, then repeat the question again until structure is understood. It might also prove helpful to vary a basic sentence several times:
Sag [Kai], daß du einkaufen gehst. (wandern, Schi laufen, spazieren, etc.)

1. Sag [Kai], daß du einkaufen gehst!
2. Sag [Ute], daß du Tomaten brauchst!
3. Sag [Kai], daß du Wurst beim Metzger kaufst!
4. Sag [Ute], daß du Kuchen beim Bäcker kaufst!
5. Sag [Kai], daß du alles in die Einkaufstasche packst!
6. Sag [Ute], daß du keine Plastiktüte kaufen willst!

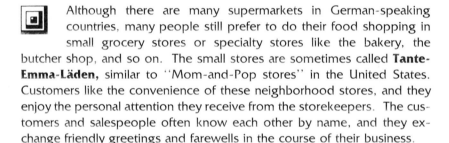 Although there are many supermarkets in German-speaking countries, many people still prefer to do their food shopping in small grocery stores or specialty stores like the bakery, the butcher shop, and so on. The small stores are sometimes called **Tante-Emma-Läden,** similar to ''Mom-and-Pop stores'' in the United States. Customers like the convenience of these neighborhood stores, and they enjoy the personal attention they receive from the storekeepers. The customers and salespeople often know each other by name, and they exchange friendly greetings and farewells in the course of their business.

234

Wurst and **Würstchen** are very popular in German-speaking countries. Almost every town, and certainly every region, has one or more sausage specialties of its own. **Würstchen** are among the foods most commonly sold at snackbars, where they are served on an unbuttered roll or with a piece of bread, often with a dab of mustard **(Senf).**

The snackbars are called by many different names, such as **Imbißstube, Kaltes Buffet,** and **Bier Würstl,** and they can be found almost everywhere — in the marketplace, in a railroad station, or in a shopping area. Besides many varieties of **Würstchen,** popular snacks include ham, cheese, or fish sandwiches, french fries, and pizza.

Some sources place the number of different kinds of *Wurst* at over a hundred. Some familiar varieties include: *Bratwurst, Leberwurst, Bockwurst, Teewurst, Knackwurst, Frankfurter Würstchen, Mettwurst, Weißwurst, Blutwurst.*

Beim Metzger

Frau Kraft kauft bei ihrem Metzger ein.

HERR LANGE	Grüß Gott, Frau Kraft! Was darf es sein?
FRAU KRAFT	Wieviel kosten die Schweinskoteletts?
HERR LANGE	7 Mark 50 das Pfund.
FRAU KRAFT	Ich brauche fünf Stück.
HERR LANGE	Gern. Sonst noch was?
FRAU KRAFT	Ich hätte gern zehn Wiener Würstchen.
HERR LANGE	So. Haben Sie noch einen Wunsch?
FRAU KRAFT	Nein. Das ist alles für heute.
HERR LANGE	Danke . . . So, bitte schön. Das macht zusammen 24 Mark 50.
	* * *
	So, Sie bekommen 50 Pfennig zurück.
FRAU KRAFT	Danke schön.
HERR LANGE	Bitte. Auf Wiedersehen, Frau Kraft.
FRAU KRAFT	Auf Wiedersehen, Herr Lange.

Good for sight-reading *mit verteilten Rollen.* First introduce typical shopping phrases and new vocabulary.

Remind students that *Grüß Gott* is a common greeting in Southern Germany and Austria.

Fragen

1. Wieviel kosten die Schweinskoteletts?
2. Wieviel Koteletts braucht Frau Kraft?
3. Was kauft Frau Kraft noch?
4. Wieviel kostet alles zusammen?
5. Wieviel bekommt Frau Kraft zurück?

Activity: Have students use names of food on p. 236 to create original dialogues. Encourage variety.

Wortschatzerweiterung

Was gibt's heute auf dem Markt?

1.	der Apfel, ¨	5.	die Kartoffel, −n	9.	der Saft
2.	die Banane, −n	6.	der Spinat	10.	die Milch
3.	die Orange, −n	7.	die Erbse, −n	11.	das Ei, −er
4.	die Erdbeere, −n	8.	die Karotte, −n	12.	die Butter
				13.	der Käse

A   The illustration above shows part of an open-air market. Ask a classmate what he/she would like to buy.

Was möchtest du kaufen?

B   Ask a classmate for her/his opinion of the food prices.

Wie findest du [die Kartoffeln] — teuer oder billig?

C   How good is your memory? Start with a simple statement about buying food and pass it on. Your neighbor repeats it and adds one more item. The next person repeats the entire statement and adds another item.

STUDENT 1: Ich gehe in den Supermarkt und kaufe Brot.
STUDENT 2: Ich gehe in den Supermarkt und kaufe Brot und Kaffee.
STUDENT 3: Ich gehe in den Supermarkt und kaufe Brot, Kaffee und . . .

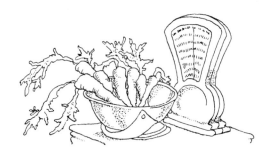

 In German-speaking countries, the metric system is used to measure volume and weight. The basic measure of volume is the **Liter (l),** and the basic measures of weight are the **Gramm (g)** and the **Kilogramm (kg).** German speakers also use the older term **Pfund (Pfd.)** for half a **Kilogramm,** or 500 **Gramm.** A **Pfund** is equivalent to 1.1 American pounds.

Units of measurement and quantity

Ich möchte vier **Kilo** Kartoffeln.	I'd like four *kilos* of potatoes.
Ich nehme fünf **Pfund** Orangen.	I'll take five *pounds* of oranges.
Er kauft zwei **Liter** Milch.	He's buying two *liters* of milk.
Sie trinkt jeden Tag vier **Glas** Wasser.	She drinks four *glasses* of water every day.
Er kauft zwei **Flaschen** Saft.	He's buying two *bottles* of juice.

In German, **der-**nouns and **das-**nouns expressing measure, weight, or number are in the singular. **Die-**nouns, for example **Flasche,** are in the plural.

D   Have a classmate take the part of a clerk. Tell her/him how much you want to buy.

■Ⅲ   Wieviel Kilo Orangen möchten Sie? Drei?   *Ja, ich nehme drei Kilo Orangen.*

1. Wieviel Gramm Butter möchten Sie? Hundert?
2. Wieviel Pfund Äpfel möchten Sie? Fünf?
3. Wieviel Kilo Kartoffeln möchten Sie? Zehn?
4. Wieviel Stück Kuchen möchten Sie? Zwei?
5. Wieviel Stück Torte möchten Sie? Vier?
6. Wieviel Flaschen Saft möchten Sie? Drei?
7. Wieviel Gramm Käse möchten Sie? Fünfhundert?

Du hast das Wort

V: *Cola, Limonade, Mineralwasser.*

Compare your eating and drinking habits with your classmates'.

Wieviel Glas Milch trinkst du jeden Tag?
Wieviel Liter Milch kauft deine Familie jede Woche? Wieviel Liter Saft?
Wieviel Stück Brot ißt du jeden Tag?
Wieviel Eier ißt du jede Woche?
Wieviel Gramm Käse ißt du jede Woche?
Wieviel Obst ißt du jede Woche?

Aussprache

┃ [ʌ]   Uhr, Klavier, fährt

When the German **r** is not followed by a vowel, it tends to be pronounced like the final sound in British English *here (hee-uh), there (thay-uh)*. The symbol [ʌ] represents this **uh** sound. In German, the sound [ʌ] occurs in the unstressed final position.

A   Practice the following words horizontally in pairs.

[R]	[ʌ]
Tiere	Tier
Paare	Paar
Uhren	Uhr
Türen	Tür
fahren	fährt
fahre	fahr
Klaviere	Klavier
schwere	schwer

B   Practice the sounds [ʌ] and [R]. Read the sentences aloud.

1. Warum brauchen wir soviel Papier?
2. Birgit sammelt gern Bierdeckel.
3. Jörg, darf ich die Tür hier aufmachen?
4. Hannelore spielt wirklich gut Klavier.

Additional Proverb: *Wer gern lernt, lernt schneller.* (He who likes to learn, learns more quickly.)

Proverb: Happy is the one who forgets about what can't be changed. (Don't worry about what you can't change.)

Glücklich ist, wer vergißt, was nicht mehr zu ändern ist.

Übungen

Conversational past with auxiliary sein

Be sure students don't confuse this form with the English present progressive: *is going, is coming,* etc.

Help students see what is meant by "change of condition":
Condition: *I'm in bed.*
Change: *I get up.*
New Condition: *I'm up.*
Can they name other such verbs in English? (*fall asleep, wake up, die, disappear,* etc.)

Erika **ist** spät nach Hause **gekommen.**   Erika came home late.
Sie **ist** erst um acht **aufgestanden.**   She didn't get up until eight.

Ich **bin** gestern in die Stadt   I went into town
    gefahren.   yesterday.

Some verbs require **sein** as an auxiliary in the conversational past. These verbs have no direct object and denote a change in location (for example, **kommen**) or a change in condition (for example, **aufstehen**).

ich **bin** gefahren		wir **sind** gefahren
du **bist** gefahren	Sie **sind** gefahren	ihr **seid** gefahren
er/sie **ist** gefahren		sie **sind** gefahren

A   You're talking about vacations. Tell your friends who went on vacation alone, and then ask where various other people went.

It is probably best to avoid the term "verb of motion", since many *haben*-verbs show motion: e.g. *spielen, tanzen,* etc.

V: Repeat using *gekommen.*

◼◗   Gretl ist allein gefahren.   *Jürgen und Paul sind allein*
    (Jürgen und Paul)   *gefahren.*

1. ich   3. Erika
2. die Jungen   4. wir

◼◗   Wohin ist Regina ge-   *Wohin ist Udo gefahren?*
    fahren? (Udo)

5. du   7. deine Freundin Inge
6. ihr   8. Richard

INFINITIVE	PAST PARTICIPLE	CONVERSATIONAL PAST
aufstehen	(ist) aufgestanden	Sie **sind** spät **aufgestanden.**
fahren	(ist) gefahren	Sie **sind** in die Stadt **gefahren.**
gehen	(ist) gegangen	Sie **sind** ins Kino **gegangen.**
kommen	(ist) gekommen	Sie **sind** um acht **gekommen.**
laufen	(ist) gelaufen	Sie **sind** nach Hause **gelaufen.**
wandern	(ist) gewandert	Sie **sind** durch die Stadt **gewandert.**

B

Past participles of other familiar *sein*-verbs are listed in the *Grammatische Übersicht*, p. 246.

Point out that *laufen* is sometimes used to mean *to walk (zu Fuß gehen).*

You and your friends are talking about leisure activities. Restate the following exchanges in the conversational past.

▪ Wandert ihr im Sommer viel?
Ja, wir wandern ziemlich viel.

Seid ihr im Sommer viel gewandert?
Ja, wir sind ziemlich viel gewandert.

1. Wohin fährst du?
Ich fahre in die Stadt.
2. Wir gehen ins Kino.
Gehen eure Freunde mit?
3. Lauft ihr jeden Tag?
Nein, wir laufen nur am Samstag.
4. Wann kommst du nach Hause?
Ich komme erst um acht.
5. Gehst du im Winter Schi laufen?
Ja, ich gehe ziemlich oft Schi laufen.
6. Stehst du spät auf?
Nein, ich stehe um sieben auf.
7. Kommt dein Bruder mit?
Nein, er geht ins Theater.

Du hast das Wort

Ask a classmate the following questions. He/she will answer and then ask you the same question.

▪ Wann bist du heute morgen aufgestanden?

Um sieben. Und wann bist du aufgestanden?
Um [acht].

Wann bist du in die Schule gegangen?
Bist du gefahren oder gelaufen?
Wann bist du in die Stadt gefahren?
Wo bist du einkaufen gegangen?
Wann bist du nach Hause gekommen?
Wohin bist du am Wochenende gegangen?
Wann bist du am Samstag aufgestanden?

Im Supermarkt muß man die Lebensmittel selbst einpacken.

Narrative past of **sein**

Optional: Review days of week: *Heute ist [Montag]. Welcher Tag war gestern? vorgestern? vorvorgestern?*

You may wish to explain briefly that a "second past tense" exists. It never has a *ge*-prefix or a helping verb.

ich **war** müde		I *was* tired
du **warst** müde		you *were* tired
er/sie **war** müde		he/she *was* tired
wir **waren** müde		we *were* tired
ihr **wart** müde		you *were* tired
sie **waren** müde		they *were* tired
Sie **waren** müde		you *were* tired

Although **sein** does have a conversational past, the most commonly used past-tense forms are **war, warst,** and so on. These forms are called the *narrative past.*

C   Restate the following conversational exchanges in the narrative past.

Personalize: *Warst du gestern krank? fleißig, müde, sauer, faul, kaputt?*

> ■◗ Wie ist das Fußballspiel?   *Wie war das Fußballspiel?*
>   Es ist langweilig.   *Es war langweilig.*

1. Wo bist du Samstag abend?
   Ich bin im Jugendzentrum, wie immer.
2. Wo seid ihr am Sonntag?
   Wir sind zu Hause.
3. Wie ist das Konzert?
   Es ist klasse.
4. Warum sind die Jungen am Wochenende zu Hause?
   Sie sind doch nicht zu Hause.

Special **der**-nouns in the accusative singular

NOMINATIVE	ACCUSATIVE
Wie heißt **der Junge** da? Wie heißt **der Herr** da?	Kennst du **den Jungen**? Kennst du **den Herrn**?

A few **der**-nouns add **-n** in the accusative singular.

Additional practice: Let students respond freely with either *den Herrn* or *den Jungen: Wen hast du gesehen? (gefragt, eingeladen, angerufen, gehört,* etc.)

D   Jörg is telling you about various people. Inquire about some other people you're curious about.

> ▪▥   Ich habe Frau Braun einge-   *Hast du auch Herrn Braun*
>   laden. (Herr Braun)   *eingeladen?*

1. Ich habe Frau Wagner angerufen. (Herr Wagner)
2. Ich habe Frau Lenz gesehen. (Herr Lenz)
3. Ich kenne das Mädchen dort. (der Junge)
4. Ich finde das Mädchen doof. (der Junge)
5. Ich kenne die Kundin dort. (der Kunde)
6. Ich finde Herrn Klein nett. (der Kunde)

Prepositions with the accusative case

durch	through	Gabi geht **durch das Geschäft**.
für	for	Gabi kauft ein Buch **für ihren Vater**.
gegen	against	Sie hat nichts **gegen ihren Freund**.
ohne	without	Frank macht die Hausaufgaben **ohne mich**.
um	around	Er geht **um das Haus**.

Review accusative forms of *der-* and *ein-* words, pp. 119–120.

The prepositions **durch, für, gegen, ohne,** and **um** are always followed by the accusative case.

E   Gerd suggests going through various buildings to get out of the pedestrian zone by a shortcut. Insist that it won't work.

Cue with visuals.

■∥   Versuchen wir mal das Café!   *Man kann doch nicht durch das Café gehen.*

1. Versuchen wir mal den Supermarkt!
2. Versuchen wir mal das Lebensmittelgeschäft!
3. Versuchen wir mal das Musikgeschäft!
4. Versuchen wir mal das Jugendzentrum!
5. Versuchen wir mal die Bäckerei!

F   You're showing Sabine all the presents you've bought. Specify whom they're for.

Precede with simple substitution drill: *Das Geschenk ist für seinen Bruder. (Freund, Vater, Lehrer, Mutter, Schwester, Lehrerin)*

■∥   Ist die Bluse für deine Mutter oder deine Schwester?   *Für [meine Mutter].*

1. Ist der Pulli für deinen Vater oder deinen Bruder?
2. Ist das Buch für Herrn Lenz oder Frau Lenz?
3. Ist die Platte für deine Freundin oder deinen Freund?
4. Ist der Kuli für deinen Bruder oder deine Schwester?

G   Frau Lerner doesn't like any of the people she deals with. Try to find out what she has against each of them.

■∥   Frau Lerner hat ihren Apotheker nicht gern.   *Was hat sie denn gegen ihren Apotheker?*

1. Sie hat auch ihren Bäcker nicht gern.
2. Auch ihren Metzger hat sie nicht gern.
3. Ihren Elektriker findet sie schlecht.
4. Sie findet auch ihren Friseur schlecht.
5. Sie hat ihren Arzt nicht gern.

H

Precede with simple substitution drill: *Frau Braun kommt ohne ihre Familie.* *(ihr Mann, ihre Schwester, ihr Bruder, ihr Vater, ihre Mutter)*

You and Gerd want to go on a picnic but your friends have to work. Suggest going without the individuals mentioned.

> ▪ɪɪɪ   Jürgen muß arbeiten.   *Dann gehen wir ohne ihn.*

1. Bruno muß arbeiten.
2. Heidi muß arbeiten.
3. Ich muß arbeiten.
4. Lore und Jutta müssen arbeiten.
5. Frank und Udo müssen arbeiten.

I

Review accusative pronouns, p. 215.

Reassure Jutta that you have nothing against the people who will be at her party.

> ▪ɪɪɪ   Hast du etwas gegen Franz?   *Nein, ich habe nichts gegen ihn.*

1. Hast du etwas gegen Marianne?
2. Hast du etwas gegen Herrn Lenz?
3. Hast du etwas gegen mich?
4. Hast du etwas gegen uns?
5. Hast du etwas gegen Stefan und Thomas?

J

It might be helpful to do Ex. J first with books open. May also serve as a written review.

Substitute the cued words for the italicized words in the following sentences. Make any necessary changes.

> ▪ɪɪɪ   Ursel geht durch *das Geschäft.* (der Super-markt)   *Ursel geht durch den Super-markt.*

1. Walter geht durch *das Haus.* (die Stadt)
2. Volker will nichts gegen *seine Freundin* sagen. (sein Freund)
3. Ingrid hat etwas gegen *ihren Bruder.* (ihre Schwester)
4. Trudi kauft den Pulli für *ihre Mutter.* (ihr Vater)
5. Sie kauft die Platte für *ihre Freundin.* (ihr Freund)
6. Christl kommt ohne *ihre Schwester.* (ihr Bruder)
7. Ich möchte einmal ohne *meinen Bruder* zelten gehen. (meine Eltern)
8. Arbeitest du für *deine Mutter?* (dein Vater)

Du hast das Wort

Tell your classmates what you would like to buy as a birthday present for some of your friends and relatives.

> ▪ɪɪɪ   dein Vater   *Für meinen Vater möchte ich [ein Buch] kaufen.*

deine Mutter
dein Bruder [Volker]
deine Schwester [Margit]
dein Freund [Ralf]
deine Freundin [Ilse]

Frau Kraft kauft ihr Gemüse auf dem Markt.

Accusative prepositional contractions

Frank geht **durchs** Geschäft. Ute kauft etwas **fürs** Haus. Ingrid geht **ums** Haus.	durch das > **durchs** für das > **fürs** um das > **ums**

The prepositions **durch, für,** and **um** often contract with the definite article **das** to form **durchs, fürs,** and **ums.**

K   Restate, using contractions.

■III   Eva ist durch das Haus ge-   *Eva ist durchs Haus gegan-*
        gangen.   *gen.*

1. Hugo ist durch das Geschäft gegangen.
2. Petra hat das Geld für das Radio bekommen.
3. Hast du die Karten für das Konzert gekauft?
4. Hast du schon den Arbeitsplan für das Wochenende gemacht?
5. Michael hat einen Spaziergang um das Haus gemacht.

Du hast das Wort   Ask a classmate about her/his plans for the weekend.

Was hast du fürs Wochenende vor?
Gehst du ins Kino?
Hast du Geld fürs Kino?

Grammatische Übersicht

Conversational past with auxiliary **sein**   (A-B)

ich **bin gekommen**		wir **sind gekommen**
du **bist gekommen**	Sie **sind gekommen**	ihr **seid gekommen**
er/sie **ist gekommen**		sie **sind gekommen**

Wir **sind** spät **gekommen.**	We came late.
Gabi **ist** spät **aufgestanden.**	Gabi got up late.

Some verbs require **sein** instead of **haben** as an auxiliary in the conversational past. Verbs that require **sein** must meet two conditions:

1. They must be intransitive verbs (verbs without a direct object).
2. They must indicate a change of location (as in **kommen**) or a change of condition (as in **aufstehen**).

In the vocabularies of this book, verbs that require **sein** are indicated as follows: **kommen (ist gekommen).** The following verbs require **sein** as an auxiliary in the conversational past.

INFINITIVE	PAST PARTICIPLE
aufstehen	(ist) aufgestanden
fahren	(ist) gefahren
fallen	(ist) gefallen
gehen	(ist) gegangen
kommen	(ist) gekommen

INFINITIVE	PAST PARTICIPLE
laufen	(ist) gelaufen
reiten	(ist) geritten
schwimmen	(ist) geschwommen
segeln	(ist) gesegelt
wandern	(ist) gewandert

Narrative past of **sein**   (C)

ich **war**		wir **waren**
du **warst**	Sie **waren**	ihr **wart**
er/es/sie **war**		sie **waren**

Wo **warst** du gestern?	Where *were* you yesterday?

The most commonly used past-tense forms of **sein** are **war, warst,** and so on. These forms are called *narrative past.* **Sein** also has a conversational past, which you will learn in *German Today, Two.*

Special **der**-nouns in the accusative singular (D)

Wie heißt **der Junge?**	Meinst du **den Jungen** da?
Wie heißt **der Kunde?**	Meinst du **den Kunden** da?
Herr Lenz ist mein Freund.	Ich kenne **Herrn Lenz** nicht.

Most nouns have the same form in the nominative and the accusative. A few **der**-nouns, including **Junge, Kunde,** and **Herr,** add **-n** in the accusative singular. Note that the **-n** must be added even when **Herr** is used as a title.

In the vocabularies of this book, special **der**-nouns will be followed by two endings: **der Herr, -n, -en.** The first ending is the accusative singular; the second ending is the nominative plural.

Prepositions with the accusative case (E-J)

durch	Tanja geht **durch** die Stadt.	Tanja is going *through* the city.
für	**Für** wen kauft sie die Platte?	*For* whom is she buying the record?
gegen	Sie hat nichts **gegen** den Jungen.	She has nothing *against* the boy.
ohne	Sie beginnt **ohne** Herrn Bauer.	She's beginning *without* Mr. Bauer.
um	Sie geht **um** das Haus.	She's going *around* the house.

Accusative prepositional contractions (K)

Erika geht **durchs** Zimmer.	durch das > durchs
Jörg kauft ein Geschenk **fürs** Kind.	für das > fürs
Torsten geht **ums** Haus.	um das > ums

The prepositions **durch, für,** and **um** may contract with the definite article **das.**

In dieser Bäckerei bekommt man auch frischen Kaffee.

Wiederholung

A   Your grandmother wants to know who's done various tasks. Confirm her guesses.

   ■Ⅲ   Wer hat den Bäcker angeru-   *Ja, ich habe ihn angerufen.*
             fen? Du?

1. Wer hat den Metzger angerufen? Du?
2. Wer hat das Haus aufgeräumt? Ihr?
3. Wer hat die Möbel abgestaubt? Karin?
4. Wer hat das Geschirr abgetrocknet? Karl und Erik?
5. Wer hat die Fenster aufgemacht? Du?
6. Wer hat die Wurst eingepackt? Deine Mutter?

B   Read the following statements about various foods and quantities of foods. Correct the statements that aren't logical.

   ■Ⅲ   Ich möchte zwei Meter   *Ich möchte zwei Pfund*
             Bananen.   *Bananen.*

1. Ich möchte zwei Liter Würstchen bitte.
2. Sind die Tomaten frisch?
3. Fleisch und Schinken kaufe ich immer beim Bäcker.
4. Ich brauche auch fünf Stück Milch bitte.
5. Kartoffeln kosten eine Mark das Gramm.
6. Im Supermarkt darf man das Obst nicht anfassen.
7. Butter kostet 6 Mark 50 das Kilometer.
8. Ich trinke jeden Tag zwei Glas Milch.

C   Everyone has chores to do today. Form complete sentences in the present tense, using the cues provided.

1. Andrea / müssen / spülen / Geschirr
2. ich / sollen / decken / Tisch
3. Werner / aufräumen / Garage
4. du / füttern / Katze
5. wir / abstauben / Möbel
6. Werner / backen / Kuchen
7. ich / müssen / raustragen / Mülleimer

D   List at least five things you sometimes do after school or in the evening. You may wish to include some of the following activities.

Remind students to use only familiar vocabulary and structures in Ex. D and E.

Hausaufgaben machen   einkaufen gehen   zu Hause helfen
tanzen gehen   ins Konzert gehen   fernsehen

E What are the following people and animals doing? Write a sentence related to each picture, using the preposition given.

▪▥ um

Sie laufen um die
Frau herum.

1. ohne

2. für

3. gegen

4. durch

Kulturlesestück

Der Markt

Viele Deutsche gehen nicht nur einmal° in der
Woche einkaufen. Sie gehen zweimal oder
öfter°, denn sie wollen frisches Obst und
Gemüse haben.

5   Sie kaufen ihr Obst und Gemüse oft auf
dem Markt. Hier kann man es direkt von den
Bauern° kaufen. Der Markt ist oft im Zentrum einer° Stàdt, auf dem Marktplatz° vor
dem Rathaus°. Die Verkäufer haben ihre
10   Waren unter° großen Schirmen°. Diese
Schirme haben viele Farben — rot, blau oder
grün. So sieht der Markt schön bunt° aus.

In großen Städten ist jeden Tag Markt, in
kleinen Städten ein- oder zweimal in der
15   Woche. Man findet oft auch Brot, Käse und
Eier, Fleisch und Wurst und Fisch° da. Und
Blumen°. Viele Blumen. Einige° Städte haben
sogar° einen besonderen° Blumenmarkt.

one time

more often

farmers
of a / market place
town hall
under / umbrellas

colorful

fish
flowers / some
even / special

A Choose the phrase that best completes each sentence, based on the reading.

1. Viele Deutsche gehen zweimal oder öfter in der Woche einkaufen, denn ...
   a. sie wollen nicht soviel tragen.
   b. sie wollen immer alles frisch haben.
   c. sie haben kein Auto.
   d. man kann Gemüse nur von den Bauern kaufen.
2. Die Deutschen kaufen gern auf dem Markt, denn ...
   a. im Supermarkt ist alles frisch.
   b. in kleinen Geschäften ist alles billig.
   c. die Bauern haben alles frisch.
   d. man muß nicht so weit gehen.
3. Auf dem Markt sieht man viele bunte ...
   a. Bauern
   b. Verkäufer
   c. Rathäuser
   d. Schirme
4. In ... ist jeden Tag Markt.
   a. großen Städten
   b. kleinen Städten
   c. allen Städten
   d. keiner Stadt

B Which of the following would generally be available at an open-air market in a German-speaking country?

Möbel, Äpfel, Kartoffeln, Cassetten, Fernseher, Käse, Eier, Wurst, Briefmarken, Blumen, Flugzeugmodelle, Fisch, Gemüse, Brot

Whenever possible, Germans prefer food without preservatives, untouched by insecticides, and grown without chemical fertilizers. They do not decorate their cakes and cookies with bright, artificial colorings the way Americans sometimes do. Given this preference for naturalness, it is not surprising to find that there are many health food stores (**Reformhäuser**) in the German-speaking countries.

Naturalness is prized in other products as well. Advertisements proclaim soaps with natural oils, hair-care products made with herbs, and clothing made of natural fibers.

Germans stand by their concern for naturalness even in sickness. People often seek relief from their illnesses in one of the many spas in the German-speaking countries. Depending on their location, the spas might feature mineral waters for drinking or bathing, mud baths, herbal medicines, or just good clean air.

Vokabeln

Kapitel 12

Guten Appetit!

Essen bei Familie Wolf

Was gibt's zum Frühstück?

Additional *Fragen:*
Ist das amerikanische
Frühstück wie das
deutsche? Um wieviel
Uhr frühstückst du an
Wochentagen? Am
Samstag? Am Sonntag?

Familie Wolf frühstückt um sieben. Zum Frühstück gibt es Brot und
Brötchen mit Butter und Marmelade, manchmal auch ein Ei, Käse oder
Wurst. Der Vater und die Mutter trinken Kaffee, und Gabi trinkt Scho-
kolade oder Milch.

Other American breakfast items:
Orangensaft, ein weichgekochtes
Ei, Rührei, Spiegelei, Speck,
Schinken.

Fragen

Some of the foods men-
tioned here are for rec-
ognition only.

1. Wann frühstücken Wolfs?
2. Was essen und trinken Wolfs zum Frühstück?
3. Was ißt und trinkst du zum Frühstück? Eier? Corn-flakes? Brot?
   Toast? mit Butter und Marmelade? Saft? Milch? Kaffee?

Was gibt's zum Mittagessen?

Personalize:
Wann ißt du zu Mittag?
Ißt du ,,warm'' oder
,,kalt''? Ißt du gewöhn-
lich in der Schule zu
Mittag? Ißt du gern in
der Schule? Ist das
Essen in der Schule
gut?

Um ein Uhr ißt Familie Wolf zu Mittag. Zum Mittagessen gibt es Suppe,
dann Fisch oder Fleisch mit Kartoffeln und Gemüse und manchmal auch
Salat. Zum Essen trinken sie gewöhnlich nichts. Nur am Sonntag trinken Herr und Frau Wolf vielleicht ein Glas Wein, und Gabi trinkt Saft.
Als Nachtisch gibt es vielleicht Orangen oder Bananen oder einen Pudding.

Fragen

1. Wann essen Wolfs zu Mittag?
2. Was essen Wolfs zu Mittag?
3. Was ißt du mittags°? Thunfisch? Schinkenbrote°? Wurst? Würstchen? Salat? Suppe? Pommes frites°? Chips? Pizza?
4. Was trinkst du zum Mittagessen?

Was gibt's zum Abendessen?

Most people in
German-speaking
countries do not drink
water from the tap.
When they are thirsty,
they prefer mineral
water *(Mineralwasser)*
or soda water *(Sprudel).*

Um sieben ißt die Familie zu Abend. Zum Abendessen gibt es Brot mit
Wurst und Käse. Der Vater und die Mutter trinken oft ein Glas Bier oder
eine Tasse Tee. Gabi trinkt kein Bier, sondern Limonade oder eine Cola.
Wasser trinken sie nicht, denn es schmeckt nicht so gut wie Cola oder
Tee.

Fragen

Additional *Fragen:* Eßt
ihr ,,warm'' oder
,,kalt''? Wer kocht das
Essen?

1. Wann essen Wolfs zu Abend?
2. Was essen Wolfs zu Abend?
3. Was ißt du abends? Steak? Rindsbraten? Schweinskoteletts? Huhn?
   Fisch? Würstchen? Kartoffeln? Gemüse? Nachtisch?
4. Was trinkst du zum Abendessen?

One of Gabi Wolf's chores is to set the table before each meal: fork **(die Gabel)** on the left of the plate, knife **(das Messer)** on the right, and spoon **(der Löffel)** above the plate. When people in German-speaking countries eat, they keep the fork in the left hand and the knife in the right, using both utensils at once. Germans keep their left hand on the table instead of in their lap, as Americans do.

Before beginning to eat, the head of the household may say **Guten Appetit** or **Mahlzeit,** short for **Gesegnete Mahlzeit** (''wishing everyone a good meal''). The rest of the family often responds with **Danke gleichfalls** (same to you).

Im Restaurant

Encourage students to create their own skits based on these dialogues.

Familie Wolf ißt auch gern mal im Restaurant.

OBER	Guten Tag! Möchten Sie etwas trinken?
FRAU WOLF	Ach ja. Ich habe so einen Durst. Ein Mineralwasser bitte.
HERR WOLF	Ich trinke auch ein Wasser.
OBER	Zwei Wasser.
GABI	Ich möchte eine Cola bitte.
OBER	Danke.
HERR WOLF	Und die Speisekarte bitte.

Der Ober bringt die Getränke.

OBER	Möchten Sie jetzt bestellen?
FRAU WOLF	Ja bitte. Ist der Rindsbraten zart?
OBER	Oh ja. Den kann ich empfehlen.
FRAU WOLF	Also, dreimal Rindsbraten mit Kartoffelpüree und Salat.
GABI	Ich will kein Kartoffelpüree.
FRAU WOLF	Hast du denn keinen Hunger?
GABI	Doch. Aber ich esse lieber Pommes frites.
FRAU WOLF	Wie du willst.

Point out how guest orders: *einmal Rindsbraten, zweimal Wiener Schnitzel.*

* * *

OBER	So, hat's geschmeckt?
FRAU WOLF	Ja. Der Braten war ausgezeichnet.
HERR WOLF	Ich möchte gern zahlen.
OBER	Bitte sehr. Das macht zusammen 43 Mark und 50 Pfennig.
HERR WOLF	Machen Sie es 45.
OBER	Vielen Dank.

Fragen

Point out to students that while they eat "hamburgers" and "frankfurters", Germans like to eat *Amerikaner* (a kind of cookie) and *Berliner* (similar to a donut).

1. Ißt Familie Wolf immer zu Hause? Wo essen sie auch gern?
2. Warum bestellt Frau Wolf ein Mineralwasser?
3. Was trinkt Gabi?
4. Wer bringt die Speisekarte?
5. Was empfiehlt der Ober?
6. Was bestellt Frau Wolf?
7. Warum will Gabi kein Kartoffelpüree?
8. Wie hat der Braten geschmeckt?
9. Wer bezahlt?

Du hast das Wort

A. Ask a classmate whether he/she likes to eat certain foods.

Ißt du gern	Kartoffelpüree? Fisch? Gemüse?

Ja, sehr gern.
Ja, [Kartoffelpüree] schmeckt gut.
Ich esse es, aber nicht gern.
Nein, [Kartoffelpüree] esse ich nicht gern.
Nein, [Kartoffelpüree] mag ich nicht.

Teacher may wish to choose which foods on p. 256 should be learned or may substitute others. In any case it is probably desirable that students learn food items via exercises and frequent class references rather than having a long list assigned to memorize.

B. Take a poll of your classmates on their preferences for foods and beverages.

Was ißt du lieber — Kartoffelpüree oder Pommes frites?
　　　　　　　　　Eier oder Corn-flakes?
　　　　　　　　　Fleisch oder Fisch?
　　　　　　　　　Orangen oder Bananen?
　　　　　　　　　Wurst oder Käse?

Was trinkst du lieber — Cola oder Kaffee?
　　　　　　　　　　Saft oder Milch?
　　　　　　　　　　Tee oder Wasser?

Most restaurants in German-speaking countries post the menu outside so that customers may decide whether they wish to or can afford to eat there. The price includes a value-added tax **(Mehrwertsteuer)** and a service charge **(Bedienung)** of 15%. To ask for the bill one can say **Zahlen bitte!** or **Ich möchte gern zahlen.** The waiter or waitress will total the bill and make change right at the table. Although no extra tip is usually left, the customer often rounds off the bill to the next appropriate figure.

Speisekarte

Suppen

Hühnersuppe	DM 2,50
Gemüsesuppe	DM 3,00
Tagessuppe	DM 2,00

Fleisch und Fisch

Filetsteak	DM 13,00
Rindsbraten	DM 10,50
Schweinskotelett	DM 9,50
Wiener Schnitzel	DM 10,50
Schinkenbrot	DM 6,50
Würstchen	DM 3,00
Fisch	DM 9,00
Hering	DM 3,50

Gemüse und Salate

Erbsen	DM 2,00
Karotten	DM 2,00
Spinat	DM 2,00
Pommes frites	DM 1,50
Kartoffelpüree	DM 1,50
Salat	DM 3,00
Tomatensalat	DM 3,50
Wurstsalat	DM 5,00

Zum Nachtisch

Eis	DM 3,50
Pudding	DM 2,00
Apfelkuchen	DM 2,00
Erdbeertorte	DM 2,50
Käse	DM 3,50
Obst	DM 3,00

Getränke

Kaffee	DM 1,80
Tee	DM 1,80
Schokolade	DM 1,80
Apfelsaft	DM 2,50
Cola	DM 2,30
Limonade	DM 2,00
Milch	DM 1,50
Mineralwasser	DM 2,00
Bier	DM 2,30
Wein	DM 4,30

A You have been given 18 German marks (DM 18,00) to spend on a restaurant meal. The restaurant you have chosen offers the items shown on the menu above. What will you eat? Begin with *Ich nehme . . .* and list the items you wish to order.

B Create a skit with a partner. One of you takes the role of a waiter or waitress. The other orders dinner or a snack from the menu.

A **Frühstück** ordered in a restaurant or hotel usually consists of a hot beverage, an assortment of rolls and breads, butter, and jam or jelly. This is what is referred to in the United States as a "continental breakfast." When people in German-speaking countries have eggs for breakfast, they generally have soft-boiled eggs **(weichgekochte Eier).** Scrambled eggs **(Rühreier)** and fried eggs **(Spiegeleier)** are eaten more for supper.

Pancakes are generally not a breakfast food in German-speaking countries. German **Pfannkuchen** are thinner and lighter than American pancakes, more like French **crêpes.** They are often filled with applesauce or jam and then rolled up and dusted with sugar.

Kleine Kochschule

der Löffel	spoon	**der Teig**	dough
der Teelöffel	teaspoon	**bestreichen**	to spread
der Eßlöffel	tablespoon	**bestreuen**	to sprinkle
die Prise	pinch	**erhitzen**	to heat
die Pfanne	pan	**gießen**	to pour
der Topf	pot	**schneiden**	to cut
die Schüssel	bowl	**verrühren**	to stir, to beat
die Zutaten	ingredients		

The list above includes some of the more common German terms used in cooking. It should help you read the following recipe for **Pfannkuchen.**

Zutaten

375 Gramm Mehl°   flour
3 Eier
1 Prise Salz°   salt
¾ Liter Milch
Butter oder Margarine
150 Gramm Marmelade
Puderzucker° zum Bestreuen   confectioner's sugar

Mehl, Eier, Milch und Salz zu einem dünnen, glatten° Teig verrühren. In   smooth
einer Pfanne etwas Butter oder Margarine erhitzen, den Boden° dünn mit   bottom
Teig ausgießen und die Pfannkuchen auf beiden Seiten° goldgelb backen.   sides
   Dies so lange wiederholen°, bis der Teig aufgebraucht° ist. Jeden   repeat/used up
Pfannkuchen mit Marmelade bestreichen, einrollen° und mit Zucker   roll up
bestreuen.

Aussprache

[ə]	bitt**e**, b**e**stimmt
[ən]	spiel**en**, geh**en**
[ər]	Spiel**er**, bitt**er**, V**er**käuf**er**

Write the second and third of the columns in Ex. A on the board. Ask students to identify whether you are pronouncing an [ə] or an [ər] sound.

The [ə] sound occurs in unstressed **-en** and **-e** endings and is similar to English *e* in *boxes, pocket.*

The [ər] sound occurs when the sequence **er** stands at the end of a word, before a consonant, or in an unstressed prefix. The **-r** is not pronounced as an [R], but sounds much like the final *-a* in English *sofa.*

A   Practice the following words horizontally.

Activity: Make up more sentences using [ə] and [ər] sounds. Suggest words if students can't think of them: *danke, müde, gute Nacht; Schwester, Lehrer, Schüler.*

[ən]	[ə]	[ər]
bitt**en**	bitt**e**	bitt**er**
denk**en**	denk**e**	Denk**er**
fahr**en**	fahr**e**	Fahr**er**
fehl**en**	fehl**e**	Fehl**er**
leid**en**	leid**e**	leid**er**
nenn**en**	nenn**e**	Nenn**er**

B   Practice the sounds [ə], [ən], and [ər]. Read the sentences aloud.

1. Wo haben Sie diese Platten gekauft, Frau Leber?
2. Unser Cassetten-Recorder ist wieder kaputt.
3. Die Hose ist nicht teuer, aber ich kann sie nicht kaufen.

Proverb: Tomorrow, tomorrow, just not today, that's what all the lazy people say.

Morgen, morgen, nur nicht heute, sagen alle faulen Leute.

Übungen

Dieser-words in the nominative and accusative

Help students discover that endings of *dieser*-words are the same as the definite article endings.

dieser

NOMINATIVE			ACCUSATIVE		
Der Dieser	Fernseher ist preiswert.		Kaufst du	den diesen	Fernseher?
Das Dieses	Radio ist preiswert.		Kaufst du	das dieses	Radio?
Die Diese	Stereoanlage ist preiswert.		Kaufst du	die diese	Stereoanlage?
Die Diese	Cassetten sind preiswert.		Kaufst du	die diese	Cassetten?

Dieser follows the same pattern of endings in the nominative and accusative as the definite article.

A   You and Martina are shopping for clothes. Compare the prices of the articles she asks about with the ones you're looking at.

Other nouns for further practice: *Anzug, Bluse, Handschuhe, Krawatte, Mantel, Rock, Socken.*

■Ⅲ   Ist die Jacke da teuer?   *Ja, aber diese Jacke hier ist nicht teuer.*

Before Ex. B, a quick review of accusative (p. 119) may be useful.

1. Ist die Hose da teuer?
2. Ist der Gürtel da teuer?
3. Ist der Pulli da teuer?
4. Ist das Hemd da teuer?
5. Ist das Kleid da teuer?
6. Sind die Schuhe da teuer?
7. Sind die Jeans da teuer?

B   You work in a market where customers often ask about the quality of various foods. Recommend all the food items mentioned.

Personalize, using pictures to cue:
T: *Kannst du diese Suppe empfehlen?*
S: *Ja (Nein), ich kann diese Suppe (nicht) empfehlen.*

Other words: *Kartoffeln, Kuchen, Obst, Tomaten, Fisch, Marmelade, Pudding.*

■Ⅲ   Ist dieser Salat frisch?   *Ja, ich kann diesen Salat empfehlen.*

1. Ist diese Wurst gut?
2. Ist dieser Käse gut?
3. Ist dieser Schinken frisch?
4. Ist dieses Brot frisch?
5. Sind diese Brötchen frisch?
6. Sind diese Tomaten gut?

welcher/jeder

Welcher Fernseher Welches Radio Welche Stereoanlage	ist teuer?

Jeder Fernseher Jedes Radio Jede Stereoanlage	ist teuer.

Welcher and **jeder** have the same endings as **dieser**. **Jeder** is used in the singular only.

C　Matthias has a habit of making vague statements. Ask him to clarify what he's talking about.

Personalize, using clothing illustrations. One student would like something; another student asks which one:
S¹: *Ich möchte den Pulli haben.*
S²: *Welchen Pulli?*

■▥　Ich habe das Buch zweimal gelesen.　*Welches Buch?*

1. Ich habe das Poster nicht gekauft.
2. Ich habe den Kugelschreiber leider verloren.
3. Ich habe den Pulli gestern getragen.
4. Ich habe die Platte schon gehört.
5. Ich habe das Spiel natürlich gewonnen.
6. Ich habe die Schuhe nicht gekauft.
7. Ich habe die Uhr selbst bezahlt.

D　Your hobby is collecting things. When a friend questions whether you actually like certain items, say that in your opinion every item has its merits.

Additional practice: Substitute article of clothing; cue with pictures:
Findest du diesen Pulli schön? (Anzug, Bluse, Hemd, Jacke, Kleid, Mantel, Rock, Schuhe)

■▥　Findest du diese Uhr schön?　*Ja, für mich ist jede Uhr schön.*

1. Findest du diese Ansichtskarte interessant?
2. Findest du diesen Bierdeckel interessant?
3. Findest du diese Briefmarke schön?
4. Findest du dieses Poster schön?
5. Findest du diese Platte gut?

mancher/solcher

Manche Bücher sind zu teuer.   *Some* books are too expensive.
Solche Bücher kaufe ich nicht.   I wouldn't buy *such* books.

Solcher and **mancher** have the same endings as **dieser,** but they are used almost exclusively in the plural.

E   The clerk at the market offers you less-than-perfect fruits and vegetables. State emphatically that you wouldn't buy such produce.

Encourage students to give more explicit answers by asking:
T: *Warum nicht?*
S¹: *Sie sind zu klein.*
S²: *Sie sind zu teuer.*
(*nicht frisch,* etc.)

◾⫿   Möchten Sie diese Kartoffeln?   *Nein, solche Kartoffeln kaufe ich nicht.*

1. Möchten Sie diese Erdbeeren?   4. Möchten Sie diese Tomaten?
2. Möchten Sie diese Orangen?   5. Möchten Sie diese Erbsen?
3. Möchten Sie diese Äpfel?

F   It's easy to make generalizations. Say that each of the following statements is true of many things and people.

May wish to review plural forms of nouns before doing Ex. F.

◾⫿   Das Mädchen trägt Jeans.   *Manche Mädchen tragen Jeans.*

1. Die Frau kauft im Supermarkt ein.   4. Das Haus ist klein.
2. Der Junge kocht gern.   5. Die Platte ist schlecht.
3. Das Geschäft ist teuer.   6. Die Party ist langweilig.

Time expressions in the accusative case

Wann kommt Karl-Heinz?   **Diesen** Sommer.
Wie oft spielt er Tennis?   **Jeden** Samstag.
Wie lange arbeitet er im Geschäft?   **Einen** Monat.

Time expressions that answer the questions **wann?, wie oft?,** and **wie lange?** are in the accusative case. Such expressions indicate a definite time or period of time.

G   Confirm the answers to the following questions.

Personalize:
Wie oft gehst du in die Schule? Jeden Tag? Wann machst du Hausaufgaben? Jeden Abend? Wann gehst du Schi laufen? Diesen Winter?, etc.

Be sure students keep infinitive at the end.

◾⫿   Wie oft kommt Michael? Jeden Abend?   *Ja, er kommt jeden Abend.*

1. Wie oft schreibt Frau Weiß? Jede Woche?
2. Wie oft geht Herr Neumeier einkaufen? Jeden Tag?
3. Wie lange arbeitet Erika schon? Einen Monat?
4. Wann gehen wir spazieren? Diesen Samstag?
5. Wie oft kommen Ingrids Freunde? Jedes Jahr?
6. Wann gehst du tanzen? Jedes Wochenende?

Du hast das Wort

A. Ask your classmates the following questions about their routine activities.

◼▮ Arbeitest du jeden Abend?   *Ja, jeden Abend. / Nein, nicht jeden Abend. Ich arbeite [nur am Montagabend].*

Frühstückst du jeden Morgen?
Gehst du jeden Tag tanzen?
Trägst du jeden Tag Jeans?
Gehst du jede Woche einkaufen?
Siehst du jeden Abend fern?
Treibst du jeden Nachmittag Sport?

B. Ask your teacher the following questions.

◼▮ Frag, ob er/sie jeden   *Treiben Sie jeden*
Samstag Sport treibt!   *Samstag Sport?*

Frag, ob er/sie jeden Abend arbeitet!
Frag, ob er/sie jeden Morgen frühstückt!
Frag, ob er/sie jede Woche einkaufen geht!
Frag, ob er/sie jeden Abend fernsieht!

Present tense to express duration of time

Wie lange **lernst** du **schon** Deutsch?	How long *have* you *been studying* German?
Erik **arbeitet schon** zwei Monate im Supermarkt.	Erik *has been working* for two months in the supermarket.

To express action that started in the past and extends into the present, German uses the present tense plus a time indication, usually accompanied by **schon**.

H   Gerd wants to know how long various people have been doing certain things. Confirm his guesses.

V: Have students add 2 to each number.

◼▮ Wie lange arbeitest du schon im Supermarkt? Zwei Wochen?   *Ja, ich arbeite schon zwei Wochen im Supermarkt.*

You may wish to have students translate into English to make clear the difference between English and German construction.

1. Wie lange lernst du schon Deutsch? Sechs Monate?
2. Wie lange wohnt Beate schon in München? Zwei Jahre?
3. Wie lange sammelt Dirk schon Bierdeckel? Ein Jahr?
4. Wie lange sammelt Heike schon Briefmarken? Drei Jahre?
5. Wie lange arbeitet Rudi schon im Musikgeschäft? Einen Monat?

Coordinating conjunctions: **aber, denn, oder, sondern, und**

Uwe trinkt Kaffee, **aber** ich trinke lieber Milch.
Ich trinke morgens Milch, **denn** ich mag keinen Kaffee.

Coordinating conjunctions are used to connect two independent clauses.
They do not affect word order of subject and verb.

Be sure students understand why subject precedes verb in I and follows in J.

I Explain to your teacher that the following persons did not do their homework last night for the reasons given.

V: Have students finish the sentence with their own reasons.
T: *Ich gehe morgen nicht in die Schule . . .*
S¹: *Ich gehe morgen nicht in die Schule, denn ich bin sehr müde.*
S²: *Ich gehe morgen nicht in die Schule, denn ich gehe Schlittschuh laufen.*, etc.

■▥ Ingrid hat Tennis gespielt.

Ingrid hat die Aufgaben nicht gemacht, denn sie hat Tennis gespielt.

1. Jan hat keine Zeit gehabt.
2. Dieter ist ins Kino gegangen.
3. Gisela hat Musik gehört.
4. Erik hat Platten gespielt.
5. Astrid hat gearbeitet.
6. Gabi ist tanzen gegangen.
7. Ich war auf einer Party.

J State your plans for several days next week by combining each pair of sentences with *und.*

If students have difficulty remembering sentences, practice with books open.

■▥ Samstag gehen wir einkaufen. Dann gehen wir ins Kino.

Samstag gehen wir einkaufen, und dann gehen wir ins Kino.

1. Sonntag wandern wir. Dann trinken wir Kaffee.
2. Montag abend mache ich Mathe. Dann sehe ich fern.
3. Mittwoch arbeite ich im Supermarkt. Dann gehe ich tanzen.
4. Donnerstag spielen wir Tennis. Dann machen wir Hausaufgaben.
5. Freitag gehe ich einkaufen. Dann mache ich Abendessen.

K Sabine often changes her mind so you're never quite sure what she's going to do. Inquire about her plans.

Have students make up sentences connected by *oder.*

■▥ Arbeitest du? Gehst du jetzt schwimmen?

Arbeitest du, oder gehst du jetzt schwimmen?

1. Kommst du mit? Hast du keine Zeit?
2. Möchtest du jetzt essen? Hast du keinen Hunger?
3. Trinkst du jetzt eine Cola? Hast du keinen Durst?
4. Gehst du auf den Markt? Kaufst du im Supermarkt ein?
5. Spielst du jetzt Volleyball? Machst du Hausaufgaben?
6. Rufst du Volker an? Besuchst du ihn?

aber and sondern

Wir möchten heute abend fernsehen, **aber** unser Fernseher ist kaputt.
We'd like to watch TV this evening, but *our TV set is broken.*

Wir sehen heute abend nicht fern, **sondern** gehen ins Kino.
We aren't going to watch TV this evening, instead *we're going to the movies.*

Aber as a coordinating conjunction is equivalent to *but, nevertheless.* It may be used after either a positive or a negative clause. **Sondern** is a coordinating conjunction that is equivalent to *but, instead, on the contrary.* It is used after a negative clause only, and then only if the second clause contradicts the first clause. Otherwise **aber** is used.

L Combine each pair of sentences with *aber.*

  ■III   Frau Meier geht jeden Tag einkaufen. Sie kauft nicht viel.   *Frau Meier geht jeden Tag einkaufen, aber sie kauft nicht viel.*

1. Ich möchte einkaufen gehen. Die Geschäfte sind zu.
2. Ich möchte ins Kino. Ich habe kein Geld.
3. Die *Hot Dogs* spielen diesen Samstag. Ich möchte sie nicht hören.

M Complete the sentences with *sondern* or *aber,* as appropriate.

1. Erikas Zimmer ist nicht groß, _____ sehr klein.
2. Ihr Zimmer ist klein, _____ schön.
3. Erika arbeitet heute abend nicht, _____ geht ins Konzert.
4. Sie hat viele Hausaufgaben, _____ sie macht sie nicht.
5. Die Schuhe sind nicht teuer, _____ sehr billig.
6. Die Schuhe sind nicht teuer, _____ ich kaufe sie nicht.

May cue by using complete sentences:
Erikas Zimmer ist nicht groß. Es ist sehr klein. Ihr Zimmer ist klein. Es ist schön., etc.

Was gibt's zum Essen?

Grammatische Übersicht

Dieser-words in the nominative and accusative (A–F)

	NOMINATIVE	ACCUSATIVE
der Pulli	Dieser Pulli ist toll.	Inge kauft diesen Pulli.
das Hemd	Dieses Hemd ist toll.	Erik kauft dieses Hemd.
die Jacke	Diese Jacke ist toll.	Jan kauft diese Jacke.
die Schuhe	Diese Schuhe sind toll.	Anna kauft diese Schuhe.

Because *jener* has a specialized use today, it is not treated here. Students can learn its meaning when and if they come across it in their reading.

Dieser, jeder, welcher, solcher, and **mancher** (called **dieser**-words) follow the same pattern of endings in the nominative and accusative as the definite articles **der, das,** and **die.**

Meanings and uses of **dieser**-words

Tell students that in the singular, *so ein* is used: *So eine Uhr kostet viel.*

dieser	this; these *(plural)*
jeder	each, every *(used in the singular only)*
mancher	many a, several *(used mainly in the plural)*
solcher	such *(used mainly in the plural)*
welcher	which?

Time expressions in the accusative case (G)

Wann kommt Katrin wieder?	Sie kommt **dieses Jahr** wieder.
Wie oft spielt Jan Tennis?	Er spielt **jeden Tag** Tennis.
Wie lange bleibt Beate?	Sie kann nur **einen Tag** bleiben.

Time expressions that indicate a definite time (answering the questions **wann?, wie oft?**) or a period of time (answering the question **wie lange?**) are in the accusative case.

Present tense to express duration of time   (H)

Nun **sind** wir **schon drei Wochen** in Deutschland.	Now we've been in Germany for three weeks.
Ingrid **arbeitet schon ein Jahr** im Supermarkt.	Ingrid has been working in the supermarket for a year.

To express action that started in the past and extends into the present, German uses the present tense plus a time indication, usually accompanied by **schon.** To express the same concept, English uses such forms as *have been, has been . . . -ing.*

Independent clauses

INDEPENDENT CLAUSE	COORDINATING CONJUNCTION	INDEPENDENT CLAUSE
Wir möchten einkaufen gehen,	aber	wir haben kein Geld.
Ich kaufe die Jacke nicht,	denn	sie ist zu teuer.

An independent clause can make sense standing alone. When used as parts of sentences, two independent clauses may be connected with each other by coordinating conjunctions.

Coordinating conjunctions (I-M)

>Ich habe Hunger, **aber** das Essen ist noch nicht fertig.
>Wir können im Restaurant essen, **denn** ich habe heute Geld.
>Nimmst du den Fisch, **oder** magst du keinen Fisch?
>Er geht nicht ins Restaurant, **sondern** ins Café.
>Du nimmst ein Eis, **und** ich bestelle den Pudding.

Five common coordinating conjunctions are **aber, denn, oder, sondern,** and **und.** Coordinating conjunctions do not affect the word order of subject and verb. The conjunctions are generally preceded by a comma.

Ich schreibe Ute einen Brief **oder besuche** sie nächste Woche.	*I'll write* Ute a letter *or visit* her next week.
Sie arbeiten bis sieben **und gehen** dann ins Kino.	*They'll work* until seven *and* then *go* to the movies.

Oder and **und** are not preceded by a comma when the subject in both independent clauses is the same. The subject is not repeated in the second clause.

aber and sondern

Ich möchte im Restaurant essen, **aber** ich habe kein Geld.	I'd like to eat in a restaurant, *but* I don't have any money.
Wir gehen heute nicht ins Restaurant, **sondern** essen zu Hause.	We're not going to a restaurant today; *instead* we'll eat at home.

Aber as a coordinating conjunction is equivalent to *but, however, nevertheless.* It may be used after either a positive or a negative clause. **Sondern** is a coordinating conjunction that expresses a contrast or contradiction. It is equivalent to *but, instead, on the contrary.* **Sondern** is used after a negative clause only. When the subject is the same in both clauses, it is not repeated:

>**Wir gehen** nicht ins Restaurant, sondern **essen** zu Hause.

 *. . . und nach dem Essen*

Wiederholung

A Answer the following questions, based on your personal experience or preferences. Then ask your teacher the same questions.

1. Ißt du lieber zu Hause oder im Restaurant?
2. Wie heißt dein Lieblingsrestaurant?
3. Ist es da teuer oder billig?
4. Wie oft ißt du dort?
5. Was bestellst du gewöhnlich?
6. Welchen Nachtisch bestellst du gern?

B Ilse is talking to her friends about a dinner she had last night at a restaurant. Express their conversational exchanges in German.

1. Did you eat in a restaurant yesterday?
   Yes. Sabine and Ralf also went along.
2. Why didn't you invite me?
   We called you up. You weren't home.
3. Did you order the roast beef?
   Yes. The waiter recommended it.
4. Did it taste good?
   Yes. It was very tender.
5. What did Ralf eat?
   He had the ham.
6. How much did you pay?
   Nothing. We didn't have any money.
7. And why did you come home so late?
   We washed the dishes.

C Ask the questions that the following sentences answer. Use the following interrogatives:

**Wann?   Wen?   Wer?   Was?   Wie?   Wo?   Wohin?
Wie oft?   Wie lange?**

1. Detlev sammelt *alte Ansichtskarten.*
2. Benno findet Ansichtskarten *langweilig.*
3. Kurt segelt *jeden Samstag.*
4. Martina geht oft *ins Jugendzentrum.*
5. Ute arbeitet schon *ein Jahr* im Supermarkt.
6. Gerd kauft seine Briefmarken *in Hamburg.*
7. *Petra* hat kein Hobby.
8. Lothar ruft *seine Freunde* oft an.
9. Frank sieht *abends* fern.

D   Begin each sentence with the word or phrase in italics, and make the necessary changes in word order.

1. Peter spielt *jeden Tag* Tennis.
2. Er sieht *abends* fern.
3. Er hat *gestern* Gartenarbeit gemacht.
4. Seine Schwester Petra hat *heute morgen* das Auto gewaschen.
5. Sie fahren *am Wochenende* nach Bremen.
6. Sie kommen *Sonntag abend* wieder nach Hause.

E   Replace each word in italics with the appropriate antonym.

einfach   frisch   hübsch   kaputt
langweilig   leicht   verloren

1. Unser Fernseher ist wieder *repariert.*
2. Wir haben das Fußballspiel *gewonnen.*
3. Dieses Hobby ist wirklich *interessant.*
4. Unsere Matheaufgabe ist heute *kompliziert*, nicht?
5. Chemie finde ich aber *schwer.*
6. Ist das Brot da *alt?*
7. Die Bluse da ist wirklich *häßlich*, nicht?

F   Change one German word to another by changing a single letter. Use the English cues as guidelines.

◼▥   we > how   *wir > wie*

1. then > because
2. beautiful > already
3. then > thin
4. of course > you *(acc.)*
5. now > only
6. four > much
7. go > against
8. still > after
9. butter > mother
10. can > know

G   In six to eight sentences describe a party you gave recently. You may wish to include answers to the following questions.

Wieviel Personen hast du eingeladen?
Wann hat die Party begonnen?
Was habt ihr alles gemacht?
Habt ihr getanzt? Musik gehört?
Was habt ihr gegessen und getrunken? Wie war die Party?

Kulturlesestück

Kaffeestunde

Am Sonntag trinken viele Deutsche nachmittags Kaffee. Sie trinken aber
natürlich nicht nur Kaffee, sondern sie essen auch Kuchen. Manche Familien trinken fast jeden Nachmittag Kaffee, nicht nur am Sonntag.

Es ist besonders° schön, nachmittags in ein Café oder in eine Kondi-
torei° zu gehen. Da gibt es viele Torten und Kuchen. Alles schmeckt
ausgezeichnet, besonders mit Sahne°.

Oft kommen Freunde zum Kaffee zusammen. Frau Weiß lädt Familie
Kuhn ein: „Können Sie am Sonntag zu uns zum Kaffee kommen? Sagen
wir um halb fünf?"

Pünktlich° um halb fünf stehen° Herr und Frau Kuhn vor der Tür.
Herr Kuhn hat Blumen° in der Hand. Er gibt sie Frau Weiß. Der Kaffee-
tisch sieht° sehr schön aus: Auf dem Tisch liegt eine schöne weiße
Decke°; Tassen und Teller° sind aus Porzellan°; die Blumen sind frisch;
und natürlich gibt es viel Kuchen und Sahne. Ein schöner Nachmittag.

Margin glosses:

especially

shop serving pastries
  and coffee
whipped cream

punctually / stand
flowers
sieht . . . aus: looks
tablecloth / plates /
china

A Choose the word or phrase that best completes each statement, based on the reading.

1. ... jeden Tag Kaffee.
   a. Kein Deutscher trinkt
   b. Viele Deutsche trinken
   c. Alle Deutschen trinken
   d. Alte Deutsche trinken

2. Wenn man „zum Kaffee" kommt, bekommt man ...
   a. nur Kaffee.   b. Kaffee und Kuchen.   c. ein warmes Essen.   d. nur Kuchen.

3. „Kaffee" trinkt man ...
   a. morgens.   b. zu Mittag.   c. nachmittags.   d. abends.

4. ... gibt es nachmittags viele Torten und Kuchen.
   a. Auf dem Markt   b. In einem Supermarkt   c. In einem Geschäft   d. In einer Konditorei

5. Wenn man zum Kaffee eingeladen ist, bringt man oft ...
   a. Blumen.   b. Bücher.   c. einen Kuchen.   d. Tassen und Teller.

6. Ein Stück Torte schmeckt besonders gut mit ...
   a. Butter.   b. Sahne.   c. Porzellan.   d. Kaffeedecken.

B Which of the following things would you expect to find when invited *zum Kaffee?*

Torte, eine weiße Kaffeedecke, Wurst, Tomaten, Teller aus Porzellan, Pudding, frische Blumen, Tee, Speisekarte, Salat, Sahne, Kaffee

When Germans eat dessert with the main noon meal, it is often pudding or fruit rather than baked goods. Cakes and pastries are eaten during the **Kaffeestunde** later in the afternoon.

Vokabeln

SUBSTANTIVE

das Abendessen　supper
das Bier　beer
das Brötchen, -　hard roll
die Cola (*also* **das Cola**)　cola drink
der Durst　thirst
das Eis　ice cream; ice
der Fisch, -e　fish
das Getränk, -e　beverage
das Huhn, -̈er　chicken
der Hunger　hunger
das Kartoffelpüree　mashed potatoes
die Limo(nade)　soft drink
die Marmelade　jam
das Mineralwasser　mineral water
der Mittag　noon
das Mittagessen　lunch
der Nachtisch　dessert
der Ober, -　waiter
die Pommes frites (*pl.*)　french fries
der Pudding　pudding
das Restaurant, -s　restaurant
der Rindsbraten　roast beef, pot roast
der Salat, -e　(head of) lettuce; salad
das Schinkenbrot, -e　ham sandwich
die Schokolade, -n　chocolate, hot chocolate;
　bar of chocolate
die Speisekarte, -n　menu
die Suppe, -n　soup
die Tasse, -n　cup
der Tee　tea
der Wein　wine

VERBEN

bestellen　to order
bringen (gebracht)　to bring
empfehlen (ie; empfohlen)　to recommend
frühstücken　to have breakfast
zahlen　to pay

ANDERE WÖRTER

als　as
ausgezeichnet　excellent
gewöhnlich　usually
mancher　some, several
manchmal　sometimes
mittags　at noon, at lunch time
nachmittags　in the afternoon
nicht nur ... sondern auch　not only ... but
　also
sondern　but (on the contrary)
zart　tender, delicate

BESONDERE AUSDRÜCKE

Durst haben　to be thirsty
Hunger haben　to be hungry
guten Appetit!　enjoy your meal
ich esse lieber ...　I prefer to eat ...
zum Frühstück　for breakfast
zum Mittagessen　for lunch
zum Abendessen　for supper
zu Abend essen　to have supper
zu Mittag essen　to have lunch
bitte sehr　certainly
vielen Dank!　thank you very much
wie lange?　how long?

Kapitel 13

Über das Wetter kann man immer sprechen

Ein Quiz

Was weißt du über das Wetter in Deutschland?

Weißt du,

wo es im Sommer wärmer ist — in Ohio oder in Deutschland?
was wärmer ist — 60 Grad Fahrenheit oder 20 Grad Celsius?
wo es im Winter kälter ist — in Pittsburgh oder in Bonn?
welche Stadt nördlicher liegt — New York oder München?
welche Stadt südlicher liegt — Chicago oder Frankfurt?
wo es im Winter mehr schneit — in Minnesota oder in
    Norddeutschland?
wo es öfter regnet — in den Smoky Mountains oder im Schwarzwald°?   Black Forest

Let students make up similar quiz questions using the world map and a variety of cities in your area. The class could present its own quiz show.

How did you do? Answers are printed on page 279.

■ Bonn lies approximately on the 51st parallel, roughly on the same latitude as James Bay, Canada (south of Hudson's Bay). No major population centers in Canada or continental U.S. extend as far north as Bonn. For example, Winnipeg lies below the 51st parallel, Boston below the 42nd. New York is around the 41st parallel, the same as Naples, Italy.

In Deutschland ist das Wetter anders

Jim aus° St. Louis besucht seinen Freund Klaus in Kassel. Klaus findet es heiß — Jim findet es warm.   from

Es ist Juli. In Kassel ist das Wetter gut. Die Sonne scheint. Jim ist gerade erst drei Tage in Kassel, da sagt Klaus: „Heute ist es wirklich heiß, furchtbar heiß." Jim aber denkt: Heiß? Hier? Jetzt? Nein! Schön warm.

In Deutschland ist das Wetter anders, denn Deutschland liegt weiter nördlich als Amerika. Bonn, die Hauptstadt der° Bundesrepublik Deutschland, liegt circa° 1300 Kilometer weiter nördlich als Washington, die amerikanische Hauptstadt. Auch beeinflußt° der Atlantische Ozean das Klima°. So ist das Wetter oft kühl im Sommer und nicht so kalt im Winter. Der Wind kommt gewöhnlich von Westen und bringt vom Atlantischen Ozean Regen mit. Es regnet also viel; und Jim lernt, daß man einen Regenschirm mitnimmt, wenn man spazierengeht.

of the
approximately
influences
climate

Fragen

1. Liegt St. Louis oder Kassel weiter nördlich?
2. Wie heißt die Hauptstadt der Bundesrepublik?
3. Wie heißt die Hauptstadt der USA?
4. Wie ist das Wetter in Deutschland im Sommer oft?
5. Was kommt von Westen?
6. Was bringt der Wind mit?
7. Was nimmt Jim mit, wenn er spazierengeht?

Wie ist das Wetter?

Im Frühling

Questions and answers are useful for warm-up once dialogues are practiced:

STEFAN	Was meinst du? Regnet es morgen wieder?
KARIN	Wahrscheinlich.
STEFAN	Das ist wirklich dumm!
KARIN	Warum?
STEFAN	Mein Regenschirm ist kaputt.

1. Wie ist das Wetter heute (jetzt)? — Das Wetter ist furchtbar (gut, schlecht); Es ist kalt (warm, schön).
2. Wie ist das Wetter im Herbst (Sommer, Winter, Frühling)? — Das Wetter ist furchtbar (gut).

Im Sommer

DIETER	Heute ist es schön, nicht?
INGRID	Ja, endlich ist es mal warm.
DIETER	Hoffentlich wird es nicht zu heiß.
INGRID	Lieber heiß als kalt.

3. Wann ist das Wetter oft furchtbar (gut)? — Im Winter (Herbst, etc.).
4. Ist es schon richtig Herbst (Winter, etc.)? Ja, es ist schon richtig Herbst.

Im Herbst

FRAU KRAFT	Schönes Wetter, nicht?
HERR WOLF	Ja, ich habe diese Jahreszeit besonders gern. Es ist so schön kühl.
FRAU KRAFT	Das ist gutes Wanderwetter.
HERR WOLF	Zu dumm, daß wir arbeiten müssen.

5. Wie lange regnet es schon? Es regnet schon drei Tage (vier, eine Woche).

Im Winter

RALF	Der Wind ist aber ganz schön kalt heute morgen.
ILSE	Ja, es hat letzte Nacht gefroren.
RALF	Heute nachmittag soll es schneien.
ILSE	Das ist ja prima. Dann können wir rodeln gehen.

(die Rodel, der Schlitten)

1. Warum ist Stefan unglücklich?
2. Hat Ingrid es lieber warm oder kalt?
3. Warum findet Herr Wolf den Herbst schön?
4. Was macht Ilse gern im Winter?

Du hast das Wort

Expand: Welche Kleider trägt man im Sommer? Im Winter? Was ist deine Lieblingsjahreszeit? Warum?

V: Students ask teacher the same questions.

A. Ask a classmate questions about the weather.

Hast du den Winter oder den Sommer lieber? Den Frühling oder den Herbst?
Hast du es lieber kalt oder warm?
Welchen Sport treibst du im Winter? Im Sommer?
Welchen Sport treibst du im Frühling? Im Herbst?
Hast du Regen gern? Schnee°?
Wie ist das Wetter heute?
Wie war es gestern?
Wie soll es morgen sein?

On board draw a happy face (agree), an unhappy face (disagree), and a question mark (doubt). Make a comment about the weather as you point to one of the figures. The student must make an appropriate response. Let students take turns leading this.

B. A classmate is trying to make conversation by talking about the weather. Do you agree with, disagree with, or doubt her/his comments?

Morgen soll es wieder regnen.
Heute ist es schön.
Es hat letzte Nacht gefroren.
Heute abend soll es schneien.
Jetzt regnet es schon eine Woche.
Morgen soll es wieder [heiß] werden.
Schönes Wetter heute, nicht?

Das stimmt.
Das finde ich auch.
Du hast recht°.
Das glaube ich nicht.
Das kann nicht stimmen.
Du spinnst°.
Meinst du?
Glaubst du?

Sag!

Sag [Ute], daß es morgen regnen soll!
Sag [Kai], daß es schon drei Tage regnet!
Sag [Ute], daß der Wind kalt ist!
Sag [Kai], daß es letzte Nacht gefroren hat!
Sag [Ute], daß das Wetter furchtbar ist!
Sag [Kai], daß es übermorgen schneien soll!

Although summers in Germany are usually moderate, it does get warm at times. School is in session well into July, so the classrooms may get very warm. If the temperature reaches 27°C (about 81°F) by the end of the third period, which comes about 10:30 A.M., the general practice is to declare **hitzefrei,** and to dismiss school for the rest of the day.

Remind students of for-
mula to convert from
Celsius to Fahrenheit:

Wortschatzerweiterung

$$\text{C to F: } \frac{C \times 9}{5} + 32 = °F$$

$$\text{F to C: } \frac{F - 32 \times 5}{9} = °C$$

For a quick estimate use:
$(C \times 2) + 32 = F$
$\frac{1}{2}(F - 32) = C$

Das Thermometer

37°C = 98.6°F

−18°C = 0°F

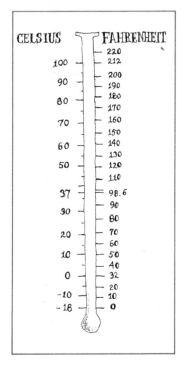

100°C = 212°F

0°C = 32°F

Game: Guess the prob-
able season: 30 Grad;
15 Grad; −5 Grad.

In German-speaking countries the Celsius thermometer is used. To find out the temperature, a German asks: **Wieviel Grad haben wir heute?** The answer may be **Es sind** [15] **Grad** or **Heute haben wir** [15] **Grad.**

A What's the temperature in degrees Celsius? *Wieviel Grad Celsius sind ...*

1. 12°F
2. 98.6°F
3. 68°F
4. 32°F
5. 212°F
6. 80°F

Answers to the weather-quiz:
1. Ohio 2. 20 Grad Celsius 3. Pittsburgh 4. München
5. Chicago 6. Minnesota 7. Schwarzwald

Das Wetter und ein Bericht

Optional vocabulary: *Es ist naßkalt, neblig (der Nebel), sonnig, schwül; es gießt in Strömen.* "Weather report" = *der Wetterbericht, die Wettervorhersage.*

Es schneit.
Die Straßen sind glatt.

Es regnet.
Die Straßen sind naß.

Es ist windig.
Es ist kalt.

Es ist bewölkt.
Es ist kühl.

Die Sonne scheint.
Es ist warm.

Es ist heiß.
Es ist trocken.

B   Jim made a report of the weather in Kassel in early March for his class at home. Using his report as a model, keep your own daily record of the weather for a week, recording the temperature in degrees Celsius.

Review other time expressions: *den ganzen Morgen, am Montag, nachmittags, gestern morgen,* etc.

Personalize: *Wie heißen die [Wintermonate]? Welchen Monat hast du gern? Warum? Wie ist das Wetter [im Januar]? Welchen Sport treibst du [im Winter]? Wann spielst du [Baseball]? Wann läufst du [Schi]? Wann gehst du [schwimmen]?*

Montag	Es hat den ganzen Tag geregnet. Es war kalt; nur 6 Grad.
Dienstag	Bewölkt und kühl. Es waren 8 Grad.
Mittwoch	Die Sonne hat endlich geschienen. Es war fast warm — 12 Grad.
Donnerstag	Es war wieder kühl und windig. Es waren 10 Grad. Furchtbares Wetter.
Freitag	Es war sehr kalt. Es hat wieder geregnet. Temperatur: 7 Grad.
Samstag	Am Morgen war es noch kühl. Aber am Nachmittag hat die Sonne geschienen. Es waren 13 Grad. Abends ist es wieder kühl geworden.
Sonntag	Es war sehr schön — die Sonne war fast heiß. Es waren 18 Grad.

Aussprache

▮ [χ]   a**ch**, no**ch**, Bu**ch**, au**ch**

The sound [χ] is made in the back of the mouth, where the sound [k] is pronounced. It is produced by forcing air through a narrow opening between the back of the tongue and the back of the roof of the mouth. To produce the sound [χ], keep the tongue below the lower front teeth and, without moving the tongue or lips, make a gentle gargling noise. Do not substitute the [k] sound for the [χ] sound.

The [χ] is produced in the back of the throat, in proximity to the back and center vowels (a, o, u, au).

A   Practice the following words horizontally in pairs.

[k]	[χ]	[k]	[χ]
na**ck**t	Na**ch**t	lo**ck**en	lo**ch**en
Sa**ck**e	Sa**ch**e	Po**ck**en	po**ch**en
la**ck**en	la**ch**en	bu**k**	Bu**ch**
Do**ck**	do**ch**	Hau**k**e	hau**ch**e

The sound [χ] is represented by the letters **ch** and occurs after the vowels **a, o, u,** and **au.**

B   Practice the following words.

Be sure students produce short o correctly in doch, noch, kochen.

ach, m**a**chen, n**a**ch   Bu**ch**, K**u**chen, versu**ch**en
n**o**ch, d**o**ch, k**o**chen   au**ch**, brau**ch**en, t**au**chen

C   Practice the sound [χ]. Read the sentences aloud.

1. Frau Meier bäckt jede Woche einen Kuchen.
2. Was machen wir noch?
3. Heute nachmittag besuchen wir Herrn Luckenbach.

Proverb: He who laughs last, laughs best.

Wer zuletzt lacht, lacht am besten.

Comparison of adjectives and adverbs

Comparison of equality

Bernd ist **so alt wie** Jens.	Bernd is *as old as* Jens.
Er arbeitet aber nicht **so viel wie** Jens.	He doesn't work *as much as* Jens, however.

The construction **so ... wie** is equivalent to English *as . . . as*.

A   Inge comments on her friends' interest and ability in sports. Ask Inge whether theirs match hers.

V: *Ich spiele nicht so gut wie Ulrike.*

■||| Ulrike spielt gut Tennis.   *Spielt sie so gut wie du?*

1. Dieter schwimmt gut.
2. Anja spielt oft Volleyball.
3. Benno geht oft bergsteigen.

4. Kirstin reitet viel.
5. Jörg segelt viel.

Comparison of inequality

Base form	klein	Ute ist **klein.**	Ute is *small.*
Comparative	kleiner	Ute ist **kleiner als** Petra.	Ute is *smaller than* Petra.

The comparative of an adjective or adverb is formed by adding **-er** to the base form. The word **als** is equivalent to *than*.

B   You are shopping for clothing with Gerda. Compare the articles she points out with the ones you see.

Use clothing illustrations to elicit free response:
T: *Ist der Pulli so schön wie der Mantel?*
S: *Der Pulli ist viel schöner.*
T: *Ist die Bluse so toll wie das Hemd? Jeans / billig / Hose? Jacke / schwer / Mantel?* etc.

■||| Der Pulli da ist schön.   *Ja, aber der Pulli hier ist noch schöner.*

1. Die Bluse da ist schön.
2. Das Hemd da ist dünn.
3. Der Gürtel da ist toll.
4. Der Mantel da ist leicht.
5. Die Krawatte da ist furchtbar.
6. Die Jacke da ist billig.
7. Die Schuhe da sind schwer.
8. Die Socken da sind billig.

	Base form	**groß**	Petra ist **groß**.	Petra is *tall*.
	Comparative	**größer**	Petra ist **größer als** Ute.	Petra is *taller than* Ute.

Many one-syllable adjectives and adverbs show umlaut in the comparative: **älter/jünger; kürzer/länger; wärmer/kälter; größer; dümmer.**

C

Michael is misinformed about a number of things. Correct him by saying that everything is the opposite of what he thinks.

■ııı   Ulf ist älter als Katja, nicht?   *Unsinn, er ist jünger.*

1. Aber Katja ist jünger als Susanne, nicht?
2. Katja ist kleiner als Susanne, nicht?
3. Aber Katja ist kleiner als Ulf, nicht?
4. Es ist heute wärmer als gestern, nicht?
5. Aber es war gestern kälter als am Samstag, nicht?
6. Dieses Jahr ist es wärmer als letztes, nicht?

	Base form	gern	gut	viel	hoch
	Comparative	lieber	besser	mehr	höher

A few adjectives and adverbs are irregular in the formation of their comparatives.

D

You and Klaus are discussing mutual acquaintances. Provide Klaus with more information about the people he mentions.

■ııı   Liese spielt gern Basketball.   *Sie spielt lieber Tennis.*
          — Und Tennis?

1. Ernst spielt gern Klavier. — Und Gitarre?
2. Jens reitet gut. — Und Erik?
3. Eva tanzt gut. — Und Cornelia?
4. Ingrid singt hoch. — Und Heike?
5. Dietmar arbeitet viel. — Und sein Bruder?
6. Karin liest viel. — Und ihre Schwester?

Du hast das Wort

Ask a classmate which of two things he/she prefers.

Was spielst du besser — Tennis oder Basketball?
Was machst du lieber — Schi laufen oder rodeln?
Was hörst du lieber — Geige oder Klavier?
Was trinkst du lieber — Cola oder Milch?
Wohin gehst du lieber — ins Theater oder ins Kino?
Wo ißt du lieber — zu Hause oder im Restaurant?

Personalize:
T: *Du bist größer als Barbara, nicht?*
S¹: *Ja, ich bin größer.*
S²: *Nein, ich bin kleiner.*
Then expand personalization: *Bist du so groß wie (Trudi)? Bist du so alt wie (Fritz)? War es gestern so warm wie heute? War es Donnerstag so kalt wie Freitag?*

Suggestion: Use comparative to review metric measurements.
T: *Katja ist ein Meter 58; Susanne ist ein Meter 56.*
S: *Katja ist größer als Susanne; Susanne ist kleiner als Katja.*

V: *Was spielst du lieber — Fußball oder Basketball? Was hörst du lieber — Gitarre oder Flöte? Wann ißt du mehr — zu Mittag oder zu Abend? Was lernst du lieber — Deutsch oder Englisch? Wann arbeitest du besser — morgens oder abends?*

The verb **werden**

Remind students that the plural, as with all verbs except *sein*, can be derived from the infinitive.

Present tense of **werden**

ich werde			wir werden
du **wirst**	Sie werden		ihr werdet
er/es/sie **wird**			sie werden

The verb **werden** is irregular in the **du-** and **er/sie-**forms of the present tense.

E On a picnic you and your friends have been playing games all afternoon. Say that everyone is getting tired.

V: *krank, sauer.*

Optional: Review professions from ch. 4. *Was willst du werden? Arzt? Ärztin? Lehrer? Lehrerin? Arbeiter? Apothekerin?*, etc. Remind students that German does not use the indefinite article with professions.

▪ⅲ Erik *Erik wird müde.*

1. Petra
2. ich
3. Christl
4. du

5. wir
6. ihr
7. Hans und Karin

Conversational past of **werden**

Ich **bin** müde **geworden.** I've become tired.
Herr Lenz **ist** alt **geworden.** Mr. Lenz has grown old.

Because the verb **werden** expresses a change of condition, it requires **sein** as an auxiliary in the conversational past.

F Agree with your friend that the following people have changed in the last few years.

Wer nichts wird, wird Wirt.

▪ⅲ Herr Fischer ist aber alt, nicht? *Ja, er ist wirklich alt geworden.*

1. Dieter ist aber groß, nicht?
2. Herr Schmidt ist aber dick, nicht?
3. Frau Meier ist furchtbar dünn, nicht?
4. Peter ist sehr faul, nicht?
5. Ingrid ist schön schlank, nicht?

Du hast das Wort Ask various classmates questions about their age.

▪ⅲ Wie alt wirst du dieses Jahr? *Ich werde [sechzehn].*

▪ⅲ Wann wirst du zwanzig? *[1987] werde ich zwanzig.*

Strandkörbe —
gegen Wind und
Wetter (Kiel)

Indirect statements

Direct statement	Petra sagt: „Jan spielt morgen Tennis."
Indirect statement	Petra sagt, **daß** Jan morgen Tennis **spielt**.

An indirect statement is a dependent clause. A dependent clause is introduced by a subordinating conjunction, for example **daß**. In a dependent clause, the verb is in final position.

G Report to a mutual friend what Jens says and does.

■))) Der Pulli ist häßlich. *Jens sagt, daß der Pulli häßlich ist.*

Ex. G-J may be done first with books open, then repeated with books closed.

1. Er kauft ihn nicht.
2. Er findet die Jacke aber schön.
3. Sie kostet aber viel.
4. Sie ist zu teuer.
5. Er kauft sie auch nicht.

Direct statement	Petra sagt: „Jan ruft uns später an."
Indirect statement	Petra sagt, **daß** Jan uns später **anruft**.

In a dependent clause, the separable prefix is attached to the base form of the verb, which is in final position.

H Pass on to Carola what Ingrid and Gisela recently told you.

■))) Stehen Ingrid und Gisela immer früh auf? *Sie sagen, daß sie immer früh aufstehen.*

1. Kommen sie heute mit?
2. Rufen sie uns später noch an?
3. Kaufen sie morgen ein?
4. Haben sie Samstag etwas vor?

Direct statement	Petra sagt: „Jan muß jetzt gehen."
Indirect statement	Petra sagt, **daß** Jan jetzt **gehen muß.**

In a dependent clause, the modal auxiliary follows the infinitive and is in final position.

I   Marianne has a busy day ahead of her. Inform Jens that you think his information about Marianne's activities is correct.

> ▣   Will sie arbeiten?   *Ja, ich glaube, daß sie arbeiten will.*

1. Muß sie zu Hause helfen?
2. Soll sie das Essen kochen?
3. Will sie dann fernsehen?

4. Muß sie noch Mathe machen?
5. Kann sie um zehn Uhr anrufen?

Direct statement	Petra sagt: „Jan hat Mathe gemacht."
Indirect statement	Petra sagt, **daß** Jan Mathe **gemacht hat.**

In a dependent clause in the conversational past, the auxiliary verb **haben** or **sein** follows the past participle and is in final position.

J   Someone did a lot of work around your house last week. Tell your parents that your brother Frank claims he did it.

> ▣   Wer hat die Garage   *Frank sagt, daß er die*
>   aufgeräumt?   *Garage aufgeräumt hat.*

1. Wer hat die Fenster geputzt?
2. Wer hat Staub gesaugt?

3. Wer hat die Wäsche gewaschen?
4. Wer hat die Torte gebacken?

Schikjöring — ein ungewöhnlicher Wintersport (Stuttgart)

286

Indirect questions

Specific questions

Direct question	**Wer ist** das Mädchen?
Indirect question	Paul möchte wissen, **wer** das Mädchen **ist**.

An indirect question is a dependent clause; therefore, the verb is in final position. In indirect *specific* questions (that is, questions introduced by an interrogative like **wer**), the interrogative functions as a subordinating conjunction.

K

Alternate exercise: Students say they would like to know various things. *Wann gehen wir ins Theater? — Ich möchte wissen, wann wir ins Theater gehen.*

Günter is having a birthday party. Ask your classmates for information about the party.

■▮▮ Wo ist die Party?   *Weißt du, wo die Party ist?*

1. Wen hat Günter eingeladen?
2. Was machen wir?
3. Was gibt es zu essen?
4. Wer soll den Kuchen backen?
5. Was soll ich mitbringen?
6. Wie alt wird Günter?

General questions

V: Frag, ob es heute schön ist! Frag, ob es heute warm ist! Frag, ob es morgen regnet! Frag, wieviel Grad es sind! Frag, ob es gestern schön war! Frag, ob es Montag kalt war!

Direct question	**Kommt** Inge zur Party?
Indirect question	Günter möchte wissen, **ob** Inge zur Party **kommt**.

In indirect *general* questions (that is, questions that can be answered by **ja** or **nein**), the indirect-question clause is introduced by **ob** (*whether, if*).

L

Show students how they can express curiosity with an independent *ob*-clause: *Ob Peter schon zu Hause ist?* ("I wonder whether Peter is already at home.") *Ob er uns angerufen hat?* ("I wonder whether he called us.")

On Monday morning you run into a friend who is curious about what Petra and Rainer did over the weekend. Express your ignorance about their activities.

■▮▮ Hat Rainer gearbeitet?   *Ich weiß nicht, ob er gearbeitet hat.*

1. Hat Petra zu Hause geholfen?
2. Sind sie schwimmen gegangen?
3. Sind Dieter und Inge mitgefahren?
4. Haben sie einen Spaziergang gemacht?
5. Sind sie zusammen tanzen gegangen?

Heute ist es aber kalt!

Grammatische Übersicht

Comparison of adjectives and adverbs (A-D)

Regular forms

Base form	**leicht**	easy	**schön**	beautiful
Comparative	**leichter**	easier	**schöner**	more beautiful

German forms the comparative of adjectives and adverbs by adding the suffix **-er** to the base form. Note that English can form the comparative either by adding **-er** to the base form or by using the modifier *more*.

Forms with umlaut

Base form	alt	groß	jung
Comparative	älter	größer	jünger

Many one-syllable adjectives and adverbs add umlaut in the comparative: **älter, dümmer, größer, jünger, kälter, kürzer, länger, wärmer.** From now on, adjectives and adverbs of this type will be listed in the vocabularies of this book as follows: **kalt (ä).**

Irregular forms

Base form	gern	gut	hoch	viel
Comparative	lieber	besser	höher	mehr

A few adjectives and adverbs are irregular in the comparative form.

so . . . wie

Bernd spielt nicht **so gut wie** Jens.   Bernd doesn't play *as well as* Jens.

The construction **so . . . wie** with the base form of the adjective or adverb is used to make comparisons of equality. It is equivalent to English *as . . . as.*

Comparative with als

Jens ist **größer als** Erik.   Jens is *taller than* Erik.
Petra tanzt **besser als** Gretl.   Petra dances *better than* Gretl.

The comparative form of the adjective or adverb with **als** is used to make comparisons of inequality. **Als** is equivalent to English *than.*

The verb **werden** (E-F)

Present tense

ich werde		wir werden
du **wirst**	Sie werden	ihr werdet
er/es/sie **wird**		sie werden

Werden is irregular in the **du-** and **er/sie-**forms of the present tense.

Ich **werde** müde.   I *am getting* tired.
Der Mann **wird** alt.   The man *is growing* old.
Wie alt **wirst** du?   How old *are you going to be*?
Was möchtest du **werden?**   What would you like *to be*?

English uses a number of different verbs to express the many ideas of **werden** in German.

Conversational past

Frank **ist** krank **geworden.**   Frank *became* ill.

Because the verb **werden** expresses a change of condition, it requires **sein** as an auxiliary in the conversational past.

Word order in dependent clauses   (G-L)

INDEPENDENT CLAUSE	SUBORDINATING CONJUNCTION	DEPENDENT CLAUSE
Ute sagt,	daß	sie morgen Tennis spielt.
Sie möchte wissen,	ob	du auch spielen willst.

A dependent clause cannot stand alone as a complete sentence. It is introduced by a subordinating conjunction such as **daß** or **ob.** The conjunction is always preceded by a comma.

Verb in final position

1. In a dependent clause, the verb is in final position:
   Ingrid sagt, daß sie in die Stadt **fährt.**

2. A separable prefix is attached to the base form of the verb, which is in final position:
   Sie sagt, daß Astrid **mitfährt.**

3. A modal auxiliary follows the infinitive and is in final position:
   Sie sagt, daß sie in die Stadt **fahren müssen.**

4. In the conversational past, the auxiliary verb **haben** or **sein** follows the past participle and is in final position:
   Sie sagt, daß sie gestern nicht **gefahren sind.**

Indirect statements

Direct statement	Ingrid sagt: „Jan macht jetzt Mathe."
Indirect statement	Ingrid sagt, **daß** Jan jetzt Mathe **macht.**

Indirect statements are introduced by the subordinating conjunction **daß** (*that*).

Indirect specific questions

Direct question	**Wann** macht Jens Mathe?
Indirect question	Ich möchte wissen, **wann** Jens Mathe **macht**.

Indirect specific questions are introduced by the same interrogatives that are used to introduce direct specific questions.

Indirect general questions

Direct question	**Macht** Ingrid jetzt Mathe?
Indirect question	Ich weiß nicht, **ob** Ingrid jetzt Mathe **macht**.

Indirect general questions are introduced by the subordinating conjunction **ob** (whether, if).

Wiederholung

A   Make three sets of comparisons for each pair of sentences.

    ■Ⅲ   Ich bin 1,40 m groß. Mein   *Ich bin größer als mein*
            Bruder ist 1,30.   *Bruder.*
                                              Mein Bruder ist kleiner als
                                              ich.
                                              Mein Bruder ist nicht so groß
                                              wie ich.

1. Ich bin sechzehn Jahre alt.
   Meine Schwester ist erst dreizehn.
2. Dieser Bleistift ist 17 cm lang.
   Dieser Kugelschreiber ist nur 13 cm lang.
3. Im August haben wir oft 30 Grad.
   Im Januar haben wir oft 0 Grad.
4. Gisela läuft einen Kilometer in drei Minuten.
   Jan läuft einen Kilometer in vier Minuten.

B   Form sentences in the present tense, using the cues provided.

1. Trudi / helfen / viel / zu Hause
2. sie / raustragen / der Mülleimer
3. am Wochenende / sie / waschen / das Auto
4. sie / müssen / auch / machen / Gartenarbeit
5. sie / werden / einfach / nicht / müde
6. sie / tragen / gern / alte Jeans
7. ihr Vater / lesen / abends / gern
8. ihr Bruder / fernsehen / lieber

May wish to practice
orally in class and then
assign as written home-
work.

C   Jörg and Sabine are discussing a typical weekend. Show that it was the same last weekend by restating their conversation in the conversational past.

1. Stehst du früh auf?
   Nein, ich schlafe bis neun.
2. Fährst du in die Stadt?
   Nein. Birgit und ich gehen windsurfen.
3. Macht das Spaß?
   Nein. Ich falle zu oft ins Wasser.
4. Wann kommt ihr nach Hause?
   Um fünf. Wir essen um sechs zu Abend.
5. Seht ihr fern?
   Nein. Wir gehen ins Kino.

D Complete each sentence with one of the following prepositions.

durch   **für**   **gegen**   **ohne**   **um**

1. Gerd geht _____ den Supermarkt.
2. Er kommt oft _____ seine Familie.
3. _____ seinen Bruder Otto kauft er 100 Gramm Schokolade.
4. Er kauft nichts _____ Trudi.
5. Hat er etwas _____ seine Schwester?
6. _____ drei Uhr kommt er wieder nach Hause.

E Choose the appropriate conjunction to connect each pair of sentences.

> ▪▮ Willst du heute abend fern-   *Willst du heute abend fern-*
>   sehen? (oder, aber)   *sehen, oder willst du*
>   Willst du lieber ins Kino?   *lieber ins Kino?*

Precede with review of coordinating conjunctions.

1. Ich kann ins Kino. (oder, denn)
   Ich habe meine Hausaufgaben schon gemacht.
2. Meine Hausaufgaben sind nicht fertig. (sondern, aber)
   Ich kann sie später machen.
3. Ich lade Paula ein. (und, sondern)
   Du kannst Heidi einladen.
4. Ich möchte nicht Heidi einladen. (aber, sondern)
   Ich möchte Ute einladen.
5. Ruf sie jetzt an! (denn, oder)
   Es wird zu spät.

F Give the individual words that make up the compounds, and supply the definite article for each noun. Then give the English equivalents of the compounds.

> ▪▮ die Wintersonne   *der Winter, die Sonne (winter sun)*

1. der Sonnenschirm   3. die Windjacke   5. der Schneemann
2. der Wetterbericht   4. der Stadtplan   6. der Regenmantel

G Express the following conversation in German.

DIETER Hi, Gisela. How are you?
GISELA Hi, Dieter. Fine, thanks.
DIETER Do you have anything planned for today?
GISELA This morning I have to wash our car and clean out the garage. But this afternoon I'm free.
DIETER Would you like to go swimming?
GISELA Glad to. It's hot.
DIETER I'll pick you up at two-thirty.
GISELA Great. See you later.

Kulturlesestück

Geographie

Deutschland liegt im Zentrum Europas und hat neun Nachbarländer°:
im Norden Dänemark; im Westen die Niederlande, Belgien, Luxemburg
und Frankreich; im Süden die Schweiz und Österreich; und im Osten
die Tschechoslowakei und Polen. Man spricht nicht nur in Deutschland Deutsch, sondern auch in Österreich und in einem Teil° der
Schweiz. Seit° 1949 gibt es zwei deutsche Staaten — im Osten die
Deutsche Demokratische Republik (DDR) und im Westen die Bundesrepublik Deutschland (BRD).

    In Deutschland ist das Land im Norden flach°. In der Mitte gibt es
die Mittelgebirge°. Im Süden liegen die Alpen, ein Hochgebirge°. Die
großen Flüsse° — der Rhein, die Weser, die Elbe und die Oder —
fließen° von Süden nach Norden in die Nordsee und in die Ostsee. Nur
die Donau fließt von Westen nach Osten.

    Im Norden sind die großen Hafenstädte°: Bremen an der Weser,
Hamburg an der Elbe und Rostock an der Ostsee. In der Mitte gibt es im
Westen viel Kohle°. Daher° ist an der Ruhr das deutsche Schwerindu-
striezentrum°. Nur ein kleiner Teil von Deutschland liegt in den
Alpen. Aber Österreich und die Schweiz sind vor allem° Alpenländer.
Hier findet man daher die international bekannten° Wintersportzen-
tren wie Zermatt und St. Moritz oder Innsbruck und Kitzbühel.

	neighboring countries
	part
	since
	flat
	low mountains / high mountains
	rivers
	flow
	port cities
	coal / therefore
	center of heavy industry
	above all
	famous

Richig oder
falsch?

1. In Deutschland liegen die Berge im Norden.
2. Das Land im Süden ist flach.
3. Die Weser und die Elbe sind Flüsse.
4. Die Donau und die Oder fließen von Westen nach Osten.
5. Der Rhein fließt in die Nordsee.
6. Hamburg ist eine Hafenstadt.
7. Die Ruhr ist ein Alpenland.
8. Die deutsche Schwerindustrie liegt im Hochgebirge.
9. Kitzbühel liegt in den Alpen.

Vokabeln

SUBSTANTIVE

der Atlantische Ozean   Atlantic Ocean
der Bericht, -e   report
der Grad   degree
die Hauptstadt, ̈e   capital city
die Jahreszeit, -en   season, time of the year
der Norden   north
der Osten   east
der Regen   rain
der Regenschirm, -e   umbrella
der Schnee   snow
die Sonne   sun
der Süden   south
die Temperatur, -en   temperature
das Thermometer, -   thermometer
der Westen   west
das Wetter   weather
der Wind   wind

VERBEN

denken (gedacht)   to think
frieren (gefroren)   to freeze, to be very cold
liegen (gelegen)   to lie, to be (situated)
mit·nehmen (i; mitgenommen)   to take along
regnen   to rain
rodeln (ist gerodelt)   to toboggan
scheinen (geschienen)   to shine
schneien   to snow
sprechen (i; gesprochen)   to speak
werden (wird; ist geworden)   to become

ANDERE WÖRTER

amerikanisch   American
anders   different
besonders   particularly, especially
bewölkt   cloudy, overcast
da   then
endlich   finally
glatt   slippery
heiß   hot
kalt (ä)   cold
kühl   cool
naß   wet
nördlich   northern, north of
südlich   southern, south of
trocken   dry
über   about, above, over
wahrscheinlich   probably
weiter   further
wenn   if, when
windig   windy

BESONDERE AUSDRÜCKE

du hast recht   you're right
du spinnst   you're crazy
lieber haben   to like better, to prefer
noch [schöner]   even more [beautiful]

Kapitel 14

Christa macht den Führerschein

296

After material has been read, ask specific questions for vocabulary control.

Aus Briefen an Jochen

Christa wird bald achtzehn und darf dann den Führerschein machen. Sie schreibt oft an ihren Freund Jochen und erzählt von ihren Fortschritten.°

progress

Mittwoch, den 16.° Januar

sechzehnten: sixteenth

... Du weißt, ich werde am Samstag 18. Dann kann ich endlich meinen Führerschein machen. Heute haben meine Eltern mich gefragt, was ich zum Geburtstag haben möchte. Vielleicht bezahlen sie ja das Geld oder wenigstens etwas Geld für die Fahrschule. . . .

Samstag, den 19. Januar

Help students correctly read the dates in Christa's letters. The ordinal numbers are for passive recognition only. They are presented in *German Today, Two*, Chapter 9.

... Ich bin sehr glücklich. Ich habe von meinen Eltern das Geld für die Fahrschule bekommen. Vielleicht kann ich nächste Woche den Sehtest° machen und mit dem Erste-Hilfe-Kurs° beginnen. . . .

eye test
first aid course

Dienstag, den 5. Februar

... Mit dem Erste-Hilfe-Kurs bin ich fertig. Mit dem Sehtest auch. Ich bin zur Fahrschule gegangen. Am Montag beginnt der theoretische° Unterricht; meine erste Fahrstunde ist am Dienstag. . . .

theoretical

Montag, den 18. Februar

... Der theoretische Unterricht ist furchtbar langweilig. Niemand macht ihn gern, aber er muß ja wohl sein. Die theoretische Prüfung soll sehr kompliziert sein. Hast Du auch gehört, daß 40%° durchfallen? . . .

Prozent: per cent

Freitag, den 7. März

... Der Fahrlehrer ist sehr nett. (Brauchst aber nicht eifersüchtig zu werden!) Es ist nur gut, daß er auch eine Bremse hat. Ich habe zu meinen Freunden schon gesagt, sie sollen abends zwischen 6 und 7 zu Hause bleiben. Da mache ich die Straßen unsicher . . .

Mittwoch, den 23. April

Show students how Germans wish someone good luck by pressing the thumbs of each hand with their four fingers.

... Morgen ist die praktische Prüfung. Halt mir die Daumen, daß ich sie bestehe . . .

Donnerstag, den 24. April

... Heute habe ich die Fahrprüfung bestanden. Endlich! Die Prüfungsfahrt° ist gut gegangen. Ich habe aber auch etwas Schwein gehabt. Nicht viele Autos auf den Straßen . . .

road test

Dienstag, den 6. Mai

... Heute habe ich einen gebrauchten° VW gekauft. Was sagst Du nun?   used
Jetzt kann ich endlich an den See fahren, wenn *ich* es will. Jetzt bin ich
am Wochenende endlich unabhängig. ...

Mittwoch, den 7. Mai

... große Diskussion mit meinen Eltern: Soll ich mit dem Auto zur° Ar-   to
beit fahren? Es ist natürlich toll, mit dem Auto in die Stadt zu fahren.
Aber Zug und Straßenbahn sind billiger. Dann können wir am Wochenende mehr fahren. Ich fahre also jeden Tag mit dem Zug. Und dann mit
der Straßenbahn. Leider! ...

Have students read the preceding text in the 3rd person. Begin with *Sie wird am Samstag 18 ...*

Richtig oder falsch?

Questions for general discussion:
1. *Wie alt muß man hier sein, um den Führerschein zu machen?*
2. *Was lernt man im theoretischen Unterricht? Im praktischen Unterricht?*
3. *Wie lange dauert ein Fahrkurs in Amerika?*
4. *Sind die Prüfungen leicht? schwer? Was muß man machen?*

1. In Deutschland macht man gewöhnlich erst mit achtzehn den Führerschein.
2. Christa möchte nichts zum Geburtstag.
3. Christa beginnt ihren Fahrkurs mit dem praktischen Unterricht.
4. Christa kann gut sehen.
5. Der theoretische Unterricht ist interessant.
6. Die theoretische Prüfung soll nicht schwer sein.
7. Christa fällt in der theoretischen Prüfung durch.
8. Christa bleibt abends zwischen sechs und sieben zu Hause.
9. Christa hält die Bremse mit den Daumen.
10. Das Auto macht Christa am Wochenende unabhängiger.
11. Christa will nicht mit dem Auto zur Arbeit fahren.
12. Christa fährt mit dem Zug und mit der Straßenbahn, denn es ist billiger.

Du hast das Wort

Let students make up their own questions about the text and ask them of each other. Some of the more interesting questions may be written on the board.

Ask a classmate about driver's education.

Wieviel kostet die Fahrschule hier?

Hast du schon einen Fahrkurs gemacht?

Hast du schon die Fahrprüfung gemacht? Hast du sie bestanden? Wieviele sind durchgefallen?

Wieviele Bremsen hat dein Auto?

Für die theoretische Prüfung muß man die Verkehrszeichen lernen.

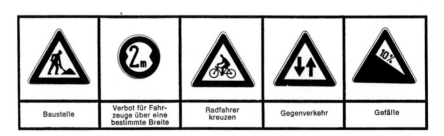

| Baustelle | Verbot für Fahr-zeuge über eine bestimmte Breite | Radfahrer kreuzen | Gegenverkehr | Gefälle |

To practice the expression *Was für ein,* collect pictures of foreign and domestic cars. Hold up a picture for identification: *Was für ein Auto ist das? Das ist ein VW.* Let students quiz each other.

The **BRD** has an extensive highway system. Superhighways **(Autobahnen)** link major cities, and numerous other roads crisscross the country. With few exceptions, there is no speed limit **(Geschwindigkeitsbegrenzung)** on the **Autobahn,** and some people tend to drive at very high speeds when traffic and weather conditions permit.

The large number of vehicles in circulation (about one car for every two people) results in numerous traffic jams **(Staus),** especially on weekends and holidays. The traffic jams on the **Autobahn** are particularly bad at the beginning and end of school vacations, despite the fact that each German state has different vacation dates in an attempt to stagger arrivals and departures.

Dein Auto, dein Traum-Auto

Manche Teenager kaufen oder bekommen ein Auto, wenn sie den Führerschein machen. Wie ist es bei dir°? Hast du ein Auto? Oder hast du vielleicht nur ein Traum-Auto? Beschreibe es!

bei dir: in your case

1. Was für ein Auto hast du? Was für ein Auto möchtest du haben?
2. Hast du das Auto gebraucht oder neu gekauft?
3. Ist das Auto groß oder klein?
4. Braucht das Auto viel Benzin? 1 Liter auf 10 Kilometer? 1° Gallone auf 20 Meilen°?

eine
20 miles to the gallon

5. Läuft es gut?
6. Reparierst du gern alte Autos? Ist das dein Hobby?
7. Fährst du gern schnell oder lieber langsam?
8. Wie schnell fährst du auf der Landstraße°? Auf der Autobahn? In der Stadt? 90 Kilometer pro Stunde? 55 Meilen pro Stunde?

highway

Du hast das Wort

Activities:
(1) Have students create skits or brief dialogues using this material.

Interview your classmates about their cars (real or imagined). Take brief notes, then share the information with the class.

Ist dein Auto alt oder neu?
Welche Farbe hat dein Auto?
Ist dein Auto amerikanisch?

(2) Have students write a narrative containing the answers to the questions.

Wortschatzerweiterung

Wie fährt man?

das Fahrrad (das Rad)

das Mofa

das Motorrad

der Bus

die Straßenbahn

die U-Bahn

der Zug

das Flugzeug

das Schiff

A   Ask a classmate the following questions about transportation.

The word *Mofa* is derived from the word *Motorfahrrad.* There are *Mopeds* in Germany as well.

1. Hast du ein Fahrrad? Ist es neu? Alt?
2. Fährst du gern mit dem Rad?
3. Möchtest du eine lange Radtour machen? Wohin?
4. Hast du letzten Sommer eine Radtour gemacht? Wohin?
5. Hast du ein Motorrad? Ein Mofa? Ist es neu? Alt?
6. Fährst du gern mit dem Motorrad? Mit dem Mofa?
7. Bastelst du gern am Fahrrad oder am Motorrad?
8. Hat deine Stadt eine Straßenbahn?

B   Ask your teacher some questions about transportation.

Activity: Have students make crossword puzzles using words related to transportation.

1. Wie fahren Sie zur Schule? Mit dem Bus? Mit dem Rad? Mit dem Mofa? Mit dem Auto?
2. Wie kann man von Österreich in die Schweiz kommen? Von Deutschland in die Schweiz?
3. Fliegen Sie gern? Wie oft sind Sie schon geflogen? Wohin?
4. Wie möchten Sie nach Europa fahren? Mit dem Schiff oder mit dem Flugzeug? Warum?

Kilometer und Meile

1 (ein) Kilometer = 0,62 Meilen
1 (eine) Meile = 1,6 Kilometer

C   You are driving in Germany but have an American car showing only miles. How fast can you drive in miles per hour when you see these German signs?

▪▥   50 km   *31 Meilen pro Stunde*

1. 80 km   2. 100 km   3. 20 km   4. 120 km

Although some young people in Germany have cars, most teen-agers take public transportation, use mopeds or bicycles, or walk to school and work. The minimum age for a driver's license is eighteen (though exceptions are sometimes made for sixteen-year-olds who need a car to make a living). Very few schools have driver-education courses. Taking a course in a private driving school **(Fahrschule)** and passing a test are required in order to get a license. The course in a **Fahrschule** is rather expensive, and insurance costs a great deal, two more factors that reduce the number of teen-agers who drive. But once one gets a license, it is valid for life.

Aussprache

After doing A–C, practice the following lists both vertically and horizontally. *buk, Buch, Bücher, Büsche; Lack, lachen, lächeln, löschen,* etc.

I [ç]   Mil**ch**, schle**ch**t, Bü**ch**er

The sound [ç] is similar to that used by many Americans for the *h* in such words as *hue, huge, Hugh.* The sound [ç] is represented by the letters **ch** when they occur after the vowel sounds written as **e, i, ie, ü, äu, eu,** and **ö,** and after consonants.

A   Practice the following words.

| mi**ch** | re**ch**t | eu**ch** | man**ch** | Bü**ch**er |
| endli**ch** | mö**ch**te | Bräu**ch**e | dur**ch** | Tü**ch**er |

B   Practice the following words horizontally in pairs, to contrast [ʃ] (as in *Fisch* and *waschen*) with [ç].

[ʃ]	[ç]	[ʃ]	[ç]
Kir**sch**e	Kir**ch**e	Men**sch**	Mön**ch**
fi**sch**te	Fi**ch**te	Bü**sch**e	Bü**ch**er
fri**sch**	fre**ch**	mi**sch**	mi**ch**

C   Practice the following words horizontally in pairs.

[x]	[ç]	[x]	[ç]
do**ch**	di**ch**	Bu**ch**	Bü**ch**er
Da**ch**	Dä**ch**er	Brau**ch**	Bräu**ch**e
To**ch**ter	Tö**ch**ter	Lo**ch**	Lö**ch**er

D   Practice the sound [ç]. Read the sentences aloud.

1. Hoffentlich hast du nichts gegen Bücher!
2. Er spricht gut Deutsch.
3. Ich möchte ein Glas Milch, aber frisch, bitte.

Proverb: Birds of a feather flock together.

Gleich und gleich gesellt sich gern.

Was ist mit dem Auto los?

Übungen

Dative case of definite articles and nouns

Singular

NOMINATIVE
Der Fernseher ist kaputt.
Das Radio spielt nicht.
Die Platte ist schlecht.

DATIVE
Was hast du mit **dem Fernseher** gemacht?
Was hast du mit **dem Radio** gemacht?
Was hast du mit **der Platte** gemacht?

Students should recognize that *-m* and *-r* cue dative.

The dative case is used with certain prepositions, one of which is **mit.** The definite article changes form in the dative case.

A Jörg cites the reasons for avoiding various means of transportation. Reply that you're not traveling by those means anyway.

You may want to review nominative and accusative forms.

▪▦   Der Bus ist zu langsam.   *Ich fahre doch nicht mit dem Bus.*

1. Die Straßenbahn fährt nach zwölf nicht mehr.
2. Die U-Bahn fährt um diese Zeit nicht.
3. Das Auto läuft nicht.
4. Das Motorrad ist kaputt.
5. Und das Fahrrad ist leider auch kaputt.

Additional cues: *Mofa, Zug.*

Plural

Remind students that -n is the sign of the accusative singular of articles and other determiners before der-nouns as well as the sign of the dative plural.

NOMINATIVE
Die **Fernseher** sind kaputt.
Die **Radios** spielen nicht.
Die **Platten** sind schlecht.

DATIVE
Was hast du mit **den Fernsehern** gemacht?
Was hast du mit **den Radios** gemacht?
Was hast du mit **den Platten** gemacht?

The dative plural form of the definite article is **den.** In the dative plural, an **-n** is added to the plural form of the noun, unless the plural already ends in **-n** or in **-s.**

B Christl says she no longer collects the following things. Ask her what she did with them.

■⊪ Ich sammle keine Briefmarken mehr.

*Was hast du denn mit den
Briefmarken gemacht?*

1. Ich sammle keine Ansichtskarten mehr.
2. Ich sammle keine Poster mehr.
3. Ich sammle keine Bierdeckel mehr.
4. Ich sammle keine Schallplatten mehr.
5. Ich sammle keine Flugzeugmodelle mehr.

Ex. B may be done first with books open.

Dative case of **dieser**-words

Von **welchem** Fernseher sprichst du?	Von **diesem.**
Von **welchem** Radio sprichst du?	Von **diesem.**
Von **welcher** Stereoanlage sprichst du?	Von **dieser.**
Von **welchen** Platten sprichst du?	Von **diesen.**

Dieser-words **(dieser, jeder, solcher, mancher, welcher)** follow the same pattern of endings in the dative case as the definite articles. The dative case is used with the preposition **von.**

C At a party Ingrid offers you various refreshments. Thank her and tell her which ones you'd like.

■⊪ Möchtest du etwas Käse?

*Ja, bitte. Ich nehme ein Stück
von diesem hier.*

1. Möchtest du etwas Wurst?
2. Willst du etwas Brot?
3. Möchtest du etwas Kuchen?
4. Willst du etwas Torte?

D   Hans-Jürgen is commenting on some clothes in the men's department, but you're not paying attention. Ask him which items he means.

V¹: Place Ex. D in women's department: *Bluse, Gürtel, Hemd, Hose, Jeans, Kleid, Rock, Schuhe.*
V²: Show 2 pictures of each item. Make a related comment, and student must ask of which you are speaking.

◼⫯   Dieser Anzug ist aber teuer.   *Von welchem Anzug sprichst du?*

1. Diese Jacke ist ja toll.
2. Dieser Pulli ist wirklich klasse.
3. Diese Schuhe sind aber billig.
4. Diese Krawatte ist aber häßlich.
5. Dieser Mantel ist zu dick.
6. Diese Handschuhe sind wirklich warm.

Dative case of indefinite articles and **ein**-words

> Erika hat das von **einem** Mann im Geschäft gehört.
> Dieter hat das von **einem** Mädchen im Café gehört.
> Uwe hat das von **einer** Frau im Supermarkt gehört.
>
> Gabi hat das von **ihren** Freunden gehört.

Indefinite articles and **ein**-words (**mein, dein, sein,** and so on) follow the same pattern of endings in the dative as **dieser-**words.

E   Gisela wants to find out what various people think about the new horror movie. Say that you haven't spoken to them yet.

◼⫯   Was denkt dein Bruder?   *Mein Bruder? Mit meinem Bruder habe ich noch nicht gesprochen.*

1. Was denkt deine Schwester?
2. Was denkt dein Vater?
3. Was denkt deine Mutter?
4. Was denken deine Freunde?

F   Silke claims people are saying the weather will change drastically tomorrow. Express surprise that they're all talking about it.

◼⫯   Unser Metzger hat es gesagt.   *Wirklich? Von eurem Metzger habt ihr es gehört?*

1. Unser Bäcker hat es auch gesagt.
2. Unser Elektriker hat es auch gesagt.
3. Und unsere Friseuse hat es gesagt.
4. Unser Lehrer hat es gesagt.
5. Und unsere Ärztin hat es gesagt.

Make a series of statements to a classmate. Your classmate will tell you whether the statements make sense and correct them if they don't.

- ■Ⅲ Man schreibt mit einem Buch, nicht? — *Unsinn! Man schreibt mit einem Bleistift.*
- ■Ⅲ Man spült Geschirr mit Wasser, nicht? — *Ja, das stimmt.*

Man fährt mit dem Rad von hier nach Österreich, nicht?
Man bäckt eine Torte mit Eiern, nicht?
Man spricht mit dem Deutschlehrer Deutsch, nicht?
Du fährst mit der Straßenbahn zur Schule, nicht?

Dative case of special der-nouns

Have students tell whether *Junge* is accusative singular or dative plural in: *Ich sehe den Jungen; ich spreche mit den Jungen; Ich arbeite mit dem Jungen.*

Nominative	Wie heißt der Herr da?
Accusative	Kennst du **den Herrn** da?
Dative	Willst du mit **dem Herrn** arbeiten?

Special **der**-nouns that add an **-n** or **-en** in the accusative also add **-n** or **-en** in the dative singular. The special **der**-nouns you know are **Herr, Junge, Kunde.**

G

V: Students respond quickly to question (give cue): *Mit wem arbeitest du? (Junge)*

Clarify with whom you did various things, using the cues in parentheses.

- ■Ⅲ Hast du mit dem Mädchen da gearbeitet? (Junge) — *Nein, mit dem Jungen da.*

1. Bist du mit der Frau da gefahren? (Herr)
2. Hast du mit dem Verkäufer da gesprochen? (Kunde)
3. Hast du mit dem Jungen da Tennis gespielt? (Herr)
4. Hast du mit dem Mädchen da gegessen? (Junge)

H

Test drill: genders are varied. Repeat each item that causes difficulty.

Say that Gabi spoke with the persons mentioned.

- ■Ⅲ die Frau da — *Gabi hat mit der Frau da gesprochen.*

1. der Herr da
2. der Junge da
3. der Friseur da
4. der Kunde da
5. die Männer da
6. die Verkäuferin da
7. die Frauen da
8. das Mädchen da

Mit dem Mofa geht's besser.

Dative case of **wer**

Review accusative case of *wer*.

Nominative	**Wer** ist das?	*Who* is that?
Dative	Mit **wem** spricht Gabi?	With *whom* is Gabi speaking?

The dative form of the interrogative pronoun **wer** is **wem.**

I Ask Christl to say again with whom various friends are doing things this weekend.

Have students answer questions:
T: *Mit wem gehst du?*
S: *Ich gehe mit meinem Bruder (Freund, etc.).*

■▮▮ Erik geht mit seinem Bruder ins Kino.   *Mit wem geht er ins Kino?*

1. Andrea spielt mit ihrer Schwester Tennis.
2. Eva geht mit einer Freundin schwimmen.
3. Volker geht mit seiner Freundin einkaufen.
4. Dirk fährt mit seinen Freunden an den See.
5. Karin kommt mit Paul zur Party.
6. Ingrid fährt mit Dieter in die Stadt.

Du hast das Wort State with whom you did various things during the last few weeks. If necessary, invent an answer.

■▮▮ Mit wem bist du einkaufen gegangen?   *Mit meinem Vater. / Mit einer Freundin.*

Mit wem bist du ins Kino gegangen?
Mit wem bist du zum Basketballspiel gegangen?
Mit wem bist du tanzen gegangen?
Mit wem hast du Musik gehört?
Mit wem hast du ferngesehen?
Mit wem bist du auf die Party gegangen?
Mit wem bist du schwimmen gegangen?

Wie fährt man? Young people often decorate their cars with colorful stickers. Others like to build their own contraptions. Bottom left: A driving school in Munich. Bottom right: River traffic on the Rhine near Niederlahnstein.

HALT
FÜR FAHRZEUGE
Rad-u-Mopedfahrer
absteigen
FAHRZEIT ab 6⁰⁰ 22⁰⁰ hr

ROMANTICA

309

Dative case of articles and nouns (A-F)

	SINGULAR			PLURAL
Nominative	der	das	die	die
Accusative	den	das	die	die
Dative	**dem**	**dem**	**der**	**den**
	die**sem**	die**sem**	die**ser**	die**sen**
	ein**em**	ein**em**	ein**er**	—
	sein**em**	sein**em**	sein**er**	sein**en**

In addition to nominative and accusative, German has a third case called dative. It is used with certain prepositions, two of which are **mit** and **von.**

The definite article has three forms in the dative case: **dem, der,** and **den. Dieser**-words **(dieser, jeder, welcher, solcher, mancher),** the indefinite article, and **ein-**words **(kein, mein, dein, sein,** and so on) follow the same pattern of endings in the dative case as the definite article.

NOMINATIVE	DATIVE
Der Fernseher ist kaputt.	Was hast du mit **dem Fernseher** gemacht?
Das Radio spielt nicht.	Was hast du mit **dem Radio** gemacht?
Die Platte ist schlecht.	Was hast du mit **der Platte** gemacht?
Die Fernseher sind kaputt.	Was hast du mit **den Fernsehern** gemacht?
Die Radios spielen nicht.	Was hast du mit **den Radios** gemacht?
Die Platten sind schlecht.	Was hast du mit **den Platten** gemacht?

In the singular, the dative form of a noun is identical with the nominative and accusative forms.

In the plural, the dative form of a noun adds an **-n** unless the plural form of the noun already ends in **-n** or in **-s.**

The letters before the dash on a German license plate tell you where the car is registered. Single letters stand for large cities (**N** is **Nürnberg);** three letters identify the smallest townships.

Dative case of special **der**-nouns (G-H)

Nominative	der Herr	der Junge	der Kunde
Accusative	den Herr**n**	den Jung**en**	den Kund**en**
Dative	dem Herr**n**	dem Jung**en**	dem Kund**en**

Special **der**-nouns that add **-n** or **-en** in the accusative also add **-n** or **-en** in the dative singular.

Dative case of **wer** (I)

Nominative	Wer ist das?	*Who* is that?
Dative	Mit **wem** gehst du?	With *whom* are you going?

The dative form of the interrogative pronoun **wer** is **wem.**

_____ Wiederholung _____

A   Lore was quite surprised when she saw Dieter yesterday. Read the following dialogue and then relay the content of the dialogue to a friend from Lore's point of view.

May wish to perform as skit.

LORE	Mensch, Dieter, habe ich richtig gesehen?
DIETER	Wie soll ich das wissen? Was hast du denn gesehen?
LORE	Du bist ja mit dem Rad gefahren.
DIETER	Na und?
LORE	Tu nicht so dumm! Du weißt schon, was ich meine. Wo ist denn dein Mofa?
DIETER	Kaputt.
LORE	Aha! Und jetzt bist du sauer.
DIETER	Ja, natürlich, und wie! Komm, ich fahr dich zu Großinger. Ich lade dich zu einer Cola ein.
LORE	Schön. Aber nicht mit dem Fahrrad. Ich nehme dich auf (*on*) meinem Mofa mit.

You may want to begin your narrative as follows:

Gestern habe ich Dieter gesehen. Er ist . . .

B Indicate with whom Mr. Wolf is speaking. Base your choice on the content of Mr. Wolf's statements.

Ärztin   Bäcker   Fahrlehrer   Elektriker
Metzger   Verkäuferin

■⫯ „Haben Sie noch Brot von   *Er spricht mit dem Bäcker.*
gestern?"

1. „Das Licht im Badezimmer ist kaputt. Können Sie es heute noch reparieren?"
2. „Ich möchte ein Kleid in Blau für meine Frau. Ich glaube, sie trägt Größe 40."
3. „Das habe ich wieder falsch gemacht, nicht? Autofahren ist nicht leicht zu lernen."
4. „Ich bin den ganzen Tag müde und habe keinen Appetit."
5. „Ich hätte gern ein Pfund von dem Schinken da."

C Form sentences about clothes shopping, using the cues provided.

For oral and written practice.

1. ich / möchten / kaufen / jedes Hemd hier
2. warum / manche Kleider / sein / so teuer / ?
3. was / ich / sollen / machen / mit / dieser Mantel / ?
4. welcher / Rock / ich / sollen / nehmen / ?
5. du / können / bezahlen / dieser Anzug / ?
6. du / finden / solche / Schuhe / schön / ?

D Change each English word to its German equivalent by changing one or two letters.

■⫯ milk   *Milch*

1. word   6. long
2. friend   7. green
3. water   8. new
4. thick   9. half
5. for   10. was

E Complete each of the following sentences with the appropriate form of the words in parentheses.

1. Christa und Jochen sind durch _____ gefahren. (die Stadt)
2. Du hast doch hoffentlich _____ nicht wieder verloren. (dein Führerschein)
3. Frank muß für _____ lernen. (die Fahrprüfung)
4. Er ist durchgefallen, aber er hat nichts gegen _____. (sein Fahrlehrer)
5. Mußt du für _____ viel lernen? (der Fahrkurs)
6. Petra kann nicht ohne _____ fahren, denn sie hat noch keinen Führerschein. (ihr Fahrlehrer)

Students may wish to make up their own sentences and have classmates guess with whom they are speaking.

Review any prepositions with which students have difficulty.

F   Complete the following dialogue by using words from the list below.

Karten   Kino   Lust   sicher   teuer   Vorstellung

FRANK   Hast du ____, heute abend ins Konzert zu gehen?
PAUL   Wann beginnt die ____?
FRANK   Ich bin nicht ____. Ich glaube, um halb acht.
PAUL   Was kosten die ____?
FRANK   25 Mark.
PAUL   Mensch, das ist viel zu ____. Ich gehe ins ____.

G   Prepare a paragraph of from eight to ten sentences about the illustration below. You may wish to include answers to some of these questions.

1. Wie ist das Wetter heute? Scheint die Sonne? Regnet es?
2. Welche Jahreszeit ist es?
3. Wieviel Personen sind hier?
4. Wer sind sie?
5. Was tragen sie? Warum?
6. Wohin wollen sie fahren?
7. Was haben sie vor? Gehen sie Schi laufen? Zelten sie? Besuchen sie Freunde?
8. Wie lange bleiben sie?
9. Wann kommen sie zurück?

May be done orally as class project. Then assign as written homework.

Kulturlesestück

Die Bahn

In den deutschsprachigen° Ländern gibt es viele Autos. Aber viele Leute°
fahren auch noch mit der Bahn°. Die Züge sind modern, schnell und
fast immer pünktlich°. Man kann alle Städte und fast alle Städtchen°
mit dem Zug erreichen°. Und es gibt jeden Tag genug° Züge, so daß man
5 nicht viele Stunden warten° muß.

    Viele Leute fahren mit dem Zug zur Arbeit. Sie nehmen den Nah-
schnellverkehrszug°. Zwischen den großen Städten gibt es die Inter-City-
Züge. Von Land zu Land fahren die TEE-Züge°. In diesen Zügen ist der
Service besonders gut. Man kann gut essen, man kann telefonieren, man
10 kann Briefe diktieren°. Natürlich sind diese Züge teuer. Billiger sind die
D-Züge (Schnellzüge)° für weitere Reisen° und die Eilzüge° für kürzere
Reisen. Aber auch für diese Züge sind die Karten nicht gerade billig.
Trotzdem° produziert die Bahn jedes Jahr ein Defizit. Der Staat° deckt°
dieses Defizit und bezahlt jedes Jahr viele Millionen, denn alle Bahnen
15 sind staatlich°.

German-speaking /
  people
railroad
punctual / small towns
reach / enough
wait

local train
TEE =
Trans-Europ-Express
dictate
express trains / trips /
  semi-fast trains
nevertheless / state /
  covers
owned by the state

Additional information
to line 5 of reading: For
example, there are ap-
proximately 45 trains
daily from Hamburg to
Hannover, and about
5-6 daily from Frankfurt
to Munich, depending
on the day of the week
and the season.

1. In den deutschsprachigen Ländern fahren viele Leute mit der Bahn, denn es gibt wenige Autos.
2. Die Züge sind fast immer pünktlich.
3. Mit dem Zug kann man alle Großstädte erreichen.
4. Leider muß man oft lange warten, denn es gibt nicht genug Züge.
5. Zur Arbeit nehmen alle Leute einen Inter-City-Zug.
6. Von der Schweiz nach Dänemark kann man mit einem TEE-Zug fahren.
7. Für lange Reisen fährt man mit dem Eilzug.
8. Es ist nicht teuer, mit dem Zug zu fahren, denn der Staat bezahlt jedes Jahr Millionen.
9. Die Bahn verliert jedes Jahr viel Geld.
10. Die Bahn in den deutschsprachigen Ländern ist privat.

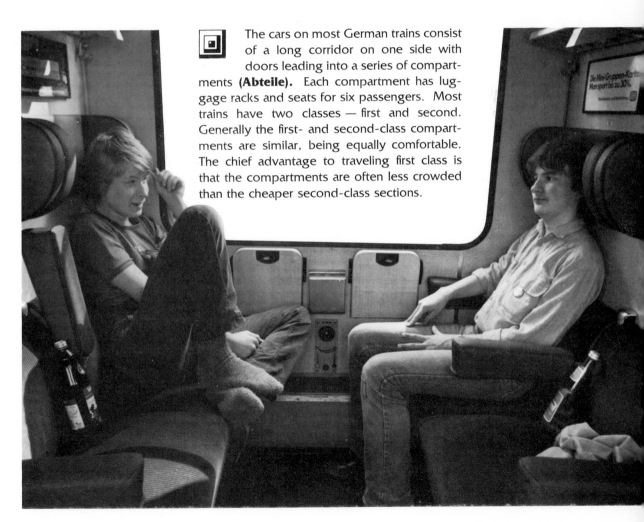

The cars on most German trains consist of a long corridor on one side with doors leading into a series of compartments **(Abteile).** Each compartment has luggage racks and seats for six passengers. Most trains have two classes — first and second. Generally the first- and second-class compartments are similar, being equally comfortable. The chief advantage to traveling first class is that the compartments are often less crowded than the cheaper second-class sections.

Vokabeln

SUBSTANTIVE

die Autobahn, -en   expressway
das Benzin   gasoline
die Bremse, -n   brake
der Bus, -se   bus
die Diskussion, -en   discussion, debate
das Fahrrad, ⸚er   bicycle
der Fahrlehrer, -   driving instructor
die Fahrschule, -n   driving school
die Fahrstunde, -n   driving lesson
das Flugzeug, -e   airplane
der Führerschein, -e   driver's license
der Kurs, -e   course
das Mofa, -s   moped, motorbike
das Motorrad, ⸚er   motorcycle
die Prüfung, -en   exam, test
das Rad, ⸚er   bicycle (*short for* **das Fahrrad**); wheel
das Schiff, -e   ship
der See, -n   lake
die Straßenbahn, -en   streetcar
die Tour, -en   tour, trip
der Traum, ⸚e   dream
die U-Bahn, -en   subway
der Unterricht   lesson, instruction
der VW   (Volkswagen)
der Zug, ⸚e   train

VERBEN

beschreiben (beschrieben)   to describe
bestehen (bestanden): die Prüfung bestehen   to pass a test
durch·fallen (ä; ist durchgefallen)   to fail, to flunk
erzählen   to tell
fliegen (ist geflogen)   to fly

ANDERE WÖRTER

auf (+ *acc. or dat.*)   on
eifersüchtig   jealous
langsam   slowly
mit (+ *dat.*)   with; by (*of vehicles*)
niemand   no one
praktisch   practical
pro   per
schnell   fast
unabhängig   independent
unsicher   dangerous; unsure, insecure
was für ein   what kind of
zwischen (+ *acc. or dative*)   between

BESONDERE AUSDRÜCKE

halt mir die Daumen   cross your fingers for me (*literally:* hold your thumbs for me)
Schwein haben   to be lucky
1 Liter auf 10 Kilometer   10 kilometers to the liter
an den See   to the lake

Ein Stadtbesuch

Wohin gehen wir denn nun?

The frequency of the *Klassenfahrt* depends on the school, teacher, and students involved.

Kai, Lore und Dieter gehen in Frankfurt zur Schule. Fast jedes Jahr macht ihre Klasse eine Klassenfahrt. Dieses Jahr sind sie nach Bayern gefahren, nach München. Am Tag besuchen sie Museen und Kirchen; oder sie bummeln durch die Fußgängerzone, vom Rathaus zum Karlsplatz und zurück. Aber abends wollen sie keine Museen und Kirchen sehen; abends wollen sie tanzen gehen.

Karlsplatz is also known in Munich as *Stachus*.

Jetzt stehen Kai und Lore vor ihrem Hotel.

The *Western Club* is a fictitious discotheque.

KAI	Wollen wir hier noch lange stehen? Wohin gehen wir denn nun?
LORE	Dieter sagt, daß die Musik im *Western Club* ganz toll ist. Aber wo ist denn der *Western Club*?
KAI	Da kommt der Dieter. Frag ihn doch! Er weiß ja immer alles.
LORE	Dieter, sag mal, wo ist der *Western Club*?
DIETER	In Schwabing.
KAI	Mensch, das ist aber weit! Wie kommen wir denn nach Schwabing?
DIETER	Ihr könnt mit der U-Bahn fahren, mit der Drei oder der Sechs. Ihr könnt aber auch laufen.
KAI	Zu Fuß nach Schwabing?
DIETER	Ja, es ist nur eine halbe Stunde von hier.
LORE	Willst du nicht mitkommen?
DIETER	Ach nein.
LORE	Warum denn nicht?
DIETER	Weil ich zu müde bin.
KAI	Das kannst du doch sehen, Mensch. Er schläft ja schon fast.
LORE	Na gut, dann gehen wir also allein. Gute Nacht, Dieter, schlaf gut!

The American West has long been a popular subject in Germany. Students may be interested in hearing about Karl May and his widely read books with characters such as Old Shatterhand, Winnetou, Sam Hawkins, etc.

Fragen

1. Wo wohnen Kai und Lore?
2. Wie oft macht ihre Klasse eine Klassenfahrt?
3. Wo sind die Schüler dieses Jahr?
4. Was besuchen die Schüler am Tag? Wo bummeln sie?
5. Was machen sie am Abend?
6. Wo ist die Musik ganz toll?
7. Mit welcher U-Bahn können Lore und Kai fahren?
8. Warum geht Dieter nicht tanzen?

Du hast das Wort

Ask a classmate how he/she came to school today.

Wie bist du heute zur Schule gekommen?

Zu Fuß.
Mit dem Rad / Bus / Auto.
Mit der Straßenbahn / U-Bahn.
[Mein Vater] hat mich gefahren.

Du hast das Wort

Ask a classmate to locate various landmarks on the map of Munich.

1. Wieviele Museen kannst du auf dem Stadtplan finden? Wie heißen sie? Wo sind sie?
2. Wieviele Kirchen kannst du finden? Wieviele Theater? Tore°? Märkte?

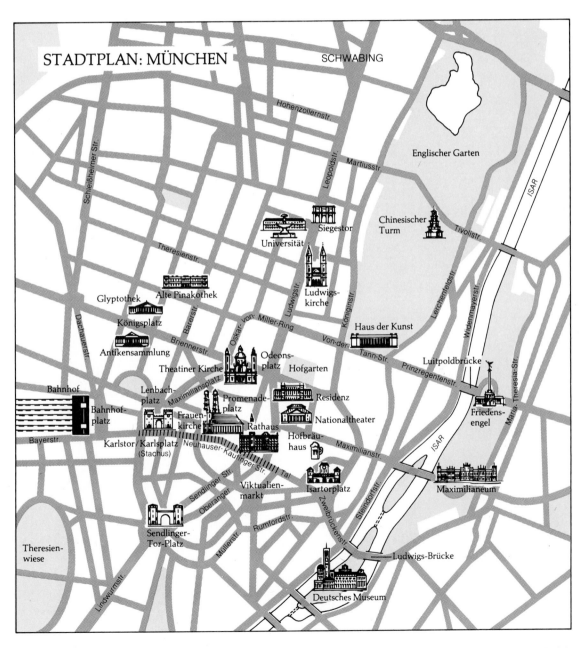

STADTPLAN: MÜNCHEN

SCHWABING

Hohenzollernstr.

Englischer Garten

Martiusstr.

Leopoldstr.

Schleißheimer Str.

Chinesischer Turm

Tivolistr.

ISAR

Universität

Siegestor

Theresienstr.

Barerstr.

Ludwigstr.

Glyptothek

Alte Pinakothek

Ludwigs-kirche

Königsplatz

Oskar-von-Miller-Ring

Brienerstr.

Haus der Kunst

Lerchenfeldstr.

Widenmayerstr.

Antikensammlung

Von-der-Tann-Str.

Luitpoldbrücke

Prinzregentenstr.

Theatiner Kirche

Odeons-platz

Hofgarten

Maria-Theresia-Str.

Dachauerstr.

Bahnhof

Lenbach-platz

Maximiliansplatz

Promenade-platz

Residenz

Friedens-engel

Bahnhof-platz

Frauen-kirche

Rathaus

Nationaltheater

Bayerstr.

Karlstor / Karlsplatz
(Stachus)

Neuhauser-Kaufinger-Str.

Tal

Hofbräu-haus

Maximilianstr.

ISAR

Steinsdorfstr.

Maximilianeum

Sendlinger Str.

Viktualien-markt

Isartorplatz

Oberanger

Müllerstr.

Rumfordstr.

Zweibrückenstr.

Sendlinger-Tor-Platz

Ludwigs-Brücke

Lindwurmstr.

Theresien-wiese

Deutsches Museum

Wie kommen wir zum Western Club?

Jetzt sind Kai und Lore in Schwabing, aber sie können den Western Club nicht finden.

KAI	Ich bin froh, daß wir mit der Bahn gefahren sind.
LORE	Ja, aber wo ist denn nun der *Western Club*?
KAI	Schau doch mal in den Stadtplan!
LORE	Ich habe ihn nicht. Hast du ihn denn vergessen?
KAI	So scheint's. Dann müssen wir wohl jemanden fragen. Entschuldigung! Können Sie uns sagen, wie wir zum *Western Club* kommen?
STUDENT	Ja, das kann ich. Ihr geht geradeaus bis zur Ampel. Bei der Ampel geht ihr rechts. Dann wieder geradeaus, bis ihr zu einem Platz mit einem Brunnen kommt. Da geht ihr links. Dann seht ihr das Schild mit dem großen Stiefel schon.
KAI	Vielen Dank!
STUDENT	Bitte schön. Oh, Moment mal. Da fällt mir gerade ein — der *Western Club* hat heute zu.
LORE	Nein, so ein Pech! Was machen wir denn nun?
STUDENT	Geht doch zu *Alfons.* Bei *Alfons* ist auch viel los. Das ist auch ein Studentenlokal.

Students may enjoy word *Pechvogel.*

Fragen

1. Wie sind Kai und Lore nach Schwabing gekommen?
2. Wer hat den Stadtplan?
3. Wen fragen sie, wo der *Western Club* ist?
4. Was für ein Schild hat der *Western Club*?
5. Warum können Lore und Kai nicht in den *Western Club*?
6. Was für ein Lokal ist *Alfons*?

Du hast das Wort

Take the role of a native of Munich. Have a classmate take the role of a stranger who asks for directions.

Entschuldigung, wie komme ich vom Bahnhof° [zum Karlsplatz]?
Entschuldigung, ich suche° [die Marienkirche].

Gehen Sie immer geradeaus!
Gehen Sie diese Straße entlang°, bis Sie zu [einer Kirche / einem Tor] kommen!
Gehen Sie die nächste Straße [rechts]!
An der Kreuzung° biegen° Sie [links] ab!
Gehen Sie um die Ecke°!

Schwabing started as a village populated by Swabians, who came from Baden-Württemberg. They continued to speak their Swabian dialect for a while and the village remained outside the Munich city limits. Today Schwabing is a district of Munich which is often compared with the Latin Quarter in Paris. Its close proximity to the university and the Academy of Fine Arts attracts many people with artistic and intellectual interests.

Schwabing is an exciting place to live in and visit. The streets come alive in the early afternoon, and during the **Kaffeestunde** the many sidewalk cafés are filled with people. Sidewalk artists attract onlookers and young people peddle paintings, jewelry, and other handmade items.

By evening, it is often hard to make one's way through the crowded streets as local inhabitants and tourists head for the more than 300 restaurants, pubs, or wine taverns. Like Lore and Kai, young people also come to Schwabing to hear jazz or rock or to dance in the discos.

Wortschatzerweiterung

Was findet man in einer Stadt?

1. die Bank
2. die Kirche
3. das Museum
4. der Park
5. die Post
6. das Rathaus
7. die Schule
8. der Supermarkt
9. die Tankstelle
10. das Warenhaus

Have students guess meaning of new words from pictures.

Other familiar places: *Café, Disco, Jugendzentrum, Kino, Restaurant.*

Listening comprehension: Give orally a series of directions based on material from the *Wortschatzerweiterung*, while students look at the *Stadtplan* on p. 319. Ask students frequently, *Wo sind wir?*

A You are expecting some exchange students from Austria. In order to give them some advance information, describe briefly your home town. You may wish to prepare a map to make your description clearer. Be sure to mention the size, what state it's in, the chief public buildings, and transportation.

Points of the compass

Game: Teacher or students describe familiar landmarks and their location. Others try to identify them:
T: *Es liegt in der Cabotstraße. Hier kann man Lebensmittel für die Woche kaufen.*
S: *Star-Supermarkt!*

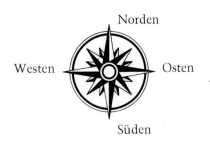

Norden
Westen
Osten
Süden

der Norden	nördlich	Norddeutschland
der Osten	östlich	Ostdeutschland
der Süden	südlich	Süddeutschland
der Westen	westlich	Westdeutschland

The four points of the compass are **der**-nouns. Adjectives related to the four points of the compass end in **-lich.** The names of the points of the compass can form noun compounds.

B   Complete the statements by choosing one of the alternatives. You may wish to refer to the atlas section at the beginning of your book.

■III   München liegt in ____.   *München liegt in*
a. Norddeutschland   *Süddeutschland.*
b. Süddeutschland

1. Italien liegt in ____.   a. Südeuropa   b. Nordeuropa.
2. Kanada liegt in ____.   a. Nordamerika b. Südamerika
3. China liegt im ____.   a. Westen   b. Osten
4. Hamburg liegt in ____.   a. Norddeutschland b. Süddeutschland
5. Schweden liegt in ____.   a. Nordeuropa   b. Südeuropa

Word families

die **Arbeit**	the work
arbeiten	to work
die **Arbeit**erin	the worker

Like English, German has many words that belong to "families" which are derived from a common stem.

C   Give the English equivalents of the following words.

1. die Klasse, die Klassenfahrt, der Klassenlehrer, die Klassenarbeit
2. einkaufen, kaufen, der Käufer, die Verkäuferin, verkaufen, das Kaufhaus, der Einkäufer, der Kauf, der Verkauf

Some of the sights in Munich: **Nymphenburg Palace** was built in the 17th century for the Bavarian rulers. The **Karlstor** stands at one end of the pedestrian **Neuhauser-Kaufinger Straße**. At the other end is the neo-Gothic **Neues Rathaus** with its famous **Glockenspiel**.

324

Aussprache

| [l]   al**l**e, **l**ese, vie**l**, küh**l**
| [ŋ]   Ju**ng**e, Hu**ng**er, Sä**ng**er

To produce the German **l,** place the tip of the tongue against the upper gum ridge, as in English, but keep the tongue flat. A very tight smile helps. Many Americans use this *l*-sound in such words as *million*, *billion*, and *William*.

    The combination **ng** is pronounced [ŋ], as in English *singer*. It does not contain the sound [g] as in English *finger*.

Additional proverbs: *Mit gefangen, mit gehangen. Einem geschenkten Gaul sieht man nicht ins Maul.*

A   Practice the following words vertically in columns.

[l]		[ŋ]	
al**l**e	**l**assen	Ju**ng**e	Fi**ng**er
Ju**l**i	**l**esen	Frühli**ng**	lä**ng**er
wei**l**	**L**ehrer	Vorstellu**ng**	Hu**ng**er
Fi**l**m	B**l**ume	kli**ng**eln	si**ng**en
to**ll**	F**l**amme	Di**ng**e	hä**ng**en

B   Practice the sounds [l] and [ŋ]. Read the sentences aloud.

1. Im Frühling werden die Tage länger.
2. Der Junge kauft eine tolle Platte.
3. Du hast das Flugzeugmodell wohl selbst gebastelt.

Proverb: Good things come in threes.

Aller guten Dinge sind drei.

Das Olympiagelände ist jetzt ein Park.

—————— Übungen ——————

Prepositions with the dative case

The prepositions **aus, außer, bei, mit, nach, seit, von,** and **zu** are always used with the dative case.

mit   with, by means of

Ingrid fährt **mit** dem Zug.   Ingrid goes *by (means of)* train.
Sie fährt **mit** ihrer Schwester.   She goes *with* her sister.

A   Erik wants to go to the Olympic Village in the northern part of Munich. Assure him that he can use any of the following means of transportation.

■⫿   Kann ich die Straßenbahn nehmen?   *Natürlich kannst du*
                                            mit der Straßen-
                                            bahn fahren!

1. Kann ich den Bus nehmen?   3. Kann ich das Auto nehmen?
2. Kann ich die U-Bahn   4. Kann ich das Rad nehmen?
   nehmen?

bei   at, with

Brigitte ist **bei** ihren Großeltern.   Brigitte is *at* her grandparents'.
Kurt wohnt **bei** seinen Großeltern.   Kurt lives *with* his grandparents.

B   Gisela wants to know what your plans are. Tell her with whom you're going to do various things.

> ▪ꜱ   Ißt du bei deinen Groß-   *Ja, bei meinen Großeltern.*
> eltern zu Mittag?

1. Trinkst du bei deiner Schwester Kaffee?
2. Siehst du bei deinem Bruder fern?
3. Spielst du bei Rudi Karten?
4. Hörst du bei Monika Musik?

Du hast das Wort   Ask a classmate with whom he/she does various things.

Bei wem ißt du zu Abend?
Bei wem hörst du Musik?
Bei wem siehst du fern?

aus   out of, from (= is a native of)

Udo kommt **aus** dem Haus.   Udo comes *out of* the house.
Monika kommt **aus** Frank-   Monika comes *from* Frankfurt.
furt.

C   State that the following people have just come from the places named.

Other places: der Su-permarkt, der Club, die Diskothek, die Kirche, das Kino, das Museum.

> ▪ꜱ   Paul und Dieter / Lokal   *Paul und Dieter kommen gerade*
> *aus dem Lokal.*

1. Lore und Frank / Café   4. Grete und Liese / Bank
2. Paula und Regina /   5. Ingrid und Jan / Post
   Warenhaus
3. Gerd und Ilse / Restaurant

D   You've met some new people at the youth hostel, and you want them to meet your friends. Introduce them as in the model.

> ▪ꜱ   Maria / München   *Das ist Maria. Sie kommt aus*
> *München.*

1. Gerhard / Frankfurt   4. Rudi / Bern
2. Anja / Hamburg   5. Helga / Berlin
3. Günter / Wien

von   from

Was hörst du **von** deiner
Freundin Meike?

What do you hear *from* your
friend Meike?

E   Jan has just heard from various reliable sources that summer vacation
will start a week early. Ask him for reassurance that he really did hear
the news from those sources.

■ⅱ   Mein Bruder hat es gesagt.

*Hast du das wirklich von
deinem Bruder gehört?*

1. Meine Schwester hat es gesagt.
2. Mein Vater hat es gesagt.
3. Meine Lehrerin hat es gesagt.
4. Meine Großeltern haben es gesagt.

*Additional cues: mein
Lehrer, mein Freund,
meine Mutter, unser
Arzt, unser Metzger,
unser Bäcker.*

Point out that there are
two prepositions in Ger-
man for English "from":
aus and *von*. *Von* is
used with names of cit-
ies, countries, etc. to
denote departure after
a temporary stay; *aus* is
used to indicate place
of birth: *Der Zug ist
gerade* von *Köln ge-
kommen. Carlos ist* aus
Mexiko.

zu   to

Help students discover that going *zu* a person can
mean going to that person's house.

Ich gehe heute abend **zu**
meinem Freund Udo.

I'm going *to* my friend Udo's this
evening.

F   You're visiting your pen pal in Frankfurt, and you've received many invitations from her friends and relatives. Ask her to specify the time of each
invitation.

■ⅱ   Mein Freund Jochen hat
uns für Dienstag eingela-
den.

*Um wieviel Uhr gehen wir
zu deinem Freund?*

1. Meine Freundin Christl hat uns für Donnerstag eingeladen.
2. Meine Großeltern haben uns für Samstag eingeladen.
3. Meine Schwester hat uns für Sonntag eingeladen.
4. Mein Bruder hat uns für Montag eingeladen.

Vary with additional
cues:
T: *Wohin gehst du
heute abend?*
S: *Ich gehe zu Udo
(mein Lehrer, meine
Lehrerin, Frau Schmidt,
Herr Lange, etc.).*

nach   to, after

Wir fahren **nach** München.

We're driving *to* Munich.

The preposition **nach,** used with cities and countries, is equivalent to
English *to (in the direction of).*

Nach dem Essen gehen wir
ins Kino.

After dinner we'll go to the movies.

The preposition **nach** is also equivalent to English *after.*

G   Say that you're going to visit the places your friend asks about.

■ⅲ   Möchtest du Deutschland sehen?   *Ja. Ich fahre im
                                            Sommer nach
                                            Deutschland.*

1.   Besuchst du auch Bayern?
2.   Dann besuchst du sicher auch München?
3.   Du möchtest dann auch Österreich sehen, nicht?
4.   Und Wien?

H   Ask whether the following people are really coming home after the time
mentioned.

■ⅲ   Schmidts bleiben zwei   *Kommen sie dann nach
        Monate in Berlin.   zwei Monaten zurück?*

1.   Schneiders bleiben einen Monat in Zürich.
2.   Hofers bleiben zwei Wochen in Zermatt.
3.   Langes bleiben zehn Tage in Salzburg.
4.   Wagners bleiben eine Woche in Kiel.

Du hast das Wort   Ask a classmate when he/she does various things.

Wann gehst du ins Kino? Nach dem Essen?
Wann spielst du Tennis? Nach der Schule?
Wann machst du Hausaufgaben? Nach der Arbeit?

Blick auf das Alte Rathaus (links unten) in München.

seit since, for

Christl ist **seit** einem
  Monat in München.

Christl has been in Munich *for* a
  month.

To express an action or condition that started in the past but is still continuing in the present, German often uses the present tense and a time phrase with **seit**.

I Lore asks you how long certain things have been going on. Confirm her guesses as to the exact period of time.

■ⅲ Wie lange ist Gerd schon in   *Ja, seit einem Monat.*
    Hamburg? Einen Monat?

1. Wie lange ist Gabi schon in Österreich? Ein Jahr?
2. Wie lange ist Frank schon krank? Vier Wochen?
3. Wie lange hat er nichts gegessen? Drei Tage?
4. Wie lange ist dein Auto schon kaputt? Eine Woche?

Free response:
T: *Wie lange spielst du schon Tennis?*
S: *Seit zwei Jahren (einem Monat, gestern, etc.).*
T: *Wie lange wohnst du schon in ...? Wie lange lernst du schon Deutsch? Wie lange läufst du Schi? etc.*

außer besides, except

Was hast du **außer** dem
  Museum gesehen?

What did you see *besides* the
  museum?

Ich habe nichts **außer** dem
  Museum gesehen.

I saw nothing *except* the museum.

J Birgit lists the sights she and her classmates saw in Munich. Inquire what else they saw.

■ⅲ Wir haben das Rathaus gesehen.   *Was habt ihr außer dem*
                                          Rathaus gesehen?

1. Wir haben das Hofbräuhaus gesehen.
2. Wir haben die Fußgängerzone gesehen.
3. Wir haben die Frauenkirche gesehen.
4. Wir haben die Isar gesehen.
5. Wir haben die Straßencafés gesehen.
6. Wir haben die Theater gesehen.

Point out that the two meanings in English — *except for, besides* — depend on whether the sentence is positive or negative.

330

Dative prepositional contractions

Unser Radio ist **beim** Elektriker.
Ich komme gerade **vom** Elektriker.
Gehst du jetzt **zum** Supermarkt?
Ja, ich gehe auch **zur** Bank.

bei dem > **beim**
vom dem > **vom**
zu dem > **zum**
zu der > **zur**

The contractions **beim, vom, zum,** and **zur** are frequently used.

K Say you already have been at the places mentioned. Use the appropriate dative prepositional contractions.

■║ Gehst du jetzt zum Bäcker? *Nein, beim Bäcker war ich schon.*

1. Gehst du jetzt zum Metzger?
2. Gehst du jetzt zum Elektriker?
3. Gehst du jetzt zum Friseur?
4. Gehst du jetzt zum Arzt?

L You are lost in a strange city. Ask a police officer for directions to the following places.

■║ die Post *Können Sie mir sagen, wie ich zur Post komme?*

1. die Bank
2. das Museum
3. das Rathaus
4. der Bahnhof
5. die Fußgängerzone
6. der *Western Club*
7. das Theater

M You're thinking of accompanying Petra on her errands, but you're tired. Ask her how far it is from one place to the next.

May be done with
books open.

■║ Ich muß zum Bäcker und zur Apotheke.

Wie weit ist es vom Bäcker zur Apotheke?

■║ Dann gehe ich zum Metzger.

Wie weit ist es von der Apotheke zum Metzger?

1. Ich muß dann zum Markt.
2. Dann gehe ich zum Warenhaus.
3. Und dann gehe ich zum Elektriker.
4. Ich gehe dann zur Post.
5. Dann muß ich noch zur Bank.

Du hast das Wort

A. Tell various classmates they need an item and ask where they would go to get it.

▪▥ Du brauchst [Wurst]. Wohin gehst du?   [*Zum Metzger.*]

Du brauchst | Brot.
Briefmarken.
Milch.
Geld.
Benzin.
Obst.

B. You notice that various classmates have bought certain items. Ask them where they were.

▪▥ Du hast [Brot] gekauft. Wo warst du?   [*Beim Bäcker.*]

Du hast | Gemüse | gekauft.
eine Torte
einen Mantel

Schools in the **BRD** occasionally close for a day so that teachers and students can go on an outing. On these days **(Wandertage)** the classes go hiking or visit a local place of interest — Roman ruins, an old castle, or a hill used by glider pilots, for example. The relatively short distances between historical sights make it possible to have several interesting **Wandertage** in a year.

An individual class sometimes takes a longer trip **(Klassenfahrt).** In the winter or early spring they may go on a week-long skiing trip. Other classes may choose to visit some city in order to explore its museums, churches, and historical sights. These trips are part of the school program and expenses are kept down by subsidies from the town.

Nächstes Jahr fährt unsere Klasse nach Heidelberg.
(Alte Brücke und Schloß)

Grammatische Übersicht

Prepositions with the dative case (A-J)

aus	Udo geht **aus** dem Haus.	Udo goes *out* of the house.
	Andrea kommt **aus** Wien.	Andrea comes *from* Vienna.
außer	**Außer** meinem Freund war mein Bruder da.	*Besides* my friend, my brother was there.
	Ich esse alles gern **außer** Fisch.	I like everything *except* fish.
bei	Sonja ist **bei** ihrer Freundin.	Sonja is *with* her friend.
		Sonja is *at* her friend's.
mit	Rita spricht **mit** dem Verkäufer.	Rita is speaking *with* the salesman.
	Udo fährt **mit** dem Bus.	Udo is going *by* bus.
nach	Gabi fliegt **nach** Berlin.	Gabi is flying *to* Berlin.
	Nach dem Essen gehen wir schwimmen.	*After* dinner we're going swimming.
seit	**Seit** dem Essen habe ich Durst.	I've been thirsty *since* dinner.
	Schmidts wohnen **seit** einem Jahr in Berlin.	Schmidts have been living in Berlin *for* a year.
von	Günter kommt gerade **von** der Party.	Günter is just coming *from* the party.
	Das Geschenk ist **von** seinen Eltern.	The present is *from* his parents.
	Sprichst du **von** meinem Freund?	Are you speaking *of* my friend?
zu	Petra geht **zu** ihrer Freundin.	Petra is going *to* her friend's.
	Sie hat sie **zu** einer Party eingeladen.	She invited her *to* a party.

The prepositions **aus, außer, bei, mit, nach, seit, von,** and **zu** are always used with the dative case.

Nach, used with cities and countries, is equivalent to English *to.* In most other instances the equivalent of *to* is **zu.**

Seit + present tense is used in German to express an action or condition that started in the past but is still continuing in the present. English uses the present perfect tense with *since* or *for.*

Dative prepositional contractions (K-M)

Unser Fernseher ist **beim** Elektriker.	bei dem > **beim**
Ich komme gerade **vom** Elektriker.	von dem > **vom**
Gehst du **zum** Supermarkt?	zu dem > **zum**
Ja, und dann gehe ich **zur** Post.	zu der > **zur**

The contractions **beim, vom, zum,** and **zur** are frequently used.

Wiederholung

A   Choose the place in column B that is associated with each statement in column A. Supply the definite article for each noun in column B.

A	B
1. Ich brauche Geld.	a. Bahnhof
2. Ich habe Briefmarken gekauft.	b. Bank
3. Ich möchte einen neuen Mantel kaufen.	c. Café
4. Am Sonntag machen wir immer einen schönen Spaziergang.	d. Kino
5. Orangen sind heute besonders preiswert.	e. Park
6. Frank ist leider durchgefallen.	f. Post
7. Die Vorstellung beginnt um sieben Uhr.	g. Schule
8. Möchtest du eine Cola trinken?	h. Supermarkt
9. Wir fahren mit dem Zug nach Salzburg.	i. Warenhaus

B   Complete each sentence with an appropriate dative preposition.

1. Am Montag bin ich _____ meinem Bruder gefahren. Er wohnt in München.
2. Ich habe _____ meinem Bruder und seiner Frau in Schwabing gewohnt. Sie wohnen _____ einem Jahr da.
3. Mein Bruder hat nicht immer in München gewohnt. Er kommt _____ Köln, wie ich.
4. Ich bin oft _____ meinem Bruder und seiner Frau im Englischen Garten spazierengegangen.
5. _____ seinem Haus bis zum Englischen Garten ist es nicht so weit.
6. In die Stadt sind wir dann _____ der U-Bahn gefahren.
7. Am Freitag muß ich _____ Köln zurück.
8. In den fünf Tagen habe ich sehr viel _____ München gesehen.

C   Make sense out of the following sentences by replacing the italicized phrase with the phrase in parentheses. Make any other necessary changes.

1. Frau Wächter geht mit *ihrer Geige* einkaufen. (ihr Mann)
2. Sie bummelt durch *den Brunnen*. (die Fußgängerzone)
3. Frau Wächter arbeitet bei *der Ampel*. (die Post)
4. Frau Wächter schreibt ihre Briefe mit *einer Flöte*. (ein Kugelschreiber)
5. Sie kauft oft Geschenke für *ihren Metzger*. (ihre Familie)
6. Sie geht nicht ohne *ihren Fernseher* in die Stadt. (ihre Einkaufstasche)
7. Frau Wächter trinkt Cola aus *einer Socke*. (ein Glas)

D   Compare the following items, using the adjective or adverb in parentheses.

1. Schallplatten sind ＿＿ als Cassetten. (billig)
2. Dieses Radio ist nicht so ＿＿ wie dieser Cassetten-Recorder. (teuer)
3. Kostet der Cassetten-Recorder so ＿＿ wie der Plattenspieler? (viel)
4. Dieser Plattenspieler ist viel ＿＿ als der Plattenspieler da. (gut)
5. Der Preis im Radiogeschäft ist viel ＿＿ als der Preis im Warenhaus. (hoch)
6. Ich spiele Platten ＿＿ als Cassetten. (gern)

E   Complete the second sentence in each pair by reporting what Kai and Lore said.

    ■III   Kai sagt: „Ich bin mit meiner Klasse nach München gefahren."
            Kai sagt, daß er *mit seiner Klasse nach München gefahren ist.*

1. Kai sagt: „Wir haben eine Klassenfahrt gemacht."
   Kai sagt, daß sie . . .
2. Lore fragt: „Habt ihr viele Museen und Kirchen besucht?"
   Lore fragt, ob sie . . .
3. Kai sagt: „Wir sind ins Deutsche Museum gegangen."
   Kai sagt, . . .
4. Lore fragt: „Seid ihr auch durch die Fußgängerzone gebummelt?"
   Lore fragt, . . .

Viele Münchner fahren nach Garmisch-Partenkirchen zum Schifahren.

335

F Express the following dialogue in German.

May personalize and
perform as skit.

GISELA	Do you know where the Western Club is?
SABINE	Naturally. In Schwabing.
TORSTEN	Is that far from here?
SABINE	To Schwabing? No. You can go by subway.
GISELA	Can we go on foot?
SABINE	Sure. I'll come along.
TORSTEN	Ask Anke whether she wants to come along too.
SABINE	All right. She likes to dance.

G Write two postcards from Kai and Lore telling about the highlights of their class trip to Munich. Have Kai write to his parents, while Lore writes to one of her friends. You may want to mention some of the following places and activities.

Schwabing   mit der U-Bahn fahren
Museen   bummeln
Fußgängerzone   tanzen

Munich, with its population of over 1 million, is one of the most popular cities in the BRD. Located on the Isar river, only an hour's ride from the Alps and famous lakes such as the Tegernsee, Chiemsee, and Starnberger See, Munich attracts tourists from other parts of Germany as well as from other countries. The city has many beautiful churches, impressive palaces, important museums, excellent theaters, and extensive parks. The following places are just some of the attractions.

The **Deutsches Museum** is an important museum devoted to science and technology.

The **Alte Pinakothek** contains one of the most famous art collections in the world.

The **Frauenkirche,** with its onion domes, has long been one of the symbols of Munich.

The **Hofbräuhaus** is a popular tourist attraction, offering music, beer, sausages, and atmosphere.

The **Englischer Garten,** a large park with lakes and wooded areas, is a popular place for afternoon strolls.

Wien

Touristen in Österreich wollen oft *eine* Stadt ganz bestimmt° sehen: definitely
Wien, die Hauptstadt. Wien hat viele schöne alte Kirchen wie zum Bei-
spiel° den Stephansdom. Und es hat schöne Schlösser°. Schloß Schön-   for example / palaces
brunn ist die frühere° Sommerresidenz der Kaiser°. Mitten° in der Stadt   former / der Kaiser: of the emperors / in the middle
5 steht die Hofburg, die frühere Winterresidenz der Kaiser.

    Wien hat berühmte° Cafés. Das Kaffeehaus *Zur blauen Flasche* soll   famous
das älteste° in der deutschsprachigen° Welt° sein. Und Wien hat The-   oldest / German-speaking / world
ater und Museen. Das Kunsthistorische Museum gehört° zu den besten   belongs
Museen in der Welt.

10   Wenn man an Wien denkt, denkt man vor allem° an Musik. Viele   vor allem: above all
kennen die Wiener Operetten und den „Walzerkönig"° Johann Strauß.   Waltz King
Mozart und Beethoven haben lange in Wien gelebt°. Die Wiener Sän-   lived
gerknaben° geben Konzerte in Wien und in der ganzen Welt.   Boys' Choir

    Touristen besuchen Wien gern. Aber auch für die Österreicher spielt
15 Wien eine große Rolle°. Es liegt am Rand° von Österreich, ziemlich weit   spielt . . . Rolle: is important / edge
im Osten. Trotzdem° ist es das politische und das kulturelle Zentrum   nevertheless
von Österreich.

A Match the items in column B with the information in column A.

A	B
1. eine schöne alte Kirche	a. Wien
2. der Walzerkönig	b. der Stephans-dom
3. die Hauptstadt von Österreich	
4. dieses Schloß steht mitten in der Stadt	c. die Hofburg
5. viele Touristen besuchen es	d. ein Wiener Kaffeehaus
6. Operetten	
7. liegt ziemlich weit im Osten	e. Musik in Wien
8. die frühere Winterresidenz der Kaiser	
9. Mozart	
10. das politische und kulturelle Zentrum von Österreich	
11. Sängerknaben	
12. das älteste in der deutschsprachigen Welt	

Schloß Belvedere in Wien

Vokabeln

SUBSTANTIVE

die Ampel, -n traffic signal
die Bahn, -en train, railway
der Bahnhof, ⁻e train station
die Bank, -en bank
Bayern Bavaria
der Besuch, -e visit
der Brunnen, - fountain, well, spring
der Club, -s club
die Ecke, -n corner
die Fußgängerzone, -n pedestrian zone
die Kirche, -n church
die Klassenfahrt, -en class trip
die Kreuzung, -en intersection
das Lokal, -e place to eat, drink, dance; restaurant
das Museum, die Museen museum
der Park, -s park
der Platz, ⁻e square
die Post post office, mail
das Rathaus, ⁻er town hall
das Schild, -er sign
der Stadtplan, ⁻e city map
der Stiefel, - boot
der Student, -en, -en/die Studentin, -nen student (at a university)
die Tankstelle, -n service station, gas station
das Tor, -e gate
das Warenhaus, ⁻er department store

VERBEN

ab·biegen (ist abgebogen) to make a turn
bummeln (ist gebummelt) to go for a stroll, for a walk
schauen to look
stehen (gestanden) to stand
suchen to look for
vergessen (i; vergessen) to forget

ANDERE WÖRTER

allein alone
aus (+ *dat.*) out of, from
außer (+ *dat.*) besides, except for
bis zu up to
froh glad, happy
jemand someone
links (to the) left
rechts (to the) right
seit (+ *dat.*) since, for
weil (*sub. conj.*) because
zu shut, closed

BESONDERE AUSDRÜCKE

so scheint's so it seems
Moment mal just a moment
da fällt mir gerade ein it just occurs to me
es ist viel los there is a lot going on
so ein Pech what bad luck, how unfortunate
zu Fuß on foot
immer geradeaus straight ahead
die Straße entlang along (down) the street

A **Besuch.** Your pen pal (from the end of Stage 2) has just written that he/she will soon have the opportunity to visit you and would like to know what to expect. Write a reply in which you explain what your friend may find different in your area. You may wish to compare some or all of the following: geography, landscape, weather, food, meals, transportation to school and into town, and town landmarks such as a market, pedestrian zone, town hall, museums.

B **Guten Appetit!** As a class project, assemble a German meal. Plan a menu, with individual students or small groups volunteering to prepare the various foods. At the dinner, each student should receive a booklet in English and German containing the menu and the recipes for each dish. Be sure to set the table and to eat as a German family would.

As an extension of this activity, or as an alternative, your class may want to compile a cookbook of favorite German recipes. If there are German-speaking people in the community, members of the class could ask them for suggestions as to what to include.

C **Eine deutsche Stadt.** In groups of four to five, prepare poster displays of a city in a German-speaking country. Provide a map of the city; draw or cut out of magazines pictures of famous buildings, and label them. Select a speaker to present a brief report on the city, using the poster.

D **Ein Geschenk.** You've been spending the summer with a family in Switzerland. Now that you're about to leave, you want to get them a present to express your gratitude; but you're not sure what to buy. Choose a partner to take the role of a salesperson in a department store. Create a dialogue in which the salesperson tries to help you make a decision by asking questions about the family's tastes and interests. As the salesperson finds out more about the family, he/she can offer various suggestions. You may want to bring in props to help you perform the dialogue.

E **Im Verkehrsamt.** Because you can speak German, you have been given a job in an information center **(das Verkehrsamt)** of the city of your choice (for example, Hamburg, Berlin, Salzburg, or Basel). Your task is to assist strangers in town. Learn about the sights in these cities. Several of your classmates will then play the role of tourist. When they ask which sights you recommend and how to get there, you give them the correct information. You may want to begin by asking how long they are staying and what their particular interests are — museums, theater, shopping, and so on.

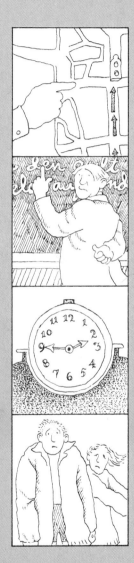

F **Deutsche in Amerika.** At the end of Stage 1, one of the suggested activities was to look briefly into the extent of German influence in your area — German city names and names in a telephone book. Now go into this question more deeply. Are there any stores or shops near you owned or managed by native speakers of German? Members of local government? Teachers or others employed in an educational capacity, such as in a museum or in an institute on German culture? Perhaps there is a town or a historic sight with a German name you can investigate. If possible, you may want to conduct interviews or prepare a description.

G **Ein Spiel.** The class is divided into two teams. Each team has 15 minutes to compile a list of questions that elicit information from Chapters 10–15. The questions may concern either the introductory reading material in each chapter, or the **Kulturlesestücke.** For example, a question from Chapter 14 might be, "Mit wieviel Jahren darf man in Deutschland Auto fahren?" Members of both teams take turns asking the questions of members of the opposing team. The team with the most correct answers wins.

H **Kleines Theater.** The class is divided into pairs or small groups. Each group or set of partners makes up a skit consisting solely of dialogue lines from Chapters 1–15. Try to invent comical situations or funny sequences of lines. A variation of this activity would be to have the class as a whole make up a dialogue, with students adding lines spontaneously.

Ein Problem. Create a skit in which you must solve a problem. In it, be sure to include expressions of apology, agreement, or disagreement. Use one of the following situations, or invent one of your own.

1. You've planned to spend an evening at a disco, then discover that it is closed. Find out where you can go instead.
2. After you have eaten a meal in a restaurant, you discover that you have no money to pay the bill.
3. You are in a German supermarket with an American friend who knows no German and isn't familiar with German customs. When your friend does something wrong — such as touching the vegetables, or not packing the groceries — you must apologize and explain to the clerks.

Ein Kreuzworträtsel. In small groups, prepare a crossword puzzle (**das Kreuzworträtsel**), using a single set of words: vocabulary relating to weather, transportation, buildings, food, shopping, and so on. When the puzzles are finished, each group exchanges its puzzle for that of another and tries to solve it.

Deutsche Touristen. You've just been approached by some German tourists who want to know what there is to see in your town. Tell them about some of the major points of interest, and direct them how to get there.

One of the tourists would like to know what is being performed at the local theater or concert hall. Tell her what's playing and explain how to get tickets.

Wo möchtest du sein? Look at the photographs on pages 225–231. In which place would you most like to be? Which person would you most like to meet? Would you choose a situation in which you feel at home and comfortable, or one which is new and different? In German, discuss your answers and the reasons for them. Then pretend that you are actually in one of the situations shown, and make up and enact a suitable dialogue. As necessary, select several classmates to work with you.

Reference

Lieder

Der Mond ist aufgegangen

Der Mond[1] ist auf-ge-gan-gen[2], die gold-nen Stern-lein[3]
der Wald[7] steht schwarz und schwei-get[8] und aus den Wie-sen[9]

pran-gen[4] am Him-mel[5] hell[6] und klar;
stei-get[10] der wei-ße Ne-bel[11]
wun-der-bar.[12]

1. moon 2. risen 3. little star 4. sparkle, shine 5. heaven 6. bright(ly) 7. forest 8. be silent 9. meadow
10. rises 11. fog, mist 12. wondrously

Himmel und Erde müssen vergehen

(Kanon)

Him-mel[1] und Er--de[2] müs-sen ver-gehn[3],

a-ber die Mu-si-ci[4], a-ber die Mu-si-ci,

a-ber die Mu-si-ci blei-ben be--stehn[5].

1. heaven 2. earth 3. pass away 4. musicians 5. last, continue

Ich bin ein Musikante[1]

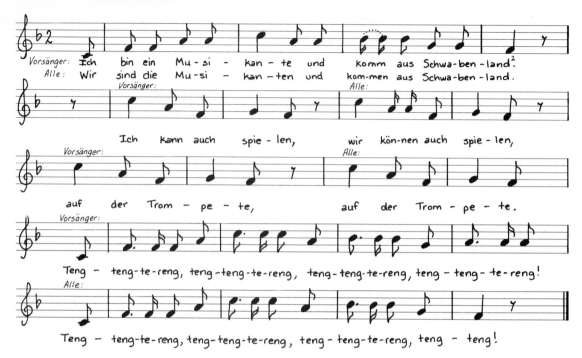

Vorsänger: Ich bin ein Mu-si-kan-te und komm aus Schwa-ben-land.[2]
Alle: Wir sind die Mu-si-kan-ten und kom-men aus Schwa-ben-land.

Vorsänger: Ich kann auch spie-len,
Alle: wir kön-nen auch spie-len,

auf der Trom-pe-te, auf der Trom-pe-te.

Vorsänger: Teng — teng-te-reng, teng-teng-te-reng, teng-teng-te-reng, teng-teng-te-reng!

Alle: Teng — teng-te-reng, teng-teng-te-reng, teng-teng-te-reng, teng-teng!

2. Auf meiner Geige,
   vidi-gei-gei-gei.

3. Auf meiner Flöte,
   didi-lid-lid-lid.

4. Auf der Klarinette,
   didi-dum-dum-dum.

5. Auf meiner Trommel,
   ti-rom-dom-dom.

6. Auf meiner Pauke,[3]
   bum-bum-de-rum.

7. Auf dem Klaviere,
   greif hier mal hin, greif da mal hin.[4]

1. musician   2. Swabia   3. drum   4. **greif . . . hin:** hit this key here, hit that key there

Heim, heim, heim

(Kanon)

Heim, heim, heim, heim, heim, heim, heim woll'n wir gehen. Lied[1] ist aus[2], Spiel ist aus,

Tanz[3] ist aus, al-les ist aus! Heim, heim, heim, heim, heim, heim, heim woll'n wir gehen!

1. song   2. over   3. dance

Gedichte

Es war ein alter König
Heinrich Heine   (1797–1856)

Es war[1] ein alter König,[2]
Sein Herz[3] war schwer, sein Haupt[4] war
 grau;
Der arme[5] alte König,
Er nahm[6] eine junge Frau.

Es war ein schöner Page,[7]
Blond[8] war sein Haupt, leicht[9] war sein
 Sinn;
Er trug[11] die seidne[12] Schleppe[13]
Der jungen Königin.[14]

Kennst du das alte Liedchen?[15]
Es klingt[16] so süß,[17] es klingt so trüb;[18]
Sie mußten[19] beide sterben,[20]
Sie hatten sich viel zu lieb.[21]

1. **Es war:** there was 2. king 3. heart 4. head (of
hair) 5. poor 6. took 7. page 8. blond 9. light,
cheerful 10. disposition, temperament 11. carried
12. silken 13. train of a dress 14. queen 15. little
song 16. sound 17. sweet 18. dark, gloomy
19. had to 20. die 21. **Sie . . . lieb:** they loved each
other too much

Erinnerung[1]
Johann Wolfgang von Goethe
(1749–1832)

Willst du immer weiter schweifen?[2]
Sieh, das Gute[3] liegt so nah.[4]
Lerne nur das Glück[5] ergreifen,[6]
Denn das Glück ist immer da.

1. reminder 2. wander, rove 3. the good 4. near
5. good fortune, happiness 6. seize

Septembermorgen
Eduard Mörike   (1804–1875)

Im Nebel[1] ruhet noch die Welt,
Noch träumen Wald und Wiesen:[2]
Bald siehst du, wenn der Schleier[3] fällt,
Den blauen Himmel unverstellt,[4]
Herbstkräftig[5] die gedämpfte[6] Welt
In warmem Golde fließen.[7]

1. fog, mist 2. meadow 3. veil 4. unconcealed
5. full of autumnal vigor 6. muted, quieted 7. to flow,
be awash

Ein Jüngling[1] liebt ein Mädchen
Heinrich Heine

Ein Jüngling liebt ein Mädchen
Die hat einen andern erwählt;[2]
Der andre liebt eine andre,
Und hat sich mit dieser vermählt.[3]

Das Mädchen heiratet aus Ärger[4]
Den ersten besten Mann,[5]
Der ihr in den Weg gelaufen;[6]
Der Jüngling ist übel dran.[7]

Es ist eine alte Geschichte,
Doch bleibt sie immer neu;
Und wem sie just[8] passieret,[9]
Dem bricht das Herz[10] entzwei.[11]

1. young man 2. chose 3. married 4. **aus Ärger:**
from vexation 5. **den . . . Mann:** the first man
6. **der . . . gelaufen:** who crossed her path 7. **ist . . . dran:**
is in a bad fix 8. by chance 9. happens to 10. heart
11. **bricht . . . entzwei:** breaks in two

ich bin total abgeschlafft I'm worn out

ein Schlaffi someone without much energy

Alte/Alter girlfriend/boyfriend (also mother/father)

anmachen: ich mache ihn an I'm trying to get to know him

mach mich nicht an! leave me alone!

Bock: ich hab' Bock auf Rock I like rock, I'm into rock

ich hab' null Bock auf Hausaufgaben I don't like homework

brettern: wir sind über die Autobahn gebrettert we drove fast down the highway

drauf sein: ich bin heute finster drauf I'm in a bad mood today

er ist ja heute irre drauf he's in a great mood today

echt very

echt gut! really good!

echt? really?

also echt (protest) aw, come on!

einsam excellent

eine echt einsame Show a really good show

die Gurke, der Ofen motorcycle

das ist ein Hammer that's unbelievable

die Karre, die Kiste automobile

die Kohle, Knete, Pinke money

labbern to talk nonsense

nerven: das nervt mich that gets on my nerves

das ist echt ein Schlauch that's exhausting

schnallen to understand

das hab' ich geschnallt I understood it

stark, groovy, super, irre great, really nice

mir stinkt's I've had enough, I'm tired of it

da tick' ich voll durch! I get it!

tote Hose: alles ist tote Hose nothing's going on

Trouble haben, bekommen, machen to have, get, make trouble

wegflippen to lose one's nerve

ich flip' gleich weg I'm losing my nerve

German first names

The following list includes some of the most popular German names. It is not a complete list of first names.

girls

Alexandra	Jutta
Andrea	Karin
Anita	Katja
Anja	Katrin
Anke	Kerstin
Anne	Lore
Antje	Margit
Astrid	Margret
Barbara	Maria
Beate	Marianne
Bettina	Marion
Birgit	Martina
Brigitte	Meike
Carola	Melanie
Christa	Michaela
Christine	Monika
Claudia	Nadine
Cornelia	Nicole
Dagmar	Nina
Daniela	Petra
Doris	Regina
Elisabeth	Renate
Erika	Rita
Elke	Ruth
Ellen	Sabine
Gabi	Sandra
Gabriele	Silke
Gisela	Sonja
Grete	Stephanie
Gudrun	Sybille
Hannelore	Sylvia
Heidi	Susanne
Heike	Suse
Ilse	Tanja
Inge	Ulla
Ingrid	Ulrike
Irene	Ute
Iris	Veronika
Isabelle	Yvonne
Julia	

boys

Alex	Lars
Alexander	Lothar
Andreas	Lutz
Axel	Manfred
Benjamin	Mark
Benno	Markus
Bernd	Martin
Burkhard	Matthias
Christian	Michael
Christoph	Niels
Daniel	Olaf
Detlev	Oliver
Dieter	Paul
Dietmar	Peter
Dirk	Phillip
Erik	Rainer
Felix	Ralf
Florian	Richard
Frank	Robert
Gerd	Rolf
Gerhard	Rudi
Günter	Sascha
Gustav	Stefan
Hajo	Steffen
Hans	Thilo
Hargo	Thomas
Heinz	Till
Helmut	Torsten
Holger	Udo
Jan	Ulf
Jens	Urs
Joachim	Uwe
Jochen	Volker
Jörg	Wim
Jörn	Wolfgang
Jürgen	
Kai	
Karsten	
Klaus	
Kurt	

English equivalents of dialogues

Below you will find English equivalents of the dialogues in this book. Because the English dialogues are not literal translations they sometimes contain words that do not have exact equivalents in the German text. Don't let this bother you. Two languages often express the same idea in different ways.

chapter 1   Hi! How are you?

What's your name?

UTE BRAUN	What's your name?
UTE SCHMIDT	Ute.
UTE BRAUN	Amazing! My name is Ute, too.

How are you?

INGRID	Hi, Gisela. How are you?
GISELA	Fine, thanks.
INGRID	Hi, Dieter. How are you?
DIETER	Bad.
INGRID	Well, what's the matter?
DIETER	I'm tired.

Are you satisfied?

VOLKER	Well, Monika, are you satisfied?
MONIKA	Yes, very much. You too?
VOLKER	No, I'm really unhappy.
MONIKA	I'm sorry.

Why is Volker so cross?

FRANK	How's Volker?
MONIKA	Bad.
FRANK	Is he sick again?
MONIKA	Nonsense! He's just lazy.

chapter 2   How old are you?

Young or old?

HEIKE	How old is Michael?
DIRK	Sixteen.
HEIKE	And you?
DIRK	Sixteen too. We're both sixteen.
HEIKE	Are you both *really* sixteen?
DIRK	Of course. Why?
HEIKE	You're so young.
DIRK	Well, how old are *you*?
HEIKE	Already seventeen.
DIRK	That really is very old!

When is your birthday?	PETRA	My birthday's in March. Yours too, isn't it?
	DIRK	No.
	PETRA	Well, when is your birthday?
	DIRK	In April.
	PETRA	Oh. Isn't Gerd's birthday in April, too?
	DIRK	No, it's not until May.
	PETRA	Oh yes, that's right.

chapter 3   This afternoon

Where do you live?	ERIK	Are you going home now?
	SABINE	Yes.
	ERIK	Where do you live?
	SABINE	On Garden Street.
	ERIK	Is that far from here?
	SABINE	No, just ten minutes.

What are you going to do?	JAN	Are you staying home this afternoon?
	GISELA	Yes, of course.
	JAN	What are you going to do?
	GISELA	Homework. What else?

chapter 5   Do you need new clothes?

That's too expensive	ASTRID	How expensive is that dress over there?
	GISELA	20 marks, and that's too expensive.
	ASTRID	What do you mean by that?
	GISELA	I think it's ugly.
	ERIK	Those jeans are really terrific.
	ASTRID	You think so? How much do they cost?
	ERIK	50 marks.
	ASTRID	50 marks! That's a bargain. Are you going to buy them?
	ERIK	Yes.

What size do you wear?	ASTRID	Here's a coat in brown. Nice, isn't it?
	ERIK	Yes, terrific. It's also nice and warm.
	ASTRID	Does it fit?
	ERIK	Unfortunately not. It's too big.
	ASTRID	What size do you wear?
	ERIK	Size 40.
	ASTRID	Here's your size.
	ERIK	But that's not a coat. That's a jacket.
	ASTRID	Oh yes. Too bad.

chapter 6   The school day

In the classroom

GISELA	What do we have at nine? Chemistry?
DIETER	No, we don't have chemistry today. We have math.
GISELA	Oh, great!
DIETER	You think math is great?
GISELA	Yes, I think math is interesting. Math's my favorite subject.

During recess

KARIN	Have you finished your homework assignments yet?
NORBERT	Which one? The math assignment?
KARIN	No, the chemistry assignment.
NORBERT	That I'll do tonight. What are you doing this afternoon?
KARIN	I'm doing biology.
NORBERT	Oh, man! We have homework in biology, too?
KARIN	Of course.

What time is it?

DIETER	What time is it?
SABINE	It's five after ten.
DIETER	Oh no! I'm going to be late again!
SABINE	That's not so bad. You're good in chemistry after all.

chapter 7   Do you want to go to the concert?

Concert at the youth center

INGRID	Hey, Dieter, the *Hot Dogs* are playing tonight.
DIETER	Boy, that's dumb. I can't go tonight, unfortunately.
INGRID	And tomorrow night?
DIETER	Tomorrow night will be all right. Do you think we can still get tickets?
INGRID	Well, we can give it a try.

At the box office

INGRID	Do you still have tickets for tomorrow night?
MAN	I'm sorry. There's nothing left for tomorrow night. I do have a couple of tickets for the day after tomorrow.
INGRID	*(To Dieter)* What do you think?
DIETER	*I* can make it. But don't you have to work then?
INGRID	Yes, I do. But I can certainly get time off. I just have to hear the *Hot Dogs.*
DIETER	OK, that's settled.

chapter 8   What are your plans?

Picture postcards are interesting

THOMAS	Say, just why do you collect picture postcards?
PETRA	I don't know. It's fun.
THOMAS	Really? I don't understand that.
PETRA	It's very simple. Old postcards are interesting and valuable as well.

Thomas needs a hobby	GERD	That Thomas is really a bore.
	PETRA	Yes, he's always tired. And he always thinks everything is boring.
	GERD	He never feels like doing anything, either.
	PETRA	What he needs is a hobby.
	GERD	Maybe ham radio operator.
	PETRA	Or ceramics.
What are you planning to do today?	ASTRID	Hey, Klaus, what are you going to do this afternoon?
	KLAUS	We're going to Hamburg.
	ASTRID	Are you going shopping?
	KLAUS	Yes, we're going to buy Gerd's birthday present.
	ASTRID	Where?
	KLAUS	I don't know yet. At Karstadt's maybe.
Why don't you come along?	ASTRID	Are you coming along this afternoon?
	ERIK	Where to?
	ASTRID	Downtown. To *Musikhaus Schumann*.
	ERIK	Today, on Saturday?
	ASTRID	Yes, today is "long Saturday," you know.
	ERIK	Oh yes, that's right. The stores won't close until five. What do you want at Schumann's?
	ASTRID	To buy the new record by Katja Peters. All right, do you want to come along now or not?
	ERIK	I really don't have time.
	ASTRID	Oh, come on!
	ERIK	Well, OK.

chapter 9   I helped around the house

I straightened up my room	NORBERT	What did you do over the weekend?
	KARIN	I slept.
	NORBERT	Oh, come on! You can't be serious!
	KARIN	Yes. I am! Honest! Then on Sunday I built a model airplane. And what did you do?
	NORBERT	I worked — as usual.
	KARIN	What do you mean you worked?
	NORBERT	I have to help at home. I straightened up my room and washed the car.
	KARIN	You call that working?
	NORBERT	Well, at least it's more than sleeping.
I baked a layer cake	SABINE	What did you do last weekend?
	PAUL	Not much. I baked a cake for my mother. She invited my grandparents over for coffee and cake.
	SABINE	How interesting!
	PAUL	Don't be so sarcastic! You did ask, you know.
	SABINE	Did the cake at least taste good?
	PAUL	I don't know. I picked up Gerda and we took a walk. Then we had coffee and cake with Gerda's parents.

chapter 10   Sports and leisure time

Who won?

GISELA	What did you do yesterday?
JAN	We played soccer.
GISELA	Against whom?
JAN	Oberndorf.
GISELA	Did you win?
JAN	No, we lost two to three.
GISELA	Oh man, I'm really sorry. But two to three against Oberndorf isn't really so bad.
JAN	That's true. Oberndorf is good.
GISELA	Well, maybe next time we can at least play a tie game.

I'm inviting you

INGRID	What do you have planned for tonight?
DIETER	I'm going to a party. What are you going to do?
INGRID	Nothing, actually.
DIETER	Nothing? That's great. Then you can come along.
INGRID	Where? To the party?
DIETER	Of course.
INGRID	But you're not giving the party.
DIETER	No, Gerd is. But I can invite you.
INGRID	Don't be silly. You can't do that.
DIETER	Sure I can. You know him pretty well, don't you?
INGRID	Yes . . . Well, all right. When does it start?
DIETER	At eight, I think. I'll call you.
INGRID	OK. So long. See you later.

chapter 11   Baker, butcher, supermarket

At the butcher shop

MR. LANGE	Hello, Mrs. Kraft. May I help you?
MRS. KRAFT	How much are the pork chops?
MR. LANGE	7 marks 50 a pound.
MRS. KRAFT	I'll need five chops.
MR. LANGE	Fine. Anything else?
MRS. KRAFT	I would like ten frankfurters.
MR. LANGE	There you are. Would you like something else?
MRS. KRAFT	No. That's all for today.
MR. LANGE	Thank you . . . So, here you are. That will be 29 marks 50 all together. * * * Here you go. You get 50 pfennigs back.
MRS. KRAFT	Thank you very much.
MR. LANGE	You're welcome. Good-by, Mrs. Kraft.
MRS. KRAFT	Good-by, Mr. Lange.

chapter 12   Enjoy your meal!

At the restaurant

WAITER	Good day, would you care for something to drink?
MRS. WOLF	Oh yes. I am so thirsty. One mineral water, please.
MR. WOLF	I'll have a mineral water too.
WAITER	Two mineral waters.
GABI	I'd like a cola, please.
WAITER	Thank you.
MR. WOLF	And the menu, please.
WAITER	Would you like to order now?
MRS. WOLF	Yes, please. Is the roast beef tender?
WAITER	Oh yes. I can recommend it.
MRS. WOLF	Well then, three roast beef dinners with mashed potatoes and salad.
GABI	I don't want any mashed potatoes.
MRS. WOLF	Aren't you hungry?
GABI	Yes, I am, but I'd rather eat French fries.
MRS. WOLF	Whatever you want.

* * *

WAITER	Well now, did you enjoy your meal?
MRS. WOLF	Yes. The roast was excellent.
MR. WOLF	I'd like the check, please.
WAITER	Very well. All together it comes to 43 marks and 50 pfennigs.
MR. WOLF	Make it 45.
WAITER	Thank you very much.

chapter 13   You can always talk about the weather

How's the weather?

In the spring

STEFAN	What do you think? Is it going to rain tomorrow?
KARIN	Probably.
STEFAN	That is really dumb!
KARIN	Why?
STEFAN	My umbrella is broken.

In the summer

DIETER	Nice today, isn't it?
INGRID	Yes, it's finally getting warm.
DIETER	I hope it won't get too hot.
INGRID	I'd rather have it hot than cold.

In the fall

MRS. KRAFT	Beautiful weather, isn't it?
MR. WOLF	Yes, I really like this season. It's so nice and cool.
MRS. KRAFT	This is good hiking weather.
MR. WOLF	Too bad that we have to work.

In the winter

RALF	The wind is rather cold this morning.
ILSE	Yes, there was a frost last night.
RALF	This afternoon it's supposed to snow.
ILSE	That's great. Then we can go sledding.

Where shall we go now?

KAI	Are we going to stand here forever? Where are we going to go now?
LORE	Dieter says that the music at the Western Club is terrific. But where in the world is the Western Club?
KAI	Here comes Dieter now. Why don't you ask him. He always knows everything.
LORE	Dieter, tell us, where is the Western Club?
DIETER	In Schwabing.
KAI	Boy, that's a long way from here. How are we going to get to Schwabing?
DIETER	You can go by subway — take the 3 or the 6. You can also walk.
KAI	To Schwabing on foot?
DIETER	Yes, it's only about a half an hour from here.
LORE	Don't you want to come along?
DIETER	No.
LORE	Why not?
DIETER	Because I'm too tired.
KAI	You can see that, man. He's almost asleep already.
LORE	Well OK, then we'll just go alone. Good night, Dieter. Sleep well (pleasant dreams).

How do we get to the Western Club?

KAI	I'm glad that we took the subway.
LORE	Yes, but now where is the Western Club?
KAI	Why don't you look at the map!
LORE	I haven't got it. Did you forget it?
KAI	So it seems. Then we'll just have to ask someone. Excuse me. Can you tell us how we can get to the Western Club?
STUDENT	Yes, I can. You go straight ahead to the traffic light. Turn right at the light. Then go straight ahead again until you come to a square with a fountain. There you turn left. Then you'll see the sign with the big boot.
KAI	Thanks a lot.
STUDENT	Don't mention it. Oh, wait a minute. It just occurred to me — the Western Club is closed today.
LORE	No, what rotten luck. What are we going to do now?
STUDENT	Why don't you go to Alfons. At Alfons there's always something going on. It's also a student hangout.

Grammatical summaries

Pronouns

personal pronouns

	SINGULAR					PLURAL			FORMAL
Nominative	ich	du	er	es	sie	wir	ihr	sie	Sie
Accusative	mich	dich	ihn	es	sie	uns	euch	sie	Sie
Dative	mir	dir	ihm	ihm	ihr	uns	euch	ihnen	Ihnen

interrogative pronouns

Nominative	wer	was
Accusative	wen	was
Dative	wem	

demonstrative pronouns

	SINGULAR			PLURAL
Nominative	der	das	die	die
Accusative	den	das	die	die
Dative	dem	dem	der	denen

Words that introduce nouns

definite article

	SINGULAR			PLURAL
Nominative	der	das	die	die
Accusative	den	das	die	die
Dative	dem	dem	der	den

dieser-words

	SINGULAR			PLURAL
Nominative	dieser	dieses	diese	diese
Accusative	diesen	dieses	diese	diese
Dative	diesem	diesem	dieser	diesen

The **dieser**-words are: **dieser, jeder, mancher, solcher,** and **welcher.**

indefinite article and **ein**-words

	SINGULAR			PLURAL
Nominative	ein	ein	eine	keine
Accusative	einen	ein	eine	keine
Dative	einem	einem	einer	keinen

The **ein**-words are **kein** and the possessive adjectives:

mein	my	**unser**	our
dein	your (*fam.sg.*)	**euer**	your (*fam.pl.*)
sein	his, its	**ihr**	their
ihr	her, its	**Ihr**	your (*formal*)

Noun plurals

		SINGULAR	PLURAL
Pattern 1	no change in plural	das Mädchen	die Mädchen
	plural adds umlaut	der Bruder	die Brüder
Pattern 2	plural adds **-e**	der Freund	die Freunde
	plural adds **-e** and umlaut	der Rock	die Röcke
Pattern 3	plural adds **-er**	das Kind	die Kinder
	plural adds **-er** and umlaut	der Mann	die Männer
Pattern 4	plural adds **-n**	die Familie	die Familien
	plural adds **-en**	die Frau	die Frauen
	plural adds **-nen**	die Schülerin	die Schülerinnen
Pattern 5	plural adds **-s**	der Pulli	die Pullis

Special **der**-nouns

	SINGULAR	PLURAL
Nominative	der Herr	die Herren
Accusative	den Herrn	die Herren
Dative	dem Herrn	den Herren

The special **der**-nouns include **der Junge, der Kunde,** and **der Student.**

Comparison of irregular adjectives and adverbs

Base form	gern	gut	viel	hoch
Comparative	lieber	besser	mehr	höher

Prepositions

WITH ACCUSATIVE	CONTRACTIONS
durch	durch das > durchs
für	für das > fürs
gegen	um das > ums
ohne	
um	

WITH DATIVE	CONTRACTIONS
aus	bei dem > beim
außer	von dem > vom
bei	zu dem > zum
mit	zu der > zur
nach	
seit	
von	
zu	

Numbers

0 = null	14 = vierzehn	28 = achtundzwanzig
1 = eins	15 = fünfzehn	29 = neunundzwanzig
2 = zwei	16 = sechzehn	30 = dreißig
3 = drei	17 = siebzehn	40 = vierzig
4 = vier	18 = achtzehn	50 = fünfzig
5 = fünf	19 = neunzehn	60 = sechzig
6 = sechs	20 = zwanzig	70 = siebzig
7 = sieben	21 = einundzwanzig	80 = achtzig
8 = acht	22 = zweiundzwanzig	90 = neunzig
9 = neun	23 = dreiundzwanzig	100 = hundert
10 = zehn	24 = vierundzwanzig	101 = hunderteins
11 = elf	25 = fünfundzwanzig	102 = hundertzwei
12 = zwölf	26 = sechsundzwanzig	121 = hunderteinundzwanzig
13 = dreizehn	27 = siebenundzwanzig	500 = fünfhundert
		1.000 = tausend

Verbs

regular verbs

Infinitive	kommen	finden[1]	tanzen[2]
Present	ich komme	finde	tanze
	du kommst	findest	tanzt
	er/sie kommt	findet	tanzt
	wir kommen	finden	tanzen
	ihr kommt	findet	tanzt
	sie kommen	finden	tanzen
	Sie kommen	finden	tanzen
Imperatives	komm!	finde!	tanz!
	kommt!	findet!	tanzt!
	kommen Sie!	finden Sie!	tanzen Sie!
Conversational past	ich bin gekommen	habe gefunden	habe getanzt

1. A verb with stem ending in **-d** or **-t** has an **-e** before the **-st** and **-t** endings.
2. The **-st** of the **du-**form ending contracts to **-t** when the verb stem ends in a sibilant (**-s, -ss, -ß, -z,** or **-tz**). Thus, the **du-** and **er/sie-**forms are identical.

verbs with stem-vowel change

Infinitive	geben (e > i)	lesen (e > ie)	fahren (a > ä)
Present	ich gebe	lese	fahre
	du gibst	liest	fährst
	er/sie gibt	liest	fährt
	wir geben	lesen	fahren
	ihr gebt	lest	fahrt
	sie geben	lesen	fahren
	Sie geben	lesen	fahren
Imperatives	gib!	lies!	fahr!
	gebt!	lest!	fahrt!
	geben Sie!	lesen Sie!	fahren Sie!
Conversational past	ich habe gegeben	habe gelesen	bin gefahren

The following verbs used in this text have stem-vowel changes:
e > i: essen, geben, helfen, nehmen, sprechen, vergessen
e > ie: empfehlen, lesen, sehen
a > ä: backen, einladen, fahren, fallen, schlafen, tragen, waschen
au > äu: laufen

irregular verbs

Infinitive	sein	haben	werden	wissen
Present	ich bin	habe	werde	weiß
	du bist	hast	wirst	weißt
	er/sie ist	hat	wird	weiß
	wir sind	haben	werden	wissen
	ihr seid	habt	werdet	wißt
	sie sind	haben	werden	wissen
	Sie sind	haben	werden	wissen
Imperatives	sei!	habe!	werde!	
	seid!	habt!	werdet!	
	seien Sie!	haben Sie!	werden Sie!	
Conversational past	ich bin gewesen	habe gehabt	bin geworden	habe gewußt

present tense of modal auxiliaries

	dürfen	können	müssen	sollen	wollen	mögen	
ich	darf	kann	muß	soll	will	mag	möchte
du	darfst	kannst	mußt	sollst	willst	magst	möchtest
er/sie	darf	kann	muß	soll	will	mag	möchte
wir	dürfen	können	müssen	sollen	wollen	mögen	möchten
ihr	dürft	könnt	müßt	sollt	wollt	mögt	möchtet
sie	dürfen	können	müssen	sollen	wollen	mögen	möchten
Sie	dürfen	können	müssen	sollen	wollen	mögen	möchten

principal parts of irregular weak verbs

INFINITIVE	PAST PARTICIPLE	ENGLISH EQUIVALENT
bringen	gebracht	to bring
denken	gedacht	to think
kennen	gekannt	to know
nennen	genannt	to name
wissen	gewußt	to know

principal parts of strong verbs used in this text

Compound verbs (like **mitgehen**) are not included when the basic form of the verb (like **gehen**) is included, since the principal parts are the same. Stem-vowel changes in the present tense are indicated in parentheses after the infinitive. For additional meanings, see the German-English Vocabulary.

INFINITIVE	PAST PARTICIPLE	ENGLISH EQUIVALENT
ab·biegen	(ist) abgebogen	to turn
an·rufen	angerufen	to telephone
backen (ä)	gebacken	to bake
beginnen	begonnen	to begin
bekommen	bekommen	to get, to obtain
bestehen	bestanden	to pass (a test)
bleiben	(ist) geblieben	to stay
ein·laden (ä)	eingeladen	to invite
empfehlen (ie)	empfohlen	to recommend
essen (i)	gegessen	to eat
fahren (ä)	(ist) gefahren	to drive
fallen (ä)	(ist) gefallen	to fall
finden	gefunden	to find
fliegen	(ist) geflogen	to fly
frieren	gefroren	to freeze
geben (i)	gegeben	to give
gehen	(ist) gegangen	to go
gewinnen	gewonnen	to win
heißen	geheißen	to be called
helfen (i)	geholfen	to help
kommen	(ist) gekommen	to come
laufen (äu)	(ist) gelaufen	to run
lesen (ie)	gelesen	to read
liegen	gelegen	to lie
nehmen (nimmt)	genommen	to take
reiten	(ist) geritten	to ride (horseback)
scheinen	geschienen	to shine
schlafen (ä)	geschlafen	to sleep
schreiben	geschrieben	to write
schwimmen	(ist) geschwommen	to swim
sehen (ie)	gesehen	to see
sein	(ist) gewesen	to be
singen	gesungen	to sing
sprechen (i)	gesprochen	to speak
stehen	gestanden	to stand
tragen (ä)	getragen	to wear; to carry
trinken	getrunken	to drink
tun	getan	to do
vergessen (i)	vergessen	to forget
waschen (ä)	gewaschen	to wash
werden (wird)	(ist) geworden	to become

Supplementary word sets

The following word lists will help you to increase the number of things you can say and write during your study of each chapter. Some of the words may be introduced as active vocabulary later than the chapters for which they are given here.

chapter 1

ADJECTIVES FOR MOOD OR PERSONALITY

ausgezeichnet excellent
erstklassig first-rate
furchtbar horrible
klasse terrific
miserabel miserable
schrecklich dreadful

ADJECTIVES FOR PERSONALITY

clever clever
doof idiotic
dumm stupid
fies disgusting
klug smart
lahm tired
langsam slow
langweilig boring
nett nice
verrückt crazy

FAREWELLS

auf Wiederhören! good-by *(on the telephone)*
bis bald! see you soon
bis dann! see you later
mach's gut! take it easy
tschau! so long

chapter 3

MUSICAL INSTRUMENTS

das Akkordeon accordion
die Blockflöte recorder
das Cello cello

das Fagott bassoon
die Harfe harp
der Kontrabaß double bass
die Oboe oboe
die Orgel organ
das Saxophon saxophone
die Posaune (+blasen) trombone
die Trompete (+blasen) trumpet
die Tuba (+blasen) tuba
das Waldhorn (+blasen) French horn

SPORTS AND GAMES

Billard billiards
Dame checkers
Federball badminton
Golf golf
Handball (Hallenhandball) handball
Hockey hockey
Mühle Chinese checkers
Schach chess
Tischtennis ping pong (table tennis)
Wasserball water polo

chapter 4

PROFESSIONS

ein Angestellter/eine Angestellte employee
der Ingenieur/die Ingenieurin engineer
der Krankenpfleger/die Krankenschwester nurse
der Mechaniker/die Mechanikerin mechanic
der Rechtsanwalt/die Rechtsanwältin lawyer
der Sekretär/die Sekretärin secretary
der Steward/die Stewardeß steward(ess)

FAMILY MEMBERS

die Tante aunt
der Onkel uncle
die Kusine cousin *(f.)*
der Cousin (der Vetter) cousin *(m.)*
die Oma grandma
der Opa grandpa
die Großmutter grandmother
der Großvater grandfather
die Stiefmutter stepmother
der Stiefvater stepfather
die Schwiegermutter mother-in-law
die Schwägerin sister-in-law
der Schwager brother-in-law

PHYSICAL DESCRIPTION OF PEOPLE

blond blond
dick fat
dunkel brunette
fett fat
häßlich ugly
hübsch pretty
mager thin
normal normal
schwach weak
stark strong
süß sweet

chapter 5

CLOTHING FOR MEN AND WOMEN

der Anorak jacket with hood
der Hut hat
die Kniestrümpfe *(pl.)* knee socks
die Latzhose overalls
die Mütze cap
der Parka parka
der Regenmantel raincoat
der Rollkragenpullover turtleneck
die Sandalen *(pl.)* sandals
der Schlafanzug pajamas
die Shorts shorts
die Strickjacke knitted jacket
das T-Shirt t-shirt
der Trainingsanzug warm-up suit
die Weste vest, cardigan
der Wintermantel winter coat

CLOTHING FOR WOMEN

der Badeanzug bathing suit
das Dirndl(kleid) dirndl
der Hosenanzug pants suit
der Hosenrock culottes
das Kostüm suit
das Trägerkleid jumper

CLOTHING FOR MEN

die Badehose bathing trunks
der Blazer blazer
der Freizeitanzug leisure suit
das Freizeithemd casual shirt
das Polohemd polo shirt

COLORS

orange orange
purpurrot crimson
rosa pink
violett violet
hell(blau) light (blue)
dunkel(blau) dark (blue)

chapter 6

SCHOOL SUBJECTS

Französisch French
Gemeinschaftskunde social studies
Griechisch Greek
Informatik computer science
Italienisch Italian
Religion(skunde) religion
Spanisch Spanish
Werken shop

CLASSROOM OBJECTS

die Federmappe pencil case
der Filzstift felt pen
das Klassenbuch record book
der Klassenschrank cupboard
das Klassenzimmer classroom
die Kreide chalk
der Kurs course
die Landkarte (Wandkarte) map
der Papierkorb wastebasket
das Ringbuch loose leaf binder
der Schwamm sponge
das Sprachlabor language lab
die (Wand)tafel chalkboard

PHYSICAL ATTRIBUTES OF OBJECTS

aus Glas   glass
aus Holz   wooden
aus Metall   metal
aus Papier   paper
dunkel   dark
hell   light
farbig (bunt)   colorful
hart   hard
weich   soft
biegsam   pliable
bequem   comfortable
gemütlich   cozy

chapter 8

STEREO AND AUDIO-VISUAL EQUIPMENT

der Farbfernseher   color television
der Kopfhörer   headphone
der Lautsprecher   loudspeaker
das Mikrophon   microphone
der Radiorecorder   cassette radio
der Schwarzweißfernseher   black-and-white
   television
das Tonband   tape
das Tonbandgerät   tape recorder (reel-to-reel)
der Tuner   tuner
der Verstärker   amplifier

HOBBIES

angeln   to fish
Blumen (z.B. Rosen, Dahlien, Lilien)   flowers
   (e.g., roses, dahlias, lilies)
der Garten   gardening
malen   to paint
schreiben (Gedichte, Geschichten)   to write
   (poems, stories)
zeichnen   to draw

COLLECTIBLES

alte Flaschen   old bottles
Glas   glass
Insekten   insects
Münzen   coins
Pflanzen (getrocknet)   plants (dried)
Puppen   dolls
Silber   silver
Streichholzschachteln   match covers
altes Zinn   old pewter

chapter 9

CHORES

(die) Fenster putzen   to clean windows
(das) Mittagessen kochen   to cook dinner
(das) Abendessen vorbereiten/machen   to
   prepare supper
meinem Vater helfen   to help my father
meiner Mutter helfen   to help my mother
(die) Wäsche bügeln   to iron (clothes)
Wäsche/Kleider flicken   to mend clothes
das Haus/den Zaun/das Boot streichen   to
   paint the house/the fence/the boat
(den) Rasen mähen   to mow the lawn
(die) Bäume beschneiden/pflanzen/fällen
   to prune/to plant/to cut trees
die Hecke schneiden   to trim the hedge
(das) Unkraut jäten   to pull out weeds
(das) Holz sägen/spalten/hacken   to saw/to
   split/to chop wood
(den) Schnee fegen (kehren)/schippen   to
   sweep/to shovel snow

chapter 10

SPORTS

das Ballonfahren   ballooning
das Boxen   boxing
das Fallschirmspringen   parachute jumping
fechten   to fence
Freiübungen   gymnastics
das Gewichtheben   weightlifting
das Jagen   hunting
das Kegeln   bowling
die Leichtathletik   track and field
der Radsport   bicycling
das Ringen   wrestling
rudern   to row
das Schießen   shooting
das Segelfliegen   glider flying

chapter 11

SMALL SPECIALTY SHOPS

die Apotheke   pharmacy
das Blumengeschäft   florist
die Chemische Reinigung   dry cleaner
die Drogerie   drugstore
das Eisenwarengeschäft   hardware store
das Elektrogeschäft   appliance store
das Feinkostgeschäft   delicatessen
das Fotogeschäft   camera store
der Juwelier   jeweler
der Klempner (Spengler)   plumber
die Konditorei   coffee and pastry shop
das Milchgeschäft   dairy store
der Optiker   optician
das Papiergeschäft   stationery
das Sportgeschäft (Sportausrüstungen)
   sporting goods store (sporting goods)

chapter 12

BREAKFAST FOODS

der Honig   honey
der Joghurt   yogurt
die Margarine   margarine
der Orangensaft   orange juice
der Tomatensaft   tomato juice
das Graubrot   light rye bread
der Pumpernickel   pumpernickel bread
das Schwarzbrot   dark rye bread
das Vollkornbrot   coarse whole grain bread
das Weißbrot   white bread

LUNCH FOODS

die Erbsensuppe   pea soup
die Fruchtsuppe (kalt)   fruit soup (cold)
die Kartoffelsuppe   potato soup
der Bratfisch   fried fish
das Fischfilet   filet of fish
der Kochfisch   boiled fish
der Bohnensalat   bean salad
der gemischte Salat   tossed salad
der grüne Salat   lettuce salad
die Ente   duck
die Gans   goose
die Leber   liver
die Nieren   kidneys
das Reh   venison

die Kasseler Rippchen   smoked pork chops
die Roulade   beef rolls filled with bacon
Königsberger Klopse   meatballs
die Schweinshaxe   pigs feet
die Klöße (*pl.*)/**Knödel** (*pl.*)   dumplings
die Kartoffelknödel (*pl.*)   potato dumplings
die Leberknödel (*pl.*)   liver dumplings
die Dampfnudeln (*pl.*)   steamed dumplings
die Spätzle (*pl.*)   noodles
das Sauerkraut   sauerkraut
die Pilze (*pl.*)   mushrooms
der Rotkohl   red cabbage
der Spargel   asparagus
die Zwiebel   onion

SUPPER FOODS

das Beefsteak Tartar   spiced, raw ground beef
der Räucherfisch   smoked fish
der Speck   bacon
der Quark   cream cheese
der Schnittkäse   sliced cheese
der Streichkäse   spreadable cheese

DESSERTS

das Kompott   stewed fruit
die Melone   melon
die Schokoladencreme   chocolate mousse
der Stachelbeerpudding   gooseberry pudding
die Zitronencreme   lemon mousse

TABLE SETTING

das Besteck   flatware
der Eierbecher   egg cup
der Eßlöffel   tablespoon
das Gedeck   table setting
die Kaffeekanne/die Teekanne   coffee pot/
   teapot
das Milchkännchen   milk pitcher
die Schüssel   bowl
die Serviette   napkin
der Teelöffel   teaspoon
der Teller   plate
die Tortenplatte   cake plate
die Untertasse   saucer
die Zuckerdose   sugarbowl

chapter 13

WEATHER EXPRESSIONS

der Wetterbericht   weather report
die Wettervorhersage   weather prediction
die Warmfront   warm front
die Kaltfront   cold front
der Niederschlag   precipitation
der Schneefall   snowfall
der Hagel   hail
der Landregen   all-day rain
das Schauer   shower
der Nieselregen (Sprühregen)   drizzle
der Luftdruck   air pressure
das Gewitter   thunderstorm
der Blitz/der Donner   lightning/thunder
die Windrichtung   wind direction
es gießt (in Strömen)   it's pouring
es regnet Bindfäden   it's raining cats and dogs
es ist naßkalt   it's damp and cold
neblig (der Nebel)   foggy (fog)
sonnig   sunny
schwül   humid
eisig   icy cold
wolkenlos   cloudless
heiter   fair
bedeckt   overcast

GEOGRAPHICAL TERMS

die Anhöhe (der Hügel)   hill
der Atlantik   Atlantic
der Bach   brook
der Berg   mountain
das Bundesland   (federal) state
der Bundesstaat   (American) state
die Ebbe, die Flut   low tide, high tide
der Fluß   river
das Gebirge   mountain range
der Gipfel   peak
der Gletscher   glacier
die Hauptstadt   capital
die Insel   island
der Kanal   canal; channel
die Küste   coast
das Meer   sea
der Pazifik   Pacific
der Strand   beach
das Tal   valley

der Teich   pond
das Ufer   shore
der Wald   woods
die Wiese   meadow

chapter 14

MODES OF TRANSPORTATION

der Pferdewagen   horse-drawn wagon
die Kutsche   carriage
der LKW (= Lastkraftwagen)   truck
der PKW (= Personenkraftwagen)   passenger car
der Anhänger   trailer
die Eisenbahn   train, railway
der Güterzug   freight train
die Bergbahn   mountain railway; cable car
die Fähre   ferry
der Schleppkahn   barge
das Boot   boat
das Ruderboot   rowboat
das Segelboot   sailboat
das Motorboot   motor boat
das Segelschiff   sailing ship
der Tanker   tanker
das Containerschiff   container ship
der Frachter   freighter
der Passagierdampfer   passenger ship
das Propellerflugzeug   propeller plane
der Jet   jet
der Hubschrauber   helicopter
das Segelflugzeug   glider plane

PARTS OF A BICYCLE

die Handbremse   hand brake
die Kette   chain
die Klingel (Glocke)   bell
die Lampe   headlight
der Lenker   handlebar
die Luftpumpe   air pump
das Pedal   pedal
das (Vorder-, Hinter-) Rad   (front, back) wheel
der Rahmen   frame
der Reifen   tire
der Sattel   seat
das Schloß   lock
der Schlüssel   key

PARTS OF A CAR

die Batterie   battery
der Blinker   turn signal
die Bremse (das Bremspedal)   brake (pedal)
das Gas (das Gaspedal)   gas (pedal)
die Handbremse   hand brake
der Kofferraum   trunk
der Kotflügel   fender
der Kühler   radiator
die Kupplung (das Kupplungspedal)   clutch (pedal)
das Lenkrad   steering wheel
die Motorhaube   hood
der Rückspiegel   rear-view mirror
der Scheibenwischer   windshield wiper
der Scheinwerfer   headlight
der Sitz   seat
die Stoßstange   bumper
die Wasserpumpe   water pump
die Windschutzscheibe   windshield
die Zündkerze   spark plug

chapter 15

LANDMARKS

**die Autobahnauffahrt, die Autobahnaus-
fahrt**   expressway on-ramp, off-ramp
die Bahnlinie   railroad (tracks)
der Bauernhof   farm
die Brücke   bridge
die Bundesstraße   federal highway
die Burg   fortress
das Denkmal   monument
das Dorf   village
die Fabrik   factory
der Flugplatz   airport
der Friedhof   cemetery
der Funkturm   radio and TV tower
der Fußweg   footpath
die Kapelle   chapel
das Kloster   monastery
die Mühle   mill
die Ruine   ruin
das Schloß   castle
der Tunnel   tunnel

ASKING DIRECTIONS

Wo ist [der Bahnhof]?   Where is the [train station]?
Wie weit ist es [zum Bahnhof]? nach [Stuttgart]?   How far is it [to the train station]? to [Stuttgart]?
Wie komme ich am schnellsten [zum Bahnhof]?   What is the quickest way [to the train station]?
Wo ist hier in der Nähe [ein Café]?   Is there [a café] around here?
Wissen Sie den Weg nach [Oberndorf]?   Do you know the way to [Oberndorf]?
Wir wollen nach [Stuttgart]. Wie fahren wir am besten?   We're going to [Stuttgart]. What is the best route?
Wo geht's hier [zum Bahnhof]?   How do you get [to the train station] from here?
Wir wollen nach [München]. Müssen/ Können wir über [Augsburg] fahren?   We're going to [Munich]. Must/can we go by way of [Augsburg]?
Was ist näher? Ist das näher?   What is closer? Is that closer?

GIVING DIRECTIONS

Sind Sie zu Fuß oder mit dem Auto?   Are you walking or driving?
Da nehmen Sie am besten [ein Taxi, die Bahn].   It's best if you take [a taxi, the streetcar].
Da fahren Sie am besten mit [der U-Bahn].   It's best if you go by [subway].
Nehmen Sie die [Drei].   Take number [three].
[Dort/An der Ecke/An der Kreuzung] ist die Haltestelle.   The stop is [over there/on the corner/at the intersection].
[Zum Bahnhof] sind es [zehn Minuten].   It's [ten minutes] to the [train station].
An der [ersten/zweiten] Kreuzung gehen Sie [rechts].   At the [first/second] intersection turn [right].
Gehen Sie die [erste] Straße [rechts]!   Take the [first] street [to the right].
Gehen Sie [am See/an der Mauer] entlang!   Go along [the lake/the wall].
Fahren Sie um [die Kirche] herum!   Drive around [the church].
Lassen Sie [die Kirche] links liegen!   Keep [the church] on your left.

Supplementary expressions

1. EXPRESSING SKEPTICISM

rede keinen Unsinn/Stuß
ist das dein Ernst?
meinst du? wirklich? meinst du das wirklich?
das ist ja komisch/eigenartig
irgendetwas stimmt hier nicht
ist das wahr?
wer sagt das? wer hat das gesagt?
woher weißt du das? wo/von wem hast du das
   gehört?

2. EXPRESSING INSECURITY OR DOUBT

das ist unwahrscheinlich
es ist unwahrscheinlich, daß . . . [sie das gesagt hat]
das ist zweifelhaft
ich glaube nicht, daß . . . [er das gesagt hat]
ich glaube das nicht
das kann nicht sein

3. EXPRESSING ANNOYANCE

Quatsch; Unsinn; Blödsinn
Blödmann; Dussel; Idiot
der hat/du hast wohl nicht alle Tassen im Schrank
bei der/bei dir ist wohl eine Schraube los
hör mal
geh
also, wissen Sie; wirklich; tsk, tsk, tsk
(das ist doch) nicht zu glauben
(das ist) unerhört/unglaublich
(das ist eine) Schweinerei
das tut/sagt man nicht
das kannst du doch nicht machen/sagen

4. STALLING FOR TIME

also; na ja; ja nun
hmmmmmmm
laß mich mal nachdenken
darüber muß ich (erst mal) nachdenken
das kann ich so (auch) nicht sagen

5. BEING NONCOMMITTAL

(das ist ja) interessant
hmmmmmmm
wirklich?

6. EXPRESSING GOOD WISHES

ich halte (dir/Ihnen) die Daumen
Gesundheit
(ich wünsche) guten Appetit/gesegnete Mahlzeit
Prost; auf Ihr/dein Wohl; zum Wohl
herzlichen Glückwunsch
ich wünsche dir/Ihnen gute Reise
                 gute Besserung
                 viel Glück
                 viel Vergnügen/Spaß
                 alles Gute

7. COURTESY EXPRESSIONS

bitte (sehr/schön)
danke (sehr/schön)

8. SAYING "YOU'RE WELCOME"

bitte (sehr/schön)
gern geschehen
nichts zu danken

9. EXPRESSING SURPRISE

ach nein
(wie) ist das (nur) möglich?
das hätte ich nicht gedacht
das ist ja prima/toll/klasse
ich werd' verrückt
(das ist ja) nicht zu glauben
ich bin von 'n Socken

10. EXPRESSING AGREEMENT (AND DISAGREE-MENT)

natürlich (nicht); selbstverständlich (nicht)
warum denn nicht?
das kann (nicht) sein
(das) stimmt (nicht); richtig/falsch
das finde ich auch/nicht
genau; eben

11. RESPONDING TO REQUESTS

bitte; selbstverständlich; natürlich
gern; machen wir; mit Vergnügen
(es tut mir leid, aber) das geht nicht
ich kann (das) nicht ... [reparieren]
das habe ich nicht
das ist zu schwer/groß/teuer

12. EXPRESSING REGRET

das tut mir leid
es tut mir leid, daß ... [ich nicht kommen kann]
leider ... [kann ich morgen nicht]
es geht leider nicht
unglücklicherweise ... [war ich gestern nicht zu
   Hause]

13. EXCUSING ONESELF

Entschuldigung; Pardon; Verzeihung; entschuldigen Sie
entschuldigen Sie bitte, daß ... [ich erst jetzt
   komme]
hier ist meine Entschuldigung
meine Mutter hat mir eine Entschuldigung
   geschrieben
das ist keine Entschuldigung

14. EXPRESSING INDIFFERENCE

das ist mir egal
es ist mir egal, ob ... [er kommt]
das macht mir nichts aus
es macht mir nichts aus, daß ... [sie mehr verdient]
das ist mir wurscht
das kannst du machen, wie du willst
das kannst du halten wie ein Dachdecker
so kann man das auch machen/sagen
ich habe nichts dagegen

15. EXPRESSING ADMIRATION

ach, wie schön; dufte; klasse
erstklassig; ausgezeichnet
das ist aber nett (von dir, Ihnen, *etc.*)
der/die ist nett
das sind nette Leute

16. EXPRESSING JOY AND PLEASURE

wir freuen uns
wir freuen uns auf ihn/seinen Besuch/die Ferien
wir sind froh
wir sind froh (darüber), daß ... [er wieder arbeitet]
es freut mich, daß ... [sie gekommen ist]
das tun/kochen/essen wir gern
das macht mir/uns Spaß
das machen wir zum Vergnügen

17. MAKING REQUESTS

hätten Sie Lust ... [mitzukommen]?
hätten Sie Zeit, ... [uns zu besuchen]?
hätten Sie etwas [Zeit] für mich?
ich hätte gern ... [ein Pfund Äpfel]
könnten Sie ... [mein Auto reparieren]?
würden Sie bitte ... [um zehn Uhr hier sein]?
hätten Sie etwas dagegen?
hätten Sie etwas dagegen, wenn ... [ich mit-
   komme]?
dürfte ich ... [ein Stück Kuchen haben]?
macht es Ihnen etwas aus?
macht es Ihnen etwas aus, wenn ... [mein Bruder
   mitkommt]?
würden Sie so freundlich sein und ... [den Brief
   schreiben]?
ich möchte fragen, ob [ich mitkommen] darf/
   kann?
könnte ich ... [um neun Uhr zu Ihnen kommen]?

18. ASKING FOR FAVORS

könntest du mir einen Gefallen tun und ... [mich
   mitnehmen]?
ich hätte eine Bitte: könntest/würdest du ...
   [mich mitnehmen]?

19. MAKING SURMISES

ich denke ja; ich glaube schon
ich glaube (schon), daß ... [sie das gesagt hat]
das dürfte/könnte wahr/richtig sein
wahrscheinlich; wahrscheinlich [stimmt das]
sicher; ich bin sicher; ich bin ziemlich sicher, daß
    ... [er das gesagt hat]
ich nehme (das) an; ich nehme das (nur) an
ich nehme an, daß ... [das stimmt]
das scheint ... [nicht zu stimmen]

20. EXPRESSING EXPECTATION

hoffentlich; hoffentlich ... [kommt sie]
ich hoffe (es) (sehr)
ich hoffe, daß ... [sie das Paket bekommen hat]
ich freue mich auf ... [die Ferien]

21. EXPRESSING FEARS

ich fürchte, daß ... [sie nicht kommt]
ich habe Angst
ich habe Angst, ... [nach Hause zu gehen]
davor habe ich Angst
ich habe Angst vor ... [dem Hund]
[ich bleibe] lieber [hier]

22. GIVING ADVICE

ich schlage vor, daß ... [wir um acht anfangen]
ich rate dir, ... [zu Hause zu bleiben]
das würde ich dir (nicht) raten
das würde ich machen/sagen
das würde ich anders/so machen
das mußt du so machen
ich zeige dir, ... [wie man das macht]

23. CORRECTING MISUNDERSTANDINGS

das habe ich nicht so gemeint
das habe ich nur aus Spaß gesagt
das war doch nicht so gemeint
das war nicht mein Ernst

German-English vocabulary

The German-English vocabulary contains the basic words and expressions listed in the chapter vocabularies, plus words that occur in headings, captions, cultural notes, and reading material. The symbol ~ signifies the key word (minus the definite article, if any) for that entry. For example, **guten ~ !** under **Abend** means **guten Abend!** The numbers in italics following the definitions refer to the chapters in which the active words are introduced.

Nouns are listed with their plural forms: **der Abend, -e.** No plural entry is given if the plural is rarely used or non-existent. Both the dative and the plural endings are given for special **der-**nouns: **der Herr, -n, -en.**

Strong and irregular weak verbs are listed with their principal parts. Vowel changes in the present tense are noted in parentheses, followed by the past participle forms. All verbs take **haben** in the past participle unless indicated with **sein.** For example: **fahren (ä; ist gefahren).** Separable-prefix verbs are indicated with a raised dot: **auf·stehen.**

Adjectives and adverbs that take umlaut in the comparative are noted: **warm (ä).**

ab·biegen (ist abgebogen)   to make a turn, *15*

der Abend, -e   evening; **guten ~ !**   good evening! *1*; **zu ~ essen**   to have supper, *12*

das Abendessen   supper, *12*; **zum ~**   for supper, *12*

abends   evenings, in the evening, *4*

die Abendvorstellung   evening performance

aber   *flavoring word with the meaning of* really, certainly, *2*; *(coord. conj.)* but; however, *3*

ab·holen   to call for, to pick up, *9*

ab·räumen   to clear, to remove, *9*

ab·stauben   to dust, *9*

das Abteil   (train) compartment

ab·trocknen   to dry up, to wipe dry, *9*

ach   oh, *6*; **~ so**   oh, I see! *2*

acht   eight, *2*

achtzehn   eighteen, *2*

achtzig   eighty, *4*

adieu   good-by

alle   all, everyone, *9*

allein   alone, *11*

alles   all, everything, *7*; **~ Gute (zum Geburtstag)**   all the best (on your birthday)

das Alphabet   alphabet

als   than, *9*; as, *12*

also   well, *8*

alt (ä)   old, *2*

am (= an dem)   in the; **~ Samstag**   on Saturday, *4*

(das) Amerika   America

amerikanisch   American, *13*

die Ampel, -n   traffic signal, *15*

an (+ *acc. or dat.*)   at, *7*; to

ander   other

ändern   to change

anders   different, *13*

an·machen   to switch on (*the light*), *8*

an·rufen (angerufen)   to call, to telephone, *10*

die Ansichtskarte, -n   picture postcard, *8*

der Anzug, ̈e   man's suit, *5*

der Apfel, ̈   apple, *11*; **der Apfelkuchen**   cake topped with sliced apples

die Apotheke, -n   pharmacy

der Apotheker, -/die Apothekerin, -nen   pharmacist, *4*

der Appetit: guten ~ !   enjoy your meal, *12*

der April   April, *2*

die Arbeit, -en   work, *9*

arbeiten   to work, *4*

der Arbeiter, -/die Arbeiterin, -nen   worker, *4*

der Arzt, ̈e/die Ärztin, -nen   doctor, physician, *4*

der Atlantische Ozean   Atlantic Ocean, *13*

auch   also, too, *1*

auf (+ *acc. or dat.*)   on; at; **~ eine Party gehen**   to go to a party, *10*

die Aufgabe, -n   homework, lesson

auf·hängen   to hang up

auf·machen   to open, 8
auf·räumen   to put in order, 9
auf·stehen (ist aufgestanden)   to get up, 8
das Auge, –n   eye
der August   August, 2
aus (+*dat.*)   out of, from, 15
ausgezeichnet   excellent, 12
aus·machen   to turn off (*the light*), 8
außer (+*dat.*)   besides, except for, 15
die Aussprache   pronunciation
der Ausverkauf   clearance sale
ausverkauft   sold out, 7
das Auto, –s   car, 8
die Autobahn, –en   expressway, 14

backen (ä; gebacken)   to bake, 9
der Bäcker, –/die Bäckerin, –nen   baker, 11
das Badezimmer, –   bathroom, 9
die Bahn, –en   train, railway, 15
der Bahnhof, ⸚e   train station, 15
bald   soon, 4
der Ball, ⸚e   ball
die Banane, –n   banana, 11
die Band, –s   band, 7
die Bank, –en   bank, 15
der Basketball, ⸚e   basketball, 3
basteln   to tinker (with), to work at a hobby, 9
die Baustelle   construction site
Bayern   Bavaria, 15
die Bedienung   service
beginnen (begonnen)   to start, to begin, 7
bei (+*dat.*)   at, 7; near; with; **beim = bei dem**
beide   both, 2
das Beispiel, –e   example; **zum ~** (*abbr.* **z.B.**)   for example
bekommen (bekommen)   to get, to receive, 7; **ich bekomme frei**   I'll get (the day) off, 7
das Benzin   gasoline, 14
bergsteigen gehen   to go mountain-climbing, 10
der Bericht, –e   report, 13
der Beruf, –e   occupation, profession
beschreiben (beschrieben)   to describe, 14
besonder   special; **besonders**   particularly, especially, 13
besser (*comp. of* **gut**)   better, 13
bestehen (bestanden): die Prüfung ~   to pass a test, 14
bestellen   to order, 12

bestimmt   certain(ly)
der Besuch, –e   visit, 15; guest, company
besuchen   to visit, 11
bewölkt   cloudy, overcast, 13
bezahlen   to pay, 11
das Bier   beer, 12
der Bierdeckel, –   coaster (*used under a glass*), 8
billig   inexpensive, cheap, 5
die Biologie   biology, 6; **die Bio**   bio, 6
bis   till, until, 4; **~ später**   till later, see you later, 1; **~ zu**   up to, 15
bitte   please; you're welcome, ; **~ schön**   please; you're very welcome, 7; **~ sehr**   certainly, 12
blau   blue, 5
bleiben (ist geblieben)   to remain, to stay, 3
der Bleistift, –e   (*abbr.* **der Stift**)   pencil, 6
der Blick, –e   view
die Bluse, –n   blouse, 5
der Braten, –   roast
brauchen   to need, 5
braun   brown, 5; **ein Mantel in Braun**   a brown coat, 5
die BRD   (*abbr. for* **Bundesrepublik Deutschland**)   Federal Republic of Germany
der Brei   porridge
die Breite   width
die Bremse, –n   brake, 14
der Brief, –e   letter, 4
der Brieffreund, –e/Brieffreundin, –nen   pen pal, 4
die Briefmarke, –n   postage stamp, 8
bringen (gebracht)   to bring, 12
das Brot, –e   (loaf of) bread, 11; sandwich
das Brötchen, –   hard roll, 12
der Bruder, ⸚   brother, 4
der Brunnen, –   fountain, well; spring, 15
das Buch, ⸚er   book, 6
die Buchhandlung, –en   bookstore
bummeln (ist gebummelt)   to go for a stroll, to take a walk, 15
die Bundesrepublik Deutschland   Federal Republic of Germany
der Bus, –se   bus, 14
die Butter   butter, 11

das Café, –s   café, coffee shop, 8
das Camping   camping, 10
die Cassette, –n   cassette, 8

der Cassetten-Recorder, –   cassette recorder, 8
Celsius   Celsius
die Chemie   chemistry, 6; **die Chemieaufgabe**   chemistry homework, 6
der Club, –s   club, 15
die (*also* **das**) **Cola**   cola drink, 12

da   here, there, 5; then, 13
das Dach, ¨er   roof
die Dame, –n   lady, woman, 5
der Dank   thanks; **vielen ~ !**   many thanks! 12
danke   thanks, thank you, 1
dann   then, 7
das   that, the, 5
daß   (*sub. conj.*) that, 13
der Daumen, –   thumb; **halt mir die ~**   cross your fingers for me (*literally:* hold your thumbs for me), 14
die DDR   (*abbr. for* **Deutsche Demokratische Republik**)   German Democratic Republic
decken   to set (*the table*), 9
dein   your (*fam. sg.*), 4
denken (gedacht)   to think, 13
denn   *flavoring word often used in questions,* 1; (*coord. conj.*) for, because, 11
der   the, 5
(das) Deutsch   German (language), 4
deutsch   German (*adj.*)
die Deutsche Demokratische Republik   German Democratic Republic
(das) Deutschland   Germany
der Dezember   December, 2
dich   (*acc. of* **du**) you, 10
dick   fat, thick, 6
die   the, 5
der Dienstag   Tuesday, 6
dieser   this, 6
das Ding, –e   thing
die Disco, –s   disco, discothèque, 8
die Diskussion, –en   discussion, debate, 14
doch   flavoring word used to persuade or to imply agreement, 8; yes (*in response to a negative statement or question*), 9
der Donnerstag   Thursday, 4
doof   goofy, dumb, stupid, 4
dort   there, 11
drei   three, 2
dreißig   thirty, 4

dreizehn   thirteen, 2
du   you (*fam. sg.*), 1
dumm(ü)   dumb, stupid, 7
dünn   thin, 4
durch   (+ *acc.*) through, 11
durch·fallen (ä; ist durchgefallen)   to fail, to flunk, 14
dürfen (darf)   may, to be permitted to, 7; **was darf es sein?**   what would you like?, 11
der Durst   thirst, 12; **~ haben**   to be thirsty, 12

die Ecke, –n   corner, 15
Ehrenwort!   honest! on my honor! 9
das Ei, –er   egg, 11; **weichgekochtes ~**   soft-boiled egg
eifersüchtig   jealous, 14
eigentlich   really, actually, 8
der Eimer, –   pail, 9
ein   a, an, 5
einfach   simple, simply, 7
ein·fallen (ä; ist eingefallen)   to occur to; **da fällt mir gerade ein**   it just occurs to me, 15
ein·kaufen   to shop, 8; **~ gehen**   to go shopping, 8
die Einkaufstasche, –n   shopping bag, 11
ein·laden (ä; eingeladen)   to invite, 9
einmal   once, for once; **noch ~**   once again
ein·packen   to pack, 11
eins   one, 2
der Eintritt   admissron
das Eis   ice cream; ice, 12
der Elektriker, –/die Elektrikerin, –nen   electrician, 4
elf   eleven, 2
die Eltern (*pl.*)   parents, 9
empfehlen (ie; empfohlen)   to recommend, 12
das Ende   end
endlich   finally, 13
(das) Englisch   English (language), 6
die Ente, –n   duck; **eine lahme ~**   a dull, boring person, 8
entlang   along; **die Straße ~**   along (down) the street, 15
die Entschuldigung, –en   excuse; **Entschuldigung!**   excuse me, sorry, 11
er   he, 1
die Erbse, –n   pea, 11
die Erdbeere, –n   strawberry, 11

die Erdkunde geography, 6

Ernst: das ist doch nicht dein ~ ! you can't be serious! 9

erst only; first, 2

erzählen to tell, 14

es it, 5

das Essen meal, 12

essen (i; gegessen) to eat, 10

etwas something, 8

euch (*acc. of ihr*) you, 10

euer your (*fam. pl.*), 4

das Fach, ̈er (school) subject, 6

fahren (ä; ist gefahren) to drive, to go, 8

Fahrenheit Fahrenheit

der Fahrlehrer, - driving instructor, 14

der Fahrplan, ̈e (train) schedule

das Fahrrad, ̈er bicycle, 14

die Fahrschule, -n driving school, 14

die Fahrstunde, -n driving lesson, 14

das Fahrzeug, -e vehicle

fallen (ä; ist gefallen) to fall, 10

falsch wrong, 2

die Familie, -n family, 4

die Farbe, -n color, 5; **welche ~ hat dein Pulli?** what color is your sweater? 5

fast almost, 11

faul lazy, 1

der Februar February, 2

das Fenster, - window, 8

fern·sehen (ie; ferngesehen) to watch TV, 8

der Fernseher, - television set, 8

fertig ready, finished, 6

finden (gefunden) to find, 4; **wie findest du (Rock)?** how do you like (rock music)?, 4

der Fisch, -e fish, 12

die Flasche, -n bottle, 11

das Fleisch meat, 11

fleißig industrious, diligent, 1

fliegen (ist geflogen) to fly, 14

die Flöte, -n flute, 3

das Flugzeug, -e airplane, 14

das Flugzeugmodell, -e model airplane, 9

der Fluß, ̈sse river

das Fotoalbum (*pl.* -alben) photo album, 3

fotografieren to photograph, 8

die Frage, -n question, 7

fragen to ask, 7

der Franken basic Swiss monetary unit

die Frau, -en woman, 5; wife; **~ X** Mrs. or Ms. X, 4

das Fräulein young woman, 7; **~ X** Miss X, 4

frei free, not busy, 7; **ich bekomme ~** I'll get (the day) off, 7

der Freitag Friday, 4

die Freizeit leisure time, 10

der Freund, -e/die Freundin, -nen friend, 4

frieren (gefroren) to freeze, to be very cold, 13

frisch fresh, 11

der Friseur, -e/die Friseuse, -n hairdresser, 4

froh glad, happy, 15

früh early, 11

der Frühling spring, 10

das Frühstück breakfast, 9; **zum ~** for breakfast, 12

frühstücken to have breakfast, 12

der Führerschein, -e driver's license, 14

fünf five, 2

fünfzehn fifteen, 2

fünfzig fifty, 4

für (+ *acc.*) for, 5; **fürs = für das**, 9

furchtbar terrible; terribly, 5

der Fuß, ̈e foot; **zu ~** on foot, 15

der Fußball soccer, 3

das Fußballspiel, -e soccer game, 10

die Fußgängerzone, -n pedestrian zone, 15

füttern to feed, 9

die Gabel, -n fork

die Gallone, -n gallon

ganz quite; complete(ly), 1; **~ gut** OK, pretty well, 1

gar: ~ nicht not at all, 1

die Garage, -n garage, 9

der Garten, ̈ garden

die Gartenarbeit gardening, yard work, 9

geben (i; gegeben) to give, 7; **es gibt** (+ *acc.*) there is, there are, 7

der Geburtstag, -e birthday, 2; **ich habe ~** it's my birthday, 2

das Geburtstagskind birthday girl or boy

das Gefälle incline, slope

gegen (+ *acc.*) against, 10

der Gegenverkehr oncoming traffic

gehen (ist gegangen) to go, 3; **wie geht's?** how are you? 1; **es geht** OK, can't complain, 1; it's possible, 7; **das geht nicht** that doesn't work; that won't do, 10

die Geige, –n violin, 3
das Gelände ground; site
gelb yellow, 5
das Geld money, 7
das Gemüse, – vegetable, 11
genug enough
geöffnet open
die Geographie geography
gerade exactly, precisely; just, 8
geradeaus: immer ~ straight ahead, 15
gern (lieber) gladly, with pleasure, 3; ~
  haben to like, to be fond of, 3; **ich hätte
  ~ . . .** I would like . . . , 11
das Geschäft, –e store, 8
die Geschäftsfrau, –en businesswoman, 4
der Geschäftsmann, –̈er (*also pl.* **die
  Geschäftsleute**) businessman, 4
das Geschenk, –e present; **Geburtstagsgeschenk** birthday present, 8
die Geschichte, –n story; history, 6
das Geschirr dishes, 9
die Geschwindigkeitsbegrenzung speed
  limit
sich gesellen to associate with
gestern yesterday, 9
gesund healthy, well, 1
das Getränk, –e beverage, 12
gewinnen (gewonnen) to win, 10; **wie hoch
  haben sie gewonnen?** by how much did
  they win? 10
gewöhnlich usually, 12
die Gitarre, –n guitar, 3
das Glas, –̈er glass, 11
glatt slippery, 13
glauben to believe, 7
gleich like, similar; alike
gleichfalls likewise; same to you
das Glockenspiel carillon
glücklich happy, 1
das Gold gold
graben (ä; gegraben) to dig
der Grad degree, 13
das Gramm gram, 11
grammatisch: grammatische Übersicht
  grammatical summary
das Gras grass
gratulieren to congratulate
grau gray, 5
der Groschen Austrian monetary unit (1/100
  Schilling)

groß (ö) tall, big, 4; **wie ~ bist du?** how tall
  are you? 4
die Größe, –n size, 5
die Großeltern (*pl.*) grandparents, 9
die Grube, –n hole
Grüetzi hello (*in Switzerland*)
grün green, 5
die Gruppe, –n group, 7
Grüß dich hello, hi
Grüß Gott hello, 11
der Gürtel, – belt, 5
gut (besser) good, 1; **gute Nacht!** good
  night! 1; **guten Abend!** good evening! 1;
  guten Morgen! good morning! 1; **guten
  Tag!** hello! 1; **es geht mir ~** I'm fine

haben to have, 2; **gern ~** to like, 3
halb half; **um ~ neun** at 8:30, 6
die Hand, –̈e hand
der Handschuh, –e glove, 5
häßlich ugly, 5
hätte: ich ~ gern I would like, 11
die Hauptstadt, –̈e capital city, 13
das Haus, –̈er house, 9; **nach Hause** home
  (*direction*), 3; **zu Hause** (at) home, 3
die Hausaufgaben (*pl.*) homework, 3
die Hausfrau housewife
der Hausmann "house–husband"
das Heft, –e notebook, 6
heiß hot, 13
heißen (geheißen) to be named, called, 4; **ich
  heiße . . .** my name is . . . 1; **wie heißt du?**
  what's your name? 1; **was heißt das?** what do
  you mean? 9
helfen (i; geholfen) to help, 9
Helvetia *name for Switzerland used on official
  documents*
das Hemd, –en shirt, 5
der Herbst autumn, fall, 10
der Herr, –n, –en gentleman, 5; ~ **X** Mr. X, 4
das Herz heart
herzlich cordial; **herzliche Grüße** best
  wishes, kind regards, sincerely (*closing in letters*), 4; **herzlichen Glückwunsch zum Geburtstag!** happy birthday
heute today, 3; ~ **abend** tonight; this evening, 3; ~ **morgen** this morning, 3; ~ **nachmittag** this afternoon, 3
hier here, 3

hinein in; into

das Hobby, -s hobby, *4*

hoch (höher) high, *10*; **wie ~ haben sie gewonnen?** by how much did they win? *10*

hoffentlich I hope, let's hope, *4*

höher (*comp. of* **hoch**) higher, *13*

hören to hear, *4*

die Hose, -n pants, slacks, *5*

hübsch pretty, nice, *5*

das Huhn, ⸚er chicken, *12*

der Hund, -e dog, *9*

hundert hundred, *4*

der Hunger hunger, *12*; **~ haben** to be hungry, *12*

ich I, *1*

ihn (*acc. of* **er**) him, *10*

ihr you (*fam. pl.*), *2*; her, its; their, *4*

Ihr your (*formal*), *7*

im = **in dem** in, *2*

immer always, *8*; **~ geradeaus** straight ahead, *15*

in in(to), *3*

interessant interesting, *6*

ja yes, *1*; *flavoring word confirming that what is said is self-evident*, *6*; **~, und wie!** sure, I do (I am), *7*

die Jacke, -n suit coat, jacket, *5*

das Jahr, -e year, *4*

die Jahreszeit, -en season, time of year, *13*

der Januar January, *2*

die Jeans (*pl.*) jeans, *5*

jeder each; everyone, *9*; *pl.* **alle** all

jemand someone, *15*

jetzt now, *3*

der Job, -s job

das Jugendzentrum youth center, club, *7*

der Juli July, *2*

jung (ü) young, *2*

der Junge, -n, -n boy, *5*

der Juni June, *2*

der Kaffee coffee, *9*; **~ kochen** to make coffee, *9*; **~ trinken** to drink coffee (*with breakfast or with afternoon pastries*), *9*; **zum ~ einladen** to invite for coffee and cake, *9*

kalt (ä) cold, *13*

kaputt broken, out of order, exhausted, *1*

die Karotte, -n carrot, *11*

die Karte, -n ticket, *7*; postcard, menu; (*pl.*) (playing) cards, *4*; **~ zu drei Mark** tickets at three marks, *7*

die Kartoffel, -n potato, *11*

das Kartoffelpüree mashed potatoes, *12*

der Käse cheese, *11*

die Kasse box office, *7*; cashier

die Katze, -n cat, *9*

kaufen to buy, *5*

kein not a, not any, *5*

kennen (gekannt) to know, to be acquainted with, *10*

die Keramik ceramics, pottery, *8*

das Kilo(gramm) kilogram, *11*

der Kilometer, - kilometer, *3*

das Kind, -er child, *4*

das Kino, -s movie theater, *7*

die Kirche, -n church, *15*

klar clear; **~!** sure! of course! *6*

die Klarinette, -n clarinet, *3*

klasse! terrific! *5*

die Klasse, -n grade, class, *6*

die Klassenarbeit test

die Klassenfahrt, -en class trip, *15*

das Klassenzimmer, - classroom, *6*

klassisch classical, *4*

das Klavier, -e piano, *3*

die Klavierstunde piano lesson

das Kleid, -er dress, *5*; (*pl.*) clothes

die Kleidung clothing

klein small, short, little, *4*

die Kneipe, -n pub, tavern

der Koch, ⸚e/die Köchin, -nen cook

kochen to cook, *4*

die Kohle, -n coal

kommen (ist gekommen) to come, *4*

kompliziert complicated, *8*

die Konfektionsgröße, -n clothing size

können (kann) can, to be able to, *7*

das Konzert, -e concert, *7*

kosten to cost, *5*

krank ill, sick, *1*

die Krawatte, -n necktie, *5*

kreuzen to cross

die Kreuzung, -en intersection, *15*

der Kuchen, - cake, *11*

der Kugelschreiber, - (*abbr.* **der Kuli, -s**) ballpoint pen, *6*

kühl cool, 13

die Kultur culture

der Kunde, -n, -n/die Kundin, -nen customer, client, 11

die Kunst art, 6

der Kurs, -e course, 14

kurz (ü) short, 6

die Kurzarbeit quiz

die Kürze brevity

lachen to laugh

lahm lame; **eine lahme Ente** a dull, boring person, 9

lang (ä) long, 6

lange (*adv.*) long; **wie ~?** how long? 12

die Langeweile boredom, 8; **ich habe~** I am bored, 8

langsam slow(ly), 14

langweilig boring, 6

(das) Latein Latin (language), 6

laufen (äu; ist gelaufen) to run; to walk, 10

die Lebensmittel (*pl.*) food, groceries, 11

der Lehrer, -/die Lehrerin, -nen teacher, 4

leicht easy, light, 6

leid: das tut mir ~ I'm sorry, 1

leider unfortunately, 5

lernen to learn, to study, 4

lesen (ie; gelesen) to read, 8

das Lesestück, -e reading selection

letzt last, 9

die Leute (*pl.*) people

das Licht, -er light, 8

lieber (*comp. of* **gern**) rather, 13; **~haben** to like better, to prefer, 13; **ich esse ~ ...** I prefer to eat . . ., 12

lieber/liebe dear (*opening in letters*), 4

das Lieblingsfach, -er favorite subject, 6

liegen (gelegen) to lie, to be (situated), 13

die Limo(nade) soft drink, 12

links (to the) left, 15

der Liter, - liter, 11; **1 ~ auf 10 Kilometer** 10 kilometers to the liter, 14

die Litfaßsäule, -n poster column

der Löffel, - spoon

das Lokal, -e place to eat, drink, dance; restaurant, 15

los: was ist~? What's the matter? 1; **es ist viel~** there is a lot going on, 15

los·gehen (ist losgegangen) to go, to take off, 10; **wann geht's los?** when does it start? 10

die Lust pleasure, enjoyment; **~haben** to feel like doing something, 7; **er hat zu nichts~** he doesn't feel like doing anything, 8

machen to do, to make, 3; **das macht Spaß** that's fun, 4; **das macht zusammen 10 Mark** that comes to 10 marks, 11

das Mädchen, - girl, 5

der Mai May, 2

das Mal time, occasion, 10; **nächstes~** next time, 10

mal times, 2; *flavoring word that leaves the time indefinite and softens a command*, 7

man (*indef. pronoun*) one, you, they, people, 11

mancher some, several, 12

manchmal sometimes, 12

der Mann, -er man, 5; husband

der Mantel, - coat, 5

die Mappe, -n briefcase, book bag, 6

die Mark basic German monetary unit (**DM = Deutsche Mark = 100 Pfennig**), 5

der Markt, -e market, 11; **auf dem~** at the open-air market, 11

die Marmelade jam, 12

der März March, 2

die Mathematik mathematics, 6; **die Mathe** math, 6

die Maus, -e mouse

mehr more, 7

die Meile, -n mile

mein my, 4

meinen to think; to mean, 5

der Mensch, -en, -en man, human being; **Mensch!** wow! brother! oh, boy! 6

das Messer, - knife

der Meter, - meter, 4

der Metzger, -/die Metzgerin, -nen butcher, 11

mich (*acc. of* **ich**) me, 10

die Milch milk, 11

das Mineralwasser mineral water, 12

die Minute, -n minute, 3

mit (+ *dat.*) with; **~dem Bus fahren** to go by bus, 14

mit·kommen (ist mitgekommen) to come along, 8

mit·nehmen (nimmt mit; mitgenommen) to take along, 13

der Mittag noon, 12; **zu ~ essen** to have lunch, 12

das Mittagessen warm noon meal, lunch, 12; **zum~** for the noon meal, 12

mittags at noon, at lunch time, 12

der Mittwoch Wednesday, 6

die Möbel (*pl.*) furniture, 9

möchte (*form of* **mögen**) would like to, 7

das Mofa, ‑s moped, motorbike, 14

mögen (mag) to like; **möchte** would like to, 7

der Moment moment; **einen~** just a moment, 11; **~mal** just a moment, 15

der Monat, ‑e month, 2

der Montag Monday, 4

der Morgen, ‑ morning; **guten~!** good morning! 1

morgen tomorrow, 7; **~abend** tomorrow evening, 7; **~früh** tomorrow morning

morgens in the morning

das Motorrad, ‑̈er motorcycle, 14

müde tired, 1

der Müll garbage, 9

der Mülleimer garbage pail, 9

das Museum (*pl.* **Museen**) museum, 15

die Musik music, 4

musikalisch musical, 4

die Musikbox juke box

das Musikinstrument, ‑e musical instrument, 3

müssen (muß) to have to, must, 7

die Mutter, ‑̈ mother, 4

na well, 10; **~und?** so what?, 10

nach (+ *dat.*) after; to (*with cities or countries*), 15; **~Hause** home (*direction*), 3

der Nachmittag, ‑e afternoon; **am~** in the afternoon, 6

nachmittags in the afternoon, 12

nächst next, 10; **nächstes Mal** next time, 10

die Nacht, ‑̈e night; **gute~!** good night! 1

der Nachtisch dessert, 12

der Name, ‑n (*acc. and dat.*‑**n**) name, 4

nämlich namely, you know, 11

naß wet, 13

natürlich naturally, of course, 2

nehmen (nimmt, genommen) to take, 7

nein no, 1

nennen (genannt) to name, to call, 9

nett nice, 11

neu new, 5

neun nine, 9

neunzehn nineteen, 2

neunzig ninety, 4

nicht not, 1; **nicht?=nicht wahr?** isn't that so! isn't that right? 2; **~nur ... sondern auch** not only ... but also, 12

nichts nothing, 7; **~mehr** nothing left, 7

niemand no one, 14

noch still, yet, 4; **~nicht** not yet, 7

der Norden north, 13

nördlich (von) northern, north (of), 13

der November November, 2

null zero, 2

nun now, 8

nur only, just, 1

ob (*sub, conj.*) if, whether, 13

der Ober, ‑ waiter, 12

das Obst fruit, 11

oder (*coord, conj.*) or, 2

oft (ö) often, 3

ohne (+ *acc.*) without, 11

der Oktober October, 2

die Orange, ‑n orange, 11

der Osten east, 13

(das) Österreich Austria

östlich (von) eastern, east (of)

paar: ein~ a few, some, 7

packen to pack, 11

das Papier, ‑e paper, 6; (*pl.*) papers, documents

der Park, ‑s park, 15

die Party, ‑s party, 10

passen to fit; to match, 5

die Pause, ‑n break; intermission, 6

Pech: so ein~ what bad luck, how unfortunate, 15

der Pfannkuchen pancake

der Pfennig, ‑e (*abbr.* **Pf**) German monetary unit: **1 Pf = 1/100 Mark**, 11

das Pfund (*abbr.* **Pfd.**) pound (**1 Pfd. = 500 g**), 11

die Physik physics, 6

das Picknick, ‑s picnic, 10

die Pille, ‑n pill

die Pinte, –n   pub
der Plan, ~e   plan; schedule, 6
die Platte, –n   record, 8
der Plattenspieler, –   record player, turntable, 8
der Platz, ~e   square, 15; seat
die Pommes frites (pl.)   French fries, 12
die Post   post office, mail, 15
das (also der) Poster, –   poster, 8
praktisch   practical, 14
preiswert   worth the money, reasonably priced, 5
prima   excellent, fine, great, 1
pro   per, 14
das Problem, –e   problem
die Prüfung, –en   exam, test, 14
der Pudding   pudding, 12
der Pulli, –s   pullover, 5
der Pullover   pullover
putzen   to clean, 9

Quatsch!   nonsense! rubbish! 10
das Quiz   quiz

das Rad, ~er   wheel; bicycle (short for das Fahrrad), 14
der Radfahrer   bicyclist
der Radiergummi, –s (abbr. der Gummi) eraser, 6
das Radio, –s   radio, 8
der Radioamateur, –e   "ham" radio operator, 8
der Rappen   Swiss monetary unit (1/100 Franken)
das Rathaus, ~er   town hall, 15
raus·tragen (ä; rausgetragen)   to carry out, 9
recht: ~haben   to be right, 13
rechts   (to the) right, 15
das Reden   speaking
das Reformhaus   health food store
der Regen   rain, 13
der Regenmantel   raincoat
der Regenschirm, –e   umbrella, 13
regnen   to rain, 13
reiten (ist geritten)   to ride (horseback), 10
reparieren   to repair, 8
das Restaurant, –s   restaurant, 13
richtig   correct, right, 2
der Rindsbraten   roast beef, pot roast, 12
der Rock   rock (music), 4

der Rock, ~e   skirt, 5
rodeln (ist gerodelt)   to toboggan; to go sledding, 13
rot   red, 5
das Rührei   scrambled egg

die Sache, –n   thing; (pl.) clothes, 5
der Saft, ~e   juice, 11
sagen   to say, to tell, 8
der Salat, –e   (head of) lettuce, salad, 12
Salut   hello
die Sammelfreude, –n   joy of collecting
sammeln   to collect, 8
der Samstag   Saturday, 4; am~   on Saturday, 4
sarkastisch   sarcastic, 9
sauer   cross, annoyed; sour, 1
schade   too bad, 5
die Schallplatte, –n   record, 8
schauen   to look, 15
scheinen (geschienen)   to shine, 13; to seem 15; so scheint's   so it seems, 15
der Scherz   joke
der Schi, –er (also Ski)   ski, 10
das Schikjöring   Norwegian sport in which skier is pulled by horses or motorcycles
Schi laufen (äu)   to ski, 10
schick   chic, stylish, 5
das Schiff, –e   ship, 14
das Schild, –er   sign, 15
der Schilling   basic Austrian monetary unit
der Schinken   ham, 11
das Schinkenbrot, –e   ham sandwich, 12
schlafen (ä; geschlafen)   to sleep, 9
das Schlagzeug, –e   drums, 3
schlank   slender, slim, 4
schlecht   bad, 1
schließlich   after all
schlimm   bad, 6
der Schlittschuh, –e   ice skate, 10
Schlittschuh laufen (äu)   to ice-skate, 10
schmecken   to taste (good), 9
der Schnee   snow, 13
der Schneemann   snow man
schneien   to snow, 13
schnell   fast, 14
die Schokolade, –n   chocolate, hot chocolate; bar of chocolate, 12
schon   already, 2; das ~   that's true, 7
schön   beautiful, 5; nice, 4

schreiben (geschrieben) to write, 4
der Schuh, -e shoe, 5
die Schuhgröße shoe size
die Schule, -n school, 6
der Schüler, -/die Schülerin, -nen student (in high school), 4
schwarz (ä) black, 5
das Schweigen silence
das Schwein pig; ~ **haben** to be lucky, 14
das Schweinskotelett, -s pork chop, 11
die Schweiz Switzerland
schwer difficult, heavy, 6
die Schwester, -n sister, 4
schwimmen (ist geschwommen) to swim, 3
(das) Schwyzerdütsch Swiss German (language)
sechs six, 2
sechzehn sixteen, 2
sechzig sixty, 4
der See, -n lake, 14; **an den ~** to the lake, 14
segeln to sail, 10
sehen (ie; gesehen) to see, to watch, to look, 8
sehr very, 1
sein his, its, 4
sein (ist) to be, 1
seit (+ dat.) since, for, 15
selbst oneself, myself, etc., 11
der Senf mustard
der September September, 2
Servus! hello (in Austria)
sicher sure, certain(ly), 7
sie she, 1; they, 2
Sie you (formal), 7
sieben seven, 2
siebzehn seventeen, 2
siebzig seventy, 4
das Silber silver
singen (gesungen) to sing, 4
der Sinn, -e sense; mind
so so, 1; ~ ... **wie** as ... as, 11
die Socke, -n sock, 5
solcher such, 12
sollen (soll) should, to be supposed to, 7
der Sommer summer, 10
der Sommerschlußverkauf summer clearance sale
das Sonderangebot special offer
sondern (coord. conj.) but (on the contrary), 12
die Sonne sun, 13

der Sonnenschirm sunshade, parasol
der Sonntag Sunday, 4
sonst (noch) in addition; **was sonst?** what else? 3; ~ **noch was?** anything else? 11
Spaß: das macht ~ ! that's fun! 4
spät late; **zu ~** too late, tardy, 4; **wie ~ ist es?** what time is it? 6; **bis später** till later, see you later, 1
der Spatz, -en sparrow
spazieren to walk, to stroll, to go for a walk, 3
der Spaziergang, -̈e walk, stroll; **einen ~ machen** to go for a walk, 9
die Speisekarte, -n menu, 12
das Spiegelei fried egg
das Spiel, -e game, 10
der Spielautomat slot machine, pinball machine
spielen to play, 3
die Spielsache, -n toy, plaything
der Spinat spinach, 11
spinnen to spin; **du spinnst** you're crazy, 13
der Sport sport, 6; ~ **treiben** to be active in sports, 4
der Sportfreund sports fan
der Sportverein sports club
spottbillig dirt-cheap, 5
sprechen (i; gesprochen) to speak, 13
spülen to wash dishes, 9; to rinse
die Stadt, -̈e city, 8
der Stadtplan, -̈e city map, 15
der Stau, -s traffic jam
der Staub dust, 9; ~ **saugen** to vacuum, 9
stehen (gestanden) to stand, 15
die Stereoanlage, -n stereo system, 8
der Stiefel, - boot, 15
still still, quiet; calm
stimmen to be true, correct, 13; **das stimmt** that's right, 8
der Strandkorb, -̈e (canopied) beach chair
die Straße, -n street, 3
die Straßenbahn, -en streetcar, 14
stricken to knit
das Stück, -e piece, 11
der Student, -en, -en/die Studentin, -nen student (at a university), 15
die Stunde, -n hour; class, 6
der Stundenplan, -̈e class schedule, 6
suchen to look for, 15
der Süden south, 13
südlich (von) southern, south (of), 13

der Supermarkt, ⏜e   supermarket, 11
die Suppe, -n   soup, 12

der Tag, -e   day; ~ !   hi, 1; **guten** ~!
   hello! 1
täglich   daily
die Tankstelle, -n   service station, gas station,
   15
tanzen   to dance, 4
die Tasche, -n   bag; pocket
das Taschengeld   pocket money, allowance
die Tasse, -n   cup, 12
die Taube, -n   dove; pigeon
tausend   thousand, 4
der Tee   tea, 12
der Teig   dough; batter
die Temperatur, -en   temperature, 13
das Tennis   tennis, 3
teuer   expensive, 5
das Theater, -   theater, 7
die Theaterkarte   theater ticket
theoretisch   theoretical
das Thermometer, -   thermometer, 13
tief   deep
der Tisch, -e   table, 9
toll   great, fantastic, 1; crazy
die Tomate, -n   tomato, 11
das Tor, -e   gate, 15
die Torte, -n   layer cake, 9
die Tour, -en   tour, trip, 14
tragen (ä; getragen)   to wear, 5; to carry
der Traum, ⏜e   dream, 14
treiben: treibst du Sport?   are you active in
   sports? 4
der Trimm-dich-Pfad   *marked path for jogging
   and exercising*
trinken (getrunken)   to drink, 9
trocken   dry, 13
tschüß!   so long! (*informal*), 1
tun (getan)   to do, 7
die Tür, -en   door, 8
die Tüte, -n   bag, sack, 11

die U-Bahn, -en   subway, 14
über (+ *acc. or dat.*)   about, above, over, 13
überall   everywhere
übermorgen   the day after tomorrow, 7
die Übersicht   summary

die Übung, -en   exercise
die Uhr, -en   clock, watch, 6; **um wieviel** ~ ?
   at what time? 6; **wieviel** ~ **ist es?**   what time
   is it? 6
um (+ *acc.*)   at, around, 6; ~ **ein Uhr**   at one
   o'clock, 6
unabhängig   independent, 14
und (*coord. conj.*)   and, 1
unentschieden   undetermined; tied (*in scor-
   ing*), 10
ungewöhnlich   unusual
unglücklich   unhappy, 1
uns (*acc. of* **wir**)   us, 10
unser   our, 4
unsicher   dangerous; unsure, insecure, 14
Unsinn!   nonsense! 1
unter (+ *acc. or dat.*)   under
der Unterricht   lesson, instruction, 14

der Vater, ⏜   father, 4
das Verbot   prohibition, ban
verderben (i; verdorben)   to spoil
verdienen   to earn
vergessen (i; vergessen)   to forget, 15
der Verkäufer, -/die Verkäuferin, -nen   salesperson, 4
das Verkehrszeichen, -   traffic sign
verlieren (verloren)   to lose, 10
verstehen (verstanden)   to understand, 8
versuchen   to try, 7
viel (mehr)   much, many, a lot, 3; **vielen
   Dank!**   thank you very much, 12
vielleicht   maybe, perhaps, 7
vier   four, 2
das Viertel, -   quarter, 6
vierzehn   fourteen, 2
vierzig   forty, 4
die Vokabel, -n   (vocabulary) word; (*pl.*) vocabulary
der Volleyball, ⏜e   volleyball, 3
von (+ *dat.*)   from, 3
vor (+ *acc. or dat.*)   before, 6; in front of
vor·haben   to plan, 8
die Vorstellung, -en   performance, 7
der VW (= Volkswagen)   14

wahrscheinlich   probably, 13

wandern (ist gewandert)   to hike, to go hiking, 3

das Wanderwetter   hiking weather

wann   when, 2

war (*past tense of* **sein**)   was, 11

das Warenhaus, ̈er   department store, 15

warm (ä)   warm, 5

warum   why, 1

was   what, 1; ~ **ist (denn) los?**   (well,) what's the matter?, 1; ~ **sonst?**   what else? 3; ~ **für (ein)**   what kind of (a), 14

die Wäsche   laundry, 9

waschen (ä; gewaschen)   to wash, 9

das Wasser   water, 10

weil (*sub. conj.*)   because, 15

der Wein, ‑e   wine, 12

weiß   white, 5

weit   far (away), 3

weiter   further, 13

welcher   which, 5

die Welt   world

wem (*dat. of* **wer**)   (to) whom, 14

wen (*acc. of* **wer**)   whom, 10

weniger   minus, less, 2

wenigstens   at least, 9

wenn   if, when, 13

wer   who, 2

werden (wird; ist geworden)   to become, 13

wertvoll   valuable, 8

der Westen   west, 13

westlich (von)   western, west (of)

das Wetter   weather, 13

wie   how, 1; as, 9; ~ **geht's?**   how are you (doing)? 1; ~ **alt bist du?**   how old are you? 2; ~ **(immer)**   as (always), 9

wieder   again, 1

die Wiederholung, ‑en   review

Wiederhören: auf ~   good-by (*on the telephone*)

Wiederschauen: auf ~   good-by, 11

Wiedersehen: auf ~   good-by, 1

wieviel   how much, 2; ~ **Uhr ist es?**   what time is it? 6

der Wind   wind, 13

windig   windy, 13

die Windjacke   windbreaker

windsurfen   to go wind surfing, 10

der Winter   winter, 10

der Winterschlußverkauf   winter clearance sale

das Wintersportzentrum   center for winter sports

wir   we, 2

wirklich   really, 1

wissen (weiß; gewußt)   to know, 8

wo   where, 3

die Woche, ‑n   week, 11

das Wochenende, ‑n   weekend, 4

wohin   where (to), 8

wohl   indeed, probably, 11

wohnen   to live, 3

die Wolle   wool

wollen (will)   to want, to intend to, to wish, 7

das Wort, ̈er   word

das Wörterbuch   dictionary

der Wunsch, ̈e   wish, desire, 11

die Wurst, ̈e   sausage, cold cuts, 11

das Würstchen, ‑   frankfurter, 11

die Würze   spice; flavor

die Zahl, ‑en   number, 2

zahlen   to pay, 12

zart   tender, delicate, 12

zehn   ten, 2

die Zeit, ‑en   time, 7

zelten   to camp, to pitch a tent, 10

das Zentimetermaß   measuring tape

der Zentimeter, ‑   centimeter, 4

das Zeugnis, ‑se   report card; grades

ziemlich   quite, 3

das Zimmer, ‑   room, 9

zu (+ *dat.*)   to; too, 3; shut, closed, 15; ~ **Hause**   (at) home, 3; ~ **Abend essen**   to have supper, 12; ~ **Mittag essen**   to have lunch, 12; ~ **Fuß**   on foot, 15

zufrieden   content, satisfied, 1

der Zug, ̈e   train, 14

zuletzt   last

zum (= **zu dem**); ~ **Abendessen**   for supper, 12; ~ **Frühstück**   for breakfast, 12; ~ **Kaffee einladen**   to invite for coffee and cake, 9

zu·machen   to shut, 8

zurück   back, 11

zusammen   together, 11; **das macht** ~ **10 Mark**   that comes to 10 marks, 11

zwanzig   twenty, 4

zwei   two, 2

zwischen (+ *acc. or dat.*)   between, 14

zwölf   twelve, 2

English-German vocabulary

The symbol ~ signifies the repetition of the key word in that entry.

a/an   ein, eine
able: to be ~ to   können
about   über
above   über
acquainted: to be ~ with   kennen
addition: in ~   sonst
after   nach
afternoon   der Nachmittag, –e; **this ~**   heute nachmittag; **in the ~**   am Nachmittag, nachmittags
again   wieder
against   gegen
ahead: straight ~   immer geradeaus
airplane   das Flugzeug, –e
all   alle, alles; **~ the best**   alles Gute
almost   fast
alone   allein
along   entlang; **~ the street**   die Straße entlang; **to come ~**   mit·kommen
already   schon
also   auch
always   immer; **as ~**   wie immer
am: I ~   ich bin
American (*adj.*)   amerikanisch
and   und (*coord. conj.*)
apple   der Apfel, ⁓
are: you ~   du bist, ihr seid, Sie sind; **they ~**   sie sind; **we ~**   wir sind
around   um
art   die Kunst
as   als; wie; **~ ... ~**   so ... wie
ask   fragen
at   an; auf; bei; um; **~ one o'clock**   um ein Uhr
autumn   der Herbst

back   zurück
bad   schlecht; schlimm; **too ~**   schade
bag   die Tüte, –n; **shopping ~**   die Einkaufstasche, –n
bake   backen
baker   der Bäcker, –/die Bäckerin, –nen
banana   die Banane, –n
band   die Band, –s
bank   die Bank, –en
basketball   der Basketball, ⁓e
bathroom   das Badezimmer
be   sein
beautiful   schön
because   denn (*coord. conj.*); weil (*sub. conj.*)
become   werden
beer   das Bier
before   vor
begin   beginnen
believe   glauben
belt   der Gürtel, –
besides   außer
better   besser
between   zwischen
beverage   das Getränk, –e
bicycle   das Fahrrad, ⁓er; das Rad
big   groß
biology   die Biologie
birthday   der Geburtstag, –e; **it's my ~**   ich habe Geburtstag; **happy ~!**   herzlichen Glückwunsch zum Geburtstag!
black   schwarz
blouse   die Bluse, –n
blue   blau
book   das Buch, ⁓er; **~ bag**   die Mappe, –n
bored: I am ~   ich habe Langeweile
boredom   die Langeweile

boring   langweilig; **a ~ person**   eine lahme Ente
both   beide
bottle   die Flasche, –n
box office   die Kasse
boy   der Junge, –n, –n; **oh, ~!**   Mensch!
brake   die Bremse, –n
bread   das Brot, –e
break   die Pause, –n
breakfast   das Frühstück; **for ~**   zum Frühstück; **to have ~**   frühstücken
briefcase   die Mappe, –n
bring   bringen
broken   kaputt
brother   der Bruder, ⁓; **~!**   Mensch!
brown   braun; **a ~ coat**   ein Mantel in Braun
bus   der Bus, –se
businessman   der Geschäftsmann, ⁓er (*also pl.* Geschäftsleute)
businesswoman   die Geschäftsfrau, –en
but   aber; sondern; **not only ... ~ also**   nicht nur ... sondern auch
butcher   der Metzger, –/die Metzgerin, –nen
butter   die Butter
buy   kaufen
by   bei; **to go ~ bus**   mit dem Bus fahren

café   das Café, –s
cake   der Kuchen, –; **layer ~**   die Torte, –n
call   an·rufen; nennen
camping   das Camping; **to go ~**   zelten
can   können

capital   die Hauptstadt, ⁼e

car   das Auto, –s; der Wagen, –

card   die Karte, –n, **to play ~s**   Karten spielen

carrot   die Karotte, –n

carry   tragen; **to ~ out** raus·tragen

cassette   die Cassette, –n; **~ recorder**   der Cassetten-Recorder, –

cat   die Katze, –n

centimeter   der Zenti-meter, –

ceramics   die Keramik

certain(ly)   bestimmt; sicher; bitte sehr

cheap   billig; **dirt-~** spottbillig

cheese   der Käse

chemistry   die Chemie; **~ homework**   die Chemie-aufgabe

chic   schick

chicken   das Huhn, ⁼er

child   das Kind, –er

chocolate   die Schokolade, –n

church   die Kirche, –n

city   die Stadt, ⁼e; **~ map** der Stadtplan, ⁼e

clarinet   die Klarinette, –n

class   die Klasse, –n; **~ trip**   die Klassenfahrt, –en; **~room**   das Klassenzim-mer, –

classical   klassisch

clean   putzen, auf·räumen

clear   ab·räumen

clock   die Uhr, –en

close   zu·machen; **~d**   zu

clothes   die Sachen (pl.), die Kleider (pl.)

cloudy   bewölkt

club   der Club, –s

coaster   der Bierdeckel, –

coat   der Mantel, ⁼

coffee   der Kaffee; **~ shop** das Café, –s; **to make ~** Kaffee kochen; **to invite**

for ~ and cake   zum Kaf-fee einladen; **to have ~** Kaffee trinken

cola drink   die (also das) Cola

cold   kalt

collect   sammeln

color   die Farbe, –n; **what ~ is . . .**   welche Farbe hat . . .

come   kommen; **to ~ along**   mit·kommen; **that comes to 10 marks**   das macht zusammen 10 Mark

complete(ly)   ganz

complicated   kompliziert

concert   das Konzert, –e

content   zufrieden

cook   kochen

cool   kühl

corner   die Ecke, –n

correct   richtig; **to be ~** stimmen

cost   kosten

course   der Kurs, –e; **of ~!**   klar! natürlich!

crazy: you're ~!   du spinnst!

cross   sauer

cup   die Tasse, –n

customer   der Kunde, –n, –n/die Kundin, –nen

dance   tanzen

dangerous   unsicher

day   der Tag, –e

dear (in letters)   lieber/liebe

degree   der Grad

department store   das Warenhaus, ⁼er

describe   beschreiben

dessert   der Nachtisch

different   anders

difficult   schwer

diligent   fleißig

dirt: ~-cheap   spottbillig

disco   die Disco

discussion   die Diskussion, –en

dishes (pl.)   das Geschirr; **to**

wash ~   (Geschirr) spülen

do   machen, tun; **that won't ~**   das geht nicht

doctor   der Arzt, ⁼e/die Ärz-tin, –nen

dog   der Hund, –e

door   die Tür, –en

dream   der Traum, ⁼e

dress   das Kleid, –er

drink   trinken

drive   fahren

driving: ~ instructor   der Fahrlehrer, –/die Fahr-lehrerin, –nen; **~ school** die Fahrschule; –n; **~ les-son**   die Fahrstunde, –n

drums   das Schlagzeug, –e

dry   trocken; **to ~** ab·trocknen

dumb   doof, dumm

dust   der Staub; **to ~** ab·stauben

each   jeder

early   früh

east   der Osten; **~ (of)** östlich (von)

eastern   östlich

easy   leicht

eat   essen

egg   das Ei, –er

electrician   der Elektriker, –/ die Elektrikerin, –nen

else: what ~?   was sonst?; **anything ~?**   sonst noch was?

eraser   der Radiergummi, –s

especially   besonders

evening   der Abend, –e; **good ~!**   guten Abend!; **in the ~**   abends; **this ~** heute abend

everyone   alle, jeder

everything   alles

exactly   gerade

exam   die Prüfung, –en

excellent   ausgezeichnet, prima

except   außer

excuse: ~ me Entschuldigung!

exhausted kaputt

expensive teuer

expressway die Autobahn, –en

fail durch·fallen

fall fallen

family die Familie, –n

fantastic toll

far weit

fast schnell

fat dick

father der Vater, ⸚

favorite: ~ subject das Lieblingsfach, ⸚er

feed füttern

feel: to ~ like doing something Lust haben; **he doesn't ~ like doing anything** er hat zu nichts Lust

few: a ~ ein paar

finally endlich

find finden

finished fertig

first erst

fish der Fisch, –e

fit passen

flute die Flöte, –n

fly fliegen

foot der Fuß, ⸚e; **on ~** zu Fuß

for für; seit; denn

forget vergessen

fountain der Brunnen, –

frankfurter das Würstchen, –

free frei

freeze frieren

French fries die Pommes frites (*pl.*)

fresh frisch

Friday der Freitag

friend der Freund, –e/die Freundin, –nen

from aus; von

fruit das Obst

fun: that's ~ das macht Spaß

furniture die Möbel (*pl.*)

further weiter

game das Spiel, –e

garage die Garage, –n

garbage der Müll; **~ pail** der Mülleimer

gardening die Gartenarbeit

gas station die Tankstelle, –n

gasoline das Benzin

gate das Tor, –e

gentleman der Herr, –n, –en

geography die Erdkunde, die Geographie

get bekommen; **I'll ~ the day off** ich bekomme frei; **to ~ up** auf·stehen

girl das Mädchen, –

give geben

glad froh

gladly gern

glass das Glas, ⸚er

glove der Handschuh, –e

go gehen; fahren

good gut; **~ night** gute Nacht; **~ evening** guten Abend; **~ morning** guten Morgen; **~-by** auf Wiedersehen, tschüß

gram das Gramm

grandparents die Großeltern (*pl.*)

gray grau

great prima, toll

green grün

groceries die Lebensmittel (*pl.*)

group die Gruppe, –n

guitar die Gitarre, –n

hairdresser der Friseur, –e/die Friseuse, –n

half halb; **at ~ past eight** um halb neun

ham der Schinken; **~ sandwich** das Schinkenbrot

happy glücklich, froh

have haben; **to ~ to** müssen

he er

healthy gesund

hear hören

heavy schwer

hello guten Tag; Grüß Gott

help helfen

her ihr (*adj.*); sie (*pron.*)

here da; hier

hi! Tag!

high hoch; **~er** höher

hike wandern

him ihn

his sein

history die Geschichte

hobby das Hobby, –s

home: (at) ~ zu Hause; **~ (direction)** nach Hause

homework die Hausaufgaben (*pl.*)

honest! Ehrenwort!

hope: I ~, let's ~ hoffentlich

hot heiß

hour die Stunde, –n

house das Haus, ⸚er

how wie; **~ are you?** wie geht's?; **~ old are you?** wie alt bist du?

however aber

hunger der Hunger

hungry: to be ~ Hunger haben

husband der Mann, ⸚er

I ich

ice cream das Eis

ice skate der Schlittschuh, –e; **to ~** Schlittschuh laufen

if ob (*sub. conj.*); wenn

in(to) in

indeed wohl

independent unabhängig

instruction der Unterricht

intend to wollen
interesting interessant
intersection die Kreuzung,
  −en
invite ein·laden
is: he/she is er/sie ist
it es
its ihr, sein

jacket die Jacke, −n
jam die Marmelade
jealous eifersüchtig
jeans die Jeans (*pl.*)
juice der Saft, ⁼e
just gerade, nur

kilogram das Kilo(gramm)
kilometer der Kilometer, −
know kennen; wissen

lady die Dame, −n
lake der See, −n; **to the**
  ~ an den See
last letzt
late spät; **too** ~ zu spät
later später; **see you** ~
  bis später
laundry die Wäsche; **to do**
  the ~ (die) Wäsche waschen
lazy faul
learn lernen
least: at ~ wenigstens
left links; **to the** ~ links
leisure time die Freizeit
less weniger
lesson die Aufgabe, −n
letter der Brief, −e
lettuce der Salat, −e
license: driver's ~ der
  Führerschein
light leicht; das Licht, −er
like gern haben, mögen;
  how do you ~ ...? wie
  findest du ...?; **what would**
  you ~? was darf es sein?;
  I would ~ ... ich hätte

gern ...; **he would** ~ **(to)**
  er möchte ...
liter der Liter, −; **10 kilo-**
  meters to the ~ 1 Liter
  auf 10 Kilometer
live wohnen
long lang; **how** ~? wie
  lange?; **so** ~! tschüß!
look schauen, sehen; **to** ~
  for suchen
lose verlieren
lot viel; **there's a** ~ **going**
  on es ist viel los
luck: what bad ~ so ein
  Pech
lucky: to be ~ Schwein
  haben
lunch das Mittagessen; **to**
  have ~ zu Mittag essen;
  for ~ zum Mittagessen;
  at ~ **time** mittags

make machen
man der Mann, ⁼er
many viele; **how** ~ wieviele
market der Markt, ⁼e; **at**
  the ~ auf dem Markt
match passen
mathematics die Mathematik; **math** die Mathe
matter: what's the ~? was
  ist los?
may dürfen
maybe vielleicht
me mich
meal das Essen
mean meinen; **what do**
  you ~? was heißt das?
meat das Fleisch
menu die Speisekarte, −n
meter der Meter, −
milk die Milch
mineral water das Mineralwasser
minus weniger
minute die Minute, −n
Miss Fräulein

model airplane das Flugzeugmodell, −e
moment: just a ~ Moment
  mal, einen Moment
Monday der Montag
money das Geld
month der Monat, −e
moped das Mofa, −s
more mehr
morning der Morgen, −;
  good ~! guten Morgen!;
  this ~ heute morgen; **in**
  the ~ morgens
mother die Mutter, ⁼
motorcycle das Motorrad,
  ⁼er
movie theater das Kino, −s
mountain-climbing: to go
  ~ bergsteigen gehen
Mr. Herr
Mrs. (or Ms.) Frau
much viel; **thank you**
  very ~ vielen Dank; **how**
  ~ wieviel
museum das Museum (*pl.*
  Museen)
music die Musik
musical musikalisch; ~ **in-**
  strument das Musikinstrument
must müssen
my mein

name der Name (*acc. & dat.*
  −n), −n; **my** ~ **is** ... ich
  heiße ...; **what's your** ~?
  wie heißt du?; **to** ~ nennen
named: to be ~ heißen
namely nämlich
naturally natürlich
near bei
necktie die Krawatte, −n
need brauchen
new neu
next nächst; ~ **time**
  nächstes Mal
nice nett, schön

night die Nacht, ¨e; **good ~!** gute Nacht!

no nein; ~ **one** niemand

nonsense! Quatsch!, Unsinn!

noon der Mittag; **at ~** mittags

north der Norden; ~ **(of)** nördlich (von)

northern nördlich

not nicht; ~ **at all** gar nicht; ~ **a,** ~ **any** kein

notebook das Heft, –e

nothing nichts; ~ **left** nichts mehr

now jetzt, nun

number die Zahl, –en

occur: it just occurs to me da fällt mir gerade ein

o'clock: it's (one) ~ es ist (ein) Uhr

often oft

oh ach; **~, I see!** ach so!

OK ganz gut; es geht

old alt

on auf; an; ~ **Saturday** am Samstag

one eins; man (*indef. pron.*)

oneself selbst

only nur; erst

open auf·machen

or oder (*coord. conj.*)

orange die Orange, –n

order bestellen

our unser

out: ~ of aus

pack ein·packen, packen

pail der Eimer, –

pants die Hose, –n

paper das Papier, –e

parents die Eltern (*pl.*)

park der Park, –s

party die Party, –s; **to go to a ~** auf eine Party gehen

pass: to ~ a test die Prüfung bestehen

pay bezahlen, zahlen

pea die Erbse, –n

pedestrian zone die Fußgängerzone, –n

pen: ballpoint ~ der Kugelschreiber, –; der Kuli, –s; ~ **pal** der Brieffreund, –e/ die Brieffreundin, –nen

pencil der Bleistift, –e

per pro

performance die Vorstellung, –en

permitted: to be ~ dürfen

pharmacist der Apotheker, –/die Apothekerin, –nen

photograph fotografieren

physics die Physik

piano das Klavier, –e

pick up ab·holen

picnic das Picknick, –s

piece das Stück, –e

plan der Plan, ¨e; **to ~** vor·haben

play spielen

please bitte, bitte schön

pork chop das Schweinskotelett, –s

post office die Post

postcard: picture ~ die Ansichtskarte, –n

poster das (*also* der) Poster,–

potato die Kartoffel, –n; **mashed potatoes** das Kartoffelpüree

pound das Pfund

practical praktisch

prefer lieber haben; **I ~ to eat ...** ich esse lieber ...

present das Geschenk, –e; **birthday ~** das Geburtstagsgeschenk

pretty hübsch

probably wahrscheinlich; wohl

pudding der Pudding

pullover der Pulli, –s

quarter das Viertel; ~ **to five** Viertel vor fünf

question die Frage, –n

quite ziemlich

radio das Radio, –s; **"ham" ~ operator** der Radioamateur, –e

railway die Bahn, –en

rain der Regen; **to ~** regnen

read lesen

ready fertig

really eigentlich; wirklich

reasonably: ~ priced preiswert

recommend empfehlen

record die Schallplatte, –n, die Platte, –n; ~ **player** der Plattenspieler, –

red rot

repair reparieren

report der Bericht, –e

restaurant das Restaurant, –s; das Lokal, –e

ride fahren; **to ~ horseback** reiten

right richtig; rechts; **to the ~** rechts; **to be ~** Recht haben; **that's ~** das stimmt

roast: ~ beef, pot ~ der Rindsbraten

rock (music) (der) Rock

roll das Brötchen, –

room das Zimmer, –

run laufen

sail segeln

salad der Salat, –e

salesperson der Verkäufer, –/die Verkäuferin, –nen

sarcastic sarkastisch

satisfied zufrieden

Saturday der Samstag; **on ~** am Samstag

sausage die Wurst, ¨e

say sagen

schedule der Stundenplan, ¨e; der Plan, ¨e

school die Schule, –n
season die Jahreszeit, –en
see sehen
seem scheinen; **so it seems** so scheint's
serious: you can't be ~! das ist doch nicht dein Ernst!
set: to ~ the table den Tisch decken
she sie
shine scheinen
ship das Schiff, –e
shirt das Hemd, –en
shoe der Schuh, –e
shop das Geschäft, –e; **to ~** ein·kaufen
shopping: ~ bag die Einkaufstasche; **to go ~** einkaufen gehen
short klein; kurz
should sollen
sick krank
sign das Schild, –er
signal: traffic ~ die Ampel, –n
simple einfach
simply einfach
since seit
sincerely herzliche Grüße
sing singen
sister die Schwester, –n
situated: to be ~ liegen
size die Größe, –n
ski der Schi, –er (also Ski); **to ~** Schi laufen
skirt der Rock, –̈e
sleep schlafen
slim schlank
slippery glatt
slow(ly) langsam
small klein
snow der Schnee; **to ~** schneien
so so; **~ what?** na und?; **isn't that ~?** nicht? nicht wahr?
soccer der Fußball; **~ game** das Fußballspiel, –e
sock die Socke, –n

soft drink die Limo(nade)
sold: ~ out ausverkauft
some mancher; ein paar
someone jemand
something etwas
sometimes manchmal
soon bald
sorry: I'm ~ es tut mir leid; Entschuldigung!
soup die Suppe, –n
sour sauer
south der Süden; **~ (of)** südlich (von)
southern südlich
speak sprechen
spinach der Spinat
sports der Sport; **to be active in ~** Sport treiben
spring der Frühling
square der Platz, –̈e
stamp die Briefmarke, –n
stand stehen
start beginnen; los·gehen; **when does it ~?** wann geht's los?
stay bleiben
stereo system die Stereoanlage, –n
still noch
store das Geschäft, –e; **department ~** das Warenhaus, –̈er
story die Geschichte, –n
strawberry die Erdbeere, –n
street die Straße, –n; **~ car** die Straßenbahn, –en
stroll der Spaziergang, –̈e; **to ~** bummeln, spazieren
student der Schüler, –/die Schülerin, –nen (in school); der Student, –en/die Studentin, –nen (in university)
study lernen
stupid doof, dumm
subject das Fach, –̈er
subway die U-Bahn, –en
such solcher
suit der Anzug, –̈e (for men); das Kostüm, –e (for women)

summer der Sommer
sun die Sonne
Sunday der Sonntag
supermarket der Supermarkt, –̈e
supper das Abendessen; **to have ~** zu Abend essen
supposed: to be ~ to sollen
sure sicher; **~!** klar!; **~, I do!** ja, und wie!
swim schwimmen
switch on an·machen

table der Tisch, –e
take nehmen; **to ~ along** mit·nehmen
take off los·gehen
tall groß
taste (good) schmecken
tea der Tee
teacher der Lehrer, –/die Lehrerin, –nen
telephone an·rufen
television der Fernseher, –; **to watch ~** fern·sehen
tell erzählen; sagen
temperature die Temperatur, –en
tender zart
tennis das Tennis
terrible, terribly furchtbar
terrific! klasse!
than als
thanks danke; **many ~** vielen Dank!
that das; daß (sub. conj.)
the der, das, die
theater das Theater, –; **movie ~** das Kino, –s
their ihr
them sie
then da, dann
there da, dort; **~ is, ~ are** es gibt
thermometer das Thermometer, –
they sie
thick dick

thing   die Sache, –n
think   denken, meinen
thin   dünn, schlank
thirst   der Durst
thirsty: to be ~   Durst haben
this   dieser
through   durch
Thursday   der Donnerstag
ticket   die Karte, –n
tied   unentschieden
time   das Mal; die Zeit, –en; **next ~**   nächstes Mal; **what ~ is it?**   wie spät ist es? wieviel Uhr ist es?; **at what ~?**   um wieviel Uhr?
times   mal
tinker   basteln
tired   müde
to   an; auf; nach; zu
toboggan   rodeln
today   heute
together   zusammen
tomato   die Tomate, –n
tomorrow   morgen; **~ evening**   morgen abend; **the day after ~**   übermorgen
tonight   heute abend
too   auch; zu
tour   die Tour, –en
town   die Stadt, ¨e; **~ hall**   das Rathaus, ¨er
train   der Zug, ¨e; **~ station**   der Bahnhof, ¨e
true   richtig; **that's ~**   das schon
try   versuchen
Tuesday   der Dienstag
turn   ab·biegen; **to ~ off**   aus·machen
turntable   der Platten-spieler, –

ugly   häßlich
umbrella   der Regenschirm, –e
understand   verstehen
unfortunately   leider

unhappy   unglücklich
until   bis
up   auf; **~ to**   bis zu
us   uns
usually   gewöhnlich

vacuum   Staub saugen
valuable   wertvoll
vegetable   das Gemüse, –
very   sehr
violin   die Geige, –n
visit   der Besuch, –e; **to ~**   besuchen
volleyball   der Volleyball, ¨e

waiter   der Ober, –
walk   der Spaziergang, ¨e; **to ~**   spazieren, laufen, gehen; **to go for a ~**   spazieren, einen Spaziergang machen, bummeln
want   wollen
warm   warm
was   war (past tense of sein)
wash   waschen; **to ~ dishes**   (Geschirr) spülen
watch   die Uhr, –en; **to ~**   sehen; **to ~ TV**   fern·sehen
water   das Wasser
we   wir
wear   tragen
weather   das Wetter
Wednesday   der Mittwoch
week   die Woche, –n; **~ end**   das Wochenende, –n
welcome: you're ~   bitte, bitte schön
well   (interj.) also, na; (adj.) gut; gesund; **pretty ~**   ganz gut
west   der Westen; **~ (of)**   westlich (von)
western   westlich
wet   naß
what   was; **~ kind of (a)**

was für (ein); **~'s the matter?**   was ist los?
when   wann, wenn
where   wo; **~ (to)**   wohin
whether   ob (sub. conj.)
which   welcher
white   weiß
who   wer
whom   wen, wem
why   warum
wife   die Frau, –en
win   gewinnen; **by how much did they ~?**   wie hoch haben sie gewonnen?
wind   der Wind; **to go ~ surfing**   windsurfen
window   das Fenster, –
windy   windig
wine   der Wein
winter   der Winter
wish   der Wunsch, ¨e; **to ~**   wollen
with   mit; bei
without   ohne
woman   die Frau, –en; **young ~**   das Fräulein
work   die Arbeit, –en; **to ~**   arbeiten; **to ~ at a hobby**   basteln
worker   der Arbeiter, –/die Arbeiterin, –nen
wow!   Mensch!
write   schreiben
wrong   falsch

year   das Jahr, –e; **time of ~**   die Jahreszeit, –en
yellow   gelb
yes   ja, doch
yesterday   gestern
yet   noch; **not ~**   noch nicht
you   du; ihr; Sie
young   jung
your   dein; euer; Ihr
youth center   das Jugend-zentrum

Index

Art credits

Illustrations

Anne Burgess: pp. i, xii, 11, 12, 13, 20, 26, 30, 38, 40, 44, 55, 57, 67, 69, 71, 88, 91, 92, 99, 100, 109, 110, 112, 113, 116, 120, 122, 138, 150, 160, 164, 182, 184, 194, 204, 218, 222, 223, 236, 237, 249, 256, 257, 277, 279, 280, 300, 313, 320, 322, 340, 341, 342.

Chris Demarest: pp. viii, ix, x, xi, 15, 28, 41, 58, 86, 111, 134, 162, 186, 207, 238, 259, 281, 302, 325.

Larry Johnson: pp. 52, 200, 296.

James Loates: pp. xiii, xiv, xv, 319.

Color Photographs

Cover: Owen Franken/Stock, Boston

Stage 1: Ich und du

P. 1, Carol Palmer/Andrew Brilliant; p. 2, Owen Franken/Stock, Boston; p. 3, (top) Peter Menzel, (middle and bottom) Owen Franken/Stock, Boston; p. 4, Owen Franken/Stock, Boston; p. 5, Carol Palmer/Andrew Brilliant; p. 6, Carol Palmer/Andrew Brilliant; p. 7, (background) Dave Bartruff, (insets) Carol Palmer/Andrew Brilliant; p. 8, Carol Palmer/Andrew Brilliant.

Stage 2: So leben wir
P. 73, Carol Palmer/Andrew Brilliant; p. 74, (top) Milt and Joan Mann, (bottom) Ralph Gates; p. 74–75, (background) Gunter Brinkmann/Peter Arnold, Inc.; p. 75, (left inset) Owen Franken/Stock, Boston, (right inset) World Film Enterprises/Black Star; p. 76, (background) Carol Palmer/Andrew Brilliant, (inset) Uta Hoffmann; p. 77, (top) David Moore/Black Star, (bottom) Carl Purcell; p. 78, (top) Vic Cox/Peter Arnold, Inc.; p. 78–79, (bottom) Cary Wolinsky/Stock, Boston; p. 79, Carol Palmer/Andrew Brilliant; p. 80, Carol Palmer/Andrew Brilliant.

Stage 3: Zum Städtele hinaus
P. 225, Carol Palmer/Andrew Brilliant; p. 226, (background) Jackie Foryst/Bruce Coleman, Inc., (left inset) Carl Purcell, (right inset) Owen Franken/Stock, Boston; p. 227, (top) Cary Wolinsky/Stock, Boston, (bottom) Dave Bartruff; p. 228, (top left) Carol Palmer/Andrew Brilliant, (top center) Dave Bartruff, (top right) Eric Lessing/Magnum; p. 228–229, (bottom) Vic Cox/Peter Arnold, Inc.; p. 229, (top left) Sabine Weiss/Photo Researchers, (right) Ralph Gates; p. 230, (background) Ralph Gates, (inset) Carol Palmer/Andrew Brilliant; p. 231, (top left) Owen Franken/Stock, Boston, (top right) Vic Cox/ Peter Arnold, Inc., (bottom left) Carol Palmer/Andrew Brilliant, (bottom right) Owen Franken/Stock, Boston; p. 232, Carol Palmer/Andrew Brilliant.

Black and White Photographs

All black and white photographs by Carol Palmer/Andrew Brilliant except:
P. x, Anne Converse/The Picture Cube; p. 52, (background) Owen Franken/Stock, Boston; p. 81, Fredrick D. Bodin; p. 82, Fredrick D. Bodin; p. 142, (top and bottom) Tom Bross/Studio 20; p. 148, Museum of Modern Art/Film Stills Archive; p. 173, (middle) Edith Reichmann/Monkmeyer Press Photo Service, (bottom) Peter Arnold, Inc.; p. 200, (inset) Peter Southwick/Stock, Boston; p. 216, (top right) Sven Simon/Katherine Young, (bottom left and right) German Information Center; p. 219, Sven Simon/ Katherine Young; p. 235, Tom Bross/Studio 20; p. 239, Werner H. Müller/Peter Arnold, Inc.; p. 241, Tom Bross/Studio 20; p. 242, Tom Bross/Studio 20; p. 245, Tom Bross/Studio 20; p. 266, (bottom) Tom Bross/Studio 20; p. 275, Andy Bernhaut/Photo Researchers; p. 285, Poly-Press/Katherine Young; p. 286, German Information Center; p. 288, Werner H. Müller/Peter Arnold, Inc.; p. 294, (middle) Hinz/Black Star; (right) Tim Gidal/Monkmeyer Press Photo Service; p. 296, (background) Belzeaux/Kay Reese and Associates; p. 298, Verkehrs-Verlag Crusius; p. 299, Eckhard Supp/Kay Reese and Associates; p. 309, (inset) Edith Reichmann/Monkmeyer Press Photo Service; p. 314, German Federal Railroad; p. 324, (bottom left) Katherine Young, (bottom right) Phelps/Kay Reese and Associates; p. 332, Verkehrsverein Heidelberg; p. 335, German Information Center; p. 338, Farrell Grehan/Photo Researchers; p. 343, Susan McCartney/Photo Researchers.